Water Policy:
Allocation and Management
in Practice

Water Policy: Allocation and Management in Practice

Proceedings of International Conference on
Water Policy, held at Cranfield University,
23–24 September 1996.

Edited by

P. Howsam and R.C. Carter

Silsoe College, Cranfield University,
Silsoe, Bedforshire, UK

CRC Press
Taylor & Francis Group
Boca Raton London New York

CRC Press is an imprint of the
Taylor & Francis Group, an **informa** business

A TAYLOR & FRANCIS BOOK

First published 1996 by Taylor & Francis
First Edition 1996

Published 2019 by CRC Press
Taylor & Francis Group
6000 Broken Sound Parkway NW, Suite 300
Boca Raton, FL 33487-2742

First issued in paperback 2019

No claim to original U.S. Government works

ISBN 13: 978-0-367-44846-2 (pbk)
ISBN 13: 978-0-419-21650-6 (hbk)

**Visit the Taylor & Francis Web site at
http://www.taylorandfrancis.com**

**and the CRC Press Web site at
http://www.crcpress.com**

A Catalogue record for this book is available from the British Library

Publisher's note
This book has been produced from camera ready copy by the individual contributors in order to make the book available for the conference.

CONTENTS

FOREWORD

By the Rt Hon Baroness Chalker of Wallasey
Minister for Overseas Development

Population growth and economic expansion are putting ever increasing demands on the quantity and quality of available water resources in most countries. Growing water scarcity highlights the importance of improving water policy, so that resources are managed in an integrated way whilst taking into account the social and economic value of water in different uses as well as its environmental impact. More efficient management of scarce water resources will increasingly require the reallocation of water from low value uses to high value uses, a greater emphasis on recycling and reducing wastage, and proper pricing policies to match demand to supply.

Improvement in water policy usually requires reform of institutional arrangements, which often means overcoming political, organisational or social obstacles. The role of Governments is changing from provision of supply to the facilitation and coordination of service delivery. This includes the establishment of policies and regulatory frameworks in order to ensure the better allocation of natural resources and to help mobilise non-Government resources. This may entail a greater involvement of the private sector but market mechanisms must be balanced with legislation to ensure that both the environment and disadvantaged groups are fully protected and benefits are fully realised.

Water projects are a central element of the ODA's strategy of improving the quality of life for people in poorer countries by contributing to sustainable development and reducing poverty and suffering. Water is essential for life, yet 1.3 billion people do not have access to safe supplies. While striving to address these needs, water projects must also seek to support the implementation of improved water policies that promote more efficient resource management in the light of growing water scarcity.

I welcome Silsoe College's initiative in organising an International Conference on "Water Policy: Allocation and Management in Practice". It provides an opportunity to exchange insights gained in implementing water policy reform, and to examine the application of the principles of integrated water policy which have been developed in the light of experience.

The papers presented come from many parts of the world and cover many different aspects of water policy implementation, ranging from strategic resource planning at an international level through to specific studies of water use. They rightly embrace the full range of political, legal, economic, technical, social and institutional considerations of putting policy into practice.

This compilation of papers shows that substantial scope already exists for learning from good practice in implementing new water policy approaches. It also indicates that there is still plenty of room for improvement if we are to meet the challenges ahead, and meet them we must!

Chalker of Wallasey

PREFACE

As demands on finite water resources grow, so does the need for reasoned debate on water policy. The universal need for water makes such debate as relevant to the domestic consumer in a town in the Netherlands or a village in Namibia, the irrigation farmer in Bangladesh or Britain, and the Government Minister in Israel or India. Harmony between competing uses and users depends on mutually agreed water policy, and sound implementation of that policy. However policy formulation does not always include full consideration of the practical implications for effective implementation. Moreover, the ability to implement policies in an integrated manner is often lacking. This may be due to inadequate policy formulation in the first place, but it is often compounded by limited cooperation between professions and organisations.

This book examines successes and failures in the practical implementation of water policies. It describes water policies and their implementation at local, regional, national, and international levels and in all sub-sectors - domestic, industrial, agricultural and environmental uses of water. In all cases attempts have been made to derive lessons which cross disciplines, geographical boundaries, and levels, concerning successful policy implementation. The book will therefore be of interest to policy makers as well as policy implementers, and to a wide range of disciplines including management, planning, engineering, sciences, economics, law, administration, and politics.

1 Water allocation

The primary role of policy is to allocate water between competing uses and users. This essentially political activity involves people: individuals and their aspirations; communities and their multiple requirements; and nations, whose power struggles can involve access, or denial of access, to water. In the current situation of finite and often limited water resources **Allan** advocates the concept of virtual water, i.e. that water should be considered not just directly but as a component of many other commodities. This opens up new options for water allocation, that will however require better cooperation between the wider range of professionals involved. The importance of cooperation is taken up by **Haque** in an analysis of water policy in Bangladesh. He argues that integration and water user participation are essential elements in policy formulation and implementation. **Abrams** describes the new social and political situation in South Africa and how it is providing an exciting and unique opportunity to review institutional and legal aspects of water policy and allocation in that country. The benefits of cooperation over conflict with respect to water allocation are promoted by **Kibaroglu**. In this case the discussion is at the international level, between the neighboring States of Turkey and Syria. **Al-Kloub** and **Al-Shemmeri** tackle the subject at a practical level by proposing, with reference to Jordan, the use of a strategic planning tool which can balance a range of issues when considering water allocation priorities. The allocation problems faced in the irrigation sector in the UK are described by **Weatherhead**, who points out the mixed benefits of the current licensing system.

2 Water resources

An understanding of water resources is essential if they are to be properly managed. Understanding needs to be underpinned by data collection, which is still far from complete. At the global level **Evans** advocates the need for large scale assessments of water resources, but fears that the quality of national hydrological data is deteriorating. **Appelgren** stresses the threat which water scarcity poses to national security, and argues for water policy measures that are integrated with broader national social, economic and development objectives. A brief perspective on water resources management in England and Wales is provided by **Sherriff**. Water privatisation in 1989 and the formation, in 1996, of a new Environment Agency, to provide integrated management of water resources, are key elements. A different approach to integrated water management is proposed by **Rao** for India. He stresses the importance of farmer or user management and understanding of all elements of the water cycle. **Lopez-Gunn** discusses water resource management in Spain at the level of major water transfer schemes between regions. She highlights the inadequacy of such schemes in the absence of an effective legal and institutional framework. Similar issues are raised by **Dottridge** and **Gibb** with reference to the risk of over-abstraction of groundwater in Jordan. They argue that acceptable and enforcible controls are essential for sustainable management of water resources in the long term.

3 Environment and water quality

Water quality protection and environmental health are priority issues for those involved in the management and supply of water. **Grimble et al** focus on groundwater degradation resulting from groundwater abstraction and pollution. Discussion of examples from China and Palestine, of the impact of policy, leads to a plea for more research into the practical implications of different policy and strategic options. Groundwater is again the focus in **Foster et al**'s paper but in this case it is the problems arising from rapid urbanisation in developing countries. Specific measures are proposed as part of water management strategies. Lessons learnt from the implementation of a groundwater protection policy in Oman are presented by **Adawi** and **Somaratne**. They stress the need to consider not only hydrogeology but also other aspects such as social and economic issues from which conflicts of interest arise. **Khouzam**'s concern is the quality of Nile river water. Here the focus is on water recycling, an important option which will not be successful if water quality issues are not properly addressed. He advocates that water recycling can be made more beneficial if water users adopt measures to prevent or reduce pollution. On a wider level **Gutkauskas** addresses the evolution of agricultural and environmental protection strategies in Lithuania, having learnt from the harm caused to the water environment from past agricultural policies. **Hodson** and **Jarman** tackle the issue of water quality protection in relation to small scale private water supplies. They describe a simple and practical method of water source protection which involves site inspection and risk assessment rather than chemical and microbiological analyses, which could be appropriate for rural water supplies in all countries.

4   Water supply management

Wherever water is scarce, it is important that allocated water is managed efficiently to avoid waste. **Horst** argues, with reference to irrigation water, that allocation and management, as well as social, technical and operational issues, need to considered as a whole if a fair and efficient system is to be achieved. The debate on the use of water metering is discussed by **Westerlund**. He suggests that it is a means, not only for reducing demand, but also for enhancing operation and management of the water supply system. Furthermore it is a useful way to bring home to consumers the importance and value of water. **Carter et al** tackle the issue of community water supply programs in developing countries. They argue for clearly expressed, quantified, and user-centered objectives for such projects, saying that their absence has been a key reason why too many projects have failed. In the irrigation sector **Radwan** explains that in Egypt significant inefficiencies and wastages exist. Wastage of water arises from inaccurate knowledge of irrigation needs, and this can be remedied by the Government promoting increased farmer participation. **Katko** and **Pietild** highlight the evolution of water supply and sanitation in Finland. They clearly remind us that sound management and planning of future water services depend on a good understanding of past evolution and present day circumstances. **Lankford** and **Gowing** take us to a different level in dealing with a practical implementation issue, i.e. water supply control in canal irrigation. They offer a better approach to coping with the interaction of design with management.

5   Water economics

At all levels water policy has economic and financial implications. This may concern the individual consumer of domestic or irrigation water who is concerned about the basis on which water is priced, the irrigation scheme manager whose budget for operation and maintenance depends on successful cost recovery, the community whose water supply scheme relies for its sustainability on an agreed system of water charges, or the policy-maker who has to determine the relative value of water for different competing uses. The issue of water valuation is analysed by **Winpenny**. He points out that while information on the value of water allows policy makers to compare the benefits of water allocation to different uses, to quantify the benefits of water supply and conservation, to monitor and regulate water markets, and to set better water prices, methodological problems, and variability in water values, may limit the increased use of water values as tools for policy formulation. In a similar vein **Carruthers** and **Morrison** suggest that the effective integration of water policy, institutions and economics has not been achieved in the past and that new institutional economics could provide a better framework to achieve this. A further critical analysis of water and economics is provided by **Green**, who argues that conventional economics has weaknesses in relation to analysis of water and environmental issues, in that it does not fully take into account human behaviour, values, and ethics. A more positive story comes from **Azaduzzaman** who provides a description of the successful integrated management of technical, social, economic and environmental elements in a sustainable rural development program in Bangladesh. **Morris** points out that putting policy into practice is a far cry from the simple sounding words of policy principles such as sustainability, demand management, and user participation. The issue of people and water economics comes up again in **Jackson**'s paper, where she advocates consideration of, and a balance between, user expectations and their ability to pay, and their understanding of the real costs of providing clean and adequate water supplies as well as protecting the water environment.

6   Water and politics

It is obvious that water, because of its social, economic and environmental importance at all levels and in all sectors, is very much intertwined with politics. **Mollinga** and **van Straaten** tackle the politics of water distribution by reference to the irrigation sector in South India. They explain that the performance of jointly managed irrigation schemes will be problematic if the importance of politics (social relationships of power) is not recognised. Similar issues are addressed by **Nicol** in relation to river basin management. It is suggested that the achievement of good water resource development reflects good governance. River basin management in Namibia is the concern of **Heyns**. He draws attention to the fact that disruption by other political issues (including wars) can seriously delay the implementation of projects outlined in international agreements. Conflict over water is also addressed by **Medzini**, with reference to the Middle East. He provides a more optimistic view and challenges the often quoted threat of water wars, by promoting the scope for flexibility and the possibility for circumstances to change so that fixed historical stances need not be adhered to. The Middle East is again the focus for **Netanyahu,** who deals with trans-boundary water policy coordination under uncertainty. She argues strongly that coordination is mutually beneficial. **Tolentino** highlights some of the problems faced in the Philippines in trying to implement effective groundwater management policy, and suggests that solutions lie in more coordination, training, and education of the public, and in the introduction of a more efficient decentralised licensing system.

7   Institutional issues

The workings of organisations which represent water users and consumers, and which manage water distribution to users is a key factor in the successful implementation of any water policy. **Martin** argues that while private sector participation in water projects is part of current water policy, to be successful a more comprehensive, integrated, longer term view is required. **Saunders et al** address the role of external support agencies. They argue that the adoption of ad hoc strategies for the implementation of water resource management policy, by the different agencies involved is not beneficial. They call for more coordination and more capacity building in order to achieve truly integrated water resource management. The views of SIDA are explained by **Johansson**. He also calls for more coordination along with more emphasis on user participation and affordable technologies in water resource management and water supply in developing countries. **Smith** and **Pathan** take us into the irrigation sector and the implementation of a currently popular policy of privatisation. With reference to the Lower Indus region of Pakistan they suggest that improvements could be achieved by more careful attention to water pricing and selling and to the reform of traditional methods of water allocation. Institution building for improved management of irrigation water is also the focus of **Hvidt's** paper. He discusses the evolution of different strategies, concentrating on construction, operation and maintenance, and on wider water resource management.

With an increasingly comprehensive approach, the establishment of strong and viable institutions will take on even greater importance. That the organisational structure of Jordan's Ministry of Water and Irrigation is inappropriate for the implementation of a comprehensive national water strategy is the case made by **Al-Kloub** and **Al-Shemmeri**. They offer a procedure to help Government analyse the various options and their ability to meet defined criteria. **Marshall** discusses the current policy of privatisation of the irrigation sector. Drawing on experience of this policy in Bulgaria, he stresses that implementation cannot and should not be rushed, and that flexible approaches offering a range of options are helpful.

8   Water users

There is a real risk that in the debate over the adoption of good water policy and its effective implementation, particularly at high political and economic levels, consideration of the water user is marginalised. This section addresses this concern at a range of levels and from a range of different perspectives. **Lane** tackles the improvement of public health through the provision of water and sanitation. **Quiroga et al** also address the community water supply sector, with reference to Columbia and Equador, stressing that a water supply system is only sustainable if it satisfies user expectations. The performance of many small water supply schemes is very poor due to poor catchment management, poor quality of piped distribution systems, and wasteful use of water. The solution they demonstrate lies in communities being strongly involved in problem identification, problem solving, decision-making, and management. The basic principle of a child's right to water is raised by **Cuninghame** and **Laws** in challenging the option of metering in water provision. They fear that improper introduction of water metering will impinge on the rights and health of the very poorest in a community. **Chatterton** describes Australian strategies for managing limited water resources where careful consideration of people's rights is essential. While much of the discussion in this book has concentrated on what Governments and other organisations should or should not do, **Ball** addresses the issue of what we as individuals should do in order to help improve water policy implementation. His case is made through the profession of a hydrogeologist and stems from experience of water projects around the world. He stresses the need to allow local people to cope with change and take responsibility but acknowledges that this requires a change of attitude. **Howsam** raises the issue of water rights, suggesting that in the current vogue of water policy principles the basic right of individuals to adequate and clean water is being marginalised. He argues that this trend should be reversed by placing basic rights at the core of any water policy and carefully protecting the principle by fair and firm water laws, which are administered as far as possible at local community level.

Peter Howsam & Richard Carter
Water Management Department
Silsoe College
June 1996

ACKNOWLEDGEMENTS

This publication owes its existence to all the contributors.

The conference, and therefore this publication, would not have happened without the financial and moral support from:

ODA, Overseas Development Administration, UK
Anglian Water International, UK
AIDA, International Association for Water Law
ADB, Asian Development Bank
CIWEM, Chartered Institution of Water & Environmental Management, UK
Environment Agency, UK
FAO, UN Food and Agriculture Organisation
IAWQ, International Association for Water Quality
IRC, International Water & Sanitation Centre
SOAS, Water Studies Group, University of London, UK
WMO, World Meteorological Organisation
WRAP, Water Resources Action Group, Palestine

Considerable help and guidance was freely provided by the members of the UK conference steering committee:

        Professor Tony Allan, Water Studies Group, SOAS
        Mr. Terry Evans, consultant
        Mr. Jerry Sherriff, Environment Agency
        Mr. Alistair Wray, Senior Water Resources Advisor, ODA
and by overseas members:
        Mr. Dante Caponera, AIDA
        Dr. Dieter Kraemer, WMO
        Dr. Tapio Katko, Vaasa Institute of Technology, Finland
Many thanks to all of them for all their thankless behind-the-scenes work.

Finally nothing at all would have happened without Mrs Carolyn King, Secretary, Water Management Department, Silsoe College. Carolyn bore the brunt of a tremendous workload in getting this book into shape and with patience and impressive administrative skills managed to help generate a successful conference.

Peter Howsam & Richard Carter
Water Management Department
Silsoe College
June 1996

PROFESSOR IAN CARRUTHERS

While this book was in preparation we learned of the untimely and sad death of Professor Ian Carruthers of Wye College. Ian made a major contribution to the development of water policy, through his own discipline of economics, and through his extensive international networking. Ian's paper, jointly authored with Jamie Morrison, and included in this book, represents one of his last contributions to the debate on water policy and management. Ian Carruthers will be greatly missed by those who knew him and his work.

Richard Carter and Peter Howsam

SECTION 1

WATER ALLOCATION

POLICY RESPONSES TO THE CLOSURE OF WATER RESOURCES: REGIONAL AND GLOBAL ISSUES
Policy responses to water closure

J.A. ALLAN
School of Oriental and African Studies,
University of London, London WC1H 0XG, UK

Abstract
Throughout the world national economies and even whole regions such as the Middle East might appear to have adjusted remarkably well to meeting their water resource needs over the last quarter of the twentieth century. It will be shown that the apparent adjustment has mainly been achieved through internationally available 'virtual water', that is the water moved in international trade in cereals. 'Virtual water' has enabled the water short Middle East to escape the trenchant predictions of water wars [1]
 First the paper will demonstrate that there have been a number of phases in the approaches taken by Governments to the provision of water. Secondly the study demonstrates that those who attempt to provide scientific information as an input to policy making should recognise that water management takes place in open political economies and not in closed hydrological and engineered systems. Thirdly, attention will be drawn to the new circumstances which face importers of 'virtual water' as the result of the shifts in policy on agricultural production in the US and the EU following the establishment of the World Trade Organisation in 1995.
Key words: cereal trade, 'closing a water resource', supply and demand management, 'virtual water', water deficits, water policy.

1   Introduction

The subject of water allocation and use has gained increasing prominence in the period since 1990, partly because of recognition that some regions, economies and communities have run out of water permanently, or temporarily, at least for some uses [2][3][4][5][6][7][8][9]. Permanent deficits have become evident in the Middle East region as a whole; temporary shortages have occurred during droughts in the same

Water Policy: Allocation and management in practice. Edited by P. Howsam and R.C. Carter.
Published in 1996 by E & FN Spon. ISBN 0 419 21650 2

locations and extreme drought related problems have occurred during the 1990s in southern Africa, in California and even in humid north-west Europe during particularly dry years such as the 1995 summer in the UK. Seasonal shortages are commonplace in semi-arid countries during dry summers, again there are many examples in the Middle East, in for example, Tripoli in Libya, Amman in Jordan or Damascus in Syria. These economies have not been able to supply the modest volumes of water needed to meet the requirements of urban domestic users.

In all discussions about water policy it is important to define the scope and nature of the analysis. Water is a familiar substance and a resource more ancient than the species which depend upon it. However, its role in sustaining life and livelihoods is in many ways much as it was at the dawn of settled agriculture in so far as all humans still need to drink and to eat. And it is the provision of water for crop production which has been and remains the dominant water using activity. With the development of complex industrialised economies, however, the economic significance of water has changed because the shares of food production and the trade in food in domestic and international systems has been progressively diminished.

Agricultural production systems require large volumes of water. Water for crop production comes either from naturally occurring soil moisture or as water delivered from elsewhere in the hydrological system from surface waters or from groundwater. As an economy develops and industrialises, the need for water increases. Industrial activity also requires water, although never in such volumes as does crop production. Industrialised economies progressively reduce the proportional contribution of agriculture to their GDPs; by the late 1990s agriculture contributed only two per cent to the UK GDP; but even in economies which have recently emphasised the importance of agriculture, such as Israel, the figure is only three per cent and for neighbouring Jordan it is only seven per cent. All communities gaining livelihoods in industry and services need large volumes of water to meet their food needs even if their own livelihood uses negligible volumes of water.

The difference between water use in agriculture and in industry is that the returns to water and the livelihoods supported are very different. Industry and services can provide a thousand times more jobs and 20000 times more financial return than would a crop producing enterprise using the same volume of water. [10]

The salience of water issues in a political economy is politically and economically determined. For an advanced industrialised economy water is a small economic element in the overall economy, accounting for a tiny fraction of one per cent of the total economy. Even the huge volumes of water used in agriculture can be available at zero cost for national crop production if the economy is located in humid latitudes.

In poor and subsistence economies the economic options are by contrast very limited. Crop and livestock production are major elements of these economies. The availability of soil moisture is a life and death issue and their are no economic insurances in a subsistence economy, such as would exist in a diverse and widely connected economy with more economically effective water using practices. Meeting the major water needs of subsistence economies is very different from meeting those of industrialised communities in a number of other ways. Sustainable subsistence economies need water to be available locally to meet their immediate drinking water and food production needs. Industrialised economies can access water via trade can also engineer drinking and domestic water supplies from distant sources.

If water is so varied in its role in livelihoods and in its general economic significance it is not surprising that it is difficult to identify policies and policy making procedures which are universally applicable. The purpose of this chapter is to highlight the relationship between the renewable natural resource, water and development. The relationship is a dynamic one and it is essential that it be understood by those evolving and implementing policy. Especially important is it to grasp that the options available to a poor economy are very different to those of a rich and diverse economy. Even more important is it to recognise that it will usually take about 25 years for economic circumstances and above all perceptions and politics to 'develop' to a point where economically and ecologically rational water allocation policies can be implemented.

The discussion will focus on the Middle East as this is the region which has first encountered the problem of running out of water. The region is the first major region in the world, as opposed to a single economy such as Australia or prominent one such as California, to have to consider 'closing' its water resource. It has *not* run out of water with which to develop diverse and sustainable economies; Israel has 'closed' its resource and is at the same time an example of economic vigour. The Middle East has run out of water to service indigenous agricultural sectors with a capacity to meet food needs. It will be shown that policy is evolving according to a predictable relationship between the economic capacity achieved and the water allocation policies that can be implemented. Overall economic development, it will be argued is the most important variable with respect to the development of sound water allocation and management.

The other aspect to which attention will be given is the effect of the global economy on water policy. The political economy of water in the Middle eastern countries is subordinate to the political economy of global trade in food staples. Because so much 'virtual water' enters the Middle East via trade in cereals the region can remain economically stable. There is a second consequence of the availability of 'virtual water'. 'Virtual water', priced for two decades at much less than its production costs on the world market, has been both a remedy to the Middle east's water deficit, and has at the same time allowed the political leaderships of the region to de-emphasise the water predicament. The rhetoric indicates that water problems are being addressed and indigenous water is being used more efficiently. The link between food imports and water is not emphasised and certainly not the unpleasant fact that indigenous water can never meet national food production needs.

It is the water demands for agriculture and plant production, even in the domestic garden [11], which are the uses which cause economic crises and social stress. The reason is that the needs of an individual for food are relatively inelastic. We each need about 1000 tonnes of water (cubic metres) per year to raise our food needs. We only need about one cubic meter of water to drink per year. The figure for domestic use per head can vary from as little as 3.5 cubic metres per year (10 litres per day) to a very high figure indeed - even 2000 cubic metres per year - if a family has a large garden in an arid or semi-arid country where people enjoy a high standard of living. At the same time the increased standard of living of industrialised communities bring a propensity to use more water for domestic purposes.

In any discussion of water management policy it is important to emphasise that water management has a number of dimensions which tend to be de-emphasised.

Water management is concerned with improving access to, and the efficient use of, water. Such measures will increase the volume of goods produced by increasing the availability of water and will also improve its productivity by increasing the returns to water by, for example, applying water more efficiently to irrigated crops. Just as important as these measures, however, is the effective allocation of water. This book bears the title - allocation and management - in order to emphasise the prime importance of allocation in any water management policy. Water use efficiency can just as surely be achieved by allocative measures as by investing in technology to improve productive efficiency. The problem with any allocation policy is that it requires that political as well as economic priorities be taken into account. Re-allocation normally means that one party will lose the resource in order hat it be made available to another user. That the economy as a whole might benefit from re-allocation does not impress existing users with millennia of tradition and status invested in their way of life.

2   Phases in water allocation and management in a dry region: the Middle East

The long experience of managing a water surplus in the Middle East up to 1970 was an important and in some ways unfortunate conditioning experience for water managers in the region. Scientists, officials and politicians developed an ethos that new water would always provide a solution provided that enough engineering ingenuity could be mustered. By the 1970s supply management ceased to be an option for much of the region.. However, because of the availability of international 'virtual water' it has been possible for the Middle Eastern and North African economies to balance their water budgets. The last quarter of the twentieth century has been a transitional period during which the region's water managers have been able to meet water needs without addressing the management of indigenous water with radical demand management practices. Demand management includes measures such as reducing water leakages in distribution systems, 'closing' the water resource for activities and sectors which bring a poor economic return to water and re-using urban and industrial waste water. Most Middle Eastern economies should have begun to consider 'closing' their water resource by the 1970s.

Chatterton [12] emphasises that a state authority must take a number of steps with respect to the ownership of water, including the identification of water rights. They suggest that it is very important to identify the water rights that would exist at 'closure' and the different rights that would exist for any subsequent allocation. Most important they claim is the identification of a budgeted overall allocation which must be less than existing and new water rights so that any reasonable appeals could be met. That attitudes to the value of water would change significantly with a water closure policy is inevitable and useful. That the politics of the announcement and implementation of a water closure policy would be intense goes without saying as does the need for robust institutions through which the interests of diverse and antagonistic users can be mediated.

The only economy in the Middle East which has been in the position of economic strength and institutional robustness to take the political step of announcing a need to 'close' its water resource is Israel. The realisation that closure was necessary did not take root quickly. The notion was identified in 1963 by US officials [13] and by Israeli scientists and officials [14]. But it required three sets of circumstances to come together in 1986, almost a quarter of a century later, for the policy of water closure to be politically feasible. It had been economically feasible for over a decade but economic feasibility is almost always much less important in a political economy than political expediency. The three circumstances were:

- a ten or more year discourse prior to 1986 on the issue of water use efficiency to which Israeli scientists and later Government officials contributed often vigorously. [15, 16, 17, 18]
- pressure from the US Government that Israel should get its economy into some better order with fewer subsidies. Water policy was just one aspect to be addressed. The sanction for not taking measures would be that a US$ 10 billion grant would be with-held.
- a timely drought in 1986 made it possible to communicate the seriousness of the water crisis to the Israeli public including the heavy water using interests in agriculture - using over 70 per cent of national water but only three per cent of the GDP and the water effective sectors such as industry and services - using only five per cent of national water but contributing 97 per cent of the GDP.

That 1986 was a moment in history of Israel's political economy at which it was possible to impose a water closure policy fits with some other general ideas in currency in environmental and development theory. Karshenas [19] [20] has demonstrated the relationship between environmental resource using practices at early and later phases of economic and social development. The tendency at an early phase of development is to use and degrade renewable natural resources such as water. At a later stage a more diverse and strong political economy can contemplate the reconstruction of resources negatively impacted by earlier phases of development. Grossman and Krueger [21] have suggested that a similar concept of the environmental 'Kuznets curve' (EK-curve) is a useful one. They draw attention to the similarity of the favourable trend in resource managing policies, of for example pollution, which appear to be associated with the achievement of a diverse and strong economy. In addition to arguing that economic growth is good for the environment they also suggest, more controversially, that the liberalisation of international trade can reduce aggregate environmental degradation. Ferguson et al [22] find that the EK-curve 'can say little about whether a country's economic trajectory yields a greater or reduced aggregate environmental effect' and they agree with the World Bank [23] that 'the existence of an environmental Kuznets curve, and this point cannot be emphasised enough, does not imply that countries will naturally grow their way out of environmental problems'. The Ferguson report insists that the shape of the EK-curve is 'policy determined' and that 'the nature of the relationship between economic growth and the environment .. lies largely in the hands of those responsible for environmental policy and its enforcement.' [22]. They also insist that sound futures can only be achieved through a 'timely and closer integration of economic and environmental policy-making' [22].

The Israeli case appears to fit both models as well as the notions of their critics. Its economy achieved rapid industrialisation in about 25 years between the mid-1950s and the early 1980s which would according to those finding explanation in the environmental Kuznets curve provide the conditions which enabled Israel's policy makers to take what appears to be a sound economic and environmental position on water allocation by 1986. The Israeli experience could also be taken to fit Ferguson's argument that what is required for sound policy is the existence of a political will to implement environmental policy inspired by an integration of economic and environmental principles. However, to insist that a principled environmental policy, in this case on water, could have come early in the process of industrialisation rather than late appears to fly in the face of the evidence of Israeli development history. It also contradicts basic notions on how policy determining scientific and political discourses evolve. [24] It is evident that approaches inspired by sound economic, demand management, principles and sustainable environmental principles came after supply management approaches were no longer tenable. That these sound principles have only been thoroughly adopted in the economy in the Middle East which has successfully and thoroughly diversified, namely Israel, is significant. In the other political economies the scientific discourses and hydropolitical discourses are in train. [25] [26] [27] [28]

3   International context of domestic water policy: water, food and trade

The main purpose of the chapter is to demonstrate that it is essential that those who attempt to provide an economic perspective as an input to policy making recognise that water management takes place in open political economies and not in closed hydrological and engineered systems. Policy makers in the real world seek effective operational systems with which to solve their problems and will prefer the remedies to be found in such systems rather than to seek solutions in intractable legal wrangling, in unrewarding negotiations with unyielding neighbouring riparians or in politically stressful water re-allocation at home. Policy makers in water short economies seek remedies to their water deficits in the wider global economy rather than the hydrologically defined one which constrains them. Trade provides the remedy.

It has been shown that the option of moving highly subsidised 'virtual water', that is the water contained for example in cereal imports, has proved to be an extremely effective and economically efficient method of meeting water deficits [29]. Those responsible for developing strategic policy on water will have to look closely at the availability of global water, at the performance of key economies in the global trade in cereals, both suppliers and potential consumers, and at the capacity of economies currently self-sufficient in water for agricultural production to remain self-sufficient in food [30]. They will also have to understand thoroughly the emerging international institutions [31] [32] which will affect trade in 'virtual water'. The political economy of water in a particular country or region will remain subordinate to the political economy of global trade in cereals.

The availability of 'virtual water' is of major significance in the domestic water policies of water short economies. It allows such economies to balance their water budgets without the political stress of confronting intransigent water using interests at home with the need to improve their water use efficiency. 'Virtual water' provides the ideal 'invisible solution' and allows policy makers and officials to defer painful measures such as closing the water resource. They can sustain the rhetoric of water and food self-sufficiency which accords well with the widely held traditional views on the importance of the agricultural sector in the economy as well as with the interests of the usually large rural population. Policy makers can continue to defer addressing the national water predicament. They have done so in the Middle East for the past 25 years in a transitional phase in which not only has 'virtual water' been available, but priced advantageously through subsidies born by producers in industrialised countries [33] [34]. Wheat was traded at half its production cost as a result of the USDA and the EC competing down of world grain prices [29].

The founding of the World Trade Organisation in the spring of 1995, along with a tightening of international grain reserves and evidence that China would be on the market in 1995 and subsequently, had a dramatic impact on world grain prices which doubled in the following 12 months [35] [36]. Despite this change in the prices 'virtual water' still remains a very good deal within such transactions. There is still no engineering measures which could mobilise the between 20 and 30 billion cubic metres per year of water needed to produce the grain being imported annually into the Middle East. Demographic circumstances dictate that the Middle East's food and water gaps can only increase in future. Meanwhile current and foreseeable technologies cannot provide water at costs which can be accommodated by crop production systems.

4   Evolving international economic and institutional contexts and water policy

New circumstances which face importers of 'virtual water' as the result of the shifts in policy on agricultural production in the US and the EU following the establishment of the World Trade Organisation in 1995 [36] [37]. The uncomfortable change in trading circumstances during 1995 has already sharpened awareness of the need to improve water use efficiency and make the best possible use of indigenous water. [28] [38] [39]

The Governments and peoples of the water deficient Middle East have to face the unpleasant challenge of increased staple grain prices at a point when their economies are either weakened by the price of oil. During the 1990s crude oil has only been able to command a price lower in real terms than its 1972 level. The non-oil economies face even more serious balance of payments problems.

The interpretation of whether the resource poor economies of the semi-arid Middle East can meet the additional burden of higher world grain prices depends on whether the observer tends to see the position s being 'half-full' or 'half-empty'. There is considerable evidence that coping with the ceaseless progressive demand of additional population is as much as these economies can expect to achieve. On the other hand the structural adjustments being forced on economies such as Egypt are bringing about change and inward investment is taking place.

A discussion of the future development prospects of a regional economy may seem to be distant from the making of water policy. It cannot be emphasised enough that the diversity and strength of an economy in the semi-arid Middle East is the essential feature to be considered. The strength of the economy and its capacity to trade in the world market and especially in the international grain market is a basic element in national economic and strategic security in all the countries of the region especially with respect to water. Access to 'virtual water' will also make it possible to pace the introduction of water closure policies to accord with the rate at which the associated discourses and politics can be steered.

The recent increase in grain prices could act as a catalyst to encourage the grain importers of the Middle East and North Africa, who together comprise a bloc of pivotal importers, to act together with a coherent policy to create favourable trading circumstances. Becoming expert in grain futures and even investing in secure supplies of grain from regions which enjoy a comparative advantage in soil moisture availability should be a widely recognised priority [28] [40].

5   Conclusion

Water policy is the concern of this publication. The aim of *this* contribution has been to show that there are a number of factors and pressures on policy makers at the macro, national, level which determine whether sound ideas can or need to be heard by the Government policy making community. The good ideas may be economically or environmentally very highly principled, but when put into scientific, institutional, political and media discourses they will be subordinate to the political imperatives preoccupying those in Government. Policy makers will be concerned with retaining power and with encouraging the circulation of ideas and proposals which provide opposition groups, official or unofficial, with information which could endanger their political position.   That scientists and consultants recommend policies that are environmentally sound, technically effective and economically efficient according to the internationally acclaimed principles, for example of intergenerational transfers, is of little importance if the proposals contradict immediate political imperatives. Outsiders drawing attention to weaknesses in the national economic fabric, such as the inadequacy of water supplies, does not accord with Government sanctioned discourses and attempts to focus attention on such issues will be unwelcome. Notions of food and water insecurity are not therefore heard or encouraged, and if they do enter the discourse they are opposed with rich rhetoric or more probably ignored.

Having established the difficulty of having an impact on influential discourses it has also been shown that the political economy of water and related water policy are subject to economic factors. There has been an attempt in the paper to show that the Karshenas model of environment and development, and the environmental Kuznets curve, do help in understanding the inevitably lengthy process which shapes water policy. A state authority can only implement politically stressful measures such a 'closing' a water resource when an economy is diverse and strong. A diverse and strong economy takes a minimum of 25 years to evolve. Governments running economies which have not achieved this status will go to great lengths to avoid taking measures which are economically and environmentally rational. It is politically easy in such circumstances to argue that the sound economic and environmental polices are unaffordable.

6   References

1. Bulloch, J. and Darwish, A. (1993) *Water wars: coming conflicts in the Middle East,* London: Gollancz.
2. OECD (1989) *Water resource management: integrated polices,* Paris: OECD
3. Hayward, J. (1995) *Averting a water crisis in the Middle East and North Africa: effective financing of environmentally sustainable development,* Washington DC: The World Bank. Paper at the Third annual World Bank conference on environmentally sustainable development, 25 pp.
4. Serageldin, I. (1995a) *Towards sustainable management of water resources,* Washington DC: The World Bank, 33 pp.
5. Serageldin, I. (1995b) *Water supply, sanitation and environmental stability,* Washington DC: The World Bank, 35 pp.
6. World Bank (1990) *Water resources management: a policy paper,* A World Bank Policy Paper, Washington DC: The World Bank.
7. World Bank (1993a) *A strategy for managing water in the Middle East and North Africa,* A World Bank Paper, Washington DC: The World Bank.
8. World Bank (1993b)*Water resources management,* A World Bank Policy Paper, Washington DC: The World Bank.
9. World Bank (1995) *Middle East and North Africa environmental strategy: towards sustainable development,* Washington DC: The World Bank, 120 pp.
10. Allan, J. A. (1996a) Returns to water in services, *MEWREW,* No.7, Sept. 1996.
11. OFWAT (1995) *Study of comparative water use in homes with gardens and flats (gardenless) in Eastbourne, UK,* London: OFWAT.
12. Chatterton, B., and L. (1995) Closing a water resource; some policy considerations, *MEWREW SOAS Occasional Paper,* October 1995. See the World Wide Web - http://www.soas.ac.uk/geography/waterissues/
13. Palmer, S. E. (1963) Comments of Stephen E. Palmer, Jr., at the American Embassy, Tel Aviv, on the *Jordan Waters Contingency Planning* sent to the Department of State, 23 October 1963. Ref. POL 33-1 ISA-Jordan.
14. Arlosoroff, S. (1995, Personal communication.
15. Fishelson, G. (1992) The allocation of marginal value product of water in Israeli agriculture, *Israeli Agriculture,* Reference Number WP/028.
16. Sofer, A. (1992) *Rivers on fire: the conflict of water in the Middle East,* Tel Aviv: Am Oved.
17. Just. A., et al. (1994) *Problems and prospects in the political economy of transboundary water issues,* University of Maryland, September 1994.
18. Arlosoroff, S. (1996) Managing scarce water - recent Israeli experience, in *Water, peace and the Middle East: negotiating resources in the Jordan basin,* (ed. J. A. Allan) London: Tauris Academic Studies, pp 21-48.
19. Karshenas, M. (1994) Environment, technology & employment: a definition of sustainable development, *Development & Change.,*Vol.25.2: pp.723-57.
20. Allan, J. A. and Karshenas, M. (1996) Managing environmental capital: the case of water in Israel, the West Bank and Gaza, 1947 to 1995, in *Water, peace and the Middle East: negotiating resources in the Jordan basin,* (ed. J. A. Allan), London: Tauris Academic Studies, pp 120-133.

21. Grossman, G and Krueger, A. (1994) *Economic growth and the environment,* Working Paper 4634 - National Bureau of Economic Research, Cambridge MA.

22. Ferguson, D, Haas, C, Raynard, Pand Zadek, S. (1996) *Dangerous curves: does the environment improve with economic growth?* London: World Wild-Life Fund for Nature. Prepared by New Economics Foundation, 112 Whitechapel Rd. London El 4JE, UK. email neweconomics@gn.apc.org

23. World Bank (1994) *The environmental Kuznets curve,* Environment Department, The World Bank. Washington DC: The World Bank.

24. Allan, J. A. (1996b) The role of scientific and political discourses in developing water policy, Conference proceedings, *Water in the Middle East* at the University of Exeter, in press.

25. Haddedin, M. (1996) Water problems in Jordan, Third Annual Conference on environmentally sustainable development, Washington DC: The World Bank.

26. Haddad, M. and Mizyed, N. (1996) Water resources in the Middle East: conflict and solutions, in *Water, peace and the Middle East negotiating resources in the Jordan basin,* (ed. J. A. Allan), London: Tauris Academic Studies, pp. 3-20.

27. Nasser, Y. (1996) Palestinian management options and challenges within an environment of scarcity and power imbalance, in *Water, peace and the Middle East negotiating resources in the Jordan basin,* (ed. J. A. Allan), London: Tauris Academic Studies, pp. 49-58.

28. Abdalla, I. S. (1996) The political economy of food deficits in the Arab region', in Farid, A. M., *Grains, water and the political decision, (ed. A. M. Farid),* London: Arab Research Centre.

29. Allan, J. A. (1996c) The political economy of water, in *Water, peace and the Middle East: negotiating resources in the Jordan basin,* (ed. J. A. Allan), London: Tauris Academic Studies, pp 75-119.

30. Cohen, J. (1995) *How many people can the Earth support?* New York: Norton.

31. Le Heron, P. (1993) *Globalized agriculture,* Oxford: Pergamon.

32. Martin, W. and Winters, A., 1995, *The Uruguay Round: Widening and deepening the world trade system,* Washington DC: The World Bank.

33. ABARE (Australian Bureau of Agricultural and Resource Economics) (1989) *US grain policies and the world market,* ABARE Policy Monograph No. 4, Canberra: Australian Government Publishing Service.

34. Le Heron, P. (1993)*Globalized agriculture,* Oxford: Pergamon.

35. International Grains Council (1996) *Grain market report,* March 1996, London: IGC. 1 Canada Square, canary Wharf, London E14 5AE.

36. CERES (1996) The gathering wheat crisis: Mid-East may suffer, *CERES,* spring 1996, pp 12-13.

37. Martin, W. and Winters, A. (1995)*The Uruguay Round: Widening and deepening the world trade system,* Washington DC: The World Bank.

38. Haddedin, M. (1996) Water problems in Jordan, Third Annual World Bank conference on sustainable development, Washington DC: The World Bank.

39. Farid, A. M. (editor) (1996) *Grains, water and the political decision,* (ed A. M. Farid), London: Arab Research Centre, 76 Notting Hill Gate, London W11, UK.

40. Allan, J. A. (1996d) Water deficits in agriculture in the Arab World and the need to increase water productivity, in *Water, grains and the political decision,* (ed. A. M. Farid), London: Arab Research Centre, pp. 34-48.

WATER POLICY FORMULATION AND IMPLEMENTATION IN BANGLADESH

Searching for a sustainable water policy

M.I. HAQUE

Bangladesh Water Development Board, Faridpur, Bangladesh

Abstract

This paper introduces its readers to Bangladesh, its people and its water resources potential. Bangladesh is known to have been raised from the Bay of Bengal by theilt deposits of rivers. From historical times its people lived on the banks of these rivers and have drawn their living from a water based economy. But this water has become very scarce in certain parts of this country because of cross boundary diversions. This has devastated the environment and changed completely the traditional water use pattern.

Keywords: basin development, drought, environment, flood, mass participation, water rights.

1 Introduction

Bangladesh is a tropical country in the northern hemisphere located on the 90^0 E longitude in Asia. It is bounded by India from the west, north and east but a small portion to the southeast by Mayanmar (see map). Physically this country is a vast alluvial plain sloping southward from the Himalayas to the Bay of Bengal. To the east of this plain is the Lushai hills and to the west lies the highlands of the Indian plateau. The surface area of this country is around 144,000 sq.km.

Bangladesh is a country of fertile soil and abundance of sun and water. This has made this country best for living and the densest in human population in the world. Its present population is about 120 million ie. 833 persons per sq.km. Its agriculture is highly dependent on its climate which varies significantly round the year. Being located at the confluence of the rivers Ganga and Brahmaputra, it receives a drainage discharge from a catchment 15 times larger than its surface area.

Water Policy: Allocation and management in practice. Edited by P. Howsam and R.C. Carter. Published in 1996 by E & FN Spon. ISBN 0 419 21650 2

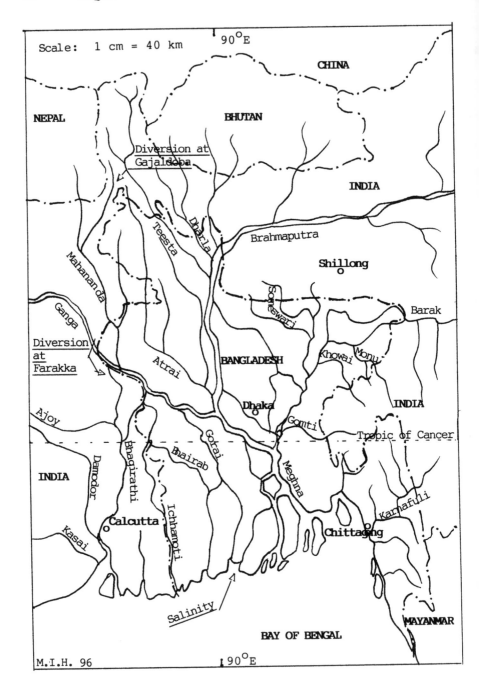

Fig. 1 Map showing the river systems of Bangladesh

The people of Bangladesh built their homes on the banks of rivers, their life supported by an ecosystem balanced and nourished by nature. They were used to the periodical floods and the low flows. But these rivers originate or pass through India before they reach Bangladesh. For the last two decades, India is diverting these rivers unilaterally, to their irrigation works, leaving the Bangladesh side dry in lean periods. This has brought serious consequences to the life of the people and threatens the whole water management policy.

2 Morphology and climate

2.1 The river systems

Bangladesh can be divided into four parts according to its river basins. The west is the basin of Ganga, the north is of the Brahmaputra, the east is of the Meghna and the southeast is of the Karnafuli(see map).

The Ganga river originates in the southern slopes of the Himalayas and carries discharge from a catchment of about 865,000 sq.km. in India, to Bangladesh. This river is the major source of silt deposits and delta formation in the Bay of Bengal.

The Brahmaputra originates in the northern slopes of the Himalayas and travels inside China to the east, then turning southward, it enters India, then to Bangladesh. Its catchment area is about 575,000 sq.km. This river is the source of snowmelt waters in the early summer.

The Meghna originates from the Lushai hills in India and flows westward by the name Barak. Entering Bangladesh it bifurcates, then meets again and renamed as Meghna. This river on its way down to the sea, receives the combined flow of the Ganga and the Brahmaputra, and forms the biggest estuary in the Bay of Bengal.

The Karnafuli is the biggest river in the southeast among three other small rivers, all originate from the Lushai hills. The Karnafuli has a reservoir in its basin to control flood and produce electricity.

2.2 The seasonal effects

The country's climate is moderate except the summer and the winter. The Bangla calendar is a solar year, of six seasons, beginning in the middle of April. These seasons have significant effects on the riverflows and the crops and vegetation on the ground. The first two months are Baishak and Jaishta, the summer. The weather is very hot and tornadoes blow almost everyday in the afternoon. The Ganga basin experiences the lowest levels in its rivers but the Brahmaputra starts rising by the snowmelt waters from the Himalayas.

The next two months, Ashar and Sravan is the monsoon and the next, Vadra and Aswin is the floods. In monsoon the country receives incessant rainfall and flash floods in the Meghna basin. In the floods, one third of the country goes under water. The autumn arrives next in Kartik and Agrahayan, the season of tropical cyclones. Then the winter, the best of all in the months of Poush and Magh. People go out in this season and enjoy the sun. Finally the spring, pleasant in the month of Falgun but hot in Chaitra.

The average annual rainfall varies in this country from 1250 mm to 3500 mm, west to the northeast.

3   Water policy formulation

3.1 Historical rights
Bangladesh is a riverine country. Its cities and villages are located on the banks of rivers. People use these rivers for washing and bathing, drainage, communications, recreation and transport of their goods. These rivers and adjacent beels and boars (marshes and lakes) supply them with fish. People dug wells and ponds along the roads and homesteads for drinking and supply in the drought.

Rice and fish are the staple food of the Bengalees. People grow rice round the year in three definite periods. The summer variety is called Aus, grown on the slopes of the depressions, becomes ready to harvest before the floods. The Amon variety grows in the floods at the depression points. The variety in winter is called Rabi, is grown over the drained up beels.

Jute is one of the major crops in Bangladesh. It is sown in the summer, but harvested in the floods. This crop is processed in the flood water. The residual moisture in the soil from the floods let the farmers grow pulses in winter. Thus, from historical times, the people of this country lived with water and their life revolved round a water based economy.

3.2 Policy demand
Rapid growth in population in the fifties and sixties brought the demand for increased food production. More lands were brought into cultivation and large irrigation projects were planned. The G.K. Irrigation Project was commissioned in 1962. At smaller scales, low lift pumps, shallow and deep tubewells were installed.

People in this country did not accept irrigation at the beginning. They thought the natural calamities are the curse of God. To motivate these people, irrigation was supplied free of cost. Soon a policy was needed to find a sustainable system.

But growth of the population crowded the villages and the cities. They were short of sanitation and water supplies. Hand tubewells were installed in the villages to supply safe drinking water. The cities improved their water supply and sewage systems.

Bangladesh is rich in groundwater. Most of the cities are fed with tubewell supplies with little abstraction from the rivers, but indiscriminate pumping lowered the groundwater table and left the streams lean. A policy was sought to bring discipline and to check over-abstraction.

3.3 Policy formulation
Water policies in Bangladesh apply at three levels : national, project and field. At national level, the Water Resources Planning Organisation (WARPO) under the Ministry of Water Resources works to plan and coordinate between Government and non-Government agencies using water. At project levels policies are sought to work between the beneficiaries and the project management. At field levels policies have been formulated by the Government to:-
1. Regulate the points and quantity of abstraction.
2. Regulate the quantity and ends of distribution.
3. Regulate the collection and route of drainage.
4. Rehabilitation of the people displaced.

5. Collection of the operation & maintenance cost.
6. Put restrictions in case of adverse effects on the environment and wildlife.
7. Settle disputes on water rights.

4   Water policy formulation

4.1 Water management
Bangladesh Water Development Board (BWDB) under the Ministry of Water Resources, is assigned to look after the water resources all over the country. Its offices are located basinwise and projectwise, with engineers, soil experts and agriculturists available in the field. They work in irrigation management, drainage and flood protection. To monitor environmental changes, BWDB has staff for recording hydrological events.

River waters are the main source of irrigation projects implemented by the BWDB. In these projects, water is lifted or diverted from the rivers and conveyed to the fields by excavated channels. Its major projects are, the G.K., Teesta, Meghna Dhonagoda, Chandpur and the Monu Irrigation Projects.

The Ministry of Local Government is assigned to supply safe drinking water to the cities and villages. Tubewells are installed for water supply. For irrigation, tubewells are installed by both Government and non-Government (NGO) agencies. The spacings maintained between tubewells :-
1. Deep tubewells   6" dia   2500-2700 ft
2. Shallow tubewells   4" dia   1000-1100 ft
3. Hand tubewells   1.5" dia   300-400 ft

4.2 Mass participation
The ideas of irrigation and growing high yield variety crops in the fields were new in this country. This needed education and training of the beneficiaries. BWDB placed its extension workers and set up training centres to introduce new systems. Water user groups were formed to manage the delivery of water at plot levels. A water policy should be for a just and sustainable endeavour. An unjust policy shall invite confrontation or can remain valid only under duress. Formation of water user groups played a very vital role in the management of irrigation systems. These groups also worked for solving social disputes, mass education and logistics distributions. Researchers could contact them for monitoring the policy impacts on the socio-culture, environment and the analysis of the reasons of violations.

4.3 Water economics
The viability of an irrigation or water development project is calculated on the preproject and postproject economics. The implementation cost is thought to be recovered indirectly from the production benefits and increased economic activities. At field level the following are the charges applied for operation & maintenance :-
1. Municipal supplies -domestic @ Tk 03.50/1000 litre(e.g. Dhaka WASA)
    - industrial @ Tk 11.35/1000 litre
2. Irrigation by -Aus (paddy) @ Tk 250/acre BWDB canals
    Amon(paddy) @ Tk 100/acre (e.g. G.K.project), Rabi(wheat) @ Tk 150/acre

For drinking water, the Government of Bangladesh has a target to install hand tubewells at every 75 persons by the year 2000. The present charges for such installations are :-
1. Deepset for saline zone - @ Tk 2000/tubewell
2. Shallow tubewells - @ Tk 750/tubewell
   (Tk 40 = 1 US $)

5   Environmental impacts

5.1 Ecology
Drawing project viability from a preproject and post-project benefits has so long been unaware of the impacts of the projects on the ecology. The projects could achieve economical gains, but affected the health and environment by crowding and pollution. Reclamation of marshes could increase crop production, but damaged wildlife. Recently the Government has attached special interest in considering environmental effects prior to project approval.

A natural lake or a marshland may be a sanctuary for the wildlife and the best fit in the local environment. Thus abstraction from it can cause adverse effects on the ecology at a considerable length. Abstraction from a stream shall affect the co-riparians and change the basin configuration. Abstraction from the groundwater can cause ecological disaster on the ground.

Study of the ecological balance should cover all species, their food habits, migratory behaviour and interdependence on the supporting resources. All development efforts should consider the resource constraints, health, education, tourism and democracy in addition to the economic gains. In no case can the historical rights of the co-habitats or the co-riparians be ignored.

5.2 Geopolitics
The rivers Ganga, Brahmaputra and the Meghna travel through the territories of India and Bangladesh, thus people of these two countries are co-riparians of the said rivers. Some tributaries of these rivers, Mahananda, Teesta, Dharla, Khowai, Gomti etc. also travel through these countries. India is diverting many of these rivers unilaterally, e.g. the Ganga at Farakka and the Teesta at Gajaldoba (see map). These diversions brought the following devastating effects on Bangladesh:-
1. The main distributories of the Ganga inside Bangladesh got delinked from November to mid-June, leaving their branches dry. Age old river routes through the Ganga and its branch the Gorai went out of order. The G.K. Irrigation project and the Teesta Irrigation project failed to supply water in the summer due to low flows.
2. The entire western part of Bangladesh faced desertification. Hundreds of small distributories became silted up and dried. Many watershed areas evaporated being delinked from the upland sources. A wide variety of fishstocks vanished for want of places to survive round the year. Big and medium rivers narrowed by siltation.
3. Traditional land use pattern changed due to dryness. A sharp fall in the groundwater levels affected the natural vegetation. A vast volume of rainforest vanished.

4. Salinity from the sea intruded deep into the countryside affecting man, animal and the crops. Industries suffered for want of sweet water in the streams to be lifted for their operation.

Efforts have been made to bring together India and its neighbours for a combined approach in basin development, but no progress has so far been achieved.

5.3 Disasters

Bangladesh is a country very much prone to natural disasters. It faces periodical floods and cyclones round the year. Drought and withdrawal of water by India in summer brings disasters on the life of plants, man and animal. At the start of monsoon sudden release of upland storage causes flash floods. In the absence of a policy for basin management across the borders, the flood havoc caused by the rivers Ganga and Brahmaputra remains unabated.

To fight flood damage BWDB has constructed flood protection dykes along the banks of major rivers. But the heights of these embankments fell short of the unprecedented flood level of 1988. A fresh attempt from the Government is being made to rebuild these embankments against floods with a 50-100 years recurrence interval.

April to November is the time for cyclones in this country. The summer one is called the Kalbaishakhi has local and scattered effects. At other times it rises up from the sea, and causes damage by strong winds and tidal surge on a large area. Efforts are underway to build cyclone shelters stronger, for the public and animals of the offshore areas. Stronger embankments are being constructed against tidal upsurge.

6   Conclusion

Water is a global resource essential for life and a treasure for all creatures on the earth. Locally it is a gift of nature distributed according to the physical environment. Any policy for diversion, storage or abstraction of the resource should not be done against the natural balance. If so done, it may sound very productive at start, but shall not be sustainable in the long run.

The contents of this paper may be summarized as follows:-

1. The people of Bangladesh live and their life revolve round a water based ecosystem. Water in the streams is their historical right.
2. Cross-boundary diversions of water by India without any agreement violates the historical rights of the co-riparians of the common rivers in Bangladesh.
3. The co-riparian nations of the river basins should make a combined approach for their development, with no damage to the historical rights of the people and to the ecosystems.
4. Beneficiary participation is a must in the formulation and implementation of a water policy.
5. Water development policies must attach special interest to assessing the environmental effects prior to their approval.
6. Water policies at project level should also aim at community development, health, education, tourism and democracy in addition to the economic gains.

7. A sustainable policy shall fit in the environment without confrontation or damage to the wildlife.

7 Bibliography

1. East Pakistan Water and Power Development Authority. (1964) Master Plan.
2. Government of Bangladesh. (1976) White Paper on the Ganges Water Dispute.
3. Government of Bangladesh. (1983) Bangladesh Irrigation Water Rate Ordinance no.31.
4. Government of Bangladesh. (1985) Groundwater Management Ordinance no. 27.
5. Government of Bangladesh. (1986) National Water Plan.
6. Government of Bangladesh, Ministry of Water Resources. (1992) Irrigation Water Rate Rules.

POLICY DEVELOPMENT IN THE WATER SECTOR - THE SOUTH AFRICAN EXPERIENCE
Water policy development in South Africa

L.J. ABRAMS
Policy Consultant, Johannesburg, South Africa

Abstract
South Africa is going through a social and political transformation after the first democratic elections in April 1994. With the introduction of a new Constitution, all law and policy is being reviewed. This has provided a unique opportunity to the public water sector to review its policy, institutional structure and legislation. This paper set out some of the objectives of policy reform in South Africa and briefly describes several specific areas of policy development which are of importance beyond the country's borders.
Keywords: development, Government, policy, sanitation, water, water supply.

1 Introduction

The political changes in South Africa, and the emergence of a democratic system based on a new Constitution with a strong human rights content, has provided an opportunity for thorough review of policy in all sectors, not least water. Since the first democratic elections in 1994, the policy of Government with regards to water has been undergoing a systematic process of change which covers all aspects from the structuring of the Department of Water Affairs and Forestry to a review of the water law of the country.

The chance provided by the political changes in the country has been regarded as a "window of opportunity" by progressive policy makers in the water sector to bring about changes which are long overdue. It is rare that such an opportunity presents itself and a great deal of energy has been spent in the past few years to take full advantage of this period of South Africa's history. The process of policy change in the water sector in South Africa is in mid-stream at present and will take some years to complete. The preface of the Water Supply and Sanitation Policy White Paper [1] of November 1994 makes the point that the last chapter in policy development is

Water Policy: Allocation and management in practice. Edited by P. Howsam and R.C. Carter.
Published in 1996 by E & FN Spon. ISBN 0 419 21650 2

never written. Policy is dynamic - it reflects the changing priorities of society and the Government.

2   National Policy Background

In order to understand the changes which have been made to water policy in South Africa, it is important to have an understanding of the national policy context. The backdrop to all political and development activity is the new Constitution. The present Constitution, which has taken the country through the elections period, is an Interim Constitution arrived at through the negotiated settlement which led to the elections. Since the elections, a Constitutional Assembly of elected persons has been drafting a final Constitution which is soon to be completed. The adoption of a new Constitution, to which all law and public policy is subject, means that all such law and policy has to be reviewed and tested against the new Constitution.

In the water sector, the introduction of a Bill of Basic Human Rights in the Constitution both demands, and provides the mandate for, far reaching policy change. Numerous sections on equality, human dignity, the rights of children, and, in Section 29, "the right of every person to an environment which is not detrimental to his or her health or well being", require a move away from the policies of the past. The broad policy framework of the new Government is contained in the Reconstruction and Development Programme (RDP). All sectoral Government policies and strategies are required to conform to the principles and strategies of the RDP. The RDP is designed to redirect public sector spending and the ethos of the public sector as a whole from the practices of the apartheid era to the new ethos.

The two main objectives of the RDP are to attain both equity and economic growth. These objectives need to be regarded in the light of the enormous poverty in the country and the fact that South Africa has the largest extreme of wealth to poverty disparity of any nation in the world. Some may argue that the simultaneous attainment of both equity and growth is not possible because of the scale of public spending that the first implies and the effect that this has on the economy. An initial reaction may be that the two objectives are mutually exclusive of each other. This is perhaps the biggest challenge to the policy makers - to ensure that the way in which each objective is pursued does not undermine the pursuit of the other objective. This is not to imply the old paradigm of assuming that equity will follow growth (the now generally discredited "trickle-down" theory). A new paradigm is being put into play based on the belief that growth is dependant upon equity; that economic stability and investment confidence is not possible in the midst of poverty and its associated anguish, crime and social disorder; and that infrastructure development is in itself the creation of real assets and constitutes growth.

3   Previous water sector Government policy

3.1 Water resources management
South Africa is a semi-arid country with unevenly distributed rainfall (43% of the rain falls on 13% of the land) and with high annual variability and unpredictability. In the

latter half of the last century and the early years of this century, the primary use of water was for agriculture, and the Governments of the period concentrated on provision of water for irrigation. By the mid 1900s the demand for water was beginning to shift towards the needs of a growing industrial economy; however the growth areas did not coincide with the availability of water. The industrial heartland of the country, the areas surrounding Johannesburg, is situated in an arid zone and straddles a continental divide. As a consequence, inter-basin transfer schemes, which are amongst the largest in the world, have been developed .

The policy and functions of the Department of Water Affairs and Forestry prior to the 1994 elections were constrained exclusively to water resource management. This included the management of the larger catchments, the administration of Government water control areas, the supply of bulk untreated water to water boards (bulk treated water supply utilities), water quality management and the administration of the Water Act.

3.2 Limitations

The Department did not regard itself as responsible for ensuring that citizens had a water supply and had no political mandate for such responsibility. Furthermore, the country was divided, starting in the 1960s, into nominally independent "homelands" as a consequence of the apartheid separate development policies, and the central Department of Water Affairs and Forestry had no jurisdiction in these areas. These were generally the more arid parts of the country where 75% of the population subsisted on 13% of the land. These areas became increasingly poverty stricken over the years with little or no effective service provision.

3.3 Consequences

The water sector consequences of these policies have been far reaching. Not only are there an estimated 12 to 14 million people without any formal water supplies and 21 million people without formal sanitation services (out of a total population of 41 million), but there are also serious environmental effects of poverty which impact on the water resource base in the country. These include encroaching desertification, deforestation, substantial loss of topsoil, widespread diffuse pollution, invasion of alien plant species and other factors which result in reduced groundwater recharge potential, increased siltation of limited storage facilities and increased danger of periodic serious flooding. All of these are now being experienced in South Africa.

The country has also faced cyclical periods of extreme drought which the poor majority is ill-equipped to resist. Without formal services of known capacity and reliability, and without responsible and capable authorities, rural communities have been left to fend for themselves. This has generally had the effect of further increasing the depth of poverty in rural areas and increasing urban migration.

These are the somewhat daunting realities which face the policy makers of the new order in South Africa.

4   Importance of policy development

The new Government in South Africa and particularly the new Minister of Water

Affairs and Forestry, together with their policy advisors, recognised very quickly that there was an urgent need for new policy in the country. New policy had to be developed for several reasons:

4.1 To provide clarity to the sector

Because of the fragmented nature of South African society which existed at the time of the political changes, all sectors were in disarray, including health, education, housing, employment, infrastructure and specifically water. There were no guidelines or common policy and as a result both the public sector and the private sector were confused and lacked direction as to how to begin to tackle the meeting of the vast needs of the people. One of the first tasks of the Ministry of Water Affairs and Forestry after the elections in April 1994 was the drafting of a White Paper on Water Supply and Sanitation which, after the holding of a national consultative conference, was published in November 1994.

Although the document was produced in a very short period of time, a great deal of effort went into its production. The position adopted was that it was more important to make clear policy available to the sector as a whole than to take months debating the finer details. The policy has proved very effective and has been heralded throughout the country and abroad for its clarity and insight into the problems facing the country and how they should be addressed. The specific areas which have been most helpful have been clarity on service levels, the definition of the minimum standard, policies on payment for services.

4.2 To reduce institutional fragmentation

The framework of institutions responsible for water resource management and water supply in the past was extremely complex with numerous areas of overlap and conflict and, as has already been mentioned above, with many areas remaining unserved. There were eleven "Governments", provincial structures, regional service providers, water boards, local Governments and a large number of NGOs.

The institutional framework for the water sector was in urgent need of simplification and clarification which the White Paper sought to provide. Water is regarded in the new policy as an indivisible national resource. In terms of the Constitution, the central Government is the custodian of the nation's water and the national Department of Water Affairs and Forestry has two primary functions :
- to manage the country's water resources, and
- to ensure that all people have an adequate water supply and sanitation service.

The responsibility, in terms of the Constitution, for the supply of water is that of local Government. It is important to note that whilst local Government has the responsibility of supplying water to consumers, it is the central Government's function to ensure that this happens in terms of the norms and standards described in the Government's policy. Where local Government fails to perform its function, the Department of Water Affairs and Forestry is empowered to take direct action to strengthen local Government and temporarily perform the functions of local Government.

Policy to enable the Department to delegate national water resource management functions to statutory catchment management structures is presently being developed. This is to ensure a more integrated approach to resource management and a greater participation of people at local level.

Water Boards have been a long standing institutional mechanism to provide treated water to large consumers in bulk. In the past this has mainly been in urban areas. The objectives of new policy with regards to Water Boards are :

- to increase the representivity of Boards,
- to rationalise the areas of service of water boards, subsequent to the reunification of the country,
- to extend water boards to eventually provide a "second-tier" water utility framework over most of the country.
-

The institutional framework of the water sector has therefore been simplified to the following:

1st tier	National Government (Department of Water Affairs and Forestry)	Water resource management, support to local Government, setting of norms and standards, monitoring and administration of the Water Act.
2nd tier	Water Boards	Supply of bulk treated water on a commercial basis.
3rd tier	Local Government	Supply of water and sanitation services to consumers.

4.3 To create a framework for investment

Clear policy provides a basis for investment in water sector infrastructure. The share of the national budget previously enjoyed by the Department of Water Affairs and Forestry was 0.3%. With the establishment of clear policy and a commitment to achieve the policy objective of "Some for all rather than all for some", the Department has been able to substantially increase its share of the budget to more than double its previous level in less than 18 months. Clear policy has enabled a relatively rapid deployment of funds which, for a Government department, is advantageous and tends to attract increasing funds.

The policy is that the Government will provide capital grants for the construction of basic services which are defined as a water supply of at least 25 litres per capita per day at a maximum cartage distance of 200m and of adequate quality. The grant includes finances for the training of communities to undertake the governance, administration, operation and maintenance of the water services as a local Government function. All recurring operation, maintenance and administration costs are to be borne by the communities. If communities desire a higher level of service, they must find the finance elsewhere than from the Government.

Strict adherence to the policy has had the effect of building confidence in the sector and attracting local and international private sector finance.

4.4 To provide an avenue for the outworking of political objectives

The highest priority of rural citizens in the country, who constitute half of the population, is water. The importance of meeting the post-apartheid expectations of the majority of the population goes beyond party political interests. Apart from the moral imperative to alleviate the plight of the poor, the normalising of South African society and the establishment of peace and prosperity is at stake, and ultimately democracy itself. Clear policy is the first step towards implementation at scale, without which development strategies cannot be established. Without clear policy, the political will to genuinely address the problems cannot be easily generated, although political will and policy formulation present a classic "chicken-and-egg" dilemma.

4.5 The importance of the process

One of the facets of the present policy making process in South Africa is the concentration on public participation. Before a White Paper, which represents official Government policy, is published, it has become practice to prepare a discussion document (usually referred to as a Green Paper). This is referred to as wide a group of interested parties as possible throughout the country and is often the topic of regional and national workshops and conferences. Special attention is given to the inclusion and briefing of those sections of the population which have not previously been engaged in such processes because of past discriminatory policies.

The importance of policy development can therefore be clearly seen in the South African context. Those sectors where policy has not been developed have clearly suffered as a result, such as in the housing, health and education sectors.

5   Current water sector policy development in South Africa

5.1 Water supply

The White Paper on Water Supply and Sanitation published in November 1994 was the starting point in the review of water policy in South Africa. The policy principles around which the policy was based are:
1. Demand driven and community based development
2. Basic services as a human right
3. "Some for all" rather than "all for some"
4. Equitable regional allocation of development resources
5. Water has economic value
6. The user pays principle
7. Integrated development.
8. Environmental integrity.

The document was written in a clear, common-English style and has been well received. Some 35,000 copies have been distributed on a demand basis which far exceeded expectation. It has formed the standard for subsequent policy documents both within the Department of Water Affairs and Forestry and within other departments.

5.2 Water demand management

As stated earlier in this paper, South Africa has a semi-arid climate. The basis of water resource management in the past has been a supply driven ethos whereby the role of the Department was to supply water for agriculture and industrial demands as and when they arose. This led to an unrealistic public assumption that water is always available in plentiful supply and that, even though there may be droughts, "a plan could always be made" to ensure the unfettered use of water. One of the main contributing factors to this ethos is the pricing structure of water and the legal framework which defines certain water as "private" and is based on the riparian rights principle. This, together with the political requirement to retain the support of the white farmers who owned most of the land in the country, has led to water being seriously undervalued and there being a general lack of conservation awareness in the country.

Policy is currently being developed which is aimed at establishing a demand management ethos in the country. This flows out of a national water conservation campaign which was launched in early 1995. The policy will be aimed at the various water user sectors in South Africa including:
- Domestic and municipal   12.0% of total
- Industry   7.6%
- Mining   2.7%
- Power generation   2.3%
- Irrigation   50.9%
- Stock watering   1.5%
- The environment   15.5%
- Forestry   7.5%

The policy will be widely consulted amongst the stakeholders in order to ensure broad acceptance and compliance. Issues to be addressed will include:
- tariff and levy policy as demand management tools
- specific policy relating to agricultural use of water
- specific policy relating to "wet" industries
- standardised water supply regulations and by-laws for the construction and plumbing industry
- retrofitting programmes
- public communication and awareness creation, particularly in schools
- loss management policy
- related land-use policy
- the impact of alien plant species in catchments
- water using appliance labelling policy

5.3 Tariff policy

The Department of Water Affairs and Forestry has been involved in reviewing its policies regarding the pricing of water for the past 18 months. The price of water sold from Government water works is set each year in April. Water is seriously undervalued in South Africa. This tends to mitigate against water being viewed as an economic good and hence being valued and conserved as it should be in a semi-arid country.

As pricing and tariff policy is developed, the underlying objective is to balance the three factors of price, cost and value of water. The price of water must reflect its cost whilst at the same time reflect that water is not only an economic commodity but also a social commodity closely related to other factors such as health and production. The price of water must therefore reflect the difficult tension between equity and economic sustainability. The cost of water should be carefully determined so as to reflect the full value of water to society, including the opportunity costs and social costs of a particular usage, over-and-above the direct costs. The adjustment of water prices to the point where they begin to reflect the full cost and value of water in South Africa will have to be done at some point if we are to continue to develop, but this will be politically difficult in the short term. Clear policy is required in order to inform the public of the processes, and careful study will have to be done to fully understand the implications of new policy on the economy as a whole and of the meeting of basic water supply needs.

5.4 Water quality management

Because water is a scare resource, water quality management becomes increasingly important in order to conserve the existing resources. The water quality vs development debate is common to most countries and, whilst various models are being reviewed at present, there is as yet no formal Government policy document on the issue. The underlying perspective which is emerging through the policy which has already been developed, both in the Water Supply and Sanitation White Paper and in the Water Law Review Principles, is that the environment should be regarded as the *resource base* on which all development depends. It should not be regarded as a competitor for water allocation along side other competing interests - it is the source from which all other users derive their water. Implementing such a policy in practice still requires difficult decisions and objective tools are needed to implement the policy in the field. The Receiving Water Quality Method is one such tool which is presently being used in South Africa.

5.5 Sanitation policy

Although sanitation is discussed extensively in the Water Supply and Sanitation White Paper, the White Paper acknowledges that a thorough process is necessary to develop a comprehensive national sanitation policy and an implementation strategy which will begin to address the backlog of services on the most basic level throughout the country. Such a process was begun in mid 1995 through the bringing together of senior politicians and public servants from a number of Ministries and Departments to provide a mandate to develop comprehensive policy, hosted by the Minister of Water Affairs and Forestry.

Sanitation traditionally receives low priority as a development issue although it has a profound effect on development potential and on poverty alleviation. One of the reasons for this is lack of co-ordination amongst public bodies concerned with the issues and another is the development of a viable institutional framework to promote and implement policy. The establishment of a multi-departmental Task Team to develop policy with the necessary political support was therefore regarded as essential to the policy development process. The following departments have been included in the process:

- The Department of Water Affairs and Forestry,
- The Department of Health
- The Department of Land Affairs
- The Reconstruction and Development Programme (Vice-President's office)
- The Department of Finance

After extensive nation-wide consultation based on a Green Paper (a discussion document), a White Paper on Sanitation is nearing completion. This sets out policy on appropriate sanitation technology, the engagement and capacity building of communities, the popular promotion of sanitation, financing options, institutional arrangements and a national sanitation development strategy. It is anticipated that this document will be to the sanitation problem what the White Paper of November 1994 was to water supply.

5.6 Local Government support

On 1 November 1995 the first democratic local elections were held in South Africa in all but a few areas. This marked a new era of challenge as many areas, particularly those areas which formed the previous black homelands, had never had any form of local Government. It is the constitutional function of local Government to provide services to local consumers and the constitutional responsibility of the central Government to ensure that this is done within the broad national policy framework and to acceptable standards. Because it will be some years before local Government will be fully functional, especially in rural areas, the Department of Water Affairs and Forestry will have a role in the medium term in supporting local Government. The challenge will be to do so in a way which does not build a large central bureaucracy at the same time as disempowering people at local level. Policy is therefore currently being prepared to guide the relationships between the two tiers of Government and to clearly set out the functions of the different institutions.

5.7 Regulatory framework for private sector engagement

There exists a dilemma in South Africa in that, although there is a weak rural local Government level, there is enormous demand, and, compared with the rest of Africa, a very well developed private consultant and construction sector. There is scope for a creative relationship between local Government and the private sector through such arrangements as delegated management concessions. The problem, however, is that there exists the possibility in such unequal relationships for exploitation and corruption. Also, because of the lack of experience of local Government personnel and the need on the part of the private sector for investment security, many potentially promising arrangements are not forged. In order to meet these concerns a regulatory framework is being designed in order to set standards and provide an "enabling" environment to create sound relationships between the various parties.

5.8 Water law review

The interplay between legislation and policy is a topic in itself which is worthy of research. Legislation provides the mandate for the activities of the public service, whereas policy reflects the priorities of the Government of the day. The existing Water Act (1956) has for many years been regarded by many experts as in need of review. As new policy is being developed, both to account for the needs of a modern developing industrial economy and to ensure equity for those who do not enjoy services at present, it has become increasingly clear that a complete re-writing of the Water Act is necessary.

The opportunity for a review of the water law is presented by the present unique period in South Africa's history. The initial phase has been the drafting of a set of principles on which a new law will be based. These are divided into 7 sections :

- The water cycle - all water is part of the hydrological cycle.
- Legal aspects of water - all water, as part of the hydrological cycle, should be treated similarly before the law thus eliminating the concepts of private water and riparianity as the primary criteria for apportionment.
- Water resource management priorities.
- Water resource management approaches.
- Water institutions - opening the possibility for the establishment of catchment management institutions.
- Existing water rights - to ensure that the new law is constitutional.
- Water services - to ensure the achievement of equity through a new law.

6   References

1. Department of Water Affairs and Forestry, South African Government (1994) *Water Supply and Sanitation Policy White Paper.*

PROSPECTS FOR COOPERATION IN THE EUPHRATES-TIGRIS BASIN
Cooperation within international river basins

A. KIBAROGLU
Bilkent University, Ankara, TURKEY

Abstract
This paper aims at providing a basis for the efforts to replace a situation of conflict between Turkey and Syria over the management and allocation of the waters in the Euphrates-Tigris river basin with one of cooperation. Within the general framework of the concept of interdependence, references will be made to the international regimes theory. Bearing in mind that the three states cutting across the rivers do not have a brilliant record of relations, identifying the principles, norms, rules and procedures of a regime concerning the management and allocation of a transboundary water-course system needs further elaboration of the proposals set forth by Turkey. Accordingly, the concept of leadership will be exploited with a view to propose that Turkey could act as a leader in the formation of a regime in that river basin. Though, in the first analysis the application of international regimes theory may seem to be conceivable for all levels of water allocation and management, each water dispute should be dealt with in an extensive manner considering the significant properties of each case.
Keywords: cooperation, Euphrates-Tigris, interdependence, international regimes, leadership.

1   Introduction

The waters of the Euphrates-Tigris emerged as a regional problem among the three major riparians because the supply of water will be short to satisfy the demand of huge development projects that these riparians implemented since the early 1970s [1]. There is a concern over how growing interdependence among the riparians of the Euphrates-Tigris river basin will influence the settlement of the water dispute in the

Water Policy: Allocation and management in practice. Edited by P. Howsam and R.C. Carter.
Published in 1996 by E & FN Spon. ISBN 0 419 21650 2

region. A recurring theme of the paper is a formulation of plausible proposals for co-operative solutions in the basin. Turkey is the upstream country in this river basin, and more than 90% of the waters of the Euphrates and 45% of Tigris are drained from Turkish territory. Accordingly, not only Syrian and Iraqi authorities, but also most of the water resources analysts [2][3][4][5] observe the irreversible dominance of Turkey which arises from its upstream position, its military power as well as its achievements so far in politico-economic terms in integrating with the international market economy.

These analysts suggest that, Turkey has no interest and no material gain from, the basin-wide cooperation. To identify Turkey on the one hand as a "hegemon" who exercises power-politics in her relations with other riparians because of her advantageous position, and on the other hand, to evaluate the positions of Syria and Iraq as disadvantageous downstream countries contributes only to the impression that the situation in the basin is unavoidably conflict-prone. Relations between Turkey and Iraq with respect to the waters of the Euphrates and Tigris constitute an important area of concern. However, substantial economic relations have existed between Turkey and Iraq since the 1980s, which have had positive impacts on the water policies of these two riparians. Most of these transactions have been frustrated since 1990 due to the Gulf crisis. But an Iraqi recovery can be anticipated following the lifting of the economic embargo imposed by the UN and, the policy-makers of Turkey and Iraq may be able to find appropriate solutions for the management and allocation of the waters of the Euphrates and Tigris.

However, the main argument in this paper is that a cooperation model could be built in the Euphrates-Tigris basin by using the major premises of the international regimes theory where, particularly between Turkey and Syria an interdependence in politico-economic terms is being observed in the post-Cold War international economic and political structure.

2   Intra-basin relations and the concept of interdependence

The distinguishing feature of transboundary rivers is the politics of their development, management, and the present and predicted use of them by the riparian states. The hydrology of a river does not change when it crosses an international frontier, only the politics change [6]. The geography of the Euphrates-Tigris river basin has an impact on relationships among the basin countries. Since our purpose is to evaluate these relations as the empirical indicators of interdependence, we should beforehand clarify what we mean by the concept of interdependence, particularly within the context of riparian imperatives of the regional states. If states are taken as economic units, interdependence denotes, in our conceptualisation, the impact of physical effects generated in one state delivered to the other via a river system. The Euphrates-Tigris river basin is such a medium by which effects of an action taken in one of the three regional states are transported to the others. Here, interdependence [7] is seen as being a structural relationship which exists among the riparian states and specifies the degree of connectedness. It does not predict what action shall be taken by either of the parties which means that the position of the riparians could be cooperative or conflict-prone.

Since the end of the 1960s when all three riparians have been engaged in starting development projects on the two river systems[1], they began to function under conditions of growing interdependence.

Increasing perceived uncertainties attended these developments and the riparians began to feel vulnerable. At the same time the international environment was becoming more complex. The uncertainties developed as the result of uncoordinated projects on the rivers in the different states, as well as through the lack of accurate and reliable data relating to the entire river basin. Information on the use of the water within the region was lacking as was a genuine regional water management institution. Inappropriate water technologies and engineering and other bilateral and trilateral issues exacerbated tensions among the riparians.[2] Most regarded the situation a zero-sum game. In practice the challenge was and remains to identify the nature of the interdependent relationship of the riparians which must cope with the implicit costs and the benefits of the development.

2.1 Regime formation for management and allocation of Euphrates-Tigris

Where interdependence is not a sufficient condition for cooperation and may even result in conflict, regimes may provide the necessary linkage between interdependence and cooperation. Regimes may help to overcome the obstacles that hinder their efforts to co-operate in an interdependent world [8][9]. Regimes are important because they can act as an intermediary between the states, decentralising the enforcement of agreements, thereby facilitating cooperation. We incur the costs of interdependence in this river basin because of the lack of institutionalised patterns of cooperation. The emergence of an appropriate regime may play a constructive role by formulating the principles, norms, rules and decision-making procedures which will enable us to reap the benefits of interdependence, and end up with joint gains. Regimes function as platforms on which participating states meet regularly, thence a certain level of institutionalisation tends to occur, though its degree may be minimal at the beginning. Concerning the Euphrates-Tigris basin we see only the Joint Technical Committee (JTC) acting as a technical forum meeting regularly for general projects discussions and exchange of hydrological data. The Joint Technical Committee was formed in 1980 between Turkey and Iraq within the framework of Joint Economic Commission Protocol, and then Syria joined in 1983. Since 1980, JTC convened for 16 times until its last gathering in October 1992. This has been a very basic form of cooperation which could not enable adequate consultation for a regime formation.

The most significant advantages of international regimes mainly follow from the fact that regimes are almost by definition organised, and even institutionalised. The JTC meetings have not been regular and the main reason why the meetings have been interrupted is said to be the reluctance of both Syrian and Iraqi authorities to put

---

[1] Such projects can be classified as Turkey's engagement in GAP (Grand Anatolian Project), or Syria's Euphrates Valley Project (Tabqa Dam), or Iraq's building of Tharthar Canal which links the Tigris to the Euphrates.

[2] In the Euphrates- Tigris river basin among the three major riparians, water is one of the factors stimulating regional tension. We could name two principal sources of friction between Turkey and Syria: one is allegations by Turkey that Syria backs the Kurdish terrorist groups, and to a lesser extent, Syria's irredentist claims to the province of Hatay. Such issues are deliberately kept beyond the scope of analysis in this research.

forward constructive proposals of water use, development and management of the Euphrates-Tigris river system. Conversely, they insisted on a sharing agreement which divides the rivers in a mathematical manner. Nevertheless, regardless of the degree of institutionalisation, such preliminary institutions are useful in the generation of information and making it available to all participating states. It is well-known that barriers to information and the lack of communication can seriously hamper interstate cooperation. The Euphrates-Tigris river basin, like all other basins in the Middle East, lacks a free exchange of reliable and accurate data and information concerning water and land resources. This constitutes a substantial obstacle for a regime formation. In that respect, Turkey's proposal for a Three Staged Plan (TSP) is worthy of serious study. The Three Staged Plan was prepared and presented by the State Hydraulic Works (DSI) of Turkey in 1985 in one of the regular meetings of the JTC. The plan contains an outline of possibilities for enhanced cooperation among the three riparians by proposing three phases to be followed jointly by the technocrats of three riparians: inventory studies for water resources; inventory studies for land resources; and evaluation of these inventory studies. By its very nature TSP is not only a substantial proposal to gather data and information concerning land and water resources of the whole region (i.e. the river basin), but also a very important step in regime formation. Its approach is special because, an upstream country, Turkey proposes that a principle of limited territorial sovereignty in the river basin be agreed rather than absolute sovereignty.

There are some major legal framework doctrines for sharing waters in transboundary river systems. Among them, absolute territorial sovereignty (Harmon Doctrine: invoked during the US-Mexican negotiations on the Rio Grande, 1895) implies that other riparian countries do not have any right to constraint a country's use of a river within its own territory. It is obviously preferred by upstream countries. The main alternative to this doctrine is defined as absolute territorial integrity which implies that each states renounces exclusive right to water exploitation. It is tended to be favoured by downstream countries. The principle of limited territorial sovereignty lies somewhere in between them, and implies that no state within a river basin should use or permit the use of its territory to cause significant harm to its neighbours.

The general tendency in transboundary river basins in the world is that, while the downstream country advocates the absolute territorial integrity of the river basin, the upstream riparian insists on the absolute territorial sovereignty so as to reap the benefits of its position [10]. Quite the contrary, in the Euphrates-Tigris case, Syria and Iraq, the two downstream countries, insist on bilateral sharing agreements depending implicitly on the principle of absolute territorial sovereignty. That is to say, since 1985, after Turkey put forward her TSP proposal, the Syrians and the Iraqis have started to pronounce a series of bilateral sharing agreements. Whereas Turkey with her proposal, made it explicit that the river basin should be treated as a whole, Syria and Iraq insisted on the apportionment of the river basin. In their reasoning, having divided the river basin, each riparian would then claim absolute sovereignty over her portion of the river basin which falls within her own territory. The TSP used the terminology developed by the International Law Commission of the UN entrusted with the codification of a "Law of the Non-Navigational Uses of International Watercourses" which may provide the norms of a water regime for the Euphrates-Tigris river basin.

The International Law Commission started working on the non-navigational uses of international watercourses, in 1971 under the auspices of the UN General Assembly, with a view to its progressive development of international law and its codification. After 23 years, the Commission came up with a document that consisted of 32 draft articles, and a resolution on confined transboundary ground water (ILC, Forty-sixth session, 2 May-22 July 1994, UN General Assembly, A/CN4/L 493, 12 July 1994). The principles and norms of an international water regime on the Euphrates-Tigris can be derived from the following six articles of General Principles: Articles 5 thru 10 concerning: equitable and reasonable utilization and participation; factors relevant to equitable and reasonable utilization; obligation not to cause significant harm; general obligation to co-operate; regular exchange of data and information; relationship between different kinds of uses.

2.2 Supplementary proposals of Turkey for cooperation

Turkey's initiatives have not been limited to the Three Staged Plan, but also continued with the proposal of the Peace Pipeline based on the idea to supply the Arabian peninsula with fresh water from the Seyhan and Ceyhan rivers in southern Anatolia. Furthermore, Turkey was eager to host a Global Water Summit in Istanbul in 1991 to discuss regional water issues, and was equally very willing to convene the multilateral talks on water issues within the framework of Middle East Peace Process. Moreover, in Turkey, scientists were very successful in convening a number of prominent conferences on the main theme of ways of cooperation in the Euphrates-Tigris river basin [11][12]. Turkey put forward many more co-operative proposals utilizing her experience in water technology and engineering skills in the use, management and development of the water resources of the river basin. Proposals for technical cooperation based on the idea of basin-wide planning process include the supply augmenting policies such as storage facilities, water transfer between rivers and non-conventional water supply methods, and demand management policies which include making more efficient use of existing supplies through structural, operational and economic means [13].

Turkey made attempts to reach sound relationship, more or less institutionalised, among the riparians so as to reap the benefits of the river basin in an interdependent context. While making use of the existing norms of ILC to form a regime, Turkey also developed a new set of norms, rules, principles and procedures which do not comprise a water-sharing agreement. For regime theorists, just like the water experts, agreements are based upon immediate self-interest, whereas regimes facilitate agreements by sacrificing instant gain. In the Euphrates-Tigris river basin a water-sharing agreement could not cope with the uncertainties of such an interdependent setting and would not solve the deficiencies in water use, management and development. In case the three countries form a series of bilateral agreements regarding the sharing of the waters of the Euphrates, since demands on water will certainly change overtime due to the rapid population growth and economic development of the riparians, there will probably be continuous shifting of alliances which might satisfy short term solutions to various problems related to the rivers. These, however, will do little to meet either the long-term internal needs of each state, or to facilitate an overall peace process involving the entire Middle East. In sum, a water-sharing agreement would tend to encourage the continuation of uncoordinated and inefficient methods of water allocation.

3   Institutional bargaining and leadership in the Euphrates-Tigris

An analysis of the relevance of international regimes theory with respect to the water issue in the Euphrates-Tigris basin should bear in mind that such regimes are not created spontaneously. Regime theorists have carried out a great deal of work on the politics of regime formation. Oran Young identifies two analytical perspectives currently dominating the study of regime formation [14]. The power theorists (realists or neorealists) emphasise the role of a hegemon in the formation of a regime. They assert that the presence of a hegemon (like the US presence in world politics after the Second World War) is a necessary condition for the emergence of institutional arrangements at the international level. On the other hand, mainstream utilitarians focus on the behaviour of rational utility maximizers and typically assume that actors of this type will reach agreement on the content of mutually beneficial institutional arrangements.

Young criticises the main premises of both schools, and presents a new model called "institutional bargaining". The model emphasises negotiations between self-interested parties as a means of dealing with collective-action problems. He asserts that institutional bargaining is likely to succeed when effective leadership emerges; it will fail in the absence of such leadership. Leadership involves a combination of imagination in inventing institutional options and skill in brokering the interests of numerous actors to line up support for such options. The Montreal Protocol on ozone depletion in 1987 is an example of a state, the USA, playing the role of a leader rather than a hegemon.

In the post-Cold War world, unlike the 1950s, it's not easy to identify any hegemon as the preponderant actor in regime formation. With the break-up of the Soviet Union there exists no hegemon over the ex-Comecon economies while in the capitalist world the USA shows little interest in playing a truly hegemonic role. Pertaining to the Middle East in particular, one may no longer talk about a superpower rivalry. Instead we observe the military posture of the US during and after the Gulf War, or its diplomatic mediator position in the Middle East Peace Process. These activities can no longer be classified as in the hegemons' dealings. Eventually, some scholars argued that the international system is not only in transition, but also that decisions and choices made by the regional actors like Turkey and Syria who find free arena to manoeveure, are likely to play an important role in the peaceful settlement of conflicts. Thus, leadership with regard to regime formation is a matter of entrepreneurship and involves the combination of imaginative institutional options with skill in clarifying the overlapping interests of the parties to work on those options. A leader in this context is a political entrepreneur who sees a potential profit in organising collaboration. Entrepreneurial leaders in regime formation are neither hegemons who can impose their will on others, nor ethically motivated actors who seek to find workable institutional arrangements as a contribution to common good. For entrepreneurship to emerge, not only must there be a potential social gain to be derived from the formation of an international regime, but the entrepreneur must expect to be able to gain more himself from investing in the regime. In addition to entrepreneurial leadership, Young classifies two more leadership categories as structural leadership and intellectual leadership. The former relates to a leader who devises effective ways to bring the state's structural power (which is based on the possession of material resources) to bear in the form of bargaining, while the latter relates to a leader who relies on the power of the ideas and experiences to shape the way in which the participants in institutional bargaining understand the issues at stake.

It is argued that Turkey acts as a hegemon in adapting water related politics vis-à-vis her downstream neighbours. Some political analysts insist on Turkey's dominance in the river basin by concentrating solely on her structural power. Yet, Turkey by proposing the Three Staged Plan and other initiatives to establish a basin-wide cooperation after a series of trilateral negotiations displays a role which is a combination of her entrepreneurial and intellectual skill and power on basin-wide issues.

4 Conclusion

In the Euphrates-Tigris river basin, there lies the problem of effective management and allocation of water. The tension over the allocation of the waters of the Euphrates-Tigris can be circumvented with the establishment of institutionalised patterns of cooperation, namely an international regime. Turkey may act as a political entrepreneur in the bargaining process which may pave the way for a regime formation. To be a far-sighted leader, Turkey should continuously assess the patterns of future use by each riparian. The two other riparians' water use, however, will depend heavily on their economic planning. In that manner, Syria could be in a position to re-examine its water allocation policy, and re-shape her strategy with respect to food self-sufficiency, and thus conclude that allocating water to agriculture is neither sustainable nor always productive in economic sense. For this purpose strong political will is required from the Syrian side, and Turkey should contribute to this by the policy of *rapprochement* to build confidence in the Syrian leadership. Although the main argument of this paper is based on regime effectiveness in the management of the waters of the Euphrates and the Tigris, one cannot make sure *a priori* whether a proposed regime will play the same role in different levels of water allocation and management. Since, it exists ample water in the Euphrates-Tigris river basin together with the considerations of co-riparians' likely *rapprochement* (stemming from their close cultural, social, economic and political ties), international regimes theory is found to be suitable in application to the case. Yet, without dealing with each case in such a manner, one cannot claim that international regimes can be a remedy for any water dispute.

5 References

1. Allan, J.A. (1993) *The Euphrates Water: Current and Future Water Sharing*, University of London, SOAS: Centre for Near and Middle Eastern Studies,

Middle East Water Database, London.

2. Naff, T. and Matson, R. (eds.), (1984) *Water in the Middle East: Conflict or Cooperation ?*, Westview Press, Boulder, Colorado.

3. Starr, J.R. and Stoll, D.C. (eds.) (1988) *The Politics of Scarcity: Water in the Middle East*, Westview Press, Boulder, Colorado.

4. Kolars, J. and Mitchell, W.A. (1991) *The Euphrates River and the Southeast Anatolia Development Project*, Southern Illinois University Press, Carbondale .

5. Lowi, M. (1993) *Water and Power*, Cambridge University Press, Cambridge.

6. LeMarquand, D. (1977) *International Rivers: The Politics of Cooperation*, University of British Columbia & Waterloo Research Center, British Columbia.

7. Keohane R.O. and Nye Jr., J.S. (1989) *Power and Interdependence: World Politics in Transition*, 2nd Edition, MIT Press, Boston, Massachusetts.

8. Haggard, S. and Simmons, B. (1987) Theories of International Regimes, *International Organisation*, Vol. 41, pp.491-517.

9. Rittberger, V. and Mayer, P. (eds.) (1993) *Regime Theory and International Relations*, Clarendon Press, Oxford.

10. Rogers, P. (1991) International River Basins: Persuasive Uni-directional Externalities, presented at the Conference on *The Economics of Transnational Commons*, Universita di Sienna, Italy, April 25-27.

11 International Conference on *Transboundary Waters in the Middle East: Prospects for Regional Cooperation*, Bilkent University, Ankara, Sept. 1991;

12 Conference on *Water as an Element of Cooperation in the Middle East*, Hacettepe University, Ankara, Sept. 1993.

13 Bilen, Ö. and Uskay, S. (1991) Comprehensive Water Resources Management Policies: An Analysis of Turkish Experience, *The World Bank International Workshop on Comprehensive Water Resources Management Policies*.

14. Young O.R. (1989) The Politics of International Regime Formation: Managing Natural Resources and the Environment, *International Organisation*, Vol. 43, pp.349-375.

COMPUTER AIDED DECISION SUPPORT SYSTEM FOR WATER STRATEGIC PLANNING IN JORDAN
A methodology for water strategic planning

B.A. Al-KLOUB and T.T. AL-SHEMMERI
School of Engineering, Staffordshire University, Stafford, UK

Abstract
The Nominal Group Technique as a structured group process and the PROMETHEE as a multi-criteria decision aid software are utilised to develop a decision support system for water strategic planning in Jordan. The system described is novel in that it integrates the various management techniques in order to increase the flexibility and efficiency of the decision making process. This system is then implemented on a sample of water projects in Jordan, and results are discussed.
Keywords: computer aided planning, demand management, multi-criteria decision aid, nominal group technique, water resources management.

1   Introduction

Water resources issue is a major complicating factor in the socio-political situation of the Middle East. The lack of efficiency in managing water resources has become one of the serious problems facing countries in the region. Jordan already suffers one of the lowest levels of water resources per capita, as well as one of the highest rates in population growth in the Middle East. Water scarcity is becoming a significant constraint to development in Jordan and the need to develop a national water strategy is imperative.

In Jordan, there is no comprehensive framework for analysing policies and prioritising options to guide decisions about managing water resources. The ranking and selection of water development projects is dominated by single criterion analysis; usually financial feasibility. Non-optimal selection of projects has resulted in knock-on effects such as waste of resources, environmental degradation, loss of opportunities for external support and inadequate community support for water

Water Policy: Allocation and management in practice. Edited by P. Howsam and R.C. Carter.
Published in 1996 by E & FN Spon. ISBN 0 419 21650 2

development projects.

In this paper a strategic planning model to guide water resources decision that is suitable for Jordan's needs is described. Due to space limitations, components and results of applying the model will be briefly described, but sufficient attention will be given to describe the general methodology adopted.

2   The model, and its application

The components of the model are shown in Fig. 1 (steps 1-6). It is a prescriptive requisite analysis, to guide the evolution of decision makers' perceptions in a dynamic, and cyclic process [1][2]. The decision makers' beliefs and preferences are assessed, modelled, and explored to derive insights and to allow revision of judgements until no further intuitions emerge. Components of the model are described in the following steps:

2.1 Step 1: identification of problems and objectives of the water sector
This is an important step to understand and define the core problem (causes-effects relationship) and objectives (means-ends relationship). The hierarchy of the national goals and objectives was broken down into lower objectives. Due to space limitations, only one example of the objective tree is shown in Fig. 2 for the objective 'water supply is increased' (level 1). Maximising water supply could be achieved by using: conventional water resources, non-conventional resources, and management and optimisation (level 2), to name a few options in order of precedence. Further specifications are shown to indicate the various levels and elements of the tree. The weights are shown in brackets which are evaluated using a specialised software (Judgmental Analysis System, JAS) to reduce subjectivity, and validate consistency [3].

2.2 Step 2: the selection and testing of the fundamental objectives, specification of attributes and weights
In order to select the set of the fundamental objectives an organised brainstorming workshop was carried out with the help of decision makers and a facilitator (co-author) in Jordan to identify the objectives, the hierarchy, the fundamental objectives, attributes and weights. The fundamental objective set satisfying certain necessary properties to be used later in the analysis [4][5][6] was selected by the decision makers and tested against these properties. The following ideas were utilised to complete the above tasks:

- *Nominal group technique* as a creative process to identify objectives.
- *Value focused thinking* to identify the fundamental objectives.
- *Demand management* to overcome the shortcomings of the existing supply augmentation approach in water resources planning.
- *Management by objectives* to create options to best achieve the values specified for the decision situation.

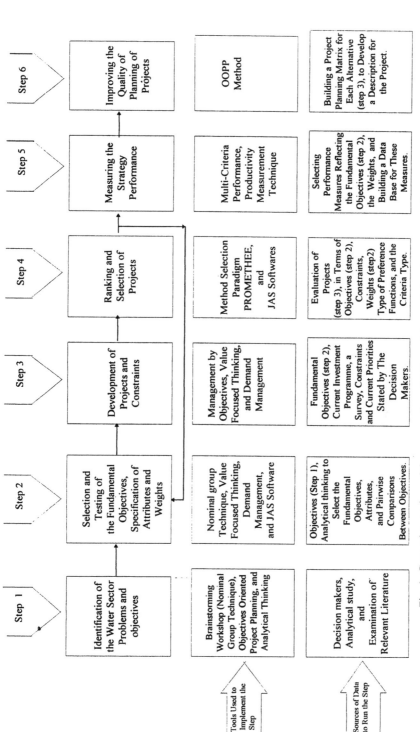

Fig. 1. General overview of the proposed model for ranking and planning water projects.

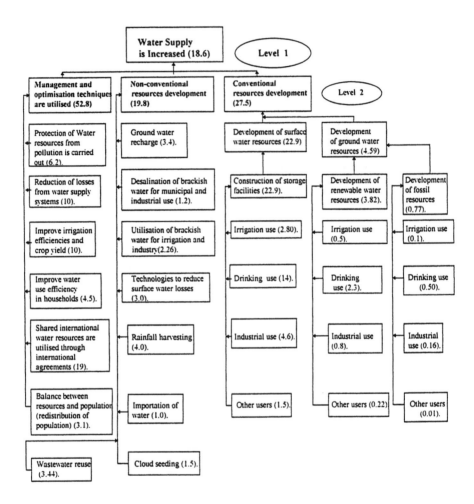

Fig. 2. The objective tree for the objective "Water Supply is Increased", and the calculated weights using the JAS software.

2.3 Step 3: development of projects, and constraints

A survey to identify possible options reflecting the values developed in the brainstorming workshop was carried out. The options were classified into five categories: **technical, regional, managerial, pricing, and regulatory.** The options were deduced from different available documents (including the new investment plan (1995-1998)). As an example, according to the values elicited, highest priorities were given to alternatives including: reducing water losses, increasing water supplies, and improving performance of the sector. The set of constraints (initial cost, operation and maintenance costs, and regional development) were defined by the group of the decision makers who participated in the brainstorming workshop.

2.4 Step 4: ranking and selection of projects

The PROMETHEE method (Preference Ranking Organisation METhod for Enrichment Evaluation) was adopted for use in this study. This method is software driven, user-friendly, provides direct interpretation of parameters, and a sensitivity analysis of results. The method incorporates the following steps [7]:

- *Building an evaluation matrix for projects*: according to a set of criteria.
- *Enrichment of the preference structure*: introducing generalised criteria to remove scaling effects.
- *Enrichment of the dominance relation*: building a multi-criteria preference index to express to which degree an option is preferred to another and an associated outranking graph and outranking flow to express how each option relates to the other options (strengths and weaknesses of the option).
- *Exploitation for decision aid*: PROMETHEE I provides a partial ranking, including possible incomparabilities. PROMETHEE II shows complete ranking of options. PROMETHEE V extends the application of the PROMETHEE II method to the problem of selection of several options to satisfy the a set of constraints.
- *The GAIA program* (Geometrical Analysis for Interactive Aid): provides a geometrical presentation of results obtained by PROMETHEE . GAIA is based on reducing the multi-dimensional criteria space to a two-dimensional criteria plane to allow direct visual presentation. Further more, it offers interactive dialogue with the user to vary certain parameters and displays the resulting changes.

A complete analysis for 72 water actions (developed in step 3 and classified into five categories) was carried out [8]. Complete ranking was demonstrated and a sensitivity analysis was undertaken by changing the weights of the criteria and observing the changes in the ranking of the actions. The following five special cases for ranking were investigated:

1. All water resources actions without introducing constraints.
2. All water resources actions after introducing cost constraint.
3. Each category of actions independently after introducing costs constraints.
4. All possible projects (this is the current situation case where implementing some of the projects is not possible due to different reasons such as political) after introducing costs constraints.
5. Technical options based on the current situation (possible projects) and introducing regional development, and cost constraints.

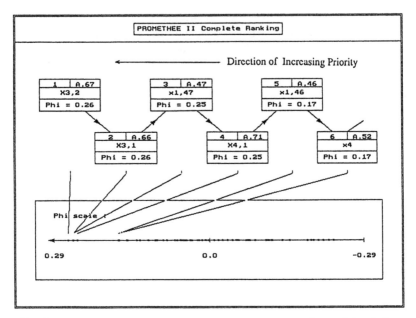

Fig. 3. A complete ranking (phi scale) of the first few alternatives and the clusters.

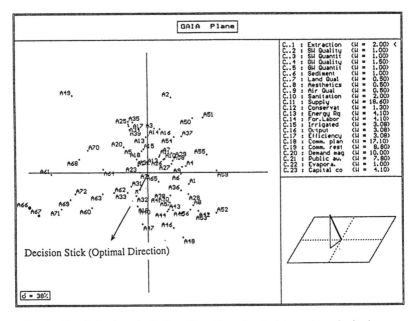

Fig. 4. The Gaia plane, including alternatives, the decision axis, and criteria.

For example, results of case 1 (part of it shown in Fig. 3) shows that the highest priority was given to managerial options $X_{3,2}$ (cease pumping from Qa-Disi aquifer (the second project in the third category)) and $X_{3,1}$ (limit of agricultural sufficiency (the first project in the third category)) respectively. This result is consistent with the values of the water sector regarding the necessary change in the way we view and use water. The water pumped from Qa-Disi is fossil non-renewable water and unfortunately it is used in agriculture, while the agricultural sector is consuming 79% of the available water resources and contributing to less than 7% of the Gross National Product (compared to industry which consumes 5% of the available water resources and contributes to 22% of the Gross National Product). Next projects in ranking are technical option $X_{1,47}$ (hydraulic analysis and improvement of water system in the country) , $X_{4,1}$ (pricing option) and again this is consistent with the values that policies should be demand driven. Next projects in ranking are regional options X_4 (Al-Wehda dam), and X_5 (Hasbani dam) and this is consistent with the values regarding obtaining the full entitlement of water resources shared with other neighbouring countries.

The associated net dominance values (Phi scale) were calculated using PROMETHEE (Fig. 2) and this shows the cluster of alternatives which are close to each other, so the first three options form a cluster, the next two in ranking form another cluster.

The GAIA plane (Fig. 4) is consistent with the results of ranking shown in Fig. 2 and the decision stick (the direction of the optimal solution) is located as far as possible in this direction and the length of this stick indicates the strength of the decision towards the optimal solution, from which it can be observed that managerial options $X_{3,2}$ (or A67) and $X_{3,1}$ (or A 66) are first priorities The PROMETHEE model solution is able to supply the intervals of weights for which the ranking does not change , for example in the first case, the "water supply" criterion with a normalised weight of 18.6%, may be weighted between 18.53% and 18.60% without affecting the ranking, all other factors remains unchanged. This indicates that the optimal solution is stable to minor changes in the weights of the criteria. Stability of results for different criteria weights is quite sensitive and using different set of weights will give another set of priorities as demonstrated in weight stability intervals and the walking weights facility in PROMETHEE which allows interactive modification of the values of the weights the resulting change on ranking.

2.5 Step 5: measuring the water sector strategy performance
An interactive computerised constantly monitored system for performance evaluation of the strategy was built, utilizing productivity as a performance measure, to monitor the changes in efficiency, effectiveness and quality [9]. The Multi-Criteria Performance/ Productivity Measurement Technique (MCP/PMT) method [9] was utilised because it links measurement and improvement to the customer needs. Different measures were elicited from the set of the fundamental objectives by the group of decision makers who participated in the brainstorming session utilizing the Nominal Group Technique method (NGT) [4]. These measures support the strategy mission, measure the performance, consider interdependencies, and stress short and long term plans. The measures, their relative importance, measurement scale and reflected fundamental objectives were developed. For each measure a long term goal

and a minimum acceptable level having significant meaning were specified by the decision makers, these two values were converted into a ten point scale.

Aggregating measures in an integrating fashion was achieved by developing a multi-attribute value function for all measures after converting all measures into a common scale, and introducing weights to measure the relative importance of each productivity measure.   Finally, an integrated value function incorporating criteria weighting to allow the development of one indicator for the overall performance of the strategy was derived.

2.6 Step 6: improving the quality of planning of projects

To address the strategic level of managing projects and to assure a successful implementation, different planning steps were followed in a narrower sense.   The Objective Oriented Project Planning (OOPP) software [8] was utilised to build a planning matrix for each project.   The Project Planning Matrix (PPM) was constructed by developing a description of the project which includes: the overall goal for the project, purposes (objectives), results/outputs, the necessary activities to implement the project, the important assumptions for success, indicators to monitor the success, and verification/sources. Analysis was carried out to check how relevant the assumptions are, what risks they entail, and if the project management can guarantee the results/outputs for each project.

3   References

1.   French, S. (1989) *Readings in decision Analysis*, Chapman and Hall, London.
2.   Phillips, L. (1982) Requisite decision modelling: a case study. *Journal of the Operational Research Society* , Vol. 33, pp. 303-311.
3.   Islei, G. and Lockett, G. (1991) Modelling strategic decision making and performance measurement at ICI pharmaceuticals. *Interfaces*, Vol. 6, pp. 4-22.
4.   Delbecq, A. and Van de Ven, A. (1976)   *Group Techniques for Program Planning, A Guide to Nominal Group and Delphi Process,* Scott Publisher, London.
5.   Keeney, R.(1992) *Value Focused Thinking*, Harvard University Press .
6.   Winpenny, J. (1994) *Managing Water as an Economic Resource*, Development Policy Studies , Overseas Development Institute, London.
7.   Brans, J., Vincke, Ph. and Mareschal, B. (1986) How to select and how to rank projects: the PROMETHEE method. *European Journal of Operational Research*, Vol. 24, pp. 228-238.
8.   Al-Kloub, B. (1995) Application of Multi-Criteria Analysis to Ranking and Evaluation of Water Development Projects, in *Critical Issues in System Theory and Practice*, (ed. Ellis, K, Gregory, A., Mears, B. and Ragsdell, G.), Plenum Publishing Corporation, pp. 89-94.
9.   Sink, S. (1985) *Productivity Management, Planning, Measurement, Evaluation, Control and Improvement,* John Wiley and Sons, NewYork.

THEORY AND PRACTICE IN IRRIGATION WATER ALLOCATION IN THE UK
Irrigation water allocation

E.K. WEATHERHEAD
Water Management Department, Silsoe College, Cranfield University, UK

Abstract
In theory, England and Wales have a comprehensive abstraction licensing system which allocates water according to reasonable need and protects the rights of existing abstractors, allowing them to invest with confidence, whilst also protecting the environment. In practice, the system is coming under increasing criticism both from farmers and environmentalists. Many of the problems can be attributed to a licensing system which is inflexible and fails to meet the needs of modern farming. Although many farmers are unable to obtain water, much of the water licensed for abstraction is unused, even in dry years. Varying licence conditions is slow and expensive, transfers between farmers are difficult and, until recently, the regulatory authorities were seen as unhelpful.

This paper reviews how licensing policies have conflicted with farmer needs in England and Wales, and discusses how changes in legislation, and better knowledge of the existing legislation, could aid irrigators and promote better use of the limited resources.
Keywords: Environment Agency, farmers, licensing, rights, water market

1 Introduction

The demand for water for agricultural irrigation in England and Wales is growing at between 1 and 2% per annum. Although this accounts for only about 1% of total water abstractions, it is a consumptive use concentrated in the driest months and in the driest regions, and can be a very significant user in some catchments. Conflicts are increasingly arising between direct summer abstraction for irrigation and other needs, particularly environmental protection.

Water Policy: Allocation and management in practice. Edited by P. Howsam and R.C. Carter.
Published in 1996 by E & FN Spon. ISBN 0 419 21650 2

2   The abstraction licensing system in England and Wales

The present framework for water allocation in England and Wales was largely introduced by the Water Resources Act of 1963. A system of abstraction licensing was set up for most abstractions, including spray irrigation. Apart from a few refinements, the concepts have remained little changed in subsequent legislation up to the latest Water Resources Act of 1991.

Licences are issued by the regulatory body, currently the Environment Agency. A lengthy application procedure has to be followed, including local and national advertising, and a study by the Environment Agency to ensure that other users and the environment will not be adversely affected. The permitted volumes are limited to "reasonable need", although the definition of this is poorly defined.

The possession of a licence for irrigation gives the abstractor a legal right to take water from the specified source for the duration of the licence or until the licence is revoked. Of course, licences in themselves cannot guarantee that the amount of water authorised for abstraction will always be available. However, subsequent applications cannot be granted if they derogate an existing licence.

To protect existing water users, the Water Resources Act of 1963 enabled them to register their abstraction and to obtain 'Licences of Right' based on their previous level of usage. The regulators had no opportunity to curtail these 'Licences of Right' providing that the abstractors demonstrated that water had been abstracted for a period of 5 years. In practice, there were few records and little attempt, or perceived need, to limit the volumes claimed. Unsurprisingly, many of the licences of right are very large. Furthermore, unlike most subsequent licences, they are not time limited and have no conditions or cessation limits. Under current legislation, these licences cannot be revoked or amended without compensation (which could now be considerable), and although many have been amended by negotiation, they have become a major problem for improving water allocation.

Most subsequent licences are time-limited, giving the regulators an opportunity to review total commitments at periodic intervals. However, although licences have often been adjusted as a condition of renewal, renewals are given priority over new applications, maintaining the first-come first-served system.

In order to protect existing abstractors and the environment, most subsequent licenses also contain conditions. Licences can specify the maximum abstraction permitted per year, per day and in some cases, per hour; these rates are independent of each other. Licences can restrict the period during which abstraction is permitted, for example during the winter only. Most specify cessation flows or levels (e.g. abstraction must cease when the river flow at a specified point drops below a specified level).

3   The farmer's perception

The licence application system is widely felt by farmers to be unnecessarily cumbersome, expensive and in particular slow. In 1996, applications in Anglia region have been taking up to six months to consider. Even if an application conforms with Environment Agency policy, e.g. to increase use of winter storage reservoirs, the full legal procedure has to be followed. This adds considerably to the cost and lead time required.   Any request by the abstractor to vary the licence also requires the full application procedure to be repeated, and the Environment Agency may impose new conditions. This applies even to minor changes, such as varying the peak flow rate to match new equipment capacities. Not surprisingly, many licence holders prefer to make do with a imperfect licence.

Licences must specify where the water is to be applied, previously interpreted to be limited to the abstractor's own land. This has meant farmers were unable to share or trade water, and hence use it where it is most beneficial. This has been a particular problem for growers renting land on a rotation and wishing to move licences to follow the irrigated crops.   A limited amount of trading has taken place, by the cumbersome method of selling the abstraction point and then varying the specified area. It appears the Environment Agency may now condone agreed transfers without land ownership changes where hydrological conditions permit, but the procedure is still too slow to be practical for short term transfers. It also seems to be permissible to include neighbours' land when requesting or renewing a licence (although it is not clear how reasonable need can then be calculated), but the legal position is untested.

Similarly, until recently, farmers could have unused water in reservoirs which they could not legally give to drought stricken neighbours. A sensible reinterpretation of the legislation by the Environment Agency now allows the reservoir itself to be specified as the application point; farmers are then free to transfer that water where it is most needed.

3   Future changes

Government agencies are presently considering changes to the licensing legislation, possibly under the policy of deregulation. The challenge will be to devise changes which encourage the efficient use of the limited resources available for irrigation whilst protecting the environment. From the farmers' viewpoint, there could be major benefits from a more flexible licensing system.   The regulatory authorities could determine how much, when and where water was available for abstraction, and then allow the farming community to allocate it themselves.

Many economists perceive some form of "water market" to be the most effective way to reallocate scarce resources to their most effective use.   Trading may also encourage farmers to adopt water conservation technology. Licences would be freely tradable, subject to the hydrological limitations of the system. The price would be set by the market, outside the regulators control.

One danger is that trading would increase total water use, as the increased flexibility allowed unused resources, particularly "sleeper" licences of right, back into circulation. This might harm both other users, with cessation limits reached earlier, and the environment. A %age clawback of traded quantities could be the best way to compensate, as it would affect only those trading.

Other problems remain to be answered about how such a system could operate. The Environment Agency would have to be clearly seen to be protecting the environment, rather than promoting the trading. It may be that most of the benefits of tradable licences could be obtained more easily by simplifying the existing system.

SECTION 2

WATER RESOURCES

WATER RESOURCES - THE NEED FOR REGIONAL CONTINENTAL AND GLOBAL ASSESSMENTS - AN AFRICAN PERSPECTIVE

Global water resource assessment

T.E. EVANS
Water Resources Consultant, Ely, Cambs, UK

Abstract

In many developing countries, the quality of national hydrological records is deteriorating at a time when water demands are starting to exceed supply. The important of regional planning is stressed. A case is put for hydrology to be seen as a global activity, rather than a national one. This is particularly important in view of the increasing dependence on General Circulation Modelling (GCM) and impact studies in the preparation of water policy strategies; although the difficulties in using GCM outputs at the present time is illustrated.

Keywords: data collection, hydrology, global, GCM, water resources.

1 Introduction

Water policy, as defined for this conference, is the set of principles or guidelines by which water resources are allocated, developed and managed. Before a national water policy can be prepared, the future water availability and the future demands need to be determined with a reasonable measure of accuracy. Without a reliable assessment then any policy is in danger of failing. The problem has been pointed out by Rodda [1], 'it is something of a paradox that, at this time when the global demand for water is rising faster than ever before, knowledge of the world's water resources is waning'.

Although there have been significant advances in rainfall runoff modelling and stochastic data generation, the science of hydrology remains firmly dependent on the collection of continuous records of hydrometric and hydro-meteorological data. It is worrying therefore, to learn that World Bank studies have confirmed the deterioration of these services, which have declined to such an extent, that in many of the developing countries of the world the collection of hydrological data is on the verge of collapse.

Water Policy: Allocation and management in practice. Edited by P. Howsam and R.C. Carter.
Published in 1996 by E & FN Spon. ISBN 0 419 21650 2

The problem is compounded in the continent of Africa due to most of the large river basins spanning the territories of many countries: Zambezi (8), Nile (9), Chari (8), Niger (9) and Zaire (7). In many river basins, a reliable assessment of current and future water availability and demands remain to be evaluated; as do the integrated river basin management studies, which are needed before realistic national water policies can be prepared.

In many regions of the World, and again Africa is a good example, there have been major shifts in rainfall patterns over the past three decades. As a result, the stationarity of river flow records is under question; as are the standard accepted procedures for evaluating the reliability of yields from water resource systems. Changes in global rainfall patterns have emphasised the inter-dependence of runoff within and between continents, and have demonstrated the inadequacies of hydrology at a national scale to solve such problems.

These changes have occurred concurrently with global warming and it is speculated that they may be connected. Whether this is so or not, is still open to debate. However, the potential dangers to future water resources, which is inherent in global warming, has led most countries to undertake climate change impact studies. The inputs to these impact studies depend on outputs from general circulation models (GCM's). GCM's simulate the hydrological interface between the atmosphere and land surfaces and between land surfaces and the oceans. Once again, the need to assess water resources on a regional, continental and global scale is a basic requirement. The failure of current GCM's to model the hydrological cycle adequately, is one of the reason that the value of impact studies based on precipitation outputs from GCM's is under question.

This short paper looks at the need for water resources to be considered as a global resource rather than a national asset and questions the value water policy decision based on climatic impact studies.

2   Data collection services in Africa

2.1 Introduction
As a result of the 1972 and 1984 droughts and famines in Africa, and the sequence of dry years in the Sahel, which have lasted almost unbroken for 30 years, the UN General Assembly in 1986 called for a concerted effort to find solutions to the growing number of problems related to water resources in the region The Sub-Saharan African (SSA) Hydrology Assessment Project was set-up by the World Bank and the UNDP and ran from 1987 to 1992 [2].

The purpose of the study was to prepare inventories and to evaluate the status of existing hydrological data, networks and collection systems in the SSA countries and to make recommendations for the improvement of the quality of data collection and for the general enhancement of the capability to measure, retrieve, process and publish hydrological data and information; the ultimate aim being to assist the countries of the region in the creation of a sound hydrometric record collection system and database for the purposes of planning and evaluating water resources development programmes.

The emphasis changed slightly as the work proceeded. Initially, a major part of the study involved the preparation of inventories and hydrogeological and hydrometeorlogical maps, but following the first regional study for the IGAAD countries, the identification of potential future projects to prevent the further decay in the water resource assessment became a major output.

Table 1. Grouping of SSA Countries

Nr	Grouping	Nr countries	Population (1994) millions	Population (2025) millions	Surface area (10^6 km^2)	Dominant rivers
1	IGADD	7	137	339	4.92	Nile
2	SADCC	11	135	276	6.80	Zambezi, Orange
3	West Africa	23	229	582	9.22	Niger, Lake Chad, Senegal and Volta
4	Central Africa	3	55	131	2.32	Zaire
5	Madagascar	1	12	34	5.82	Betsiboka and Tsiribihina
	Total	45	568	1 362	-	-

2.2 Water scarcity in Africa

The single factor responsible more than any other for creating the pressure on present and future demands on water resources is the increase in population of African countries. The population of the SADC region is likely to double in the next 30 years, whilst the regions covered by IGGAD, Central and Western Africa and forecast to increase by more than two and a half times. These estimates assume that the average fertility will reduce from 6.5 down to 3.0 over this period. Should fertility rates not reduce by this amount then the increase in population will be considerably higher.

There has been little research undertaken to evaluate the problem of water scarcity within the African continent as a whole. Falenmark [3] has made an attempt, using as a yardstick 2 000 m^3/capita/year as an appropriate requirement for Africa. The analysis was simplistic and rather crude, but in spite of these reservations the approach does highlight the serious problems which lies ahead for African development. Of the major surface water basins in Africa however, only the Zaire has resources in excess of foreseeable demands of the riparian states A reliable assessment of the Continent's water resources is needed, together with an assessment of how far it is able to meet the increasing demands which will be placed upon it in the next few decades.

2.3 Conclusion

Amongst the detailed conclusions of the Hydrology Assessment Studies a few of the main ones are listed below:

- In the past hydrological data have been grossly undervalued with all countries having data collection agencies struggling with unrealistic budgets and totally inadequate resources. Funding at present has been reduced to such an extent that many agencies are barely able to function and few function efficiently.
- Compared with meteorological services, there has been a significant deterioration in the relative effectiveness of the hydrological services, which are now very much the poor relation. This is a complete reversal of their perceived importance at the time that most countries became fully independent in the 1950's and 1960's. The reason is

mainly institutional, with the meteorological services more stable and usually located within the Ministry of Transport or Defence and better supported by the WMO, and are seen to provide a global service for air traffic, weather forecasting and, monitoring and research into global warming. Whereas, the hydrological services have in the past been project orientated and of national importance only.

- Water assessment agencies who invariably are a small unit within a large sectorial ministry, eg Agriculture and Public Works etc, have little control over their budgets. Consequently, they are a common target for budget cuts, as they are perceived to be of little importance and are given a low priority.
- In many agencies, continuous records are no longer being collected. Once a hydrological record has gaps, then its value reduces rapidly to the point where it can no longer provide information on which sound development plans can be based.
- Because of the physical and political boundaries within Africa, international river basins should be a dominant force in its economic development.

3   Recent changes in global precipitation

The global interconnections of hydrology are well demonstrated by the large area of the world in what precipitation and runoff is influenced by the Southern Oscillation.

Folland et al [4] have shown that a high proportion of the variance in Sahel rainfall can be explained by differences in sea surface temperatures on a hemi-spherical scale: higher sea temperatures in the southern hemisphere relative to the northern hemisphere and largely responsible for the Sahelian drought. The magnitude of the problem facing Lake Chad is well illustrated by Fig. 1.

Hulme et al [5] have prepared maps (see Fig. 2) showing annual and seasonal changes in precipitation between the periods 1931 to 1960, and 1961 to 1990. The two most prominent features are over northern Russia, with increased precipitation of 10 - 20% and the African Sahel, between latitudes 10°N to 30°N, with reduced precipitation between 20 - 50%. Significant changes, have occurred over all continents.

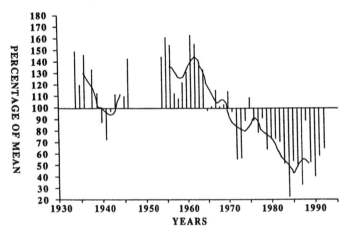

Fig. 1. Departures of annual mean flows, River Chari at N'Djamena (1934-1992)

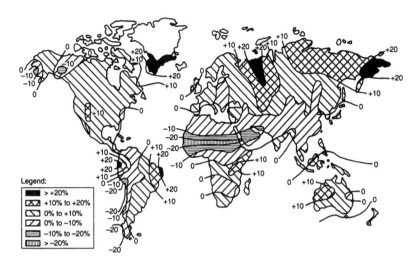

Fig. 2. %age annual precipitation change from 1931-1960 to 1961-1990 [5]

Higher precipitation over northern Russia, falling mainly as snow, has led to increased flows in the river Volga leading to fears of flooding, and impeded drainage around the Caspian sea; this in spite of the extensive water developments leading to abstractions of 40 km^3 and irrigation for 7.5 million ha of land.

The inter-dependence of water resources between the different regions of the world are now becoming better understood and indicate the importance of treating hydrology as a global science.

4 Global run-off

4.1 Published data

The 'Hydrology Assessment' studies included a brief review of available water resources, water developments and future demands of the SSA countries.

The results showed that much of the information published and available to organisations outside the countries contained anomalies.

Research into the worlds water balance has been the prerogative of the USSR for many years. The UNESCO publication prepared by the Hydrometeorological Service, USSR, Petersburg, is still a standard reference, whilst the World Resources Annual Reports continue to rely heavily on Russian sources from the 1970 and 1980's. However, much of the information published on regional water resources, particularly for Africa, are spurious.

The problem is that with river flow data being a national responsibility, data is often jealously guarded. Scientists who wish to undertake studies of such information often have to rely on data published in text books or international publications.

Table 2. Example of comparisons between GCM predictions and observed and
    naturalised flows

River	Model output (km^3)	Observed flow (km^3)	Naturalised flow (km^3)
Nile	56	9	82
Niger	577	47	240
Zaire	1 760	1 260	1 360

The most comprehensive attempt to collate hydrological data has been made by Gleick
[6]. But again a serious `health warning' is given about errors in the published data.

Part of the problem appears to be that no acceptable standards are in place for
comparing resource data. For example, it is often unclear whether the data represent:

• recorded flows
• naturalised flows
• recorded or naturalised flows with future development schemes in place.

Although the problem of anomalous published data may appear of little consequence to
the water resource planner who is immersed in a countries actual records, and is aware
of the effect of past and future developments, water resource data is being used
increasingly by scientists of other disciplines. For example, in recent Hadley Centre
transient model runs, comparisons of the model runoff outputs are compared with
observed flow data.

The model outputs in each case did not take account of manmade water development
projects. They should, therefore, have been compared with naturalised not recorded
flows. With the Aswan dam almost all the Nile flows are used. Moreover, it is important
that the high natural losses in many of the river basins, eg Sudd swamps and the Niger
Interior Delta in which half the inflow is lost, are adequately modelled. It is quite
probable that the GCM river flow outputs are much better than the Hadley Centre
realise.

4.2   Impact Studies

There are many ways of using outputs from GCM's to provide inputs into hydrological
models. The most obvious is to take the GCM simulation of daily rainfall, temperature
and other meteorological variables and feed them directly into a calibrated hydrological
model. Unfortunately, GCM's produce unrealistic simulations of day-to-day rainfall.
Alternative approaches are to use the `change' in rainfall, temperature and other climate
variables to produce a perturbed time series, or to use regional GCM generated pressure
patterns to generate sequences of rainfall and evapotranspiration (Mott MacDonald [7]).
None of the methods used give confidence that results will be other than approximate
and of limited value in water resource planning.

To date, most of the impact studies undertaken have not used hydrological models
which adequately simulate the transient nature of the parameters of the hydrological
cycle.

The Institute of Hydrology, (IH) have undertaken an impact study for 21 catchments in England and Wales (Arnell and Reynard [8]). The wettest scenario produces a general increase in average runoff across UK, whilst the driest produces a reduction. However, the most interesting findings relate to changes in evapotranspiration (ET). These different potential evapotranspiration (PET) scenarios were investigated: PET changes based on; Case 1 - increased temperatures only; Case 2 - changes in temperature, net radiation, relative humidity and wind speed; Case 3 - Case 2 plus changes in plant stomatal conductance and leaf area. The results are given in Table 3.

Table 3. Equilibrium climate change scenarios for 2050 (Arnell and Reynard [8])

Climate parameter	Annual changes in England and Wales
Temperature	+2.2°
Rainfall	+4%
PET 1	+10%
PET 2	+35%
PET 3	+24%

An important feature of the results is the quite dramatic increase in PET resulting from the inclusion of climatic elements other than temperature. A change in humidity produced the most significant increased based on the Penman-Monteith formula.

The greatest single problem in using impact studies arises from the ever changing outputs from the models, particularly for precipitation. An example of this is the latest Hadley model which includes sulphate aerosols. The effects of this single change is to alter significantly the predicted rainfall over western Europe over the next 50 years.

The value of the large number of impact studies undertaken to date lies largely in determining impact study techniques rather than providing firm data to determine water policy.

5 Conclusions

- Hydrology should be treated on a regional, continental and global scale not nationally in isolation. As with climatic parameters, river flows are related on a regional, continental and global scale. All measures which will promote this change should be supported by Governments and international agencies.
- Data collection of hydrometric data are essential for operating water resource systems. They are also essential for planning water development. It is unfortunate that in many developing countries data collection has almost been abandoned. Water resource assessment agencies are invariably small units within large sectorial ministries and perceived to be of little value. It is essential that this situation is remedied as a matter of urgency.
- World-wide climate change may exacerbate the differences between water-rich and water-poor areas. Water transfer will therefore assume increased urgency and importance.

- GCM's represent the only plausible method for predicting the effect of global warming on the hydrological cycle. Unfortunately, existing GCM's are not capable of producing realistic precipitation outputs which are required in water resource planning. This is due in part to the way clouds and precipitation are modelled, and to coarse resolution, but also to the inadequate representation of the land phase and ocean systems in existing equilibrium GCM's and also in new transient GCM's. For example, lateral water transfer and man-made influences are not accounted for. Because of the interactive relationships between the atmosphere, land and oceans, such simplications are likely to affect outputs from current GCM's.
- Predictions from the large number of impact studies undertaken to date to evaluate the effect of climate change on the hydrological cycle, can largely be discounted. Their value at present lie in improving impact study techniques rather than assisting in water development planning. However, much of the research has been directed at trying to convert inadequate outputs from GCM's to more realistic values for use in the impact studies rather than trying to target specific problem areas.

6   References

1. Rodda, J.C. (1995) *Guessing or assessing the Worlds' Water Resources?* JIWEM, 9, pp. 360-367.
2. World Bank/UNDP (1988, 1991, 1992) Sub-Saharan Africa Hydrological Assessment.
3. Falenmark, M. (1989) *The massive water scarcity now threatening Africa - why is it not being addressed?* Ambio, Vol. 18, 2, 1989.
4. Folland, C.K., Palmer, T.N. and Parker, E.D. (1986) *Sahel rainfall and world-wide sea temperatures, 1901 - 1985*, Nature, Vol 320, 17, April 1986, pp 251-254.
5. Hulme M., Marsh, R. and Jones, P.P. (1992) *Global changes in a humidity index between 1931 - 1960 and 1961 - 1990*, Climate Research, Vol 2, July 9 1992, pp. 1-22.
6. Gleick, P.H. (1993) *Water in Crisis - a guide to the world's freshwater resources*, Oxford University Press.
7. Mott MacDonald (1993) *Scenario planning and risk analysis*, Anglian Water Services Ltd, October 1993.
8. Arnell, N.W. and Reynard, N.S. (1993) *Impacts of climate change on river flow regimes in the UK*, Institute of Hydrology, NERC, Water Directorate, DOE, July 1993.

A MANAGEMENT APPROACH TO NATIONAL WATER SCARCITY
Management in national water scarcity

B.G. APPELGREN
Land and Water Development Division,
Food and Agriculture Organisation of the United Nations, Rome, Italy

Abstract
Water scarcity results from population growth, environmental change and degradation and unequal distribution of water resources. As water scarcity becomes aggravated it reaches the dimension of a national security issue that needs to be managed as a part of a larger strategy for societal change and economic reform. From this perspective, the paper provides a critical review of conceptions and options for water management, and their effectiveness in handling scarcity management at the national level.
Keywords: drought, water, water crisis, water management, water policy, water pricing, water scarcity.

> "The spate of events with which we attempt to cope and strive to control have far exceeded,
> in this modern age, the old bounds, that they have been swollen up to giant proportions,
> while all the time the stature and intellect of man remain unchanged."
>
> Winston S. Churchill (1948)

1 Water scarcity in a national context

Water scarcity is the result of pressures from population growth, of environmental change and degradation and unequal distribution of water resources. With increasing competition for limited supplies, conflicts among water users intensify. Water scarcity and resultant conflict are often consequences of inappropriate or inadequate management frameworks, linked to general economic policy and Government structures, with solutions depending on national and regional geo-political realities.

Shared, transboundary water resources and import of water are realities in water scarcity management. For example, an overview of water resources in SADC countries

Water Policy: Allocation and management in practice. Edited by P. Howsam and R.C. Carter.
Published in 1996 by E & FN Spon. ISBN 0 419 21650 2

highlighted the regional ramifications of water scarcity, and indicated the many national and supranational issues and potential conflicts associated with sharing resources and major transfers between river basins and countries [1].

Economic theory predicts that when water becomes scarce it would be expected that water prices would increase to reflect demand pressures, and that water users would save and restrict consumption and other use to essential social and high-value uses. The market would see to it that the marginal benefit unit is the same for all uses and that therefore there is no gain from re-allocation. Prices would then cover the cost of supply to ensure continued availability. However water pricing and management and water markets are hampered by legal and institutional constraints, and traditional and regional attitudes to water, together with high transaction costs and physical limitations in handling the commodity. A system of firm and transferable rights to specified quantities of water that can be exchanged among alternative users through decentralised market processes could, however, work in a well developed economy, while it is argued developing countries require more Government control under assorted water permit systems. An example of a genuine economic approach is presented in Box 1.

The extent to which a country is vulnerable to water depends not just on the available water, its distribution over time and its quality, but more on the extent that the supplies can balance and sustain present and future demands. Climate is the principal factor in water scarcity, but population and economic development are the main influences on quality and demand that together define scarcity as the level of competition between uses. Water starts to become vulnerable when annual internal renewable water resources are less than a critical value, often being cited as 1000 m^3 per capita. Specific indicators [2] have been proposed to reflect factors such as regularity of supplies, external dependence, demand pressures, non-sustainable water use, and level of wastewater discharge, as well as water utilisation for drinking and irrigation. However, contrary to water vulnerability, scarcity occurs both in dry and humid climatic conditions, influenced by many interlinked factors, including growing water demands from economic development and inadequate management due to institutional shortcomings. While scarcity and competition for use of water are basic factors, the main issue is the institutional and economic capacity of society to manage water scarcity and make water available and suitable, in time and space, for different uses and

---

Box 1: The Harvard Middle East Water Project (HMEWP)

HMEWP proposed an economic approach to optimal social allocation of water. Water values were estimated not only as the prices in the free market but also reflecting national social aims involved in water. The cost of supplying and transporting water were estimated, and the private demand curves for households, industry and agriculture were established. Finally, national water policy was expressed as additional demand for water at different prices, and the equilibrium prices that balance supply and demand were calculated. The economic approach transferred the contentious issue of sharing of scarce water into a negotiation of monetary values [2]

secure efficient use and harmonious relations between different users.

From this aspect, the approach to water scarcity management is closely linked to the capacities of the national economy and institutions. While developed economies have the necessary economic potential to plan for and adapt to water scarcity, developing economies, generally subject to and constrained by high population growth, might not have the capacity and economic diversity to manage water scarcity. The main issue in water scarcity is time and the differences in management of water scarcity in developed and developing economies.

Studies of major drought events in the 1970s and early 1980s showed significant decline in GNP and domestic savings, worsening balances of payments, and loss of job opportunities. Water scarcity is, however, an irreversible process, affecting national economies over long time spans, and there is need to alert decision-makers to the related threats to the economy and the state. There is therefore a need to assess the social and economic costs to society of constrained and delayed social and economic development due to water scarcity.

With these dimensions, water scarcity becomes a threat that could contribute to general failure of weak developing country economies, and water scarcity has become an issue of national security. Decision-makers must be made aware of the social and economic impacts of water scarcity and the importance for the stability of the state and the economy, in order to mobilize the necessary political support for development of effective and timely measures.

2   Water and national security

Water scarcity is increasingly seen as a cause of domestic and international conflict, and therefore a risk to national stability and security. This preoccupation is reflected in an increasing number of water-scarce countries, where water is being included in the agendas of the highest authorities responsible for national security. Similarly, water scarcity and its importance for national security are being given increasing priority by international donors. Water scarcity as a national security issue [3] is developing into a useful concept for approaching the problem and in attracting attention at the political level to the importance of water scarcity as a long-term, macro-economic and sustainability issue. The security risks, deriving from environmental scarcity, population growth and unequal distribution of water, appear as reduced state capacity, and also civil violence, rather than international conflict. Water scarcity could contribute to frustration of weak national administrations, leading to breakdown of the state as water scarcity becomes a major threat in developing countries trying to achieve their social development objectives. As a consequence, when perceived as a threat to social and societal security, water scarcity should mobilize the attention of national policy-makers and the international community sufficiently soon to address the problems before they reach uncontrollable dimensions. Box 2 presents a summary of two current national water policies for addressing water scarcity: in Egypt and in Mexico.

3   Water and food security

As a result of increasing demands, the global food gap is widening. The price of food in international markets is projected to increase significantly, and weak economies are already facing increasing difficulties in buying food. At present, 2400 million people depend on irrigated agriculture for jobs, food and income. Over the next 30 years, an estimated 80% of the additional food supplies required to feed the world will depend on irrigation. Irrigated agriculture will be expected to produce much more food in the future, while using less water than it uses today.

4   Environment and health

Environmental concerns are increasingly shaping water management plans. The environmental impacts of schemes to supply and use water can have a massive hydrological impact, and impose water scarcity on other users and future generations. Crucial factors, such as minimum flows in rivers, will gain in importance and it is likely that the value that society places on water for environmental and health purposes will increase in future.

5   Management of national water scarcity

Recognition of water scarcity at an early stage in planning forms the underlying principle for any action towards water sector policy reform. Action is, however, often reactive and short term, and policy reforms and water acts are more easily accepted by the public and at the political level in crisis periods of drought and acute water shortage. Many countries, especially in humid zones, maintain a position of no problem and so no need for management, and hence react slowly, often not until water shortage or water quality degradation is constraining national social and economic development.

Approaches to water scarcity management need to be based on political recognition and general awareness of the realities of scarcity as a major national problem. While there is reluctance to deal with issues that risk being contentious, and so results in deferral of

---

Box 2: Water policy in Egypt and Mexico

Egypt: National strategies include water pricing based on agricultural production, storage in coastal lakes, desalination, water conservation in the upper Nile, re-use of irrigation drainage water, increased irrigation water use efficiency, groundwater utilisation, and modified cropping patterns.

Mexico: An alternative to economic approaches is management by fiat and Government control under water-permit systems. Mexico, in implementing the new 1992 Federal Water Act and developing a unified system for administration of water abstraction and wastewater disposal permits, is operating the system on an experimental basis in an area with competing agricultural, industrial and city water demands.

appropriate measures, the risks are accumulating of catastrophic social and economic consequences, including deteriorating food security with resultant conflict and possible collapse of state and customary institutions, thus threatening national security. Ultimately, it will be the countries themselves that will have to find their own means of adjusting to changing circumstances, or they will collapse.

Of crucial importance is that many policy measures - both traditional and of newer provenance - for operational water resources management, short-term planning and conflict resolution to free and provide more water are narrow, and, even under ideal institutional set-ups, will not work, and can even in time provide mis-directions in addressing national water scarcity. The requirement is for a broad, long-term approach, based on national security and economic growth objectives, well consolidated with national development, economic reform and macro-policy, as part of a larger strategy of long-term societal change to counteract the root causes of effects tending toward breakdown of the state (See Box 3, Yemen) [4].

6   Misconceptions on solutions to water crisis

Frederiksen [5], in a review of common misconceptions concerning the emerging water crisis, soliciting more real-world and down-to-business approaches, points out basic constraints and misconceptions, and caveats concerning current management approaches.

Scarcity of time to act to meet the needs
There is a necessity to act, even on controversial issues, and therefore to use established measures rather than to wait for new approaches that might not be implementable with available resources and capacities.

Box 3: The macro-economy and water scarcity in Yemen
Yemen is facing economic stagnation and difficulties with budget and balance of payments. Current development practice is to deplete natural resources assets, notably water, to finance consumption, unproductive industrial capital and poor savings. Low returns on investments and external indebtedness shift resources towards current use, reducing water sustainability. The losses of water assets are not recorded under current accounting practices. With capital resources injected into the import sector and inefficient production, this is not an adequate source of growth. It has therefore become necessary to consider inter-sectoral effects that derive from water-intensive economic growth which results in resource deterioration, with economic interactions between mobilization of water resources and the macro-economic and sectoral policies. The balance between macro-economic and sectorial development and sustainable protection of water resources needs to be determined as structural and policy reforms are implemented and the economy evolves.

Common misconceptions on how to free and produce needed water
Water availability is often expressed in terms of total water resources, while only the utilizable portion of the water resources can meet the needs of a nation, and there are few options for increasing this portion, such as regulation of surface flows and conjunctive use of surface and groundwater.

Diverting a share from agriculture to higher-value uses is often quoted as the solution to water scarcity. However the scope for re-allocation is often limited to the low-flow season, and does not include high-flow season water, when major cropping often takes place in irrigated areas.

Water acquisitions from agriculture for municipal and industrial uses tend to be localised, and thereby reduce the economic basis in the immediate vicinities of cities, at a social cost in lost production that might be larger than the losses from reservoir inundation.

Improved agricultural efficiency is often stated as an obvious option to save substantial quantities of water for other uses. However, irrigation projects pass unused losses to downstream users, and, as a result, basin efficiencies are generally high. Thus improved agricultural efficiency could lead to reduced supplies and potential water conflict among downstream users, and conflict with national and social and economic interests as current production might be reduced and exchanged for new production, at a cost but with no net gain. Water should, however, be saved in urban coastal cities which have low water use efficiencies of 10-15% and where return flows are lost into the sea, and in irrigation areas that discharge return flows into saline depressions. In national water scarcity management it is the basin efficiency that is relevant.

Demand management and water pricing are not likely to free large quantities of agricultural water to other uses since water is already managed as a main constraint to cropping in the water-short, low-flow season.

In addition to costly institutions and physical infrastructure needed for water markets and trading, these policies will only re-allocate water that is already used in a productive way, and is likely be counterproductive to poverty alleviation and national social and security objectives. Transfers and acquisition of water rights need to be closely linked to land rights.

As pollution control, together with recycling and desalination, cannot offer inexpensive and rapid options, and development of groundwater and natural flows are limited, one of the few option is to develop surface water storage. Improved cropping management, including production-effective and high-tolerance crops, and the use of water of marginal quality, also have a lot of promise.

Policies to mitigate shortage of funding
The major concern is that while only short-term, and often insufficient, funding is being allocated and made available to the water sector, the very large financial needs in the next decades have not even been analysed and prioritized.

Privatisation, which is often being promoted, remains dependent on the traditional source of funds - Government or beneficiaries - and has proven to be an uncertain source of financing, especially under conditions of water scarcity and economic recession.

In contrast, increased service fees and transfers of financial responsibilities to beneficiaries represents an efficient and timely option for improving funding, with major longer-term retrenchment of financial responsibilities from Government. It is consistent with, and goes in parallel with, the slower process of removal of subsidies in the water sector.

7   Conclusions

With changing social and economic conditions and weak governance in developing countries, what are considered normal conditions for water resources and the capacity to manage water scarcity can be expected to change drastically in the next decades. Current conceptions and approaches to managing water scarcity focus on use of water where it is available, and re-allocation of available water for its greatest benefits. While detailed data on water scarcity and its impacts are generally absent, there is evidence that these conceptions and the focus on demand management and non-structural policy instruments are insufficient, mis-guiding and delaying to more effective action because they do not reflect the requirement to manage water scarcity as part of the larger process of societal change. This is especially true in developing countries with weak economies and unstable state formation. Traditional approaches to water management will therefore not be sufficient in situations of extreme national water scarcity, possibly resulting in the collapse of state and customary institutions. Hence water scarcity management needs to be given a broader scope and made part of national strategies for societal and economic reform. To address these challenges, FAO is currently developing a guide to provide recommendations to member countries facing current or potential water scarcity.

Acknowledgement: This paper was prepared by B.G. Appelgren, Senior Officer (Water Policy and Planning) Water Resources Development and Management Service, Land and Water Development Division of the Food and Agriculture Organisation of the United Nations (FAO) and is reproduced here by permission of that organisation.

8   References

1.   Anon. (1994) *The Harvard Middle East Water Project.* Harvard University, Cambridge, Massachusetts, USA.
2.   Margat, M.J., Valee, D., and Louvet, J.M. (1995) *Les indicateurs (d'economie) de l'eau: ressources et utilisations.* [Draft version; June 1995] Observatoire du Sahara et du Sahel. OSS paper no. 166. Paris.
3.   Ohlsson, L. (1995) *Water and Security in Southern Africa.* University of Gothenburg, Dept. of Natural Resources and the Environment, Publications on Water Resources, No.1. 66p. SIDA, Stockholm.
4.   FAO [Food and Agriculture Organisation] (1995) Republic of Yemen. National Action Plan for Environment and Development. Policies and Guidelines. FAO, Rome.
5.   Frederiksen, H. (1996) Water crisis in the developing world: Misconceptions about solutions. *Journal of Water Resources Planning and Management,* Vol.122, No.2, pp. 79-87.

WATER RESOURCES MANAGEMENT IN ENGLAND & WALES
UK water resource management

J. SHERRIFF
Environment Agency, Bristol, UK

Summary

There have been many changes to the institutional framework for water resources management in England and Wales over the years.

In 1974, a major change took place which created 10 regional water authorities responsible for water supply, sewerage, water resources, fisheries, recreational and other functions. There were quasi-autonomous bodies under the supervision of a Government department (Department of the Environment) which provided capital funding and approved charges made by the water authorities. The creation of these authorities enabled an integrated approach to catchment management and their creation coincided with a time when there was increasing attention needing to be given to the control of effluents which was not affordable by the previously responsible bodies.

The regional water authorities remained in existence for 15 years and, without doubt, significant achievements were realised in integrated management. However, in 1989, water services were privatised and the service provision for sewerage, sewage disposal and for water supply passed into private ownership. Reasons for privatising water services include:-

- to enable the companies to obtain private funding for expenditure on water sector projects rather than having to compete against other sectors for public funds. At privatisation expenditure on water services was expected to increase in real terms for a number of years in order to recover from a period of underinvestment.
- to remove the situation where a single body has responsibilities both for provision of the service as well as certain responsibilities for authorising abstractions and discharges.
- to fulfil Government's privatisation policy.
- complexities in some of the financial arrangements which meant that some cross

Water Policy: Allocation and management in practice. Edited by P. Howsam and R.C. Carter.
Published in 1996 by E & FN Spon. ISBN 0 419 21650 2

subsidy occurred between authorities.

Privatisation of water services in 1989 created a clear separation between the regulated and the regulators. At present the 10 privatised water service companies are regulated by the Office of Water Services (OFWAT) and the Environment Agency.

OFWAT is the economic regulator of the water companies and is responsible for ensuring that companies meet specified service levels. The Director General of OFWAT is responsible for setting the price limits within which the companies can charge.

The privatisation of the water companies has meant that they have been freed from the limitations of funding and have invested heavily in infrastructure projects to make up, to some extent, for the previous underinvestment in the service. Since 1989, compliance with the drinking water regulations and discharge consents has improved significantly. However, costs of water services have increased significantly above inflation due to the required high level of investment.

Although water companies are not controlled by elected representatives, they consult customers directly. OFWAT also enable local consultation through their Customer Services Committees to obtain opinion on the necessary improvements and the willingness to pay for them.

Customers' attitudes to the privatised companies appear to have hardened since privatisation. They have received poor publicity, partly due to their performance on reducing leakage levels, partly due to perceived high levels of remuneration by top executives and partly by the need to have imposed supply restrictions during the recent drought.

The recent drought has resulted in a shift of emphasis from water quality to water quantity being a top priority for companies' future investment plans.

The creation of the National Rivers Authority in 1989 resulted in better regulation and enforcement. A single body covering the whole of England and Wales has meant that policy, legislation and regulation has been developed and coordinated at the national level.

Although the NRA was not an elected body, its appointed Board members represented a wide range of interests. Public involvement was obtained through consultation processes including the preparation of charging schemes, strategies, catchment management plans and quality objectives.

The creation of the Environment Agency in 1996 has further strengthened the integrated approach to river basin management and has specific duties associated with sustainable development and the need to take costs and benefits into account in exercising its functions.

The Environment Agency is primarily a regulator and in relation to water resources, is the body which authorises abstraction and effluent discharges of the companies. It comprises the former National Rivers Authority, Her Majesty's Inspectorate of Pollution and the waste regulation function of the Local Authorities. Local interest in its affairs is through statutory committees as well as through public consultation on its proposals and plans.

The Environment Agency is said to be the largest environmental body in Europe. It is committed to achieving the objectives of integrated catchment management and development and is a key player in furthering the Government's sustainable development policies.

'FOUR WATERS' CONCEPT IN WATERSHED MANAGEMENT IN INDIA

'Four Waters' concept in India

T. HANUMANTHA RAO
Irrigation and Water Resources Consultant
Hyderabad, India

Abstract

Watershed Management is gaining importance in India and in recent years, the Government budget in this sector had increased several fold. 'Four Waters Concept' provides a scientific and practical approach to develop a watershed using rainwater, soil moisture, groundwater and surface water, to derive the maximum benefit. It would arrest the present trend of depleting water tables year after year, and increase the water table levels appreciably over a period of time. This would mean reduction to half or one third in the power consumption charges in agricultural pumping. Soil erosion would be reduced significantly. Loss of soil moisture would be prevented and rainfed crops would give higher yields. It is possible to provide irrigation for about 40% of the cropped area in the Semi Arid tropics of India through groundwater alone, without mining. When these techniques were adopted, the streams in the watershed which were once dry, during non-rainy period, were found to have spring flows. The technology of 'Four Waters Concept' given in the paper is innovative and is generally relevant to the Semi Arid tropics in India, as well as elsewhere under similar circumstances.

Keywords: controls, 'Four Waters', groundwater, rainwater, soil moisture, surface water

1   Four Waters

Comprehensive control and management of groundwater, surface water, soil moisture and rainfall would be needed for increasing agricultural production and making safe drinking water available. This can be termed as the **Four Waters Concept**. The objective of the approach is to produce two crops per year, over the largest possible area of the watershed with limited use of surface water and groundwater. The basic innovation of this concept is the dynamic control of the aquifer by the collective participation of Farmers group. Dynamic groundwater management also makes use of the aquifer as a convenient storage media which sustains for long periods during droughts and also during the summer session. One of the significant results of the project is to bring up water table levels from the present 16 metres below ground level (mbgl.) to 3mbgl. In order to have a visible impact of watershed development, size of the watershed will have to be a minimum of 20,000 ha. Base flows in the streams will become prominent in such big watersheds. The entire area of the watershed should be covered throughout by at least one, watershed activity of the 'Four Waters', without leaving any gaps of even one hectare extent. Farmers' associations will have to be formed in the entire watershed and they should be informed about the scope and content of the activities. Planning of the activities, including selection of sites, scope of works, selection of types of works, methods of execution will have to be decided by the Farmers' Associations duly taking the guidance of Government technical staff (Civil Engineers, Agricultural Scientists etc.) The responsibility of technical features and designs will rest with the Government departments. Farmers should be informed about the principles of aquifer management to be adopted during various seasons such as rainy season, drought season, summer season etc. and they should give their total acceptance for implementing the same during the operation phase of the project.

After the above aspects are complied with, the execution of works will have to be started. Some of these issues are not complied with, in many of the watershed development programmes in India, leading to several defects and undesirable results.

Depleting water table levels, year after year is a common phenomenon observed in all the drought prone areas. In many areas, shallow dug wells are getting dried up during summer. To overcome this feature, bore wells were drilled in these areas. The increased draft through these bores are responsible for further lowering the water table. This leads to drilling deeper bores year after year, in the same area. Thus there is competition for pumping groundwater and a person who can afford the cost, gets the water however deeper the water table may be. Adequate recharge works would be the answer to such a situation. Increasing the number of wells or drilling deeper bores would not be a solution. This aspect is considered in the Four Waters Concept. Details of each of the components of this concept are now elaborated.

2   Rain water

Mean annual precipitation in drought prone areas in India varies between 500 mm to 700 mm. Rain occurs at times, with heavy intensities of 25 mm/hr. During such times, there will be run off and severe soil erosion. If the rainfall is allowed to percolate and stored in the soil, it would be useful to the crop even during drought periods. By ploughing the land across the slope, furrows are formed along the contours. These furrows will be able to hold small quantities of water and encourage percolation. In red soils (Sandy loam) the rate of percolation would be about 8 mm /hr. With good leaf litter, the percolation can be as high as 12 mm/hr. Rain water in fields will have to be managed in such a manner that it would not cause soil erosion on the farm. To facilitate this, conventional soil conservation works will have to be taken up in the entire rainfed agricultural area of the watershed, without leaving even one hectare. Many of the soil conservation programmes executed in India during the past four decades have not given the expected benefits. In many cases, it was not possible to construct bunds along the contours, since farmers preferred boundary bunds. The technical content of the programme requires revision in the light of past experiences. For example, it is preferable to provide bunds, along the field boundaries (which are usually not on contour), by providing a bigger section of bund at the lower ground levels while keeping the top of bund at the same level throughout. In such a case, it would be imperative to provide for spilling at ends of the bund at a safe level to prevent breach of bunds during high intensity of rainfalls.

Small storages with a water spread of about 0-0.5 ha can be constructed in large numbers, one for every 10 to 20 ha of catchment, and at the foot of hill slopes in the waste lands and hilly areas. These storages would attenuate the peak flood intensities during storms and would eventually reduce gully formations and soil erosion in the stream sections. Such micro storage would also ensure, soil moisture for good growth of trees raised on the downstream side. Soil erosion has therefore to be prevented, right at the source, where the rain falls on the soil. Tree planting and leaf litter on the ground will prevent soil erosion and increase percolation.

All the cultivable waste lands, within the watershed and neighbouring denuded forests if any, will have to be planted with trees. There should be a good mix of various types of trees such as fruit bearing, fuel wood, leguminons (green manure) and other local varieties which grow well for those climatic and soil conditions. Exotic species will have to be avoided. Fast growing woody shrubs should be planted in between the trees. The under growth and leaf litter will not only prevent soil erosion but reduces the soil moisture evaporation especially in summer. The Government owned lands, and denuded forest lands will have to be allotted to farmers to enable the farmers to do this. All the unproductive lands under farmers' possession should be similarly treated. Farmers' associations will have to be actively involved in this regard.

3   Soil moisture

Soil moisture is available in the unsaturated zone i.e. the zone above the water table level. This zone consists of root zone of crops and deeper layers which support tree growth. The unsaturated zone can retain moisture up to its field capacity, where water is held under capillary suspension. Any increase in water content, will gravitate further below and recharges the groundwater. In the red soils areas of drought prone regions of India, it is estimated that about 60% of annual rainfall would be stored in the unsaturated zone. The 40% balance of rainfall would be in the shape of groundwater and surface water of almost equal proportion. Apart from any %ages, it has to be appreciated that a substantial quantity of rainfall is stored as soil moisture. This competent is almost fully consumed during the cycle of a year through transpiration of crops (and trees) and evaporation. If a management practice or technical intervention can be devised to reduce the soil moisture evaporation it would be a great leap forward. This is a very crucial issue in the watershed development process, since even if about 60% of soil moisture evaporation is saved in the semi arid tropics, it would be quite huge in quantity, since it would almost be equal to the surface and groundwater resources put together in that area. Soil moisture thus conserved would be available for crops and trees. If this is achieved, there would be lesser demand for irrigation. Surface and groundwater resources can be conserved and used for other purposes as well as irrigating additional extents of areas.

The appropriate method for conservation of soil moisture is to raise green manure or cover crops in the entire dry land (rainfed agricultural lands). The technique is to grow a forage cover crop which would be left in the field to serve as a mulch cover, during periods when there is no crop on the lands. At the beginning of the next crop period, this mulch would be ploughed into the soil and the same would fertilise the soil with organic carbon and nitrogen in an abundant measure. Such bio-fertilisation would also increase the yields of crops.

Using green manure legumes has resulted in fixing the equivalent 'N' of 200 Kg ha, costing about US$ 66/ha in the form of chemical fertiliser. Green manure (g.m.) crops have the additional advantages of fixing organic carbon into the soil and smothering weed growth. It is possible to add to the soil up to 50 T/ha (green weight) of organic matter to the soil during each application. This organic matter has, in turn, a whole series of positive effects on the soil, such as improving its water-holding capacity, nutrient content, nutrient balance friability and pH. This is in addition to prevent of soil moisture evaporation during summer and non crop periods. These additions of organic matter and N are achieved with no transportation costs. They are produced right in the field, and are already well distributed. Cover crops require no capital outlay whatsoever once the farmer has purchased his first handful of seed. There is also an important factor in reducing weed control costs, when used as a mulch. After having discussed briefly the two waters, i.e. rain waters and soil moisture, let us discuss the management of the third water - Groundwater.

4   Groundwater

4.1 Water table levels

In most of the wells in command areas of tanks (small reservoirs) the water table would be one to two metres below G.L. when there is storage of water in the tank. In the areas outside the commands, which are in higher elevations, the water table would be 10 to 15 mbgl even after the post rainy seasons. The water table will get depleted by 7 m to 10 m during the summer period. Tank commands would normally extend to about 25% of the total cultivated areas. By a structured engineering intervention, it is possible to raise the water table levels in the non command areas, extending to 75% of the cropped area.

In a block period of 3 or 4 years, if the total recharge and draft balances each other, there would not be any continuous depletion of water table levels, even though there may be more draft one year or less recharge in another year. When there is any increase in draft during a block period, the recharge component should be increased adequately to match the draft. A simple way of accomplishing this, is by water spreading techniques. By execution of these works and following the management practices suggested above for 'Rain Water' and 'Soil Moisture', it is possible to maintain the groundwater table levels and even increase it to the desired level and make sufficient groundwater available for usage in a given area. By following principles of aquifer management collectively by the farmers described in para. 4.5, it is possible to bring the water table levels to 3 mbgl in a period of about 3 years. The water table would not be allowed to fall below a particular designed level, say 10 mbgl (under water table conditions). The average lift of water would then be about 6 m, compared to the earlier 15 m. For pumping the same quantity from deeper layers it would need 2 ½ times more power than pumping from the shallow depths. This is of significant benefit to the State, since agricultural power tariffs have substantial subsidies throughout the country. In physical terms, it can be projected that using the present power consumption in the drought prone areas, (where Four Waters Concept is adopted), it is possible to pump 2 ½ times more groundwater, once the water table levels are brought up.

4.2 Rationale in Government taking up recharge works

In the surface water irrigation sector (major, medium and minor irrigation projects), Government is incurring full expenditure for investigation, design and construction of water resources head works and conveyance systems for distribution of irrigation water to the farmers' fields. The entire expenditure of about US\$ 3000 per ha (1995 rates) is totally borne by the Government under its plan funds, and it is relevant to note that the beneficiaries are not contributing even a part of this capital cost. Thus the farmer who is served by surface water irrigation is able to get irrigation water to his fields without any investment. In the case of usage of groundwater for irrigation, the entire capital cost for creation of these facilities is borne by the farmer himself. Apart from meeting this capital cost, the farmer will also have to bear the full burden of operation, repairs and maintenance of groundwater system (including pumping equipment) and pay for power consumption charges. It can therefore be seen that the farmer using groundwater for irrigation is already under heavy burden of financial outlay when compared to the farmer using surface water irrigation. It is therefore rational that Government approach should change and render all possible assistance (financial and technical) to encourage the farmers using groundwater. At present the Government operations are focused in the direction of assessing groundwater and this in turn enables the farmers to obtain loans from the financial institutions. Where it is not possible to clear the well for technical reasons the farmer is denied a loan facility. Also, if he constructs a well with his own financial resources, he has to face the grave risk of inadequate groundwater in the well, and also perhaps failure of well. It has to be appreciated in this context, that when the farmer is coming forward to incur capital costs and create water resource, for his use, it should be the endeavour of the Government to ensure availability of groundwater. The regulatory function of Government namely clearing wells technically will have to be substantially modified so as to make it obligatory to provide a recharge structure to serve a group of farmers wherever technically feasible. The policy of Government should therefore be modified accordingly. It is rational and justifiable on principles of equity (between farmers using surface water and groundwater) that Government should take up this activity in watershed development in the drought prone areas on priority. Wherever it is not technically feasible for providing recharge works, emphasis should be given to take up soil conservation works to enable obtaining higher productivity in rainfed agriculture and also increase the recharge however marginal it may be.

4.3 Spreading techniques

Mini percolation tanks will have to be constructed in all the first order of catchments within the boundaries of the selected 20,000 ha watershed, and also in the boundaries of sub-watersheds, within the main watershed. By the first order of catchment, it is meant that the catchment is totally free and not intercepted and the location of the mini tank would be in a valley, dip or small stream course in the head reaches of the stream, within a distance of about 0.5 km from the ridge point. For water spreading purposes, the target should be construction of a large number of small or mini percolation tanks. It may be possible to have about 600 mini tanks (also called 'Kuntas') in a watershed of 20,000 ha area. Downstream areas of these mini tanks can be used as discharge zones and groundwater can be pumped from these zones for purposes of irrigation and other uses. Percolation tanks of capacities 5 M.cu ft (14.2 ha.m) and higher can also be constructed at suitable locations on the downstream side of watershed. These can be considered in selected and special cases since they are expensive and occupy land for submersion for considerable length of crop periods. With regard to costs, mini percolation tanks are more cost effective than percolation tanks. For effective deep percolation, a trench may be excavated parallel to the tank bund (dam).

4.4 Sub-surface dams

At the middle and in the downstream regions of the main stream of the watershed, there would be possibilities to have valley fills or alluvial stream beds. In some of the water sheds, having an extent of 200 sq.km. It is likely that the depth of alluvium may be 10 m and more. During the post rainy period, there may not be any run off and the base flow, if any, is likely to disappear by December. During the dry season from January to May, there would be flow of groundwater to the downstream side. On account of this, the groundwater levels within the stream bed alluvium, would fall down and groundwater would not be available for use within the watershed. It is in this context, sub-surface dams would be useful in storing groundwater and preventing the loss of groundwater from the watershed. A series of sub-surface storage reservoirs can be created in the alluvial river bed within the watershed area. The groundwater in the alluvial bed can also be used for drinking purposes and would be a great asset during the summer periods and during successive drought years, when they occur. The sub-surface dam can be simple and economic in design, and would comprise of 1m thick puddle clay.

4.5 Aquifer management

Collective management of the aquifer will have to be done by the farmers. Farmers will have to be informed and educated about the aquifer management principles relevant in the area. The following principles would be relevant in many of the discharge zones of red soil areas, lying on the downstream side of the mini percolation tanks.

Raising irrigated wet (paddy) crops may be done in as large an area as possible in the Khariff season only. No wet crops should be grown in the non rainy season (rabi) or summer seasons, even though a particular farmer may have adequate water in his well in the watershed. Such an activity would result in wasteful use of water, depriving the other farmers in the neighbourhood (located at higher levels), their legitimate requirements, and eventually lowering the water table below the limit set for the area.

A second irrigated dry crop can be grown in good and average years of rainfall. There should be no summer irrigated crop in any year, however good may be the rainfall in that year. This is with a view to conserve groundwater so to have adequate carryover to the next year in case the next year happens to be a low rainfall year.

In the event of a low rainfall year (drought year) a second rabi crop should not be raised. The limited groundwater should be set apart for drinking purposes and irrigating orchards and perennials.

From the above, it could be seen that the success of aquifer management solely lies within the hands of the farmers who use the groundwater. Training, extension and demonstration to farmers, and fully involving them in the whole process will have to be ensured through suitable organisational set up.

4.6 Controls

There are instances reported where several small structures constructed by different organisations are not serving the purpose for which they were meant. Some have failed and were washed away during the rains. This is due to poor design or faulty execution of works or both. Some of the organisations do not have the technical skills to undertake these works. Also technology is not properly understood in some instance. For example, small diversion weirs (called as check dams) are constructed across stream beds without proper abutments and bank connections to higher ground. In some cases, the aprons provided are not according to the design norms. Some of these structures were washed away or got outflanked, when there were heavy rains. Design and execution of mini percolation tanks and diversion weirs will have to be done under proper control, following the relevant technical guidelines.

5   Surface water

Surface water bodies relate to a) Mini percolation tanks, b) Percolation tanks, and c) Minor irrigation tanks. Item a) would be feasible and could be a few hundred numbers in a watershed of about 20,000 ha. Item b) would be feasible in some of the watersheds where the same was not already taken up earlier. Feasibility of item c) will be more situation specific and may or may not be possible in the watershed. Good design norms are available in the Government Minor Irrigation Departments for this item of works.

On account of increase in recharge, there will be increase in baseflow in the streams within the watershed. There will be groundwater flow from the catchments of mini and micro watersheds into the streams. It is likely that this spring flow would be available even during summer months. Such surface flows can be pumped and used for irrigating the areas in the banks of streams. A better method would be to divert the water, through a diversion weir located at a suitable upstream point on the stream, and command the lands through gravity flow canals. Such diversion works can be planned at suitable intervals along the stream to command sizeable extents of land located all along the banks of streams. These works are highly cost effective and the per hectare capital cost may be one fifth of the conventional storage works.

6   Experiences elsewhere in the world

The 'Four Waters Concept' has been tested and refined through several years in the Nampi experimental station in Hebei province in China. A pilot area of 23,600 ha watershed was selected for this purpose. Yields of crops increased by 77%. Through the average annual rainfall is 550 mm, it was possible to irrigate one light irrigated crop in the dry season to an extent of 43% cropped land. This was found possible without resorting to mining of groundwater or external water diversions from any other basin. Experiences gained in Xiong Xian county, in the central part of Hebei Province were similar. The water table which was previously at a dangerously low level was raised and kept between 2 mbgl and 6 mbgl This results in substantial energy saving and increased yields. The success of the method was due to a strict common resource management. Safeguards against illegal pump operations were provided and enforced through the establishment of "Village Service Teams", which were paid and supervised by the farmers themselves. The service teams were supervising and authorising operation of pumps and monitoring groundwater levels.

7   Conclusion

The 'Four Waters Concept' provides a scientific and practical approach to develop a watershed to derive the maximum benefit from the land and water resources in the area. It arrests the trend of depleting the water tables year after year and would increase the water table levels appreciably over a period of time. This would decrease the power consumption charges in agricultural pumping. Soil erosion would be reduced significantly. Loss of soil moisture would be prevented and rainfed crops would give better yields. Bio-fertilisations resulting out of mulching would improve the structure and fertility of soils. It is possible to provide irrigation for about 40% of cropped area through groundwater, without mining. It has to be stressed here that the total water resources available in any region will not get increased in the 'Four Waters Concept'. By adopting the strategies detailed in this paper, it is possible to manage more efficiently the water available in the 'Four Waters' namely rainwater, soil water, groundwater and surface water. The advantages of this concept are striking and hence it is suggested that the same is adopted for all watershed development programmes in India, duly following the checks and controls described in this paper.

8   Reference

GRID - IPTRID (International Program for Technology Research in Irrigation and Drainage), Issue 2, March 1993.

SPANISH WATER SUPPLY AND DEMAND MANAGEMENT: THE CASE OF WATER TRANSFERS

Spanish water planning and management

E. LOPEZ-GUNN
Division of Environmental Sciences, University of Hertfordshire, Hatfield, UK

Abstract
The existing Spanish legal and institutional framework has not been adequate to properly manage limited water resources. To meet water demands water planning tradition lies in supply management strategies, like inter-basin water transfers. This paper reviews the already existing Tagus-Segura transfer to highlight the main issues arising from its operation. This example could be a useful precedent for future planned transfers under the draft Spanish National Hydrological Plan. It also highlights the often ignored opportunities for demand water management.
Keywords: legal and institutional framework, Spain, water management, water planning, water transfers

1 Introduction

The scarcity of water resources in Spain is placing extreme pressure on the legal and institutional framework to manage and plan water resources for the future in a sustainable manner. In per capita terms, Spain has a slightly higher average water availability 2,924 cubic metres per person (m^3 /person) than the European average of 2,500 m^3/person. Due to seasonal and locational factors the picture is much more complex. Evapotranspiration is very high in some areas and the geographical and seasonal distribution of rainfall is unequal.

Although average rainfall is 650 mm this disguises the existence of the so called 'humid' and 'dry' Spains, a variation between northern and southern basins with 37% of rainfall falling on 11% of the territory. The rest of the country, where 1/3 of Spanish population live, has seasonally irregular rainfall, variable water flows and high potential evapotranspiration which becomes a key factor in the context of

Water Policy: Allocation and management in practice. Edited by P. Howsam and R.C. Carter.
Published in 1996 by E & FN Spon. ISBN 0 419 21650 2

irrigation projects.

In terms of water demand, Spain has the highest water consumption in the European Union and the fourth in the OECD. In Spain 80% of consumptive water is for agriculture, particularly in highly productive irrigated areas in the Mediterranean and increasingly, tourism industry, with 62 million tourists seeking sunny, water scarce areas. Agriculture, the main water consumptive use, employs 8.5% of the working population and accounts for 15% of national GDP (17% of trade exports). However, this irrigated land accounts for 60% of agricultural GDP (2 billion out of 3.6 billion pts) (1994) whilst only representing 14% of the agricultural area [1].

2   Current Spanish legal and institutional framework for water management

The main national water law is the 1985 Water Law (29/85 2nd August) . This law was based on three key principles [2]: i) public character of continental waters (surface and ground water), ii) need for hydrological planning and iii) public administration of water resources according to river basins .

Water administration in Spain has to be analysed both in terms of vertical structure (administrative tiers) and also in terms of horizontal water management (specific water organisations). Administration is underlined by the basic principle of administration based on river catchments, sometimes crossing administrative boundaries. In water management, the question whether the State or the region have full 'competence' is dependent on catchments being declared as 'inter-community' or 'intra-community'. 'Inter-community' basins, such as the Tagus and the Segura , extend over an area belonging to different autonomous regions. Yet, under the Spanish constitution, in line with most constitutions worldwide, regions such as Murcia and Castille-La Mancha, part of the Segura and Tagus catchments respectively, have powers regarding regional development, planning and environmental protection, all of which affect water planning.

In the case of horizontal water administration, the main actor in Spanish water management are the Hydrographic Commissions or Organismos de Cuenca first created in 1926. The 1985 Water Law strengthened their role as basic institutions for water administration. The Hydrographic Commissions theoretically have full functional autonomy and own legal status as 'public law' bodies, independent of the State or the Autonomous Communities. However, in reality the main official, the President of the Hydrographic Commission, is appointed by the Ministry of Public Works, Transport and Environment (or MOPTMA) Two of their key roles are: administration and control of public water domain (including some public works) and the creation, follow up and review of Catchment Plans [3].

The National Water Council, also ascribed to the MOPTMA, is the highest consultative body for water planning in relation to the National Hydrological Plan (or PHN) and catchment plans Each catchment also has its own water council. 'User associations' such as farmer associations, particularly in the Segura catchment, date back to Visigoth or Arab times. The 1985 law maintained and widened 'user associations' to include not just farmers but all types of water users and in future could play a key active role in implementing demand or supply management policy options.

3 Water planning in Spain: catchment plans and the draft Spanish Hydrological Plan

Water planning is a constitutional and 'legal duty' at regional and national levels to maximise the best use of water for economic and sectorial development [4]. The State has responsibility for developing a National Hydrological Plan (PHN) and once passed by Parliament, the PHN will have the status of Law. The draft PHN (1993) was designed by the MOPTMA and, specifically, its State Secretariat for Water and Environment Policy set up in 1991 [5]. Another important player is the Ministry of Agriculture, Fisheries and Food (MAPA) who is currently preparing a National Irrigation Plan which has to be passed before the National Hydrological Plan is approved.   In addition to national water planning, individual Hydrographic Commissions have the duty to prepare Catchment Plans. These Catchment Plans are approved by the Government at the request of the respective Catchment Water Councils. The MOPTMA can modify Catchment plans in line with the PHN and review them of their own accord or at the initiative of the Water Council. They have to be reviewed by law every 8 years. However, at the instigation of the regional party of Aragon, the P.A.R, the Senate produced a ruling which specified that the PHN could not be passed until the catchment plans were ready. Thus any modification of Catchment plans would be *'a posteriori'* of their preparation.

While Catchment Plans are being prepared, with their own preferential user lists, the 1985 Water Law (Art. 58.3) provides a general list of priority uses which can be applied. In general, preference goes first for urban water uses (including industries with low water demands) and second, for irrigation and agricultural uses. Indeed water uses in Spain have responded to this planning line, with agriculture still the main water user at both the regional and national levels. Under the 1985 Water Law Art .38 national water planning has to 'satisfy water demand to the best possible extent and to ensure balanced and smooth regional and sectorial development by increasing water availability' [6]. The draft PHN law paraphrased this article as 'to meet the current and future demand by means of the judicious use of each catchment's own resources and *balancing water availability between catchments*' (Art.2 added emphasis). One of the main strategies for meeting national water demand is based on 'joint integrated use' or in other words interbasin water transfers. Based on the concept of 'hydrological imbalance' water transfers were mentioned in 1933 by Lorenzo Pardo in the 'National Plan for Hydraulic Works'. In the 1990s, the draft PHN plans to transfer water between 'surplus regions' and 'deficit regions': 'Water transfer policy is the strategic heart of the PHN, since it is the vehicle for water resource redistribution at national level' [7]. The volume of water that will be transferred depends respectively on the demand forecasts and deficits in the exporting and importing catchments. This strategy is reinforced by the perception of a 'water-rich' north and a 'water-scarce' south. For example the Tagus basin (Mid West) receives 642 mm/year of rainfall while the Segura basin, in South East Spain, only has 380 mm/yr. The Tagus-Segura transfer was designed in order to meet the water deficit of the agriculturally productive South East of Spain.

4   Main issues on the Tagus-Segura water transfer

The Tagus Segura transfer could prove exemplary in stock taking of positive and negative experiences for future planned transfers and main water users. In this section, a brief rationale and description of the transfer will be made. A second part will reflect on the Tagus-Segura experience to analyse some of the key issues underlying water transfers: i) the concept of 'surplus' water and minimal environmental flows, ii) the argument on regional solidarity and economic development and iii) social aspects such as user participation required under the 1985 water law.

The Tagus and Segura rivers are similar in the sense that both are located in the so called 'arid' Spain and the fact that agriculture is their main activity. However, in other aspects (length, direction of flow, surface and ground water resources, population numbers, main water problems, etc.) the rivers are distinct . The Segura catchment alone represents 20% of the annual national water deficit estimated at 3,000 hm^3. To meet the Segura catchment water deficit, and in line with the mentality of the 1950s-60s use of water as the engine for regional development, plans were made in the 1960s to transfer water to the Segura catchment.

The transfer's General Preliminary Project (passed in 1968) established the regulated volume at the two headwaters dams of the Tagus river at 1,200 hm^3/yr, of which 600 hm^3/year were needed to meet the Tagus basin demand and the remaining 600 hm^3/year were classified as 'surplus' and, therefore, transferable to the Segura basin.

The transfer consists of a complex system of pipes, canals and tunnels extending over 300 km between the exporting catchment (Tagus) and the receiving catchment (Segura). In addition, there are 315 post-transfer installations to distribute the water in the Segura catchment. Since it was completed and became operational in 1979, many criticisms have been put forward in relation to both the principles of transferring water and the practice of the transfer.

First, the very concept of 'surplus water ' (pre-requisite for water transfers) is questioned by some authors. Water cannot be classified as surplus if it is the 'normal' or 'natural' flow of that river and its 'surplus' is only relative when compared to other rivers, such as the Segura . However, it could be assumed that the 'surplus' water concept is reasonable if defined in terms of the water not used or diverted for irrigation, municipal or industrial uses.

In the catchment context, legally only 'surplus' water defined by the catchment plan can be transferred. In the case of the Tagus river surplus, while the Catchment plan is prepared, this surplus is determined by the legal requirement that flow before the confluence with the Jarama tributary, in Aranjuez, has to be 6m^3 per second (m^3/sec). This pre-requisite has proved conflictive:

- an auditor's study, carried out by the Castille-La Mancha region, highlighted that this minimal flow was often not being achieved [8].
- this 6 m^3/sec proviso was altered in December 1995 by a Decree of the Council of Ministers to ensure water transfers could continue to water starved fruit trees in SE Spain.
- according to the Tagus Hydrographic Commission water collecting in the Tagus headwaters dam has been decreasing over the last 17 years, even back to 1912.

Yet in the peak of the 1990-95 drought, the Central Syndicate of Transfer Irrigation farmers in the Segura region asked for an additional transfer of 55 hm^3 for irrigation.

These examples indicate that the meaning of 'surplus' water is a flexible concept dependent on the hydrological conditions occurring at the time, to the extent that legal minimal flows (6m^3/second at Aranjuez) can be halved under drastic water shortages.

In addition, in environmental terms, 'surplus' will have to be redefined to take into account environmental concerns for 'minimum' and not 'surplus' flows. At present, minimal flows for the Tagus are defined only under 'normal' circumstances, leaving the door open for downward alterations in times of drought, when ecosystems are more vulnerable to some of Madrid's untreated sewage. In addition, water transfers, unlike dams, do not have to undergo Environmental Impact Assessment studies.

Second, the economic feasibility of the project is closely tied to national and regional economic and social benefits. In this context it is relevant to examine: a) the cost of building the project and its re-payment and b) compensation provided for the exporting region. Payment would was made through a German loan at preferential rates, while it was agreed that the importing region would have to pay for the transfer through water prices. In relation to compensation, the transfer's 'financial' regime was based on 'compensating' the exporting region via public irrigation plus water infrastructure works and tariffs to account for exported water. In the first case, many parts of the promised infrastructure are still pending, for example, many villages upstream of the Tagus (Alberche and Tietar) have had water shortages in recent years despite high rainfall, due to their lack of basic infrastructure. In addition, some experts and water users argue that the infrastructure had to be carried out in any case, regardless of the transfer, and should not be considered as compensation. In the second case, tariffs were agreed for transferring water. However, in the first phase, rates were only calculated according to 60% of investment, instead of 100%. Tariffs had to be reviewed every two years (Art 14), yet since March 1989 no review of tariffs has taken place. Furthermore, the Tagus Hydrographic Commission directly receives the transfer's compensation, and it has independence as to where and how the money is invested in the catchment. There is no proviso to invest on the area directly affected by the transfer (Tagus headwaters). This area which has given up a resource should receive some payment.

In terms of estimating the cost of the project, the only official economic study was carried out in the late 1960s, assessing the feasibility of the project assuming a transferred volume of 900 hm^3/yr at a total cost of 14,500 million pesetas [9]. On this assumption the economic study proved the transfer viable. In reality, the maximum quantity ever transferred was 377 hm^3, while the average amount transferred since the transfer started functioning is 276 hm^3. No other official public economic study has been carried out with the altered figures.

This expected water transfer required by law has been allocated as closed irrigation perimeters between Alicante, Murcia and Almeria by the Instituto de Reforma y Desarrollo Agrario (IRYDA) [10]. Expectations were created in the importing regions on the basis of the water promised in the 1960s-70s which, in reality, has been reduced to less than one fourth. In addition, this lack of realistic water planning has been compounded by the lack of adequate control on areas irrigated in the importing region. Indeed, many areas considered inadequate for irrigation have been ploughed inside irrigation perimeters. In this context, the Government of Castille-La Mancha has demanded that in future specific details are provided on which farmer, crop and number of hectares have benefited from the transfer and that irrigation areas are clearly defined so that no further expansion can take place.

Third, in social terms, the Tagus-Segura transfer can shed some light on institutional structures working in practice such as 'user participation', a legal requirement under the 1985 water law. A Central Commission was created in the 1970s with representatives of the Ministry of Public Works and the two Hydrographic Commissions, regions affected were invited as guests but with no decision powers. By law, this Commission had to maintain a minimal reserve in the Entrepeñas and Buendia dams at the end of each hydrological year (30th September) and would not accept transfers if this minimum was violated. However, in 1992, this Commission, with the backing of the Council of Ministers, agreed to transfer water despite the fact that there was no typified surplus water. This happened again in 1994. Both decisions were contested by the Castille-La Mancha regional Government at the Supreme Court and on March 1996 this Court ruled the transfers illegal. The Ministry of Public Works had argued that dialogue had to take place between basins and not regions. The perspective of regions different: hydrographic Commissions are ascribed to the Ministry, therefore not fully independent whereas regions enjoy relative autonomy.

5   Future transfers in Spanish hydrological planning?

In the current draft PHN an estimated volume of 2,370 hm^3/year in the first phase (2002) and up to 4,245 hm^3/year in the second phase (2012) could be transferred between basins [11]. According to the draft PHN the Ebro, Douro, Pyrenees and Cantabrian areas are considered as 'surplus' regions while simultaneously they do not represent the greatest growth in demand. The Ebro river alone is expected to supply 48% of the volume that will be transferred between catchments. It is interesting to assess issues already analysed in the Tagus-Segura transfer in relation to the planned transfers in the draft PHN if water transfers become the main supply management strategy adopted for future Spanish water planning.

First, according to the draft law of the hydrological plan only 'surplus' water can be transferred. In national water planning, 'surplus' has so far not been clearly defined in the draft PHN. It has only been determined *'a posteriori'* and administratively, on the basis of predicted future demand by extrapolating current demand into the future, complemented by a Government order guiding estimates. Only briefly does it discuss the possibility of actively influencing 'demand' through demand management policies. In addition, exporting regions are concerned as experience in the Tagus-Segura shows that legal ' maximums' or 'minimums' can be altered, particularly under drought conditions.

Second, the issues of payment and compensation. Current proposals for future water transfers under the draft PHN will benefit from European Union's cohesion funds, under its 'environment' section, to co-finance water infrastructure with the Spanish Government. The draft PHN law also specifies a charge be paid in compensation for water transferred. However, experience in the Tagus-Segura water transfer shows, that although money is paid to the Hydrographic Commission it is not necessarily handed back to those residents directly affected by the transfer and, in addition, the updating of the tariff is not guaranteed. In theory, the law states that 'surplus' and 'importing' regions can be altered temporarily in case of drought. However, this would be difficult to implement once supply is allocated to key economic sectors on which the national economy will rely even more at a time of drought and economic recession.

Third, in terms of sustainable regional development (in economic, social and environmental terms) in the perception of the affected 'surplus' regions, most of the planned water transfers will take water away from extensively farmed areas in the interior of the peninsula, with low incomes, to areas which already practice profitable irrigated agriculture (e.g. Almeria, Murcia, Alicante, etc.) which also increasingly use water for tourism (golf courses, large hotels with swimming pools, etc.). This would augment regional divergence in Spain between poor and wealthy regions. In the words of one of the drafters of the draft PHN: 'It is our duty to place water in acceptable conditions, where there are favourable conditions for agricultural production, so that expectations cannot be frustrated' [12]. However, if realistic water prices were applied, i.e. unsubsidised water for agricultural use, the profit from these areas would decrease considerably. Yet in terms of the national economy, the losses of Alberche and Tietar (upstream Tagus) are negligible when compared to the estimated losses in the SE Spain due to drought losses of agricultural crops estimated at 150,000 m pts.

Indeed, and thanks to the Senate decision on the need to prepare catchment plans in advance to the PHN, the Ebro river and region are maximising their water demand and allocations in order to make transfers or the existence of 'surplus' difficult if not impossible. However, this is hardly in line with sustainable water use based on conservation and demand management. Both levels of administration - central (PHN) and regional (Catchment plans) - seem to plan in line with supply management policies.

6   Demand management in Spain

Demand forecasts and priorities will be modified in line with the 'National Irrigation Plan' (PNR), passed on February 1996, establishing as priority objective the improvement, modernisation and consolidation of current irrigated areas. At present, 70% of irrigation networks are more than twenty years old and 29% are more than 200 years old. Investment on modernising irrigation networks could save between 4,000 to 5,000 hm^3/year. Yet, general policy lines remain similar (i.e. supply management and focus on productive Mediterranean areas) as the PNR states the importance of Mediterranean agriculture and urges the approval of the PHN and inter basin transfers. Spanish and international pressure groups like CODA, Greenpeace or SEO argue that much could be done on 'demand management' before any further need for increased water supply. It is estimated that as much as 40% of water is lost in distribution networks. Also, although politically expensive, Art 48.4 Water Law specifies the need for water saving techniques and dissuasive methods to reduce water use, such as the increase in water rates. A strong economic-financial system lies at the heart of rational water use in Spain, treating water as a scarce and therefore expensive, natural resource thus pushing towards a review on demand trends and estimates.

7 Conclusion

In Spain, eleven years after the passing of the 1985 Water Law which created a legal duty to carry out hydrological planning no Catchment Plan or the National Hydrological Plan have been approved. This highlights four key issues: first, the fact that potential 'surplus' regions do not feel confident enough on financial systems planned into water transfer 's management. Second, whenever someone discusses water policy in Spain, in reality, it is a discussion of agricultural policy (and increasingly tourism) as the main sector(s) which have to be targeted in order to carry out coherent and sustainable water use. Third, in view of future planned water transfers it is fundamental to seriously address the issues exposed in the Tagus-Segura experience and address the limits in practice of the current institutional and legal framework

In future, planning will have to be more sophisticated and flexible, with in-depth studies and modelling of impacts, particularly in relation to Portugal and exporting regions. There should be no predetermined bias towards opting for increased supply which encourages catchment plans to inflate demand to prevent transfers while the national plan prioritises certain (privileged?) areas. In future sustainable water management could lie on the question of demand management. It is encouraging to see the draft National Irrigation Plan appear in order to be discussed. It would be even more positive to include 'Demand Management Plans' as part of the current catchment plans which are being presented to the National Water Council.

Acknowledgements: Thanks to Dr. Ted Hollis at University College London for his advice on this paper, to Bradley Bainger for his help in preparing figures and to Jeanne Gunn for providing some key references.

8 References

1. MAPA (1995a) *Avance del Plan Nacional de Regadios: Memoria* Secretaria General de Desarrollo Rural y Conservacion de la Naturaleza (Direccion General de Planificacion Rural y Medio Natural); Octubre; Madrid.
2. Montes, C. and Bifani, C. (1990) Spain in *Wetlands: market Interventions and Failures* (ed. Turner, K. and Jones, T.), OECD, Earthscan Publications Limited, London, p. 155.
3. Delgado Piqueras, F. (1992) *Derecho de Aguas y Medio Ambiente,* Pub. Tecnos, Madrid.
4. Gallego Anabitarte, A. and Calvo Lechosa, A. (1995) Algunos aspectos de la Ley de Aguas de 1985 a los diez años de su aprobacion *El Campo Servicio de Estudios BBV 'El Agua'* Banco Bilbao Vizcaya, Bilbao, p. 172.

5. In March 1996 the new conservative Government has created a new environment ministry, which will include water as part of its roles., thus altering the old MOPTMA structure (author's note)

6. Cabezas Calvo-Rubio, F. (1994) Consideracion de los recursos hidrogeologicos y no convencionales en el Plan Hidrologico de la Cuenca del Segura in *Recursos hidrogeologicos y recursos hidraulicos no convencionales* (ed MOPTMA) Seminario de la Universidad Internacional Menendez Pelayo, Santander 30th August to 3rd September 1993, Pub. MOPTMA, Madrid p 345.

7. Manteiga, L. and Jiliberto, R. (1995) *Strategic Environmental Assessment and Hydrological Planning in Spain* SEO/RSPB, Birdlife International, Cambridge (UK) p 42.

8. Study by Doña Aurora Ruiz Alonso, notary in by Bono Martinez, J. (in press) *El rio Tajo: cauce para la solidaridad* closing day in Jornadas sobre el Tajo, organised by the Fundacion 'Puente Barcas' 22.4.95 Aranjuez.

9. In the second phase of the planned transfer an additional 300 hm3 would be set free for the transfer when the Jarama waters (Tagus tributary) were treated after supplying Madrid (JCM 1995b *Informacion sobre el Trasvase Tajo Segura* Toledo 5 June 1995 p 9).

10. Legally, one of the two transfer laws - Law 21/1971 on the 'Joint Use of the Tagus-Segura' had allocated the amount of transferred water as a maximum of 600 hm3 in the first phase going up to a maximum 1,200 hm3/yr in the second phase (author's note).

11. MOPTMA (1993) *Anteproyecto de Ley del Plan Hidrologico Nacional* Abril, Madrid, Title 2.

12. Baltanas Garcia, A. (1994) El Plan Hidrologico nacional. Situacion actual y efectos especificos sobre los regadios españoles *Revista de Estudios Agro-sociales*. No.167, January-March, 1/1994, Pub. MAPA, Madrid, p 34.

WATER FOR SUSTAINABLE DEVELOPMENT IN THE NORTH-EASTERN BADIA, JORDAN

Sustainable water development in Jordan

J. DOTTRIDGE
Department of Geological Sciences, University College, London, UK
B. GIBBS
Hydrogeology Group, British Geological Survey, Wallingford, UK

Abstract
In the arid northeast of Jordan, sustainable development relies on lasting, adequate and reliable supplies of water. As water demand rises, the gap widens between abstraction and replenishment of the main source of good groundwater, the upper aquifer of the Azraq basin. Most surface flows are lost by evaporation on the Qaa (playas). Although some uncertainty remains in the resource estimates, the most optimistic figures show that pumping is more than twice recharge. This has led to declining water levels and cessation of spring flows, causing serious environmental damage at Azraq oasis. Water allocation is a serious issue, with conflicting priorities of urban water supply, local domestic use, agriculture and wetland conservation. Despite strong Government policy to control abstraction, no firm system of water management has been implemented. The Jordan Badia Research and Development Programme aims to promote sustainable development of the desertified Badia environment and to improve the standard of living of the inhabitants. To meet these objectives, without aggravating the problems of water shortage, the programme is investigating innovative ways of maximising the usable water resources, by optimising the design of run-off harvesting schemes, use of other groundwater resources and water conservation.
Keywords: arid, groundwater, development, policy management, sustainability, water resources.

1 Introduction

In arid areas, water scarcity has traditionally restricted development; sustainable development relies on adequate, reliable and lasting supplies of fresh water. In 1992, the Jordan Badia Research and Development Programme was established, jointly by the

Water Policy: Allocation and management in practice. Edited by P. Howsam and R.C. Carter.
Published in 1996 by E & FN Spon. ISBN 0 419 21650 2

Higher Council for Science and Technology (HCST), Jordan, and the Royal
Geographical Society (RGS), UK, to promote " the sustainable development of the
desertified Badia environment and the improvement of the standard of living of the
inhabitants... under management systems which conserve the natural resources so that
production levels will be sustainable in the long term." [1][2].

The pilot area selected for the programme is in northeastern Jordan, as shown in Fig.
1, with an average annual rainfall of only 50 to 150 mm [3]. Despite the apparently
unfavourable geology and climate, the area has substantial groundwater resources and
regular winter flows in the wadis, originating from Jebel Arab in Syria. But the Badia
programme area forms part of the Azraq basin, as illustrated by Fig. 1, and the water
issues cannot be considered in isolation from the overall basin resources, and in
particular the environmental deterioration at Azraq oasis and the adjoining wetlands,
which are suffering from a reduction in spring flows [4][5]. On the basin scale,
groundwater is over-abstracted, with large scale pumping for public water supply to
Amman, Zerqa and Mafraq. This desert area is therefore an exporter of water to the
wetter but more densely populated parts of Jordan. The local population relies on
groundwater for domestic supplies, livestock and irrigation. The dilemma for the Badia
programme and others working in the area is to provide sufficient water for local needs,
without aggravating the problems of overabstraction and increasing derogation at
Azraq, which lies downstream of the programme area.

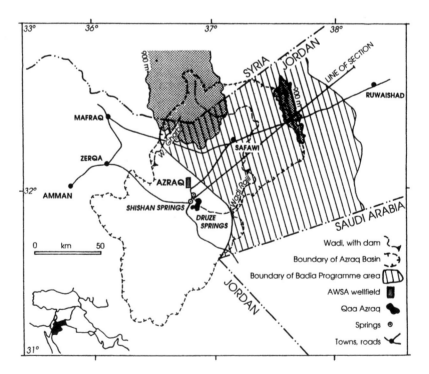

Fig. 1. Location and main features of the Badia Programme area and Azraq Basin

2 Water resources

2.1 Groundwater

Groundwater in northeastern Jordan occurs in three aquifer complexes [6][7][8], as shown in the section in Fig. 2:

- Upper aquifer, composed of Quaternary basalts and the underlying Rijam cherty limestone;
- Middle aquifer, Cretaceous limestones of the Amman-Wadi Sir and Hummar aquifers, with very variable productivity and water quality, at depths of 300 to 1000 m;
- Lower aquifer, Cretaceous and older sandstones (Kurnub and Disi formations), at depths of 1.3 to 3.4 km.

Although a recent project has explored the middle aquifer [9], only the upper aquifer is currently used. In this system, flow in the fissured basalt and Rijam limestone is approximately radial towards Azraq, with a gentle piezometric gradient of 0.001. Both depth to water and saturated thickness of the aquifers decrease southwards towards Azraq. The transmissivity of the basalts is highly variable, ranging from 5 to 30000 m^2/d [10] and shows a correlation with major faults. The major fault zones provide conduits for rapid flow of very low salinity water, while the Fuluk fault acts as a partial barrier to groundwater flow [11]. The transmissivity of the Rijam limestones is lower, 6

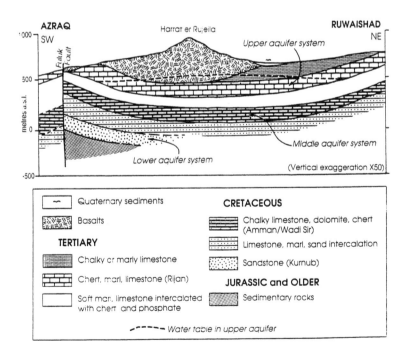

Fig. 2. Schematic section showing the main aquifers

to 230 m^2/d. The specific yield is estimated as 1 to 3% [12], although test pumping at Azraq gave higher values of 12 to 22% [13].

The water quality in the upper aquifer is extremely good, suitable for drinking or irrigation. The distribution of total dissolved solids confirms the radial flow pattern with elongated zones of low salinity, from 190 to 400 mg/l, coinciding with the permeable fault zones [14]. Water with high salinity, up to 300 000 mg/l, occurs locally in a zone of shallow water table around the playa of Qaa Azraq.

Recharge to the upper aquifer occurs mainly through direct infiltration in the wetter, northern part of the basin, above 1000m elevation, and by infiltration of wadi flows. In wet winters, some recharge may also occur in the larger, more arid area below 1000m. The estimates of annual recharge range from 0 to 67 mm^3/year, mostly averaging between 22 and 36 mm^3/year. A credible minimum value is 16 mm^3/year, which equals both the value calculated for recharge above 1000 m [15] and lowest estimate of historical flow from the springs at Azraq [16].

The main natural outlets from the basin are the springs at Azraq, the Druze springs fed by water from the north and Azraq Shishan supplied from the south. In the mid 1950s, the discharge from the Druze springs was measured as 3.5 mm^3/year, with 23 mm^3/year from the lower altitude Shishan springs [6]1 [17]. The spring flows have declined over the last forty years, until the Druze springs ceased to flow at the end of 1987 and the Shishan springs dried up at the end of 1992. The decline of spring flows and the accompanying decline in piezometric head, at rates between 0.35 and 0.6 m/year, in the central part of the basin were matched by a continual increase in pumped abstraction since the 1940s. The trends with time are illustrated in Fig. 3.

2.2 Surface water

Although there are regular, short duration floods during winter in the wadis flowing south from Jebel Arab, there were no measurements of flow until six new gauges were installed in 1995. Total flows have been estimated from rainfall data to average 27 mm^3/year. It is reported that flood frequency and magnitude have declined markedly in recent years, due to the construction of dams on the upper reaches of the wadis in Syria. A Jordanian dam was constructed on the lower reach of Wadi Rajil in the 1980s, but the reservoir has only filled once, in the winter of 1994/95.

3   Current water use

Groundwater is used for:
- large scale public water supply to the Amman area, and on a smaller scale to Mafraq;
- local small supplies for domestic use and livestock;
- industrial users, with low water demands of only 56000 m^3 /year at present;
- intensive irrigation concentrated around Azraq;
- scattered smaller scale irrigation in the north of the project area.

Abstraction rates for all sectors have increased rapidly since 1980. The single largest abstractor (18 mm^3/year since 1988, 19.2 mm^3/year in 1994) is the Amman Water and Sewerage Authority (AWSA) wellfield, north of Azraq. In 1994, only 0.87 mm^3 of this total was used for local supply, with the remainder exported from the area. A further 5.15 mm^3 from wells along the Mafraq-Safawi road was supplied to Mafraq.

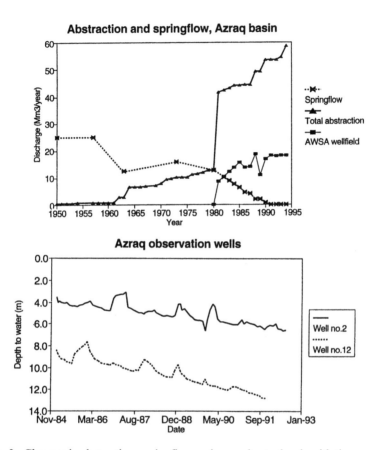

Fig. 3. Changes in abstraction, springflow and groundwater levels with time

In the northern part of the basin, local supplies in 1994 accounted for 2.6 mm³, 18% of total abstraction, but drilling of new boreholes for local public supply continued in 1994 and 1995. Losses in the distribution system are very high, estimated to be 61% [18].

Irrigated agriculture, with pumping from over 600 boreholes, is concentrated in the agricultural areas to the east of Azraq and the north of the basin. The abstraction for irrigation in the northern agricultural area was calculated as 6.6 mm³ in 1994. Although drip irrigation is used, poor design and maintenance results in moderate distribution efficiencies, represented by a measured value of 68%. This suggests that the crops' peak requirements are only just satisfied by the present systems. In the Azraq area, abstraction for irrigation was estimated to be between 25.35 mm³ [19] and 32.55 mm³ [18], with much lower efficiency, below 50%, due to the coarser soil and continuing use of channel and basin techniques.

Combining all the components leads to estimates of total basin abstraction in 1994 between 58.9 and 65.1 mm³. These figures are derived from detailed investigation of each activity, are consistent with the larger of the earlier estimates [16] and are therefore considered to be reliable and realistic. Comparison of recharge and discharge figures shows that the annual abstraction is at least two or three times the quantity replenished.

4   Water policy

In Jordan, any well or borehole abstracting more than 5 m³/hour requires a licence, but licences allow pumping in perpetuity. Licence conditions are strict, unpopular, difficult to enforce and often flouted. The controls include a minimum distance between wells, typically at least 1 km in the Badia, maximum abstraction of 50 000 m³/year, pump testing supervised by the Water Authority of Jordan (WAJ), installation of a flowmeter, restriction of irrigation to the owner's land by efficient methods and prohibition on the sale of water.

Since 1971, no new licences have been allowed in the central Azraq area; this was later extended to cover most of the northern part of the Azraq basin. In May 1992, a three year ban on the issuing of new well licences throughout Jordan was imposed, with the exception of special circumstances. Direct action to close unlicensed wells followed a Government decree in November 1988, issued in response to the 1987 Ramsar Convention's recommendations on the conservation of the Azraq wetland. The campaign resulted in plugging of 151 wells and 35 boreholes [5], but was abandoned due to problems with well owners. The decree formed part of a comprehensive set of recommendations from a Cabinet committee formed to consider Azraq's water situation, which also included restricting total abstraction to 20 mm³/year, with 14 mm³ allotted to the Amman area, only 3.5 mm³ for irrigation and minimum spring discharge of 2.5 mm³. These figures are in marked contrast with the recent estimates in section 3. Restoration of the Azraq wetland is the subject of a $ 3 million project, funded by UNDP and due for completion in 1996.

Despite the regulations, there are still large numbers of unlicensed wells and boreholes, with 203 boreholes and 164 dug wells recorded in a census in 1993 [19]. Most of these are in the Azraq area where the water table is shallow and drilling costs low; in the north, the high cost of boreholes deters farmers from drilling without a licence [18].

The Department of the Environment is responsible for the administration of the Ramsar Convention and for enforcing environmental protection measures, but the Ministry of Water and irrigation has responsibility for both regulation and development of water. This dichotomy of interest in the institutional framework leads to lack of implementation of the regulations.

5   Development options

In view of the extent of overabstraction in the Azraq basin, planning of water use for future development is problematic, and abstraction must be reduced if spring flows are to be restored. In contrast to the central part of the basin, the Badia programme's project area still has ample supplies of groundwater, recharge exceeds local abstraction and the water quality is excellent. However, additional development of groundwater would contravene Government policy and contradict the programme's aim of sustainable development, by increasing volumes of 'mined' groundwater in the Azraq basin. The programme has therefore concentrated on maximisation of water availability by evaluating alternative sources of water, including surface flows, groundwater from the middle aquifer and the adjoining Sirhan and Hammad basins, artificial recharge of the upper aquifer, reuse of waste water and leakage control.

The most substantial and under-used resource is surface flow, which is capable of providing significant additional supplies through water harvesting. There will be no significant impact downstream because, at present most of the surface water flows onto the fine silty surface of the playas (Qaas) and then evaporates. Only a small proportion of the water is used, mostly by natural vegetation on the Marebs (playa with outflow), which provide pasture, and in a few localities, water is diverted and stored for local use. The largest of these systems is at a farm on Wadi Gharbi, to the northwest of Azraq, where the wadi flows are captured by a small dam and pumped into a deep storage reservoir. The extensive fields of olive trees and presence of water in the reservoir in October 1995 demonstrate that surface water harvesting can provide a year round supply of water, providing the winter rainfall is sufficient, but a borehole is used as a reserve supply.

The feasibility and optimum methods of utilizing the surface water resources form the main objectives of the water theme for the second phase of the Badia Research and Development programme [19]. However, groundwater will continue to form the main source of water for the area, due to its reliability and widespread availability.

6   Conclusions for future resource management

When considering use of finite water resources, sustainable development policies cannot be implemented without considering the influences of water users both upstream and downstream of the project area.   For the Badia Research and Development programme's pilot area, water planning must consider the whole of the Azraq basin, including the high rainfall area in Syria and the main discharge area centred on Azraq. However, over-abstraction on the basin scale need not prevent future development, provided that alternative sources of water can be utilised. In the Badia area, the surface flows represent an additional water resource, as now, almost all the water is lost through evaporation.

Although some uncertainty remains about the scale of overabstraction in the Azraq basin, due to lack of precision in values of both recharge and abstraction, there is no doubt about the conclusion that current pumping rates are at least twice the recharge rate. The uncertainty should not therefore be a reason for lack of action to control abstraction.

The Jordanian Government has tough policies on licensing and controlling groundwater use, but these are not always enforced when other considerations receive a higher priority. Enforcement of controls and firm resource management are essential to define the strategy and priorities for water use, co-ordinate different groups with conflicting aims and to implement the management plans to safeguard the resource in the long term.

Acknowledgements: The views expressed in this paper are those of the authors alone. The authors acknowledge the contribution of the staff and researchers of the Badia Research and Development Programme, and numerous others in the water sector in Jordan. The work was made possible by the cooperation and generous provision of data by WAJ, Ministry of Water and Irrigation, Natural Resources Authority (NRA) and Ministry of Agriculture. Special thanks to the water resources staff of WAJ for their continuing expert assistance. Financial support from the RGS, HCST, Royal Society, Natural Environment Research Council and Royal Jordanian is gratefully acknowledged.

7   References

1. RGS (1992) *Framework Document, The Jordan Badia Research and Development Programme 1992-1995 (Stage One: Safawi).*
2. HCST (1993) *The Badia, Rural Development...Investing in our common future..*
3. Al-Homoud, A.S., Allison, R.J., Sunna, B. and White, K. (1995) *Geology, Geomorphology, Hydrology, Groundwater and Physical Resources of the desertified Badia environment in Jordan,* GeoJournal, vol 37.1, pp 51-67.
4. GEF (Global Environmental Facility) (1993) *Arid Region Nature and Natural Resources Conservation and Rehabilitation - Azraq component - Project Document.* For UNDP and Government of Jordan.
5. Jones, T.A. (1990) *Azraq Oasis, Jordan.* Ramsar Convention Monitoring Procedure Report No 16.
6. Parker, D.H. (1971) *The hydrogeology of the Mesozoic-Cainozoic aquifers of the Western highlands and plateau of East Jordan.* PhD thesis, University of Nottingham.
7. Core Lab (1987) *Azraq Basin Study.* Volume IIID, Reservoir Geology Hydrodynamics. For NRA, Amman, Jordan.
8. NRA (1993) *Al Azraq 3353 1.* 1:50000 Geological map.
9. Salzgitter (1994) *Middle Aquifer Exploration Project, Azraq basin.* Final report
10. WAJ (1987) *North Jordan Groundwater Project.*
11. Holden, W. (1995) *Modelling and isotope study of the Upper aquifer of the Azraq basin,* unpublished MSc thesis, University College London.
12. WAJ (1989) *Azraq Basin Water Resources Study,* Draft Final Report.
13. Howard Humphreys (1982) *AWSA Azraq wellfield evaluation.*
14. Drury, D.M. (1993) *The Hydrochemistry of the Azraq Basin, N.E. Badia.* unpublished MSc. thesis, University College London.
15. Noble, P. (1994) *Quantification of recharge to the Azraq Basin, NE Badia, Jordan,* unpublished MSc thesis, University College London.
16. Gibbs, B. (1993) *The Hydrogeology of the Azraq Basin, N.E. Badia, Jordan,* unpublished MSc. thesis, University College London.
17. WAJ (1986) *Springflow data in Jordan Prior to 1985,* Department of Water Resources Development, Technical Paper no. 51.
18. Waddingham, J. (1994) *Water demand in the north-east Badia, Jordan,* unpublished MSc thesis, University of Newcastle upon Tyne.
19. Dottridge, J. (1995) *Water Resources: Progress and Priorities,* Jordan Badia Research and Development Programme.

SECTION 3

ENVIRONMENT & WATER QUALITY

GROUNDWATER RESOURCE DEGRADATION: A FRAMEWORK FOR ANALYSIS, WITH EXAMPLES FROM CHINA AND PALESTINE

Groundwater resource degradation

R.J. GRIMBLE and G. GASS
Social Science Department, Natural Resources Institute, Chatham Maritime, UK
B. ADAMS, A.M.MACDONALD and R.CALOW
Hydrogeological Group, British Geological Survey, Wallingford, UK
D.R.C. GREY
World Bank, Washington, USA

Abstract
Groundwater resources (GWR) are vulnerable to physical degradation in the form of depletion, depletion-induced changes, and contamination. Degradation, commonly induced by human activity, has environmental, economic and social effects which in turn impact on mankind. This paper develops a broad framework for analysing groundwater degradation problems and management strategies. It then applies the framework to two contrasting groundwater resource degradation situations in developing countries.
Keywords: China, degradation, groundwater, institutions, management, Palestine, policy, sustainability.

1 The water context

Historically, water has been a grossly undervalued and often neglected resource. Slowly this is beginning to change as water scarcity, deteriorating water quality and rising marginal costs of supply have brought discussion of water management into the political arena and begun to shift perceptions of water from being an entitlement to an economic commodity [1][2]. As economic scarcity and its recognition increases, so does the threat of conflict over the allocation and distribution of water at local, national and international levels [3].

The involvement of the state in the water sector in many countries has also recently been subject to criticism. Firstly, the range and fragmentation of Governmental policy interests vested in the sector have acted against coherent and consistent policy development and public sector investment (e.g. water quantity and quality issues, and surface and groundwater management, have been insufficiently integrated) [4].

Water Policy: Allocation and management in practice. Edited by P. Howsam and R.C. Carter.
Published in 1996 by E & FN Spon. ISBN 0 419 21650 2

Secondly, considerations of economic efficiency have been marginalised, and states have followed a supply management orientation, often in the post war era with emphasis on large engineering structures. Until recently, relatively little attention has been paid to improving water use efficiency, the use of pricing and economic incentives, or to encouragement of small-scale measures for local management and supply augmentation.

2   The groundwater problem

Groundwater, even more than surface water, has suffered from undervaluation and neglect. This, one suspects, is a function of its invisibility ('out of sight out of mind'), lack of knowledge and understanding, inherent difficulty of study (or model), and the small scale of much exploitation. Under both state and private development there is evidence of non-sustainable management and groundwater resource degradation in different parts of the world. However depletion is still insufficiently recognised as a major global problem and seldom is its human significance assessed. Similarly, groundwater quality issues until recently have taken a back seat in most debates about environmental degradation.   The consequences of such neglect is serious: groundwater, though naturally suited to human consumption, is vulnerable to contamination and hard and expensive to clean up [5].

2.1 Aquifer functions
The functions of aquifers in supporting human productive and livelihood activities are considerable and diverse. As an essential part of the hydrological cycle, aquifers collect and store surface run-off that might otherwise be lost to the sea. Thus they provide natural storage of fresh water in a form that can be readily utilised by society when required. Where recharge is adequate the resource can be managed sustainably, and be used as a buffer in periods of deficit or drought, or retained for use by future generations. Other beneficial functions of aquifers include, depending on location and geology, their role in assimilation of waste, in sustaining wetlands of ecological interest, and maintaining springs and surface water supplies; they may also provide a natural storage reservoir for water surplus to immediate requirements, and be used for artificial recharge.

   Aquifer exploitation may require relatively little investment and is potentially available to any resident with overlying land, though also depends on prevailing institutional factors. Technological development has recently extended the volume of groundwater within economic range, but at the same time has increased its susceptibility to depletion.

2.2 Groundwater development
Because of its physical characteristics, groundwater is a common pool resource typically developed on a small scale, often privately by individuals and communities. Where open access ('no property') situations exist, with exploitation open to multiple users, individual rationality has often led to unsustainable competition not beneficial to society as a whole. Beyond a point, groundwater resources (GWR) are subtractible, and where there is no institutional control over sinking wells, non-sustainable

exploitation can take place - the so called 'tragedy of the commons' scenario [6][7].

Not all GWR resources, however, have been developed in an uncontrolled or laissez-faire manner. In this paper we have selected two case studies for examination that portray contrasting institutional situations: the Gaza Strip in Palestine, where management systems have failed to keep pace with socio-economic and political developments and a virtual 'pumping race' has emerged; and Yao Ba, an irrigation scheme in Inner Mongolia with a tradition of tight centralised regulation and control. As we will see, however, certain GWR degradation problems have arisen in both locations and circumstances: even where abstraction is controlled by the state, non-sustainable exploitation can occur.

3   Groundwater degradation

A general definition of GWR degradation might be 'any deterioration in the stock or quality of groundwater resources or systems'. It can occur for natural or anthropogenic reasons, although we are here primarily concerned with degradation induced by man. It can be permanent or reversible, though the cost of reversal (or treatment) may be high. In all cases, however, it has implications for the availability and cost of freshwater supplies, and for meeting the needs of future generations.

A convenient framework in which to consider the symptoms of degradation is to classify them in three categories: depletion; depletion-induced; and contamination. *Depletion* relates to a reduction in the quantity of the resource as indicated by a fall in water levels. *Depletion-induced* relates to secondary changes induced by the fall in water levels, particularly saline intrusion, land subsidence, and reduction of water storage capacity. *Contamination* relates to the loading of contaminants (pollutants) at a rate exceeding the aquifer's ability to assimilate, and is independent of depletion. A fourth degradation category, augmentation or raising of water levels, could be added as this may result in soil salinisation and water logging but this aspect is not pursued here.

Contamination can similarly be broken down into categories, referred to as point source and diffuse (or non-point) pollution. Point source pollution is traceable to a particular site or entry point, and often emanates from industrial effluent or municipal waste. Diffuse pollution is that which cannot be traced to specific sites or locations, and is typically associated with intensive agriculture, particularly the use of nitrogenous fertilisers, but also may be atmospheric in origin (e.g. acid rain). Pollutants include hydrocarbons, heavy metals, organic and bacterial compounds, nitrates and pesticides. Their presence in GWR may reduce useable water stocks, downgrade their value (e.g. change from drinking to industrial water quality), introduce health risks, and increase supply cost.

In sum, degradation can be considered as having both quantitative and qualitative aspects. This is most conveniently handled using the economic concept of value. In economic terms, degradation represents a reduction in real value of a resource stock as a consequence of deterioration in either its quantity or quality, or indeed the two together. Unless otherwise specified, we henceforth use the term degradation in this general way.

4   A conceptual framework

From a broader social science perspective, GWR degradation is part of a circular cause and effect process, illustrated schematically in Fig. 1. Degradation is viewed as the result of the operation of economic and demographic processes that over time serve to increase the demand for groundwater within the economy and the level of pollutant (or load) reaching the aquifer system. These processes are communicated to the resource via a matrix of institutional factors which serve either to limit or intensify the impact on the groundwater resource; they are defined generally to include any factor that may influence pressures on GWR, and may be legal, cultural, organisational, technological or relate to the political system. The severity of degradation is in turn influenced by the specific aquifer characteristics (such as volume, depth, heterogeneity) that limit or raise the vulnerability of the resource to degradation. Thus both institutional and physical factors govern the susceptibility and nature of GWR degradation in any particular situation.

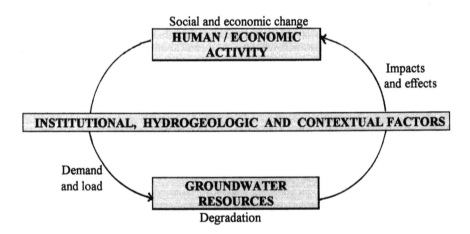

Fig 1. Human-physical inter-relationships and the degradation cycle

Once GWR have begun to degrade, effects will start to show in the human productive and livelihood systems they support. These impacts may be economic, environmental or social in nature - including, for example, increased operating costs, changes in cropping pattern, infrastructural damage, and damage to health - and be differentially distributed in society. The nature and extent of the socio-economic impact of GWR degradation in a given situation are subject to a similar set of location-specific institutional factors. Analysis to establish these linkages requires interdisciplinary effort that examines bio-physical and human variables in a 'web' of cause-and-effect relationships. Although the process is cyclical, with no start or end point, the cycle is never constant and feed-back and mutation enter the system. In this way factors can be both cause and effect at the same time.

5   Mitigation and management

Most theoretical examination of optimal natural resource exploitation policy treat resources as either *exhaustible* or *renewable* but in practice the line between the two may not be easily drawn. Groundwater is an important example of a resource that may or may not be renewable depending on physical circumstance and strategic management. The resource can be managed in one of three broad ways:

- degrade the aquifer at present or accelerated rates
- maintain the aquifer by reducing abstraction and contamination to sustainable levels
- restore the resource to original levels.

The choice of strategic option relates to basic questions of time-preference and the future value of the resource stock. Methodologies for selecting options have been discussed at a theoretical level [8] but not to our knowledge in relation to groundwater. Good policy demands making difficult temporal comparisons requiring detailed local knowledge and analysis but cannot preclude judgement. In practice, selection commonly occurs not as a result of analysis of likely costs and benefits to aggregate society, and to the various stakeholders within it, but often by default [9].

In practice the strategic options are not as stark as portrayed above and there are other important aspects of strategic management. A convenient frame of analysis is to group them into three categories, supply-side measures, demand-side measures and intermediate measures. *Supply-side* measures relate to the augmentation of existing water sources and normally involve investing in physical structures to meet a projected water 'demand curve' or to rectify a pollution problem. This has been the traditional and engineering-led approach to strategic planning of the water sector. *Demand-side* measures, on the other hand, are designed to reduce the use of water, and improve use-efficiency, through economic incentive mechanisms or by regulation. Incentives can be direct, through the use of volumetric pricing (paying for quantities of water used), or indirect through taxation or pricing of agricultural inputs. *Intermediate* measures are designed to save water by reducing wastage, such as the introduction of more water-efficient irrigation technologies and the lining of distribution canals, though only high value usage may be able to cover implementation costs. Where sufficient power is invested in the state, it may also be possible to divert water from low value usage, often thought of (not necessarily correctly) as irrigated agriculture, to higher value industrial or domestic consumption.

6   Two case studies

As part of our current ESRC research programme, we have conducted nine case studies of groundwater degradation problems in China, India, Thailand, Mexico, Ghana, Jersey and the Palestinian territories, representing a range of political, socio-economic and hydrogeological circumstances. Here we turn to site specific discussion of degradation problems and management options in two contrasting study areas.

6.1 Yao Ba oasis

Yao Ba is situated in an arid pastoral area bordered by mountains to the east and the Gobi desert to the west, in the autonomous region of Inner Mongolia. About 35 km^2 in size, its location is determined by an aquifer which underlies the area at a depth varying between 15 and 60 metres. An irrigation scheme was established in the area in 1972, since when it has become an oasis of prosperity and home to a population of over 7,000 people. Today its thriving economy is based on the irrigated production of wheat and other cereals for human consumption and livestock feed. Farmers are composed of local villagers who have turned from pastoralism to sedentary farming and settlers from impoverished and over-populated provinces who have migrated to the area. The scheme now has 250 functioning boreholes powered by electricity which gravity-feed numerous individually operated irrigation basins.

The problem. In the last six or seven years, prosperity has been threatened by the problem of rising salinity in the desert margin, a problem that will grow at present or even reduced abstraction. Changes in hydraulic gradients resulting from aquifer draw-down have led to the intrusion of saline water into the aquifer from a nearby (ephemeral) alkaline lake. Yao Ba thus demonstrates a *depletion-induced* problem which has begun to salinise soils, reduce crop yields, remove salt-sensitive crops, and in some cases force the abandonment of wells. The problem facing the authorities is how best to handle this physical problem and minimise its socio-economic impact on the local community [10].

The management system. As in the rest of China, water resources are the property of the state. In Yao Ba, water policy emanates from multiple levels of Government including the central Government in Beijing, the Government of Inner Mongolia, the Alashan League division, and the local banner or county. Day to day management of the irrigation scheme is shared between various bureaux of the banner, together with the Yao Ba administration, local administrative units called gatchas, state farms, and farmer groups. The Electricity Authority also plays an indirect if unconscious role in water management through its charging mechanisms.

The establishment of boreholes in the area is under the strict control of the water authorities, partly through licensing and partly through supplying drilling machinery and credit. While resource ownership is still firmly in the hands of the state, scheme operation is in the process of decentralisation (the 'household responsibility system'). In practical terms boreholes are now the property of the gatchas, the most local level of Government, and their management rests with farmer user-groups. Utilisation of the water itself is the responsibility of individual farmers who, since 1994, have been able to make their own cropping and water allocation decisions. Water is distributed to farmers on a strict rota basis and is virtually unpriced. However electricity charges for pumping have in the last two years been raised several-fold and their impact is beginning to affect farmers' water-allocation decisions. Decisions relating to further development or abandonment of the area's groundwater resources, however, rest largely with the Water Utilisation and Conservancy Bureau. The Bureau has responded to the growing salinity problem by restricting borehole establishment which has effectively curtailed expansion of the scheme.

Strategic options. Conceptually, as noted above, the strategic options are to *degrade, maintain* or *restore*. At the existing rate of pumping (about 30 mm^3/yr), drawdown and thereby salinity will increase over time and ultimately destroy the aquifer. While having immediate advantages, in the longer term this would have an enormous economic and social impact on local livelihood systems, and more widely on the supply of cereals and livestock feed in Inner Mongolia. On the assumption that annual recharge is of the order of only 6 mm^3/yr, the introduction of a fully sustainable policy will (*ceteris paribus*) would lead to a drastic reduction in irrigated area and have a massive impact on livelihoods. Knowledge of aquifer recharge levels is very imperfect and for this reason there are serious practical problems associated with sustainable management. The third strategic option, aquifer restoration, merits little consideration here for social and economic reasons, demanding as it would abandonment of the scheme and the loss of livelihoods by many.   In   practice, therefore, the realistic options involve a balance between the first two of these strategies.

Fortunately the position can be improved using the supply, demand and intermediate framework identified above. In Yao Ba there are few obvious supply-side measures although the drilling of interceptor wells to reduce saline accumulation has been proposed. On the other hand, there appears to be a considerable potential for reducing water demand through economic or pricing mechanisms, though implementation would not be straightforward; proposals introduced by the Bureau in 1994 were not implemented following a national decree from Beijing intended to protect farmers. Fortunately there appears to be ample potential for improving water use efficiency at both scheme and farmer levels. These include the lining of channels, replacement of basin irrigation by micro-irrigation systems, the use of plastic membranes to reduce evaporation, and changes in cropping pattern. It would also be theoretically possible to abandon the saline area and move farmers elsewhere. The problems with all such possibilities are socio-economic; such measures are socially disruptive, costly to implement and financially and economically questionable. The economics are especially difficult given the largely low-value crops produced.

To date, the institutional arrangement giving effective control of GWR to the state has not solved the degradation problem. There are two basic difficulties. Firstly, the administration is disparate and has no financial or other incentive to improve water use efficiency, though recently more decision-making responsibility has been passed to farmers. Secondly, the working of the local aquifer, including the way fresh and saline underground water moves and dissipates, is insufficiently understood to facilitate effective management. Imperfect knowledge to a degree thus negates any strategic advantages there may be in centralised management.

6.2 The Gaza Strip

The Gaza Strip lies along the south-eastern coast of the Mediterranean Sea and borders the Sinai and Negev deserts. Physically it is not unlike Yao Ba having under 400 mm of rain/yr and largely sandy soils. The Strip has a fast growing population (3.7%) of nearly one million and one of the highest population densities in the world. Over half the population live in refugee camps that are largely unsewered and have limited and often unsafe water supplies. Agriculture has traditionally been the key sector, with citrus the main crop. Fresh water is obtained solely from a coastal aquifer which is now under threat.   Historically, the area has been occupied by a succession of powers, most recently by Israel (1967-1994), which have acted against the development of effective management structures.

The problem. GWR in the Strip are threatened by depletion, contamination, and depletion-induced saline intrusion. Water table levels have dropped drastically since exploitation began early this century, although not consistently throughout the area. Data on contamination is scarce but it is clear that nitrate and probably pesticide concentrations are very high in areas with intensive agriculture and biological contamination is severe in unsewered residential areas. The Strip is surrounded by saline water including the sea and trapped saline deposits (conate water) which are intruding into the aquifer. Areas of freshwater are thus diminishing rapidly and only two areas of good quality water remain [11].

The management system. During the Israeli occupation, abstraction was strictly controlled through licensing and quotas but at levels thought to exceed aquifer recharge by 200 to 400%. With autonomous Government the control of abstraction has been relaxed much further. The system today is a prime example of 'open access' exploitation of a common pool resource, with thousands of farmers and households acting rationally as individuals but effectively mining the resource as a whole. The absence of effective Palestinian institutions for water management in Gaza is a basic problem for mitigation.

Strategic options. As elsewhere, there are three strategic options to aquifer management, to degrade, to manage sustainably, or to restore. As in Yao Ba restoring the aquifer to its previous condition is an unrealistic objective given the prevailing political, institutional and economic circumstances, and appeals only environmentally. However continued degradation is not inevitable, and sustainable management is possible though it may involve accepting the loss of high quality water and using the resource largely for irrigation. Both cases would demand institutional, legal and policy changes of very considerable magnitude, including regulation and control of a large number of individually owned pumps and operators.

Because many individuals would suffer in the process, these changes would give rise to enormous difficulties in implementation and enforcement. New institutional systems and structures, however, are vital if sustainable management is to be taken seriously. At the current rate of degradation, it has been calculated that water of drinking water standard will be available for only some fifteen or twenty years, and water for irrigation water for eighty years. If these projections are correct, at this point there will be no water in the Gaza Strip fit for any form of human activity.

9   Conclusions: policy, theory and practice

The widespread and chronic underestimation of the value of groundwater systems provides a strong a priori case for the very careful assessment of groundwater management options in the developing world where mistakes can be least afforded.

Our case studies have demonstrated the use of an analytical framework for the study of degradation and thrown light on the policy problems facing groundwater management in two contrasting situations. The GWR problems illustrated in both areas are extreme but by no means unusual; water is increasingly scarce and degraded by pollution or salinity. In both cases the local situation points to the need for a new emphasis on demand management and water efficiency, and balancing economic and equity considerations over space and time. But in both circumstances, the problems of implementation are immense.

In Gaza, the example of open access to the resource raises serious questions about sustainable management and how it could be regulated or enforced. In Yao Ba, local water authorities are strong but unable to apply sensible measures for reducing water consumption due to 'arm twisting' by central Government. At present neither public institutions, local communities nor individual farmers have sufficient incentive to economise on the use of water. The only real disincentive to wastage at present is the recently-increased cost of energy.

While the policy options vary between the two locations, certain of the problems apply generally. One overriding problem in both areas is the paucity of knowledge about the aquifer system and its behaviour, and there is a need for studies of how the aquifer will operate under different management regimes. Such research requires carefully focused and integrated socio-economic and hydrogeologic study aimed at addressing the problems and providing practical solutions. Only such research can answer how different political and institutional systems can address and adapt to the enormous problems facing efficient and sustainable groundwater management in various parts of the world.

Acknowledgement: The paper is based on an interdisciplinary study funded by the Global Environmental Change programme of the Economic and Social Research Council (ESRC) directed by Dr Grimble and Mr Adams. The study is indebted to David Grey who preceded Mr Adams as BGS project director. The paper is published with the permission of the Chief Executive of the Natural Resources Institute and the Director of the British Geological Survey.

10 References

1. Winpenny, J. (1994) *Managing Water as an Economic Resource*, Routledge, London.
2. World Bank (1993) *Water Resources Management: A Policy Paper*, World Bank, Washington D.C.
3. Ohlsson, L.(1995) *Hydropolitics: Conflicts over Water as a Development Constraint,* Zed books, London
4. Postel, S. (1992) *The Last Oasis: Facing Water Scarcity* , Earthscan, London
5. National Rivers Authority (1992) *Policy and Practice for the Protection of Groundwater*, HMSO, London
6. Hardin, G. (1968) *The Tragedy of the Commons*, Science 162: 1243-48
7. Gardner, R, Ostrom E, and Walker J.M. (1990) *The Nature of Common Pool Resources*, Rationality and Society, Vol. 2 No. 3.
8. Fisher, A. (1981) *Resource   and   Environmental   Economics*,   Cambridge University Press, Cambridge
9. Grimble, R.J, and Wellard, K. (1996) *Stakeholder Methodologies in Natural Resource Management,*   ODA Workshop on Socio-economic Methodologies, ODI, London
10. Grimble, R.J, Brown, D. and Morton J. (1996) *Groundwater Resource Degradation in Yao Ba, Inner Mongolia,* NRI, Chatham, Kent
11. Gass, G., Calow, R., MacDonald, A., and Nasser Y (1995) *Groundwater Resources Degradation in the Gaza Strip,* NRI/BGS Technical Report, Chatham, Kent

URBAN GROUNDWATER RESOURCE MANAGEMENT - PRIORITIES FOR DEVELOPING CITIES

Urban groundwater resource management

S.S.D. FOSTER, A.R. LAWRENCE & B.L. MORRIS
British Geological Survey (Groundwater & Geotechnical Surveys Division), Nottingham & Wallingford, UK

Abstract
Urban population growth in Asia and Latin America is occurring on a scale, and at a rate, unprecedented in human history. Many of the cities are sited on unconfined or semi-confined alluvial aquifers which possess abundant, but fragile, groundwater resources. It has become increasingly evident that inadequately-controlled groundwater exploitation and indiscriminate liquid effluent and solid waste disposal to the ground widely result in significant groundwater degradation, both within the urban area itself and in downstream riparian areas. This degradation is a contributory cause of escalating water-supply cost, increasing water resource scarcity and growing health hazard. Proactive, rather than passive, management of groundwater resources, based on systematically-identified priorities and simple pragmatic criteria is advocated to avoid premature loss of major investment in groundwater development.
Keywords: groundwater, management, urban.

1   Impacts of urbanisation on groundwater

1.1 Perturbations of hydrological cycle
The provision of water-supply, sanitation and drainage are key elements of the urbanisation process. Substantial differences in development sequence exist between higher-income areas, where the process is normally planned in advance, and lower-income areas, where informal settlements are progressively consolidated into urban areas, but common factors are impermeabilisation of a significant proportion of the land surface and major importation of water from outside the urban limits. Sanitation and drainage arrangements are also fundamental to consideration of the urban hydrological cycle. They generally evolve with time and vary with differing patterns of urban

Water Policy: Allocation and management in practice. Edited by P. Howsam and R.C. Carter.
Published in 1996 by E & FN Spon. ISBN 0 419 21650 2

development, but installation of mains sewerage generally lags considerably behind population growth and water-supply provision.

Urbanisation causes radical changes in the frequency and rate of subsurface infiltration (Table 1), with a general tendency for volume to increase significantly and for quality to deteriorate substantially [1]. These changes cannot be measured directly, and are thus difficult to quantify, but in turn influence groundwater levels and flow regimes in underlying aquifers. Subsequently groundwater quality degradation, both within the urban area itself and in downstream alluvial aquifers, occurs.

1.2 Quality deterioration within urban limits

Some urbanisation processes cause radical changes in the quality of subsurface infiltration (Table 1). This is widely the cause of marked, but essentially diffuse, pollution of groundwater by nitrogen compounds, increasing salinity, elevated dissolved organic carbon concentrations (which can lead to enhanced mobilisation of Fe and/or Mn) and, on a more localised basis, contamination by faecal pathogens and/or microorganic pollutants. The intensity of impact varies widely with the pollution vulnerability of underlying aquifers and with the type and stage of urban development. In alluvial formations the uppermost unit in the commonly present multi-aquifer sequence is vulnerable to pollution from human activities at the land surface, given its shallow water table.

Rapid urbanisation and industrialisation with indiscriminate use of the ground for liquid effluent and solid waste disposal presents a complex array of activities potentially polluting to groundwater. In many districts without mains sewerage, a heavy subsoil contaminant load originates from in-situ sanitation and the disposal of sullage waters increases the risk of shallow groundwater contamination, because of the presence of various household chemicals. In addition to elevated nitrogen concentrations, increased concentrations of chloride (mostly from excreta), sulphate and borate (from detergents) and bicarbonate (from oxidation of organic matter) are frequently observed. A further, increasingly-frequent, cause of shallow groundwater contamination in residential areas of developing cities is hydrocarbon fuel leakage from underground storage tanks at gasoline filling stations.

In many rapidly developing cities an increasing number of industries (such as textile mills, tanneries, metal processing, vehicle maintenance, laundry and dry cleaning establishments, printing and photoprocessing, etc) are located in the extensive fringe urban areas without mains sewerage. Most of these industries generate liquid effluents, such as spent lubricants, solvents and disinfectants, which are often discharged directly to the ground and can represent a long-term threat to groundwater quality.

Santa Cruz-Bolivia is a low-rise, relatively low density, fast growing city, whose municipal water supply is derived entirely from wellfields within the city limits, extracting from a semi-confined, outwash-plain, alluvial aquifer. The city has relatively high coverage of mains water-supply, but only the older central area has mains sewerage, and most domestic/industrial effluents and stormwater drainage are disposed to the ground. The uppermost aquifer unit thus shows substantial deterioration in groundwater quality (Fig 1) down to depths of about 40 m [2]. Groundwater abstraction from the deep alluvial aquifer has induced downward movement from the shallow horizons and a component of contaminated water is now observed at depths approaching 90m. The heavy development of the shallow aquifer for private water

Table 1: Summary of impacts of urban processes on groundwater systems

URBANIZATION PROCESS	EFFECT ON SUBSURFACE INFILTRATION			GROUNDWATER QUALITY IMPLICATION	
	Rates	Area	Timing	Scale	Contaminant Groups
(A) MODIFICATIONS TO NATURAL SYSTEM					
• Surface Impermeabilisation & Drainage					
- stormwater soakaways	increase	extensive	intermittent-to-continuous	marginally negative	Cl, HC, DOC
- mains drainage	reduction	extensive	continuous	none	none
- surface water canalisation	reduction	linear	variable	none	none
• Irrigation of Amenity Areas	increase	restricted	seasonal	variable (if wastewater used)	(N, Cl, DOC)
(B) INTRODUCTION OF WATER-SERVICE NETWORK					
• Mains Water-Supply Leakage	increase	extensive	continuous	positive	none
• Sanitation System Installation					
- in-situ sanitation	major increase	extensive	continuous	negative	N, FP, DOC
- mains sewerage (in urban areas)	major increase	extensive	continuous	positive	reduces above
- mains sewerage (downstream)	some increase	riparian areas	continuous	negative	N, Cl, DOC
(C) UNCONTROLLED AQUIFER EXPLOITATION					
• Falling Water-Table	some increase	extensive	continuous	potentially positive, except where saline intrusion can occur	
• Induced Downward Leakage	minor increase	extensive	continuous	negative, causes pollution of deep aquifers with persistent contaminants	

Cl   chloride and salinity generally
N   nitrogen compounds (nitrate or ammonium)
HC   hydrocarbon fuels
DOC   dissolved organic carbon, including possibility of microorganic pollutants
FP   fecal pathogens

supplies, however, effectively provides a degree of protection for deeper municipal wellfields by abstracting and recycling part of the polluted water, which is fortuitously good management practice provided that none of the supplies provided by these wells are destined for sensitive use.

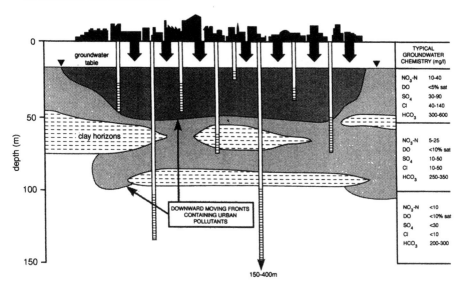

Fig. 1. Shallow groundwater pollution caused by rapid urbanisation with induced downward leakage to deep aquifers in Santa Cruz-Bolivia

In some cities located on low-lying coastal alluvium, direct disposal of wastewater to the ground via on-site sanitation is not possible and effluents are discharged into rivers and canals, which often become influent to aquifers as a result of groundwater abstraction. Hat Yai-Thailand is an example of this condition [2]. Most of its limited mains water-supply is imported from external surface water sources, but about 60% of the overall supply is provided from local groundwater resources. The disposal of domestic and industrial effluents to the ground by on-site sanitation systems is not always possible because of the shallow water table and such wastes are discharged into rivers and canals. The heavy groundwater abstraction results in induced infiltration to shallow aquifers detectable most readily by high NH_4-N concentrations, reflecting the low Eh of the aquifer system. With increasingly heavy groundwater development it is believed that induced canal seepage is now the largest component of groundwater recharge.

1.3 Downstream riparian effects

Although the provision of mains sewerage lags considerably behind population growth and water-supply provision, sewage effluent (termed here wastewater) is generated in large volumes by the majority of (but not all) rapidly-developing cities. This wastewater is normally discharged to surface watercourses after minimal treatment from where, especially in more arid climates, it is used on an uncontrolled basis for agricultural irrigation in downstream riparian areas. Such areas are usually underlain by important alluvial aquifers [3] and examples of this situation include many cities in northern Mexico and northeastern China.

Infiltration of wastewater either through agricultural soils or via stream bed recharge can result in groundwater quality degradation including elevated chloride, nitrate or ammonium and some phenols.

In Leon-Mexico, the groundwater quality of deep municipal boreholes within an area irrigated by wastewater, is being threatened by increasing salinity with downward movement of a Cl front.

1.4 Consequences of uncontrolled aquifer exploitation

Groundwater quality issues cannot be divorced from those of resource exploitation. The most common quality impact of inadequately-controlled aquifer exploitation, particularly in coastal situations, is the intrusion of saline water. For thin alluvial aquifers this takes the classical wedge-shaped form, but in thicker multi-aquifer sequences salinity inversions often occur with intrusion of modern seawater (or retention of palaeo-saline water) in near surface aquifer horizons with fresh groundwater below.

Contamination of deeper (semi-confined) aquifers, where they underlie a shallow poor quality phreatic aquifer affected by anthropogenic pollution and/or saline intrusion, is a frequent consequence of uncontrolled exploitation. This occurs as a result of inadequate well construction leading to direct vertical seepage and/or pump-induced vertical leakage, with penetration of more mobile and persistent contaminant species (Fig 4). Evidence has been accumulating since the 1980s of widespread drawdown of the piezometric surface by 20-50 m or more in various Asian megacities, as a result of heavy exploitation of alluvial aquifers, and both of the aforementioned side-effects are quite widely observed.

A recent Asian Development Bank technical cooperation programme on water resources management in megacities included case histories for 4 Asian cities in the humid tropics, which possess major alluvial groundwater resources. The results of these studies have been reviewed, and amplified by further direct data collection and other references [4][5][6][7], with the aim of drawing generic conclusions [8]. Among the cities surveyed, groundwater remains the major component of municipal (public) water supply only in Dhaka-Bangladesh (Table 2), having been substituted in other cases by long-distance imports of surface water. This was often due to quality deterioration through saline intrusion and/or anthropogenic pollution, but sometimes the result of reduction of individual borehole yields, due to falling water-table or poor well construction and maintenance.

The situation is not as simple as it might at first appear, however, since in the other cases (Bangkok, Jakarta and Manila) resultant shortage and increasing cost of water-supplies led to a major growth in private well drilling (Table 2), such that the overall exploitation of groundwater increased, despite attempts to initiate control, as a result of fears about further saline intrusion and/or land subsidence. There is little point in controlling municipal abstraction if private groundwater exploitation is not similarly managed. In effect, what has occurred in Bangkok, Jakarta and Manila is the replacement of a moderate number of municipal groundwater supplies, which were at least capable of being systematically controlled, monitored, protected and treated, by a very large number of shallower, largely uncontrolled, unmonitored and untreated sources.

Tapping groundwater at location of demand makes sense for many industrial users and for amenity irrigation, since these are difficult to supply through mains distribution. However, it is questionable in densely-populated areas, both on economic and on public health grounds, as regards domestic supplies and those for sensitive industries (such as food and beverage preparation). An added concern is illegal connection of private wells to the mains water-supply, without measures to prevent 'back syphoning' at times of reduced mains pressure, with consequent contamination of 'down-system' users.

Table 2. Recent water-supply statistics for selected Asian megacities located on coastal alluvial aquifers

CITY	POPLN (M)	POPLN DENSITY (cap/ha)	WATER-SUPPLY (Ml/d) public total (propn served)		GROUNDWATER ABSTRACTION (Ml/d) public (propn)	private
Bangkok (Thailand)	5.9	40	3220 (70%)	3840	190 (6%)	620
Dhaka (Bangladesh)	6.1	380	670 (60%)	900	670 (100%)	230
Jakarta (Indonesia)	8.2	130	1200 (45%)	1820	60 (5%)	620
Manila (Philippines)	8.3	130	2280 (75%)	3120	90 (3%)	840

2 Implications for groundwater management

Rapid urbanisation has been shown to have a profound effect on groundwater recharge, flow and quality. The scale of implications for the security and safety of developing city water-supplies is considerable. The paper has selected examples from tropical alluvial aquifers in view of their importance internationally, and brevity prevented presentation of a wider spectrum of hydrogeological conditions. Nor is it possible to discuss systematically all the resource implications and the corresponding management strategies.

While, in many instances, institutional and regulatory arrangements will need strengthening to implement management strategies, such strategies must also be soundly based on hydrogeological criteria if they are to achieve more sustainable exploitation of groundwater resources. Some of the ways in which hydrogeological considerations can be meshed into a groundwater resource management programmes are defined below.

2.1 Aquifer pollution control

Given typical socioeconomic and hydrogeological conditions, it is not realistic to attempt to protect shallow alluvial aquifers from some quality deterioration during the urbanisation process. However, it will be prudent to control those activities which most threaten groundwater quality overall, especially that in deeper (less vulnerable) aquifers.

This will be best achieved through the following strategy:
- undertake a rapid survey of subsoil contaminant loading [9] to identify those activities likely to pose the greatest threat to groundwater through mode or intensity of discharge and presence of persistent and/or toxic chemicals,
- establish the degree of existing deterioration of the uppermost aquifer unit from anthropogenic pollution by a sampling survey of representative shallow wells, with analysis for appropriate indicator determinands,
- introduce selective controls on subsoil contaminant loading (where demonstrated necessary) through extension of mains sewerage, incentives for improved handling/control of industrial chemical effluents, etc.

2.2 Resource management criteria

The use of urban groundwater also needs to be directed and rationalised, taking account of the quality distributions and trends identified. A better balance needs to be achieved between shallow and deep groundwater abstraction, for example by directing non-sensitive water users towards exploitation of groundwater of inferior quality so as to minimise the downward migration of high concentrations of anthropogenic contaminants. Municipal groundwater development strategies need to be harmonised with private groundwater use patterns and with wastewater disposal and/or reuse strategies.

The hydrostratigraphical and geohydrological complexity of tropical alluvial aquifers means that groundwater recharge evaluation is always subject to considerable uncertainty, and rarely forms a sound basis for resource management. Other simple criteria are needed and combinations of the following approaches, appropriately adapted to local hydrogeological conditions, are likely to prove more useful:

- determine the extent of vertical layering of the aquifer system, and associated hydraulic head and groundwater quality variations, by selective field data collection,
- appraise the susceptibility of the system to saline intrusion and/or land subsidence following major depression of the piezometric surface, in a qualitative sense on simple geohydrological criteria [10],
- use target piezometric levels as the resource management criterion, since this is more likely to maximise groundwater production while minimising irreversible side-effects which threaten sustainability,
- spread public water-supply abstraction geographically to avoid large cones of piezometric depression in the deeper semi-confined aquifers, especially in areas susceptible to saline intrusion and/or land subsidence,
- in situations where significant encroachment (or intrusion) of saline water has already occurred, avoid abandonment of pumping from salinised wells and try to encourage continued abstraction for appropriate uses to reduce landward hydraulic gradients,
- avoid generation of large downward hydraulic gradients by balancing the abstraction between shallow and deep aquifers, by encouraging non-sensitive users

(industrial process and cooling water, amenity irrigation, etc) to drill shallow wells and by reserving deeper aquifers for potable supplies and sensitive industrial uses; this may be achieved by direct licensing controls or differential abstraction tariffs.

Acknowledgements: This paper is published by permission of the Director of the British Geological Survey (BGS). Its aim is to highlight key messages for the sustainable development of groundwater resources arising from recent surveys of a number of developing cities, which were funded by the (British) Overseas Development Administration, the World Health Organisation and the UN Environment Programme. The major contribution of numerous national groundwater professionals and certain BGS colleagues, especially John Chilton, to these surveys is fully appreciated and gratefully acknowledged.

3 References

1. Foster, S.S.D., Morris, B.L. and Lawrence, A.R. (1994) Effects of urbanisation on groundwater recharge. Proceedings of Institution of Civil Engineers International Conference 'Groundwater Problems in Urban Areas' (London - June 1993) : 43-63.
2. Lawrence, A.R., Morris, B.L. and Foster, S.SD. (1996) Groundwater recharge - changes imposed by rapid urbanisation. *Quarterly Journal of Engineering Geology*: in press.
3. Foster, S.S.D, Gale, I. N. and Hespanhol, I. (1994) Impacts of wastewater use and disposal on groundwater. British Geological Survey Report WD/94/55.
4. Ahmed, K.M., Woobaidullah, A.S.M. and Hasan, M.A. (1995) Hydrogeology of the Dupi Tila Aquifer of Dhaka City, Bangladesh. Acta Univ Carolina Geol 39 : 113-121.
5. Munasinghe, M. (1990) Managing water resources to avoid environmental degradation: policy analysis and application. World Bank Environmental Working Paper 41.
6. Ramnarong, V. and Buapeng, S. (1991) Mitigation of groundwater crisis and land subsidence in Bangkok. *Journal Thai Geoscience* Vol. 2 : pp.125-137.
7. Schmidt, G., Soefner, B. and Soekardi, P. (1990) Possibilities for groundwater development for the city of Jakarta, Indonesia. International Association of Hydrological Sciences Publn 198 : 233-242
8. Foster, S.S.D. and Lawrence, A.R. (1996) Groundwater quality in Asia : an overview of trends and concerns. *UN-ESCAP Water Resources Journal* : in press.
9. Foster, S.S.D. and Hirata, R.C.A. (1988/1991) Groundwater pollution risk assessment: a methodology using available data (also in Spanish & Portuguese). WHO-PAHO-CEPIS Publication : 79pp.
10. Foster, S.S.D. (1992) Unsustainable development and irrational exploitation of groundwater resources in developing nations - an overview. International Association of Hydrogeologists Hydrogeology Selected paper 3 : 321-336.

FRAMEWORK OF WATER RESOURCES PROTECTION POLICIES IN THE SULTANATE OF OMAN
Water resource protection in Oman

A.A. ADAWI and N.M. SOMARATNE
Water Resources Protection Department, Ministry of Water Resources,
Ruwi, Sultanate of Oman

Abstract
Many parts of the Sultanate of Oman are, largely dependent on groundwater resources for domestic, municipal, agricultural and commercial purposes. The rapid development undertaken in the recent past and experience gained in groundwater pollution incidents, has triggered the need for a system to protect all potentially usable groundwater resources from pollution. These include point sources such as waste disposal and mine tailings, landfill leachate, underground storage tanks and diffuse source of agricultural chemicals. Management aspects of these, particularly from a water resources protection perspective, involve the wide range of physical and socio- economical factors as well as the hydrogeological conditions that favour the rapid movement of contaminant to groundwater. Wellfield protection areas are being announced and regulations have been formed and enforced by the Ministry of Water Resources. Various aspects of these are discussed. Stages of developing a protection plan, sources of pollution, abstraction control, method of determining the zone of contribution to the supply well, and conflicts of interests are also presented. The legislative framework for the protection of water resources, in particular those applicable to wellfields, are of a dual nature: (1) protection from pollution and (2) protection from over exploitation.
Keywords: pollution, regulations, water resources, wellfield protection

1   Introduction

The Ministry of Water Resources in the Sultanate of Oman manages precious water resources for municipal, industrial and agricultural uses. Recent economic development in the country, together with rapid expansion of the population has

Water Policy: Allocation and management in practice. Edited by P. Howsam and R.C. Carter.
Published in 1996 by E & FN Spon. ISBN 0 419 21650 2

increased the demand for water. These demands exacerbate the over utilisation of aquifers. A number of groundwater pollution incidents, originating from leakage of underground storage tanks and seepage of leachate from mine tailings have been reported. Agricultural developments utilizing inorganic fertilisers and pesticides are also a major concern of groundwater pollution. Increasing demand upon wellfields coupled with the rapid infrastructure development and agricultural expansion has emphasized the need to protect municipal wellfields by means of implementing legislation.

Designing a comprehensive water resources protection program, which is workable, effective and politically feasible poses a serious challenge. This process is particularly difficult in rapidly developing countries in arid region, where the available water resources are limited and the demand for water is ever increasing. Often, many communities do not have alternative water sources. Realizing this, the Ministry of Water Resources has recognised the need to protect all potentially usable water resources from pollution. The paper outlines the framework of wellfield protection plans used to protect groundwater that supplies municipal water demand.

2 Fate of contaminants in the Oman environment

Most agricultural soils in Oman are of medium to coarse textured mainly sands, loamy sands and sandy loam. The depth of soil layer may vary, typically from 0.30-1.0 metres. The organic content of these soils is low and they show high infiltration capacity. This favours rapid movement of surface applied chemicals and fertilisers to groundwater. Alluvium plains, prone to flash floods, are the main recharge zones of the aquifers. These characteristically consist of cemented alluvial fans with uncemented active fluvial channels. Further downstream, the deeper alluvium has varying degrees of clay and carbonate cementation.

For a given conservative behaviour, the surface applied chemicals in the soil environment is governed by the retention and transport processes. Presence of preferred flow paths, can cause rapid movement of contaminant to the watertable.

Derivation of protection zones for soil and hydrogeological conditions that prevail in Oman, therefore, take account of the following factors:

(a) Poorly developed to non-existing soils with low organic carbon content
(b) Little or no clay content affording minimal adsorption
(c) The presence of soil macropores causing rapid infiltration
(d) Infrequency of dilution events

Because of the velocity and areal extent of typical floods that are encountered in Oman, any point sources of pollution (otherwise far removed from wellfield areas) can be rapidly mobilized and deposited close to wellfields. Because of this "short-circuiting", the catchment boundaries are designated as the outer-limits of the protection zones. Hence control over potential contaminants and deleterious practices is exerted throughout the complete catchment.

3   Activities of concern

3.1 Sources of pollution

In drawing up water resources protection policies, an attempt is made to identify the activities that would cause pollution. The risks of contamination from conservative pollutants are obviously greatest near the source of water or immediately around the supply. Therefore, the strictest controls are applied to these areas. Major concerns are:

(a) Civil and commercial developments
(b) Solid and liquid waste disposals
(c) Underground and above ground storage tanks
(d) Landfills
(e) Sewage and drainage
(f) Burial grounds
(g) Oil wells, exploration wells and oil pipelines
(h) Agriculture
(i) Mining and quarrying
(j) Waste water injection
(k) Septic tanks

3.2 Groundwater withdrawals

Similarly, the need to control groundwater withdrawals is also recognised. This is required to minimise the effect of interference and capturing of groundwater flows destined for wellfields. Major factors in this regard are:

(a) Construction of new private wells
(b) Deepening of existing wells
(c) Metering of abstractions

4   Wellfield protection

The overall objectives of wellfield protection is to safeguard and protect the existing groundwater reservoir against over extraction, pollution and to prohibit and eliminate unauthorised land and water uses that might adversely affect the wellfield. Wellfields requiring protection plans are prioritized based on the type and severity of the water resources impairment, type of pollutant, source magnitude and transport mechanisms.

Three stages are used in the development of a protection program. In the first stage, the protection zones are delineated, pollutant sources are identified and production wells in the catchment are inventoried. Attention is also given to the identification of supporting agencies and duties. Regulations applicable to each zone are then formulated.

In the second stage, a groundwater simulation and optimization model is developed to estimate the likely safe yield and the future viability of the wellfield for a range of demands and hydrologic conditions. The most important aspect of wellfield management considered here is the development of optimum operating policies. That is, where to locate wells, the number of production wells, and how much and when to pump from each [1][2]. In the final stage, a public awareness program is developed.

A total of three zones (four zones in the case of coastal aquifers) are used for the protection of the wellfields.

Zone I (RED ZONE)	=	Inner zone, time of travel 365 days.
Zone II (ORANGE ZONE)	=	Outer zone, time of travel 10 years.
Zone III (YELLOW ZONE)	=	Remainder of the catchment upstream of the wellfield.
Zone IV (BLUE ZONE)	=	Area between the wellfield and the coast. Applicable only to coastal wellfield

The inner and outer zones of the protection areas are delineated by travel of time criteria, which determine the capture zones (zone of contribution) to the production wells of the wellfield [3]. This depends upon the hydrogeologic characteristics of the aquifer, the pumping rate of the well, number of wells and the amount of recharge the aquifer receives.

The RED zone is an area immediately surrounding the municipal wellfield in which pumping from other wells, or any release of contaminants, is likely to have an immediate and measurable effect on the quantity or the quality of the water produced by the existing or future wells. This area is designated solely for municipal wellfields.

The ORANGE zone is an area adjacent to the RED zone. This area covers land area where any pumping from other wells, or any release of contaminant, is likely to have a long-term effect on the quantity or the quality of the water produced by the existing or future wells of the wellfield.

The YELLOW zone is the remainder of the catchment upstream of the wellfield. Any uncontrolled, unplanned development may in the long-term affect the existing and future wells in the wellfield.

The BLUE zone is an area downstream of the wellfield up to the coast, in which excessive pumping is likely to cause or accelerate saline water intrusion, thus threatening water quality of the wellfield.

Regulation applicable to the wellfield protection zones are of a dual nature: regulation for the protection of water quality and that for water conservation and augmentation. Each regulation is applicable to one or more zones. Generally speaking, the lower the zone number, the stricter are the regulations that will apply to it. For the purpose of deciding which regulations are the most advantageous in terms of benefit to the wellfield, they have been given a qualitative rating for public acceptability, effectiveness and ease of implementation [4].

Since regulations vary according to the severity, practicality and urgency, they are implemented in two phases: Phase I - within one year and Phase II - within three years. Once promulgated, administration, enforcement and review are to be undertaken by the Ministry of Water Resources.

5   Areas of conflicts

In developing a water resources protection plan, there exist several areas of potential conflicting interest between water resources protection and other activities. The latter include waste disposal, agricultural activities, quarrying and mining development.

5.1 Gravel quarrying and waste disposal

When a large proportion of gravel quarrying is in operation in a wadi alluvium (that may itself be an aquifer or may directly overlie an aquifer) then this may adversely affect the wellfield by way of diverting natural flow paths and therefore flood water recharge to the aquifer. In addition, gravel pits left behind as a result of quarry operation may provide convenient but inappropriate choice for waste disposal sites. This problem is currently addressed in a way that quarrying and waste disposal are limited to a specific locality, away from wellfield catchments. A hydrogeological study is performed to evaluate the short- and long-term effects on water resources in the area. This is particularly important downstream of the site, prior to permitting such activities.

5.2 Agricultural development

Agricultural practices can lead to groundwater pollution, particularly through the increasing use of nitrogenous fertilisers in excess of the plant take-up. Policing the amount and type of agro-chemicals and fertiliser use is difficult and inappropriate, and a public awareness program may be more effective in this regard. In addition, groundwater pumping for agricultural development directly competes with the wellfield production, within the catchment. Metering of all abstractions in the inner and outer zones is an effective method of limiting abstraction to the allocation. However, unmetered abstraction from dug wells is a major problem.

5.3 Residential developments

In a developed area, such as the Capital Area of the Sultanate, the wellfield protection plan should address two equally important problems. The need for water to be protected from pollution needs to be balanced by the need for urban development. Frequent requests from land owners are received for residential developments. In a situation like this, residential developments are allowed, but no solid and liquid wastes are permitted to be disposed of in the catchment. Similarly, septic tanks are not allowed and all sewage must be dealt with either by vacuum tankers or by central sewage connection to a treatment plant.

6   Discussion

A structural approach to dealing with aquifer pollution and over extraction generally involving development of alternative sources of water supply, controlling abstraction for other uses, or recharge enhancement of the catchment are well known and currently practised. However, non-structural ways of managing the water resources such as demand side policies are also needed. This may involve coordination with people, as in most cases, problems are related to unmanaged demand. This also may be achieved through a public awareness program.

   At present, before issuing a permit for resource development, which stipulates the type, manner and means of operation (waste disposal, gravel quarrying, waste water injection etc.) as well as control and monitoring, the requesting authority is consulting the Ministry of Water Resources for a study on risk of groundwater and surface water pollution. This practice has been found to be very effective in protecting the potentially usable water resources in the Sultanate of Oman. Also the wellfield protection plans have frequently prevented large scale waste disposal in the upstream catchments.

A rigid legislation system, that is not related to the hydrogeological conditions must be avoided, whilst a balance has to be maintained between conflicting interests.

6   References

1.   Merrick, N.P. (1987)   Documentation of linear programming software for fundamental groundwater problems. *Hydrogeological Report No: 1987-3, Department of Water Resources, ISSN 0705-2782.*

2.   Punthakey, J.F., Prathapar, S.A. and Somaratne, N.M. (1992)   PUMPMAN: Optimizing pumping rates to control shallow watertables in the Wakool irrigation district. *Technical Report TS.92.0888, NSW Department of Water Resources, ISBN 0-7305-7901-8.*

3.   US-EPA Office of Groundwater Protection. (1991)   WHPA 2.0: A modular semi-analytical model for the delineation of wellhead protection areas.

4.   Somaratne, N.M. and Laver, J.C. (1994)   Al Buraymi wellfield protection zone proposal, *Draft Technical Report, Ministry of Water Resources, Sultanate of Oman.*

A WATER QUALITY MANAGEMENT STRATEGY
STUDY CASE: THE NILE RIVER
Nile Water Quality Management

R. KHOUZAM
Resource Economist, Cairo, Egypt

Abstract
Water availability in quantity and quality is a main constraint to development worldwide. Water recycling is one of the major options to meet shortage. However, recycling depends in the first place on the quality of the returning water. Several policy tools are in use in a number of countries to enhance the quality of returning water. Due to innate shortcomings, those policies have not been fully successful in achieving their goals. This paper presents an alternative policy which avoids those deficiencies. The cornerstone of this policy is to avoid pollution generation at its source. It relies on the introduction of an array of options to replace polluting inputs or techniques. Apart from being environmentally conservative, suggested substitutes are cheaper; consequently, their adoption yields greater profit. Hence, a firm, while pursuing its own self-interest, is motivated to adopt the recommended substitute. As such, improving the water environment can be achieved without making anybody worse off (a win-win approach). The applicability of the proposed policy is studied in the three most water-polluting sectors in Egypt; namely, sewage, agriculture and industry.
Keywords: agriculture, industry, management policy, Nile, policy failure, quality, recycling, sewage.

1   Introduction

In Egypt, water shortage exceeds six billion cubic meters (BCM) [1]. The deficit is covered by recycling water. Water deficit is expected to expand as a result of the increasing needs of a growing population and the implementation of ambitious land reclamation programs. With about 13 BCM of water discharged annually to the sea

Water Policy: Allocation and management in practice. Edited by P. Howsam and R.C. Carter.
Published in 1996 by E & FN Spon. ISBN 0 419 21650 2

[2], water recycling will continue to be a main source for meeting the expanding water deficit.

Improving the quality of the returning water is a multifaceted issue. The degraded quality of returning water makes recycling unsafe for public health. Even if returning heavily polluted water is not recycled, pollutants can reach man's food chain through deep and lateral percolation which, subsequently, results in the contamination of the shallow aquifer (used to support surface irrigation) and the root zone of agricultural lands, not to mention the pollution of the fresh water itself.

Enhancing the quality of returning water is not a concern of Egypt alone; it is a global question. A wide variety of policy tools are being applied by various countries to control, and if possible improve, the quality of the water environment. Those tools can broadly be classified into three categories: negative incentives, coercive schemes, and positive stimuli. These devices comprise tradeable discharge permits (as for the Colorado River in the USA), water rights registries that indicate quality and point of returning water (adopted in Peru), land use zoning (the Yellow River in China), tax relief (Malaysia), the construction of private plants to treat returning water as in Japan [3][4][5][6].

Egypt has taken several steps in that direction: (a) enacting suitable legislation (e.g. Law 4/1994, Law 48/1982), (b) establishment of specialized institutions (principally the Egyptian Environmental Affairs Agency), (c) preparation of environmental protection plans, (d) utilisation of foreign experience [7].

Evidently, the adopted policy has not been a full success in terms of achieving its goals. The National Specialized Councils (NSC) warns of the massive pollution being dumped daily by the industrial, agricultural, and sewage sectors in various water courses (NSC 1992). Another source indicates that inorganic salts, biodegradable organic matter, and chemical residues are increasing steadily in the Nile[1] [8]. The failure to effectively improve water quality is attributed to a number of reasons:

- A policy assumes that polluting firms possess identical marginal abatement costs and, consequently, they will have the same response to a policy tool [9]. Obviously, this is not necessarily true. Firms' reactions will naturally vary widely depending on several factors such as production technique, scale, etc.

The procedure followed to formalise a policy legally is lengthy and complex; that makes it rather rigid when adjusting to the ever-dynamic economic variables. What may be a prohibitive penalty today could be rendered obsolete tomorrow if its real value is eroded by economic changes.

- In most of the cases, polluters are persuaded to maintain the *status quo* because emission reduction brings about a drop in profit as a result of the costs of investment in new environmentally-conservative techniques or in the purchase of more expensive cleaner inputs.

---

[1] The word "Nile" in this text denotes the water of the Nile river, all its branches, the drainage network, and terminal lakes.

The difficulties involved in defining relevant rights and liabilities provide plenty of room for lobbying and exploitation of loopholes to undermine strict application of laws and regulations.

- Government budget constraints might limit the ability of environmental authorities to sustain continuous and alert monitoring of the extensive water network extended over the Nile valley, delta, and lakes.[2]
- A Government gets rather lenient in law enforcement if the application of a policy results in closing down an operating firm and renders its workers unemployed.
- Lack of data, information, and knowledge subverts the development of an effective policy. At least four pieces of information are needed to form a policy: a river's assimilative capacity, the amount of pollutants dumped, pollution's marginal social damage, and benefit functions. Pending on the intersection between the two marginal functions, policy makers can determine appropriate levels of pollution permitted, or penalty size, etc. Quantification of assimilative capacity and estimation of functions require considerable investment in data collection, processing, model building, and highly specialized manpower which is not likely to be available in developing countries.

To avoid these deficiencies, another policy is proposed. Firm's willingness to adopt is assessed in two point-source polluting sectors (sewage and industry) and a non-point source polluting sector (agriculture). In order to assure the suitability of the recommended policy to the Egyptian circumstances, the study is based on empirical research findings reached by Egyptian scholars. Briefly, the elimination of the pollution resulting from sewage activities is based on the treatment-for-recycling principle. Reduction of the notorious agriculture non-point pollution relied on substituting organic and biofertilization for chemical fertilisers. As for the industrial sector, results of a recently initiated pollution prevention pilot project are utilised to support the soundness of the suggested policy.

2   Sewage waste

In urban areas sewage services cover 80% of the population; in the rural regions, only 5% is served with a sewage system [10]. Sewage water is loaded with nitrogen, microbes and viruses. In areas served with a sewer system, the collected sewage is dumped (treated, semi-treated or untreated) in drainage canals via lateral and deep percolation, as mentioned above. Although the law prohibits using water of those canals, pollutants might penetrate man's food chain where the drainage canals pass through agricultural regions.

Research findings indicate that using treated sewage to manufacture compost and organic fertilisers has several benefits. While sewage waste is considered a "bad" which a society invests in order to get rid of, it can be manufactured into a useful

---

2 Actually, soil and air pollution may end up polluting water media. However, this paper is confined to direct pollution of the water medium.

product. Consequently, a demand for sewage waste is created and it becomes, subsequently, a "good" which has a positive, rather than negative, value. Selling waste for recycling provides revenues to finance the extension of sewer systems to other areas. Besides, establishing a new industry to treat waste for recycling purposes generates employment opportunities. Furthermore, organic fertilisers provides farmers with cheap and clean substitutes for chemical fertilisers which residues (estimated at 15% of the applied quantities) are carried to the Nile. Organic fertilisers manufactured from sewage and other municipal wastes were tested on-farm and gave technical positive results [11]. Full assessment of the farmers willingness to use the new option is achieved by addressing agriculture plant activities.

3   Agriculture drainage

Water pollution resulting from agricultural activities is mainly caused by the returning drainage which is loaded with residues of chemicals and soil particles. Residues reach the Nile system via 72 drains spread between Aswan and the Delta barrage [12], leaving aside drainage in regions north of the Delta barrage.

In Egypt, farmers consider chemical fertilisers an indispensable input. When fertiliser prices rose by 300% over the period 1989-1992 (during the process of economic reform), its consumption dropped only by 16% [13]. The weak price-demand responsiveness is attributed to farmers' ignorance of available substitutes and to the false low relative price of chemical fertilisers due to heavy subsidisation. The introduction of comparatively cheap organic and biofertilisers is anticipated to boost price-demand elasticity.

An agroeconomic model was built especially to assess the financial attractiveness of thirty organic and biofertilization techniques for seven crops (out of twenty two crops included in the model): wheat, broad beans, maize, barley, berseem, rice and sugar cane in addition to assessing one technique representing the prevailing practices.

Egypt was divided, according to the scheme widely used in agriculture statistics, into three regions: upper-, middle-, and lower-Egypt. Each region has its own set of monthly constraints on agriculture area and monthly labour services. Moreover, all three regions are subjected to the national constraint on total annual water supply.

The model's decision variable is land allocation among a set of selected crops defined over a matrix of technical choices which comprises, beside the thirty one fertilization techniques, three planting dates, and three irrigation levels [14]. Only crops which occupied at least 10% of a region's agriculture area are included. This criterion accommodates regional specialization. Accordingly, twenty two crops are selected; altogether, they represent 75% of the cropped area in Egypt: 10 winter crops representing 93% of the total national area of winter crops, 11 summer crops which occupy 86% of summer land and one perennial crop (sugar cane).

The data of 1993 are used in the model. Data are published by the Ministry of Agriculture and Land Reclamation (MALR) which is the prime source for agriculture data in Egypt. However, some variables had to be adjusted for each component in the choice matrix: main- and by-product yields, monthly land and labour inputs, and seasonal water requirement. Similar adjustment is applied to the costs of irrigation, chemical fertilisers, organic or biofertilisation, harvest, and transportation. Cost items left unchanged are: land preparation, seeds and cultivation, agriculture operations, pesticides and rent.

Four scenarios are simulated: a pair represents the conventional fertilization technique and the other introduces all the thirty one options. In each pair, one scenario allocates land without restriction on the area of any of the crops (termed "Free"); the other, on the contrary, does not allow a crop area to exceed 133% of its regional area in 1993 (termed "Restricted").

The objective function maximizes farms' net revenues on the ground that it is their principal concern. In addition to the objective function, the model includes a number of monitoring variables such as value added to capture society's interest, and shadow price of regional land.

Generally, clean agriculture techniques are more attractive to farmers as they provide greater net revenues under both the free and restricted scenarios (Table 1). Similarly, they are appreciated by the society as they provide higher value added in both cases and as they generate greater land prices in upper and lower Egypt.[3]   In middle Egypt, there is no impact of adopting clean agriculture on the shadow price of land if crop areas are not restricted, yet slight appreciation is indicated if crop areas are restricted.

Table 1. Summary of results of four scenarios of the agroeconomic LP model

Scenario	Free conventional	Free clean	Restricted conventional	Restricted clean
Net revenue (billion LE)	30	32	8	13
Value added (billion LE)	39	41	15	20
Land shadow price (LE)				
Upper Egypt	3512	4718	4718	1151
Middle Egypt	6165	6165	634	652
Lower Egypt	4492	4477	1039	1311

Source: Khouzam, R.F. 1996 [15].

4   Industrial effluent

Industrial pollutants dumped in the Nile river and its canals are estimated at 1151 tons/day of dissolved solids, 296 tons/day of suspended solids, 168 tons/day of oils, and 1.65 tons/day of heavy metals [12]. To counteract the situation, a pilot pollution prevention project is being implemented now in the Egyptian industrial sector by the Energy Conservation and Environmental Project/Environmental Pollution Prevention

---

[3] This result may provide an answer to another environmental problem; specifically, urban encroachment of agriculture land. An increasing shadow price of land implies a relative improvement in the competition in favour of agriculture *vis a vis* urbanization.

Project [7]. The project's records indicate that valuable progress is being made in water and other environmental media as well.[4]

Tentative project results are summarized in Table 2. Naturally, the cost of improvement varies significantly from one industry to another. While cost is estimated at LE 731 thousand in the aluminium industry, it is LE 22 thousand in the house appliances industry. Similarly, the expected water savings differed: the highest is that of the aluminium industry and the lowest in a T-shirt factory (108 and 6 thousand m³/year; respectively). The per-unit price of saved water differs from one industry to another: the price of a cubic meter is about LE 0.75. However, in some cases, water has to be treated before use as in the textile industry. In such cases, the average value of a saved cubic meter of water goes up to LE 1.65.

Table 2. Summary of results of industrial pollution prevention

Industry	Fixed Cost	Annual savings			
		Water quantity	Water value	Material value	Total value
	(000 LE)	(000 m³)	(000 LE)	(000 LE)	(000 LE)
Cars	401	34	26	381	407
Aluminium	731	108	81	361	442
House appliances	22	31	23	4	27
Fashion wear	279	79	130	223	353
T-shirts	75	6	11	360	371
Total	1508	258	271	1329	1600

Source: Khouzam, R.F. 1996 [15]

If simple payback period is employed as a criterion to evaluate the financial attractiveness of pollution prevention with respect to water savings alone, it takes less than one year to recover the fixed cost in the house appliances factory and rises to fifteen years in the car industry (with an overall average of over five years). Accordingly, the cut in the water bill alone is not enough to persuade a factory owner to adopt pollution prevention methods in all cases. Yet, attractiveness is boosted if the value of conserved material is included; in this case, the payback period drops significantly to a maximum of 1.7 years in the aluminium industry, a minimum of two months in the fashion wear factory, with an average of eleven months.

---

[4] Adoption of pollution prevention goes beyond water media to other favourable environmental impacts such as the reduction of VOC emission, material saving, energy conservation, not to mention, the positive impact on health and fire hazards. Nonetheless, this section is confined to its effect on water environment.

5   Policy recommendations

Worldwide, several endeavours have been made over the past two decades to address water shortage issues: the World Conference on Water held in Mar del Plata in 1977, the declaration of 1981-1990 as the International Drinking Water Supply and Sanitation Decade, the Copenhagen Informal Consultation on Integrated Water Resources Development and Management where 27 countries participated in 1991, the International Conference on Water and the Environment held in Dublin in 1992, Agenda 21 issued by the UN Conference on Environment and Development held in 1992 in Rio de Janeiro, the World Bank's "Policy Paper on Water Resources Management" issued in 1993, then, in the same year, the East African Water Resources Seminar held in Entebbe, Uganda. In 1994, the Development Assistance Committee of OECD dedicated its meeting to water resource management; and the statement by the Committee for Sustainable Development was issued.

The potential role of recycling used water in meeting the rising demand for water has not received suitable emphasis. For example, plans in six East African countries indicate that quantity, rather than quality, is the main issue[16].

This work brings to the fore water recycling as a path to counteract water shortage and, meanwhile, it addresses water quality issues in an economic framework. For the three polluting sectors, there exist policy components which motivate the reduction of emission levels. Motivation is provided in the form of cost reduction and, consequently, greater profit. This provides a built-in force that attracts a polluter to adopt environmentally conservative techniques. Such self motivation avoids the intrinsic deficiencies of the current policies (listed above). Nonetheless, it is extremely important to point out that the information cost involved in searching for profitable environmental techniques and the risk and uncertainty associated with their adoption are not considered in this work and will be incorporated in future phases.

In the light of the above findings, a set of policy recommendations are presented to Governmental organisations, international development agencies, and NGOs:

- Win-win policy tools (exemplified above) have to be exhausted before resorting to negative incentives and coercive tools.
- Agencies concerned with pollution should invest in the adaptation and dissemination of local and foreign research findings which supply environmentally cleaner, and at the same time more profitable, options.
- Private business should be encouraged to invest in, and open markets for, waste treatment for recycling.

Although the question addressed in this paper is presented in the Egyptian context, the ideas are applicable to other areas in the world. Incorporation of these recommendations as an integral component of environmental policies is anticipated to boost the outcome of societies' efforts to secure safe and sufficient water for their peoples.

6 Bibliography

1. Abu-Zeid, M.A. and Rady M.A. (1991), "Egypt's Water Resources Management and Policies." *Comprehensive Water Management Policy Workshop*, the World Bank, Washington D. C., Jun. 24-28.
2. Abu-Zeid, M.A. (1992), "Major Issues in Egypt's Water Resources and Irrigation Policy: To the Next Century," Key Note Address, *Roundtable on Egyptian Water Policy*, Proceedings of a Seminar on Egyptian Water Policy, sponsored by the Water Research Center, the Ford Foundation, and Winrock International, Alexandria, Egypt, April 11-13, pp. 2-10.
3. Tohamy, S. (1995), *International Experience in Controlling River Water Pollution and Policy Recommendations for Egypt*, (mimeograph).
4. Pearce, D.W. and Turner, R.K. (1990), *Economics of Natural Resources and the Environment*, Baltimore: Johns Hopkins University Press.
5. Baumol, W.J. and Oates, W.E. (1988), *The Theory of Environmental Policy*, 2nd ed., Cambridge University Press, New York.
6. Just, R. E., Hueth, D.L. and Schmitz, A. (1982), *Applied Welfare Economics and Public Policy*, New Jersey, Printice-Hall, Inc.
7. ECEP/DRTPC/TIMS/EP3 (Energy Conservation and Environmental Protection/Development Research and Technological Planning Center/Tabbin Institute for Metallurgical Studies/Environmental Pollution Prevention Project) (1995), "Pollution Prevention Assessment", several issues.
8. El Gohary, F. (1993), "Comparative Environmental Risks in Cairo, Water Pollution Problem." In PRIDE (Project in Development and the Environment) (1994), *Comparing Environmental Health Risks in Cairo, Egypt*, Vol. 3: Technical Annexes, USAID Contract Number: ANE-0178-Q-00-1047-00.
9. Gren, Ing-Marie (1993), "Alternatives Nitrogen Reduction Policies in the Malar Region, Sweden, *Beijer Reprint Series,* No. 14, Beijer International Institute of Ecological Economics, the Royal Swedish Academy of Sciences.
10. PRIDE (1994), "Environmental Assistance to Egypt," *Status Report.*
11. Awadallah, S. (1995), *Recycling Municipal and Farm Wastes for Bioagriculture in Egypt*, (mimeograph).
12. NSC 1992, Encyclopaedia of the National Specialized Councils: 1974-1992, *The Policy of Protecting the Nile River from Pollution*, Vol. 18, pp. 229-254. (In Arabic)
13. Siam, G. (1995), *Approaches for Environmentally-Conservative Agriculture in Egypt*, (mimeograph).
14. Hazell, P., Perez N., Siam G. and Soliman, I. (1994) "Effects of Deregulation of the Agricultural Production Sector on Food Availability and Resource Use in Egypt." In MALR/IFPRI, *Maintaining Food Security in Egypt During and After Agricultural and Food Policy Reform*, pt. III. (manuscript)
15. Khouzam, R.F. 1996, "Economic Incentives to Promote the Abatement of Nile Pollution," ECES Working Papers Series.
16. Lundqvist, Jan and Torkil Jonch-Clausen (eds.) (1994), *Putting Dublin/Agenda into Practice: Lessons and New Approaches in Water and Land Management.* Special Session at VIIIth IWRA World Congress, Cairo, Egypt, November 21-25.

WATER QUALITY PROTECTION POLICY AND INTEGRATED AGRICULTURAL AND ENVIRONMENTAL PROTECTION STRATEGIES IN LITHUANIA

Environmental issues in Lithuanian agriculture

A. GUTKAUSKAS
Department of Agriculture, Ministry of Agriculture, Vilnius, Lithuania.

Abstract

During the period of transition to a market economy, under conditions of economic crisis, the application of pesticides and mineral fertilisers, as well as the rate of production, decreased in Lithuanian agriculture. Traditional markets were lost and the unemployment rate increased. Consequently, environmental pollution has declined, but not due to an increased commitment to environmental protection. As economic conditions and the growth of production improve, ecological problems will reoccur. Currently, there is a unique opportunity to restore agricultural production by implementing alternative practices while, at the same time, reducing the utilisation of chemicals. In one Lithuanian region, the karst zone near Birzai and Pasvalys, a special program, supported by the Government is being implemented. Beginning in 1993, traditional agriculture began to be transformed into sustainable and organic and other environmental measures are being implemented to reduce both point and non-point source pollution.

This programme is being implemented by the Karst Fund "Tatula", which has been established for that purpose. The fund competitively awards its members with free interest credits, grants subsidies for the construction of waste water treatment facilities, and for educational activities, training, ecological monitoring and other activities. In that ecologically sensitive karst region it is necessary to protect ground water, while, at the same time, solving the marketing problems for agricultural production and unemployment issues. With the growth of the national economy the program will be expanded throughout Lithuania as is required by the Government's strategies on Environmental Protection and Climate Changes. At present the programs developed for the karst zone on education and certification of organic production have been implemented in all regions of Lithuania.

Keywords: agriculture, environmental protection, groundwater, karst.

Water Policy: Allocation and management in practice. Edited by P. Howsam and R.C. Carter. Published in 1996 by E & FN Spon. ISBN 0 419 21650 2

1   Introduction

The population of Lithuania is currently about 3.77 million, 32% of which are rural residents. The area of the country is 65.30 thousand square kilometres. Agricultural land makes up 53.8%, forests - 30.2%, water bodies - 4.0% and marsh lands - 2.4%. Due to intensive land-reclamation activities, drainage systems were installed on 3041.5 ha (about 80% of the total marsh lands have been drained).

There are 29.1 thousand rivers, small rivers and channels in Lithuania. Their total length amounts to 63.7 thousand km. In addition, there are about 3000 lakes larger than 0.5 ha and 13,940 smaller ones. The average annual river outflow is about 26 cubic km of water. About 60% of the ground water basins in Lithuania are located near river channels and are hydraulically connected to the river.

The area of protected territories is 728,042 ha or 11% of the total area of the Republic, including 5 preserves (23,508 ha or 0.4%), five national parks (138,070 or 2.0%), 30 regional parks (380, 880 ha or 5.8%), 290 state preserves (176,390 ha or 2.7%) and 62 preserves of municipalities (5,065 ha or 0.5%).

In 1990, after independence had been restored, the agrarian reform began in Lithuania. Former collective and state farms (about 1.2 thousand) were replaced by individual farmers (about 134.6 thousand) and partnerships (about 2340). Individual farms now occupy about 34.2% of the agricultural land, while partnerships occupy about 31.7%. The state property was transferred to private ownership in 1995.

2   The current state of agriculture and environmental protection

Prior to independence, an intensive agriculture dependent upon an abundant use of chemicals prevailed in Lithuania. This high-input agriculture had a negative impact on the environment: increased soil erosion and soil, water and food contamination. In 1991, the process of transformation to a market economy resulted in upheaval in the Lithuanian economy in general and the agriculture sector in particular. The use of agricultural chemicals was drastically reduced, and, as a result, agricultural production declined rapidly.

The use of mineral fertilisers (particularly nitrogen and potassium) had been increasing steadily until 1991. In 1973, 159.8 thousand tons (of active substance) of nitrogen fertilisers were used for agricultural purposes in Lithuania. In 1988 nitrogen use had increased to 267.5 thousand tons, but in 1993, use declined to only 29.8 thousand tons. The corresponding figures for potassium fertilisers were 154.5, 292.2 and 1.0 thousand tons, and for phosphorus - 83.9, 141.5 and 12.9 thousand tons. The same trends can be seen in the application of chemical plant protection measures. In 1989, 8,822 tons of pesticides were used, but in 1993, only 490 tons.

Agricultural production yields have decreased dramatically during the transition period. e.g. the grain yield decreased from 29.1 cant/ha in 1991 to 17.6 cnt/ha in 1994, for potatoes - from 161 cnt/ha to 94 cnt/ha, for sugar beets - from 313 cnt/ha to 173 cnt/ha, for fodder beets - from 535 cnt/ ha to 239 cnt/ha. One of the major factors influencing the decline in yields has been the decline in agricultural chemical use described above. It should also be mentioned that drought conditions had a negative impact on the yields as well.

It is anticipated that, if chemical use remains the same as in 1993-1994, and if no alternative farming methods are implemented, the yields will continue to decrease.

Environment pollution has also decreased over the past few years, but it is clear that this is not the result of efforts toward environmental protection and is not an indicator of the development of an environmental protection ethic, but rather simply the result of decreased chemical use and the resultant reduction in contamination sources.

Agricultural production levels will have to be restored, as the decreased production volumes are adding to the economic and social distress in rural areas. Economic changes aimed at restoring production have already begun: in 1995 the application of pesticides and mineral fertilisers was two times higher than in 1994. While the current political climate in Lithuania is unfavourable for agricultural reform, the existing economic conditions make efforts to implement such reforms potentially more successful at the farm level as demonstrations of and support for alternative agricultural practices that reduce environmental impacts while increasing production will be more readily received by farmers now than in the future when the old high-input practices have become reestablished. Alternative farming forms would reduce the need for energy and for natural resources. In addition, the levels of agriculture-related pollution would be reduced both directly (by reducing the application of pesticides and mineral fertilisers) and indirectly (by reducing the volumes of chemical production, energy resource exploitation and ag-industrial production in general).

Thus, as the national economy improves, efforts should be made by the Government to support the implementation of sustainable and organic farming. During a transitional period from traditional agriculture to sustainable and organic farming, the issues of agricultural production marketing, as well as unemployment issues must be successfully solved along with environmental protection. (32% of the population dwell in the countryside and their major activities are related to agriculture).

25% of Lithuanian residents get their drinking water from about 300 thousand shaft wells. The majority of these wells are located in rural areas. The water quality of more than half of those wells does not meet the allowed standards.

During the transitional period to a market economy, the construction of water supply systems and waste water treatment systems has been halted in rural areas. In addition, the repair and maintenance of existing facilities has been considerably slowed.

Thirty-three large-scale hog complexes (with an annual capacity ranging from 12-54 thousand head) have been constructed in Lithuania. The pollution potential from those complexes could be compared with that from a town with a population of 5 million inhabitants.

There are many unsolved environmental protection problems on smaller livestock farms and on other agricultural production units. As the transitional period continues, the prospects for many agricultural production operations are unclear, therefore it is rather risky to try to plan for support activities and their financing. According to preliminary estimates, 4 billion US dollars would be necessary to solve our rural environmental protection problems.

3   The karst zone management plan

Solutions to environmental problems have so far remained elusive, as many of them are still unidentified. However, beginning in the autumn of 1987, with the creation of the Environmental Protection Service at the Ministry of Agriculture, a number of steps have been taken by the Government and the Seimas toward providing mechanisms to address environmental issues.

Scientists concerned about these issues proposed the development of a pilot program for rural environmental protection in Lithuania by concentrating our capacities and financial resources for the solution these issues in the karst region of northern Lithuania, the most sensitive area from an environmental protection perspective. The karst region is characterized by thick layers of gypsum and dolomite lying close to the surface. The high solubility of these layers results in the formation of numerous channels and sinkholes that provide conditions favourable for rapid ground and surface water pollution.

The idea behind the karst program was to protect one of Lithuania's most vulnerable resources while at the same time gaining experience in addressing rural development and agricultural issues from both economic and environmental perspective. As the economic climate becomes more favourable, this experience will provide a base from which to expand the implementation of the program to the rest of Lithuania. These tactics are detailed in the strategies for Environmental protection and Climate changes that were prepared by the Government in 1995.

The karst region is located in a triangle encompassing portions of the Akmene, Birzai, Rokiskis, Pasvalys and Panevezys regions. It occupies an area of about 8 thousand square kilometres, or about 12% of the total area of the country. In the heart of that area, in the Birzai and Pasvalys regions, soils are very fertile, so, historically, an especially intensive agriculture, with utilisation of abundant amounts of chemicals, was developed. Because of resulting water contamination problems, there were several state resolutions (in 1977 and in 1982), drastically restricting economic activities in that region. However, these regulations were very one-sided, ignoring the economic issues associated with implementing the restrictions. Further hindering compliance were state directives to further intensify production. As a result of these problems, implementation of the protective regulations was ignored.

In the beginning of 1987 a committee of scientists was set up to define the size of the territory where restrictions should be introduced, based on agricultural, economic and geological criteria. It took two years to develop a consensus among all interested parties. The result was a defined intensive karst zone of 29.4 thousand ha and a protected region, primarily designed to restrict construction activities, of 165.4 thousand ha. Based on different geologic conditions, best characterised by the density of sinkholes per unit area, the intensive karst zone was subdivided into 4 land groups. In each of these groups, varying levels of protection are provided, depending on the severity of karst activity. ie. in the fourth land group (more than 80 sinkholes per square kilometre) the application of chemical plant protection measures, mineral fertilisers and non-composted manure is strictly prohibited, while in the first land group (fewer than 20 sinkholes per square kilometre), restrictions on farming activities are limited to prohibitions only on several types of herbicides and chloro-organic insecticides, and restrictions on application rates of mineral fertilisers to no more that 90 kg/ha (active substance) of nitrogen, phosphorus and potassium, and on manure applications to no more than 80 t/ha.

Initially, during the period while collective and state farms still existed, a special crop structure was designed for each land group. The highest restrictions were prescribed for the fourth land group, where only meadows and forests could be grown. This was seen as the only way to insure that the application of chemical substances could be strictly controlled. Currently, however, with privatisation and the breakup of the state farms, the situation is different, as it has become possible to develop sustainable and organic agriculture in the karst region. This reorientation of traditional agriculture has eliminated the need for restrictions on crop structure. Organic agriculture can be characterised as farming without chemical plant protection measures and without chemical mineral fertilisers. Alternative farming practices are introduced, based on crop rotation, installation of composting facilities and other techniques that reduce or eliminate the chemical load on the environment. Despite these measures, however, the most sensitive areas will be established as geological preserves where no agricultural activities will be allowed.

Historically, environmental protection measures were developed without regard to their economic implications such as costs required to support implementation and impacts on the affected population. The Karst Zone Management Plan was not presented for Governmental approval until all of the economic issues were addressed. In the end of 1991, after the final territorial delineation of the karst zone was defined, the Government began to develop a program to implement protective restrictions in the zone. The program addressed economic mechanisms to support implementation and the necessary financial arrangements. The program was confirmed by resolution of the Government in 1993.

There were many discussions as to who could successfully implement the program as there were few examples of successful programs to serve as a model. However, based on the experience of the Netherlands in implementing environmental protection programs in protected territories, it was decided that the program would be implemented by a special non profit organisation, the Karst Region Fund "Tatula", which is financed from the state budget and supported by the fund members. The Fund's membership can include farmers, private (non-state) partnerships, enterprises, and natural persons. The essential elements and goals of the program are as follows:

1. By 2005 - 2010, the program will reach the break point in transforming agriculture from traditional to sustainable and organic: organic agriculture should make up about 5% of all agricultural land by that time. In order to accomplish that goal, the Fund's activities will focus on expanding ecological education in the karst region, strengthening cooperation between fund members, furthering implementation of sustainable and organic farming, establishing service infrastructure (including purchasing, processing and sales of organic production materials) and market research, development and implementation of a certification and control system.
2. By the year 2000, we will be able to implement successfully the environmental protection measures for stopping point source pollution in rural areas by continuing the construction of waste treatment plants, and implementing other measures of environmental protection.

3. To become the owner of current and future nature preserves and other protected territories in the region (following the world-wide experience) by initiating amendments to the Constitution and laws.
4. To enhance programs being implemented in environmental protection, agricultural strategies and other policy and regulatory documents and thus make the Karst Program a pilot project for the whole of Lithuania.

Financing of the program comes from the state budget according to a special procedure confirmed by the Government and the Ministry of Agriculture. One million dollars US were assigned for the years 1993-1995. Implementation of the program is being assisted by Danish and American organisations, with financing from their own state budgets. There are also negotiations being held with the Netherlands, Sweden, Germany, UN-FAO and other organisations from different states. The Fund "Tatula" is:

1. an organisation providing interest free credits for farmers, large agricultural companies (partnerships) and enterprises implementing measures planned in the program. The Fund aims: to transform the farming activities in the karst zone from traditional farming to sustainable and organic farming, and establish purchasing, processing and sales infrastructure;
2. an organisation that contracts for and finances the implementation of measures directed by the program: construction of waste treatment plants and other environmental protection measures;
3. a contracting organisation, financing ecological education (including publishing) and teaching (including consulting), science, establishment of a system for certification and control, legalisation and implementation of environmental protection monitoring;
4. a co-operative, joining together efforts of its members in solving the environmental and health protection problems and social and economic issues in the karst zone.

The Fund currently has 119 members: 89 farmers, 4 enterprises, 8 large agricultural companies (partnerships) and 18 natural persons. The fund is managed by the unanimous consent of all members through the following administrative bodies:

- Observers Council (5) - elected by the members
- Inspector (1) - elected by the members
- Board (7) - elected by the Observers Council
- Administration (2) - assigned by the chairperson of the fund.

4   Summary

It is evident that non-point source pollution from agricultural practices and point source pollution from rural households and villages present a serious threat to surface and groundwater resources in the karst zone. It is equally evident that the karst zone management plan represents a comprehensive attempt to address these problems in a regional, holistic manner.

Agriculture in the karst zone is reflective of Lithuanian agriculture as a whole with large state-run enterprises being broken up into numbers of small individual operations. As a result, waste management has become a dispersed problem, much more difficult to address than in former, centralised times. Agricultural input and management practices are also more difficult to address as large numbers of individual operators are more difficult to reach than smaller numbers of state farm management teams. Nevertheless, the attitude of the individual farmers appears to reflect much more concern with environmental issues than that demonstrated by the former enterprises. he karst area management plan reflects a similar concern at the national level.

The plan appears to have been well-designed and takes into account both the prevailing economic conditions and the geophysical characteristics of the karst zone. Difficulties in implementation of the plan derive from those same economic conditions as there is a chronic lack of funding for critical major projects such as wastewater treatment plants for towns and cities in the area. Other needs, such as a widespread, ongoing monitoring program are also expensive and have yet to be implemented.

Farmers in the zone, while generally aware of the plan and the unique conditions in the area that require special practices, appear to have an unfulfilled need for education and advisory services that will enable them to implement the required practices. While the farmers appear to be concerned with their environment and willing to implement practices to protect it, the agricultural economy of the area, as in the rest of Lithuania, is such that there also is a need for the Government to develop an incentive and/or indemnity program to induce farmers to comply with restrictions that may affect their somewhat fragile economic security.

The author believes that the karst zone plan can succeed, if, as improving economic conditions allow, the Government provides the resources to construct the necessary infrastructure and support the economic integrity of area residents upon whom, ultimately, the success of the plan depends. If successful, the plan can serve as a model for regional approaches to agro-environmental problems throughout the Baltic region.

PRIVATE WATER SUPPLIES - A CATCHMENT APPROACH
A risk assessment procedure for water supplies

P.R. HODSON
Consultant
R.A. JARMAN
Environmental Practices Adviser,
The National Trust for England, Wales & N Ireland

Abstract
A technique for an environmental and health risk assessment of private water supplies has been developed for the National Trust. The risk assessment considers engineering and catchment management factors affecting water quality, has been extensively tested in the field, and may have applications for small scale water supply systems in developing countries. The results of the field trials have been compared with actual water quality data from both simultaneous and local authority tests. The results are discussed here with consideration to the application of the risk assessment as an alternative or accompaniment to water quality tests, in the UK and overseas.
Key words: engineering, intervention, potable water supplies, management, pollution, risk-assessment, survey.

1   Introduction

Although the majority of people in the U.K. now use mains water, there are still about 1% of properties on the British mainland which rely on private water supplies (PWS). This equates to some 138,000 supplies of which 55,000 are in England and Wales, [1]. The privatisation of local water authorities in the 1980's has resulted in a rapid rise in water charges and the introduction in many areas of water metering; this has provoked renewed interest in private supplies which are now being seen increasingly as an asset rather than a liability.

The introduction in January 1992 of the "Private Water Supply Regulations 1991", [2], by the Department of the Environment, completed the translation into U.K. law of the E.C. "Directive on the Quality of Water Intended for Human Consumption", [3]. In accordance with this legislation local authorities are responsible for ensuring that

Water Policy: Allocation and management in practice. Edited by P. Howsam and R.C. Carter.
Published in 1996 by E & FN Spon. ISBN 0 419 21650 2

PWS meet with the water quality criteria laid down in the regulations. Furthermore each supply is now classified according to its usage, the number of users, and the quantity of water discharged, in order to establish a frequency and figure of testing which protects public health without being prohibitively expensive.

Table 1.   Classification of private water supplies and frequency of sampling. Category I - supplies used for domestic purposes by those persons normally residing on the premises [2].

Class	Number of Users	Daily Supply M³/day	Sampling Frequency
A	>5,000	>1,000	12 times per year
B	501-5,000	101-1,000	6 times per year
C	101-500	21-100	1 time per year
D	25-100	5-20	1 time per year
E	<25 (except class F)	<5	Once every 5 years
F	single dwellings		no regular sampling

The frequency of testing can be varied by local authorities according to the water quality history of the supply, with more frequent testing where water quality is suspect. Supplies delivering over 100m³ per day in either category 1 or 2, must be tested for all 64 quality parameters specified in the Regulations; however smaller water supplies need to be tested for only 9 basic parameters including Coliform contamination.

In practice this means that the quality of water delivered by private supplies is now under systematic scrutiny for the first time, and this could have significant cost implications for private supply owners and users. Despite this, infrequent testing for some supply classes, (eg once every year for categories 1.D and 2.5), is not a reliable indicator of the risk of failure between tests as the time of sampling is critical to the result [4].

The National Trust for England, Wales and N Ireland has stewardship over some 240,000 hectares of land including 35% of the Lake District National Park, 207 historic houses open to the public, and some 20,000 other properties. A number of these properties are served by PWS, (162 in the north west region alone), and so the Trust has a vested interest from the public safety, financial and environmental standpoints, in securing reliable and safe water supplies at a minimum cost.

The problem for the Trust is that previously very little care has been taken of the PWS which they have inherited, and as a result many systems have become dilapidated with little or no attempt at source protection. In addition, modern intensive farming systems have increased the potential for pollution in rural catchments, and the increase in tourism brings in an increasing number of visitors who not only increase demand for water, but may be at increased risk from water-borne illnesses.

Where intervention is necessary to improve water quality, connection to a mains supply may not be a viable option depending on cost. In 1989 the Bristol Waterworks Company quoted a cost of £165,000 for the connection of a single property to the mains [5]; this is an extreme case but even so, replicated nationally, the potential cost of such interventions is enormous, and the PWS as valuable local resources would be lost.

The National Trust recognises the need to be proactive in addressing PWS problems, and to take the initiative in the assessment and rehabilitation of systems. The Trust's aim has therefore been to develop a risk assessment technique, simple enough to be used by its staff, which indicates the degree and source of the risk and which can therefore be useful in targeting interventions. By this method the Trust aims to ensure adequate and wholesome water supply to its properties, making the maximum use of the available water resources and with a minimum cost, disruption, or environmental impact.

What follows is an account of the development of this risk- assessment technique and its application in the field.

2   Method

In 1993 the Trust sponsored two M.Sc. projects from Silsoe College, Cranfield University, one concentrating on the engineering of PWS [6], and the other on pollution threats within the supply catchment [7]. Each project developed a risk assessment technique specific to the area of study concerned. These two techniques were later combined as part of a separate exercise to produce a single risk assessment covering both the engineering and catchment management aspects of PWS. Chronologically the research followed the following format.

2.1 Identification of risk factors

Both studies aimed to produce simple, easy to use assessment techniques which could be replicable and valid in a wide range of conditions, and give results which could be translated into logical intervention aimed at risk reduction.

For this reason the large number of potential contributing factors needed to be rationalised to include only those most likely to influence water quality in terms of frequency and magnitude. Some precision was therefore sacrificed for practicality. Hodson concentrated on the system engineering factors likely to influence water quality delivered at the point of use. To give a structure to the survey, the system was broken down into the following sections:

• Source and abstraction works
• Storage and treatment
• Distribution system

The component sections of the PWS were then scrutinised for the following factors:

• the standard of design and construction
• sanitary protection measures
• system management and maintenance
• the age of the system and materials used in its construction
• the location of, and susceptibility to, potential sources of pollution

In addition the physical characteristics of the water at the point of use, such as smell, taste and appearance were considered as indicators of potential problems within the system. Windram identified the following pollution sources typical of rural catchments:

- Livestock housing and yards
- Silage storage
- Fuel and oil storage
- Pesticide and fertiliser storage,
- Sheep dips
- Field applications of slurry, fertilisers and pesticides
- Livestock grazing
- Septic tanks
- Rubbish pits

In addition aquifer characteristics and vulnerability to contamination were considered [8].

2.2 Quantifying the risk

For a universal technique, the degree of risk attached to any one factor can be particularly difficult to quantify, dependent as the risk is on the variability of contributing and ameliorating factors. Hodson and Windram developed different scoring systems, one incremental and the other reducing, which were both based on the perceived risk from a particular factor as indicated by the frequency, nature and potential health risk associated with contamination incidents. Scores were awarded to each factor in order to quantify the associated risk to water quality. These scores were inevitably arbitrary in the first instance.

2.3 Testing the validity of the risk assessment technique

In order to put the risk assessment into an accessible and usable form, a series of questions were framed by which the relevant factors could be scrutinised, The two risk assessment techniques were then extensively tested and refined on PWS serving National

Trust properties in Cumbria and Yorkshire. Performance of the assessments conducted in Cumbria was measured against simultaneous water quality tests for coliform bacteria, while the Yorkshire risk assessments were compared with the results of previous local authority tests where available.

2.4 Combination of the risk assessment techniques

As a separate exercise following on from this work, the Trust contracted Silsoe College to combine the two separate risk assessments into a single procedure with a unified scoring system. This is incorporated into a manual on PWS written for use by Trust staff [9].

Table 2. Example of risk assessment survey scoring system:

SPRINGS - COLLECTION TANK	YES	NO
1. Is the source protected by any structure or collection tank?	2	0
2 Is the structure clean and in good repair?	2	0
3 Is the structure vermin proof?	2	0
4 Is there a well fitting lid, raised above ground level?	2	0
5 Has the structure been cleaned/disinfected in the last 12 months?	1	0
6 Has any maintenance been carried out in the last year?	1	0
TOTAL	10	

3   Results

3.1 Engineering risk assessment

The engineering risk assessment was carried out on 50 PWS in Cumbria and a further 30 PWS in Yorkshire. The results are shown below in comparison with water quality test data from simultaneous and local authority periodic tests.

Table 3. Results of engineering risk assessment:

Source of data	Number of PWS	Pass	Fail
Risk assessment	80	6%	94%
Simultaneous coliform test - tap	49	42%	56%
- source	47	24%	70%
Local authority test data (post-1985)	15	73%	27%

Comments:

1. One site identified as a pass by the risk assessment failed the simultaneous water quality test.
2. Several sites which showed imminent risk of contamination, passed the water quality test after a period of dry weather.

Classification by source:

Wells and boreholes	Springs	Surface water
3	63	19

N.B several PWS used more than one source.

3.2 Catchment risk assessment

The catchment risk assessment was evaluated on 25 PWS in Cumbria measured against simultaneous coliform tests, and a further 29 PWS in Yorkshire measured against recent local authority test results. The results are shown below.

Table 4. Results of catchment risk assessment

Source of data	Number of PWS	Pass	Fail
Risk assessment	54	22%	78%
Simultaneous coliform test	25	56%	44%
Local authority tests (post-1985)	15	73%	27%

4   Discussion

4.1 Performance of the risk assessment technique

The most obvious feature of the risk assessment compared with either simultaneous or periodic water quality tests, is that it is a much more severe scrutiny of a PWS than the water quality tests. As a result the predicted failure rate is much higher.

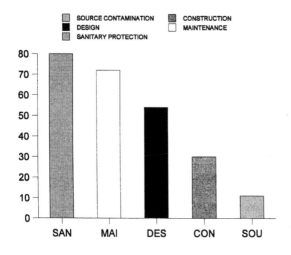

Fig. 1. Causes of failure as identified by the engineering risk- assessment.

Water quality tests are only a measure of <u>actual</u> contamination of a supply at a particular point in time. For lower category supplies which are tested infrequently, (eg once every 5 years for category 1.E. supplies), water quality tests may not identify the health hazard attached to a particular supply.

Simultaneous water quality tests corresponded more closely with the risk assessment than the available local authority tests, which suggests that more frequent testing would help to overcome this. However the high cost of tests would make this prohibitively expensive for small supplies.

4.2 Intervening to improve water supply systems

Under the conditions in which the risk assessment has been tested, the most common engineering factors contributing to failure are issues such as sanitary protection and maintenance, which are well documented in engineering manuals. The overwhelming catchment factor is grazing, which suggests that a management intervention to restrict grazing may be necessary as proposed by Valentine [10]. The structure of the risk assessment links failure of a PWS to potential causes, and can therefore aid decision making with regard to interventions.

The management and maintenance of catchments and systems on National Trust land requires either enforcement by the National Trust or participation between the Trust and its tenant(s). The Trust is attempting to introduce a participatory approach. With the recent experience of drought-affected PWS, the Trust is also promoting water conservation measures to its tenants, such as low flush or dry composting toilets, showers as alternatives to baths and rainwater harvesting for garden use.

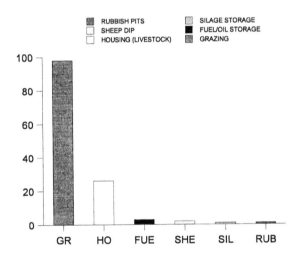

Fig.2. Causes of failure as identified by the catchment risk assessment.

4.3 Conducting risk assessment surveys

Any survey is only as good as the information it gathers. The risk assessment relies on the participation of the supply users for some of the information required, and so the timing, presentation and duration of the survey are all critical to the response obtained. It should also be considered that in some instances inaccurate verbal information can be given and so the risk assessment has been designed so that as much of the required information as possible can be physically double checked.

4.4 Is the risk assessment transferable?

The conditions under which the technique was tested were predominantly upland livestock farming areas with shallow groundwater, spring, or surface water sources.

At the time of unifying the two risk assessments into a single format, several more sites in arable farming areas in the south east of England were tested, including one artesian source. The technique appeared to work well under these conditions with a similar correlation to water quality test results to that achieved in the main study. However the number of sites tested was small [6], and a wider range of tests to include contaminants such as nitrate and pesticides should be considered.

Given this qualification the factors likely to affect water quality from private supplies remain the same and so the risk assessment survey will be applicable under a wide range of conditions. Only where specific and unusual local risks to water quality exist is there a risk that they may fall outside the scope of this risk assessment.

With consideration for local conditions therefore, risk assessment surveys could prove useful both in Europe and also in developing countries where a much higher proportion of the population depends on "private" water supplies.

5   Conclusion

A risk assessment survey of PWS is a more efficient and cost effective method of evaluating the danger of a water supply being contaminated than infrequent periodic water quality tests.

The risk assessment technique highlights the likely origin of a threat to the supply and can therefore be used to aid management decisions concerning the upgrading or improvement of a supply. It may also prevent poorly targeted interventions and thus conserve financial resources.

The risk assessment survey enables the National Trust to be proactive in identifying and rectifying water supply problems in advance of legislative enforcement once a supply has failed a local authority lest

From the evidence of the trials conducted, this kind of assessment, in conjunction with periodic tests, may be a more effective way for local authorities to implement the private water supply regulations and safeguard public health than the current regime of infrequent testing for lower category supplies.

6   References

1. Drinking Water Inspectorate. (1993) *Personal communication.*
2. Department of the Environment. (1991) *Statutory Instruments No.2790: Water, England and Wales - The Private Water Supplies Regulations* 1991. Department of the Environment, London.
3. Council of the European Community. (1980) *Council Directive Relating to Water Intended for Human Consumption.* 87/778/EEC.
4. Petrie, A. S. et al. (1994) *Seasonal Variations in the Quality of Spring Waters Used as Private Supplies.* Journal of the Institute of Water and Environmental Management, 1994. 8, June, pp 320-326.

5. Severn National Trust. (1990) *Correspondence with Bristol Waterworks* Co.

6. Hodson P.R. (1993) *Engineering and Associated Management Factors Contributing to the Non-compliance of Private Water Supplies Development of a Predictive Questionnaire.* M.Sc. Thesis, Silsoe College, Silsoe.

7. Windram, C. (1993) *Risk Assessment Procedure for Private Water Supplies.* M.Sc. Thesis, Silsoe College, Silsoe.

8. LeGrand, H.E. (1964) *System for Evaluation of Contamination Potential of some Waste Disposal Sites.* Journal of the American Waterworks Association, 56, pp 959-974.

9. Hodson, P.R. et al. (1995) *Private Water Supplies, a Guide to Design, Management and maintenance.* National Trust Cirencester.

10 Valentine, J.F. (1990) *Grazing Management.* Academic Press Inc., London.

SECTION 4

WATER SUPPLY MANAGEMENT

TECHNOLOGY IMPLICATIONS OF IRRIGATION WATER DELIVERY POLICIES

Irrigation delivery policy and technology

L. HORST
Department of Irrigation and Soil and Water Conservation
Agricultural University, Wageningen, The Netherlands

Abstract

Policy decisions on irrigation water delivery (allocation and distribution) have far-reaching consequences on the type of water division technology (structures to regulate and measure flows in the irrigation system), and subsequently on the possibilities and impossibilities of operation in terms of staff requirements, complexity, compatibility with farmers perceptions etc. This paper discusses the various policy options with special attention to the choice between delivery based on equity by means of inflexible proportional water division systems and delivery based on crop water requirements by flexible automated systems.

Key words: automation, crop growing restrictions, demand-supply considerations, irrigation, proportional division, water delivery scheduling.

1 Introduction

Possibly the most crucial policy decision in irrigation design is on how water is to be delivered (allocated and distributed) to the farmers. Each type of water delivery requires its specific water division technology. This appurtenant technology dictates the required staff in terms of numbers and skills, and determines the operational complexity, the measure of transparency and understandability of how water is divided, and the possibilities of mismanagement and collusion. In short, the selection of a certain water delivery method determines eventually the chances of success or failure.

The various water delivery methods however, should not only be judged on the above factors. Possible selection also appears to be strongly dependent on the supply of water: the sufficiency and the measure of control of the source of water.

This paper reviews the various types of water delivery scheduling (section 2) and

Water Policy: Allocation and management in practice. Edited by P. Howsam and R.C. Carter.
Published in 1996 by E & FN Spon. ISBN 0 419 21650 2

discusses their applicability in terms of demand-supply considerations (section 3). In section 4 conclusions are drawn regarding the consequences of selection of water delivery policies.

2   Water delivery scheduling

Many different water delivery schedules can be discerned [1][2]. However, the many different methods can be categorised into three main groups based on:

- equity (proportional scheduling)
- matching crop water requirements as determined by a central agency (central scheduling)
- matching crop water requirements as determined by the farmers (responsive scheduling).

The last two methods, although both based on crop water requirements, are distinctively presented here because of different technology and operation (Plusquellec et al [3] typify them as "top-down" and "bottom-up" approaches).

Method I Proportional scheduling: the flow entering the system is divided into fixed parts proportional to the subareas to be irrigated. (Deviations from this equity principle might sometimes occur due to preferential rights or taking into account expected seepage and percolation losses. The principle, however, remains the same.) The appurtenant irrigation system containing fixed structures is, at least partly, self managed requiring little operation. The flexibility is small. In case of low flows and silty water, rotation might be considered. It is often stated that proportional division should be limited to mono-cropping. Many small holder irrigation areas, however, are typified by numerous small plots with different crops under different stages of growth. In this case the average water requirement per unit area will be the same for each tertiary or secondary block. Therefore also here proportional division is applicable.

Method II Central scheduling: the water entering the system is allocated and distributed by the central agency on the basis of (surmised) actual cropping patterns and crop water requirements. In general an upstream controlled, adjustable system is required. Flows might be changed by adjusting gates or by rotation among canals. The flexibility is high but in case of manually operated structures operation is intensive and cumbersome.

Method III Responsive scheduling: here two options exist:

Method IIIA responsive-arranged: Water is divided by the central agency on the basis of farmers' requests. The system may be comparable with that of case II.

Method IIIB responsive-free: Farmers or groups of farmers can draw water if needed by means of an automatic downstream controlled system.

Clearly the policy decision on the selection of a water delivery schedule determines the type of water division technology. This selection, however, can not freely be made by adopting a certain policy on how to allocate and distribute the water (on the basis of equity or of crop water requirements, dictated by a central agency or responsive to farmers wishes). The applicability of a certain water delivery schedule should also be tested in terms of demand-supply considerations.

3   Demand-supply considerations

An important boundary condition for water delivery schedules is the availability of water in terms of quantity and timing. Hereby two elementary different types of water sources occur:
- static (lakes, reservoirs, ground water)
- dynamic (run-of-the-river flows).

If the water is not diverted from its source, in the first case water will remain stored and available for use, in the second case it is lost (in the river).

Another distinction is the adequacy of supply:
- sufficient supply throughout the year
- insufficient supply for unrestricted cropping calendars during part of the year.

The four cases are sketched in Fig. 1. In both cases A and B the operation could be simple. In view of sufficient water throughout the growing seasons, a responsive water delivery schedule (method III) might be adopted, accommodating the instantaneous needs of the farmers. An automatic downstream control system could be an option although the question arises whether this sophisticated type of technology is actually necessary: a system with proportional division structures - proportional scheduling (Method I) - running at Full Supply (FS) throughout the year will accommodate the same needs. Canals running FS also should be preferred when silt enters the system: with FS most of the silt will either leave the system or will be deposited in the fields. In both cases (automatic and proportional division) a well developed drainage system is required in order to return the excess water back to the river system.

With the cases C and D we arrive at one of the fundamental questions in irrigation: which measures should be taken for the shortage of water during part of the year? Matching supply to unrestricted demand might only be possible by building reservoirs to increase the dry season flows (creation of case A). In many parts of the world this appears rarely to be feasible however, and solutions should be found in matching demand to the actual limited supply. In principle two types of solutions might be considered: crop sanctions and water sanctions.

Crop sanctions
In order to match, during the dry season, the irrigation requirements with the water available, restrictions are issued on growing specific crops. Examples are the localization or crop zoning in India limiting the areas under 'wet' crops like rice and sugarcane and the sanctions in Indonesia for growing rice in the dry season.

These crop restrictions are based on an assessment of anticipated water availability during the dry season. Localization based on average reservoir storage (case C) or average river flows (case D) would lead to skewed water distribution during 50% of the (dryer) years, when farmers having better access to water will draw more than planned. Therefore localization is often based on 1:4 or 1:5 dry years flows, determined by statistical analysis of hydrological records of previous years.

In case C the reservoir outflow can be regulated to supply the flows required for the given restricted cropping calendar. Case D is more complex due to irregular river flows complicating operation of the system. In tropical rivers these irregularities can be large and frequent, and consequently, in practice, a considerable volume of water is not used and lost in the river (see dotted line in Fig. 1).

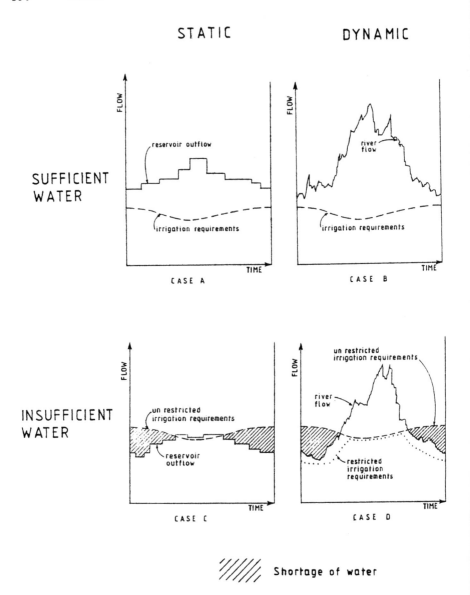

Fig. 1. Demand-supply cases

For both cases C and D proportional scheduling (method I) is often not applicable because of localised areas not being evenly distributed over tertiary and secondary blocks. In principle methods II, IIIa and b might be adopted. This institutional solution, however, only works on condition that: these sanctions on crops are strictly adhered to, the operational plan correctly represents the irrigation requirements and the water distribution is exactly according to this plan. Numerous studies [4][5][6][7] reveal that these conditions are seldom met due to the following reasons:

- the irrigation command area is designed larger than the actual water supplies justify;
- the localization is influenced by political pressure or unrealistic data leading to too large 'wet' crop areas;
- due to collusion, power pressure etc. some farmers manage to grow more 'wet' crops than sanctioned;
- due to the complicated technology the operators are unable to operate according to the operational plan.

Consequently the central and responsive-arranged schedules (methods II and IIIa) in practice result in situations of extreme inequities in terms of water distribution. Water is delivered to (groups of) farmers on the basis of negotiations, power relations, and in the worst case on the basis of chaos and catch-as-catch-can.

Method IIIb (responsive-free: automatic control system) only works when the supply *always* exceeds the demand. If not, automatic upstream control will produce shortages in the lower end of the system and downstream control in the upper end.

Water sanctions
Another possibility to solve the problem of required crop restrictions during the dry season, is to design irrigation systems which divide the water shortage equally among the farmers or groups of farmers. These systems are based on principles of proportional water division. Examples are the many traditional farmer managed irrigation schemes in e.g. Nepal, India, Bali, N-Africa, Yemen, Spain etc. In these cases the water is often divided by overflow weirs with equal crest heights and widths proportional to the areas behind them.

In regard to agency managed schemes, examples are found in the Northern parts of India and Pakistan (Punjab). Here the outlet to distributaries (secondary canals) are designed to deliver flows proportional to the command areas (tertiary units or 'chaks') when the distributaries are at Full Supply. The flow to the chak is then divided among farmers by means of a roster method called Warabandi.

The advantages of this solution lie in equity, transparency and timeliness. Instead of determining and imposing crop restrictions, here the restrictions in the form of less water than wished, are forced equally upon the (groups of) users. It is at the user's discretion to solve these restrictions either by growing 'dry' crops or leave part of their land fallow. (This is contrary to the crop sanctions where actual localization is in most cases by areas and not by a %age of each farm.)

The point of departure of water sanctions is the equal division of water. Of course collusion, power pressure etc. always will play a role where farmers try to obtain more water than allocated. Due to the fixed structures, these sources of struggles and conflicts are, at least on paper, reduced to the level of the village and tertiary unit.

Moreover the fixed structures are more transparent and the operation more understandable than in case of adjustable structures.

Finally an important advantage of water sanctions can be noted for case D (run-of-the-river schemes constituting a large part of the irrigated areas in the world). As we have seen, localization is often based on 1:4 or 1:5 dry year river flows which are much lower than the actual flows [8]. In the case of proportional division however, the actual river flows are diverted constituting a considerable extra volume of water for crop growing. Here an important aspect is the water holding capacity of the soil rendering a buffer function for irregular supplies. (In this context a remarkable feature of irrigation engineering should be noted: where in rainfed farming the vagaries of rainfall are - from sheer necessity - accepted, irregular irrigation supplies are seldom tolerated. Perry [8] citing Naryanamurthy indicates furthermore that rationing Warabandi systems farmers underirrigate in order to better exploit expected rainfall).

Another solution alleviating some of the aforementioned problems is the creation of intermediate reservoirs in the irrigation system. (Not further discussed.)

4   Concluding observations

After this review of possible policy options on how to allocate and distribute irrigation water, the consequences of these options on the appurtenant technologies, and the testing of these options to different supply situations, the following observations can be made.

The majority of Government administered small holder irrigation schemes in the world have centrally managed systems with manually operated water division structures. Clearly most of these systems operate well below expectation and many authors assent that this technology and its mode of operation simply can not work (cf Plusquellec et al. [3]: p. 24: "... a schedule defined at the central office may never materialise in the field as intended." and p. 5: "Extended gravity irrigation schemes with manually operated gates and control works rarely work, despite all efforts to improve irrigation management and the capacity of staff.")

In this context, the endeavours to introduce crop-based irrigation for these type of schemes should be considered as fallacies. Moreover to find solutions by turning over to farmers an inappropriate type of technology should be questioned.

At this point we arrive at the dilemma: should we try to find a solution on the basis of equity at the cost of flexibility or should the answer be found in automation?

During the last decade a number of authors did advocate the introduction of automation [2][3]. Most of the authors however implicitly assume sufficient supply (upstream storage reservoirs) to render automation possible (significantly the introduction to an important symposium on automation [2] states: "The reliability of the supply in its broad sense of the capacity of a major reservoir, ... is not the concern of this symposium.")

We have seen in section 3 that there is no need for automation in case of sufficient supply for unrestricted demand. We also discussed the problems encountered when crop restriction should be applied in case of insufficient supply, rendering automation problematic. The condition that restricted demand should never exceed the available supply leads furthermore to underutilisation of water in case of run-of-the-river projects.

The above mentioned dilemma, therefore, appears to be deceptive: for the majority of the projects in the world without storage facilities no other option appears to be available than some type of proportional scheduling. This policy principle based on equity deserves attention from a social as well as a technological point of view when designing either rehabilitation or new projects.

Finally, the message of this paper is applicable to irrigation in terms of water allocation strategy as well as implementation.

5   References

1.   FAO (1982). *Organisation, Operation and Maintenance of Irrigation Schemes,* Irrigation and Drainage Paper 40. FAO, Rome
2.   Zimbelman, D.D. (1987). *Planning, Operation, Rehabilitation and Automation of Irrigation Delivery Systems*, American Society of Civil Engineers, New York.
3.   Plusquellec, H., Burt, C. and Wolter, H.W. (1994). *Modern Water Control in Irrigation*, World Bank Technical Paper 246, Washington.
4.   Mollinga, P.P. (1996). *On the waterfront. Water distribution, technology and agrarian change in a South Indian large scale canal irrigation system* (Ph.D. thesis). Forthcoming.
5.   Jurriens, M. (1993). *Protective Irrigation: Essentials and Implications,* 15th ICID Congress, The Hague, The Netherlands.
6.   IIMI (1989). *Efficient Irrigation Management and System Turnover in Indonesia,* Final Report, Vol. 2. Colombo, Sri Lanka.
7.   Burns, R.E. (1993). *Irrigated Rice Culture in Monsoon Asia: the Search for an Effective Water Control Technology*, World Development Vol. 21, no. 5, pp. 771 - 789 Pergamon Press Ltd, Great Britain.
8.   Perry, C.J. (1993). *Irrigation in Conditions of Water Shortage.* mimeo

TO METER OR NOT TO METER; THAT IS THE QUESTION

To meter or not to meter?

H. WESTERLUND
The Swedish Water & Wastewater Association, Stockholm, Sweden

Abstract
The intention of this paper is to analyse the pro and cons of water metering. In certain countries such as the United Kingdom, where metering is not common, discussions are under way as to whether metering should be introduced; whereas in other countries such as Sweden, where almost every water board has introduced metering, some people argue in favour of a change to this regime.
Keywords: demand management, domestic water, industrial water, meter, metering experience, water tariffs.

1 Introduction

To meter or not to meter; that is the question. Or is it a question? As always, the question certainly has no one answer, that is generally-applicable in all countries, or perhaps I should say to all preconditions. The answer does in fact vary widely from case to case and subsequently needs to be evaluated before any clear opinion is expressed. Certainly not only technical criteria should be borne in mind.

Metering water could always be justified if it is in short supply, even if the cost of the water consists mainly of capital investment and is therefore independent of the actual amount of water used.

On the other hand, if the amount of water supplied is greater than the demand, there is justification for not metering in order to keep up the flow and subsequently the quality of the water supplied to consumers. The issue is, however, the extent to which consumers should be encouraged to deplete natural resources which, viewed from a global perspective, are scarce. In other words, which signals should be sent to the general public? To what extent should technical and financial considerations be

Water Policy: Allocation and management in practice. Edited by P. Howsam and R.C. Carter.
Published in 1996 by E & FN Spon. ISBN 0 419 21650 2

allowed to affect the efforts to bring environmental awareness to the public and to encourage them to take part in the overall Agenda 21 work on a local level?

2   Demand management

With few exceptions, people do not usually live where water supplies are to be found. For this reason satisfying the demand for water is usually no an easy task. Balancing the situation in this way is also much more expensive than demand management. The issue of whether or not to introduce water metering is also very much a matter of finding a tool for demand management. Demand could, however, be managed in various ways. Besides metering, it might also be possible to install facilities that use less water, such as WCs that use only a couple of litres of water per flush or showers that use less water. Managing demand in this manner, however, would necessitate the introduction of extremely strict building standards for both new and existing buildings, which would mean having to replace a huge number of existing facilities with new ones.

Most water industries in the Western world charge consumers for water; and even if such companies are under public control, I have never heard of anyone who does not want to gain the greatest financial benefit from the business. Convincing people to use less water and subsequently earning less money, is hardly the best way to create a supplier-customer relationship built on trust. It is similar to situations in which energy-generating companies try to make people more energy-conscious and use less energy. The only criterion for a situation like this is when the utility is unable to meet demand without making heavy investments.

If anyone here should argue against metering water supplies, it should be me: I live in a country with a plentiful supply of water. Some people in Sweden have even considered exporting water to Northern Africa and the Middle East.

There is currently a widespread consensus of opinion among the water utilities in Sweden that metering should be done. As metering reduces the consumption, this is a sort of contradiction as there   is a technical requirement to increase consumption due to oversized pipes and, of course, a wish to increase revenues for more sold water. The reason for a need of increased consumption due to oversized pipes is, that the water quality could be unacceptable if the retention time of the water in the pipes is too long. There were two reasons for oversizing the pipes: the first was that the size of the water mains was originally defined by requirements of the fire authorities. Since the water boards are financed by water charges, while fire brigades are not, the issue of whether the fire brigades or the district councils should pay for the oversized water mains is now under discussion.

The other reason for oversizing the mains was that a million new homes were built in Sweden in the 1960s and 1970s and, as usual, there was a tendency to overestimate all the statistics both concerning the number of new homes in the future as the figure of water consumption per capita.

Water consumption at that time amounted to approximately 220 l/PE a day and was expected to rise to some 250 l/PE a day around this time. Instead, consumption has fallen to 200 l/PE a day due to the effect of the combined measures mentioned here, and it would appear that consumption is still on the decline.

As a comparison, the consumption is currently five times higher or 1 m3 per PE a day in a small Swedish town, where they have chosen not to meter!

One reason for managing demand, which is obvious to utilities responsible for both water supply and waste water treatment, is that a reduced flow of water consequently means more efficient waste water treatment, as well as lower costs in general for running waste waterworks and systems.

3   Metering as incentive for saving water

Metering could primarily be a tool for keeping down water consumption where water resources are scarce but it is also the only way for managing supply correctly as leakages on the network are more or less impossible to evaluate without metering. In a country like Sweden, where there are large water supplies, the reasons for metering are often other than for managing demand. There are even those, who argue, to what extent consumers should be encouraged to save water at all. We should not forget, that the water utilities actually also make their money on selling water. With metering, there is normally a fixed tariff and a flexible tariff and with a larger consumption the utilities subsequently earn more. The relation between the fix and the flexible tariff is however normally the other way around compared with the real costs as the costs to a fairly small degree is depending on the amount of consumed water.

The saving for a water utility for reduced water consumption is the marginal cost for production, distribution, collection and treatment of water. In Sweden this marginal cost is less than 3p per m3. A typical flexible rate in Sweden is currently £1 per m3 exclusive VAT for both water supply and waste water treatment. This means that a reduced consumption will result in a higher cost as the major part of the cost not is depending on the amount of supplied water. Due to more efficient water installations and energy awareness, the trend in Sweden is currently reduced consumption and subsequently several water utilities are worried about how to design tariffs, that are more transparent.

If we look at the sewage treatment, reduced water consumption means less discharges of phosphorous and nitrogen to the recipients but not directly proportionally. 10% less water consumption means between 3 and 4% less discharges and at 20% less water consumption the same figure will be something between 5 and 8%.

A reduced turn-over of water in the network could as a matter of fact also be damaging for the over dimensioned pipes as we are currently trying to reduce the use of chlorine for protection of the water quality. To compensate this, many Swedish water utilities do currently have to flush the pipes, which requires man power and subsequently financial
resources.

Reduced water flows could also result in reduced capacity to transport matters in the sewers. In the long run, reduced water consumption could lead to the need of investments for new water pipes and sewers.

When it comes to the use of chemicals for separating phosphates, the need for that will be reduced due to lower water flows even if the requirement of chemicals mostly is depending on the amount of incoming nutrients. In order to make an environmental impact, it would be better to reduce the amount of chemicals and other not wanted matters in the waste water than actually reduce the amount of consumed water.

This is very much a Swedish viewpoint but even when saving water not is necessary, metering is still a useful tool for managing supply and for having a proper control over the network.

4   Water tariffs in Sweden

In spite of the fact that Sweden has extremely large supplies of water, practically all the water consumed is metered. The cost of producing water and treating waste water is between 7% and 15% of overall costs, depending on the amount of water involved. The variable cost element is primarily energy-related and, to a certain extent, a small quantity of chemicals. These resources are not unlimited but Swedish water utilities are now actually able to generate more energy than they consume by recovering energy for district heating from the waste water using heat pumps and by utilizing biogas for generating electricity and for other purposes – as fuel for buses, for example.

Sweden's largest waste water treatment works, the Rya works in Gothenburg, for instance, generates 20 times more energy than it consumes. This does not, however, justify unlimited consumption of water, as alternative uses for energy can always be found.

Given the water boards' well-developed energy efficiency and gradual reduction of the amount of chemicals used, the real cost of water at present definitely has nothing to do with the amount of water sold. However, maintaining public awareness of the necessity to restrict water consumption is regarded as crucial.

Permitting consumption of unlimited water amounts would seem very strange to the general public at a time when we are working very hard to convince them to take part in the creation of a sustainable society. The trend is, therefore, to operate tariffs that do not mirror the cost situation but are roughly the opposite to the mentioned cost figures in order to encourage people to be more aware of the importance of using natural resources. It could, in fact, even be justifiable to have just a single variable rate.

One crucial criterion is, of course, whether there should be a total market economy approach or an approach which supports the commitment of the public to a future sustainable society. The first case could, of course, lead to a development quite contrary to what I think is required in the long run.

A typical Swedish water consumption tariff for an average sized town would be some £80 per year for a one family house plus £1.50 per m3. Over the year, the total cost will end up around £420, of which £80 represents reinvestments, £190 capital costs and £150 maintenance.

The costs are distributed in roughly the following way:

maintenance	25%
reinvestments	20%
capital costs	45%
storm water	15%

Two-thirds of this cost go towards waste water, one-third towards water supply. The average annual meter cost for a single family dwelling is £20 for installation and maintenance, plus £10 for meter reading and billing.

The cost for other customers could be 50% higher. On top of this there is an annual meter fee, depending on the type of meter, of between £10 and £100. These costs are added up to the total fix annual charge of in average £80. Customers then just pay for water by the amount they use. If consumers' awareness of their utilisation of natural resources such as water were to lead to a reduction in their consumption of it, this could have an adverse effect for them in that the water boards would then be forced to increase their tariffs. This is very much the situation in which several Swedish water utilities find themselves. A regime with free supply of water, in other words with no metering or just a fixed tariff with a zero marginal cost, supports the people who use lots of water, whereas consumers who are more careful regarding their water consumption are penalised. This is at least not a system of which I, in my position, would approve.

For a typical Swedish water board with a connection of some 100 000 PE, it would be possible to bring down the cost of water services by some £60 000 if the water consumed for domestic purposes were to be reduced by 50%. However, the cost of maintaining the mains would increase by some £20 000. Together with the reduced sales of water services, this would have the overall effect of forcing up the water tariff by approximately 50p per m^3 or, for argument's sake, 25%. In other words, encouraging people to reduce their water consumption in return for higher water tariffs presents the water utilities with a sort of pedagogical dilemma! The only way to succeed in this mission is to make consumers more environmentally aware in general and subsequently create an acceptance for this effect.

The arguments above, that a reduced consumption could lead to higher tariffs is built on the assumption, that also higher consumption subsequently must lead to lower tariffs. This is however not always the case.

An increased consumption could very well lead to the need of more investments and end up with a requirement of a totally higher tariff. To assume, that lower consumption absolutely will lead to higher tariffs, is in other words not correct.

Normally, there are various fees depending on the size of the meter. Some utilities have however changed to just one fee independent on the size of meter. This is then a way to give a discount to large consumers.

Many countries have regulated water charges, that do not allow the utilities to do profits. This could especially be an obstacle when there is a need to fund water and sewage surplus from good times to bad times.

A regime, to handle for instance dry summers in Sweden, is now suggested in a new Water Act, which will allow utilities to have different charges over the year in order to reduce consumption over for instance dry seasons.

5   To meter or not to meter?

5.1 Reasons for not metering water supplies

The reasons for not metering water supplies could be summarized as follows:

1. Unnecessary cost of installation, and maintenance of meters plus reading in areas where plenty of water is available.
2. When the consumption of water on a *per capita* basis is no longer on the increase, the metering incentive could perhaps be discussed.
3. High levels of water consumption where pipes are oversized could be a way to ensure the quality of the water. The alternative to greater consumption would be to flush out the mains pipes, which would require a certain amount of manpower and could seem very strange to the public when they see water being flushed down the drain.
4. It could be argued whether failing to permit tariffs to reflect actual costs is honest.

5.2 Reasons for metering water supplies
The reasons for metering water supplies could be summarized as follows:

1. It is important to show the general public that the consumption of water, like that of other natural resources, should conform to the prerequisites for a sustainable society; that is to say, water is not produced freely and without the need for other resources (energy and – normally – chemicals). This should be a particularly important consideration for countries which have signed the Rio 21 treaty.
2. Sensible utilisation of water in areas where water is plentiful increases the potential for supplying water to areas where this resource is scarce.
3. Even if there is plenty of water available, an increase in demand could result in the need for new investments in the entire piping system, not only by waterworks, but also by sewage works (which also could lead to the need of higher tariffs).
4. The lower the level of water consumption, the more efficient and economical waste water treatment will be (the greater the quantity of insoluble materials, the less efficient the treatment and the greater the overall discharge of BOD, phosphates, suspended solids and other matter).
5. The greater the water flow, the more chemicals and energy are used – not only in waterworks but also in sewage works and pump stations.
6. Without water metering, it is impossible to assess leaks in the system. This means, that it is a good idea to meter, even if the purpose not is to keep down consumption.
7. To cope with seasonal demand of changes in climate.

6   Costs

When metering or not is considered, it is imperial to know all the costs involved for water supply. They could be divided into:

- Operating costs
- Financial costs, mainly depreciation and interest
- Taxes and various levies

The operating costs consist of a number of parts like:

- Personnel
- Energy
- Treatment products
- Machines and vehicles
- Maintenance of buildings and equipment
- External professional services like consultants, contractors etc
- Administrative over-head expenses

Taxes and levies could consist of:

> Tax on profit
> Tax on assets
> Property tax
> Environmental levies
> Charges for central authorities

If the water utility is a limited company, there will also be costs for equity remuneration but as well incomes beside the water charges like annual return on assets.

7   Industrial considerations

Industry plays a certain role in this instance which should not be forgotten. In Sweden, the goal is to make industry more accountable for the environmental costs attributable to it for the handling of water and, in particular, waste water.

Industry is currently responsible for 8% of the revenue paid to the water boards in Sweden. We are currently working on a new directive for industrial water tariffs which are designed to be simple and to remain stable on a long-term basis. These tariffs must, however, include charges for hazardous industrial compounds in waste water that ends up in the sewage sludge. We are currently creating a recycling system for this in association with the Swedish Farmers' Association and the Swedish Environmental Protection Agency. As the Swedish water utilities both provide water and treat waste water, our water industry is responsible for recycling water, nutrients and solids.

8   Experience

The Swedish Water and Wastewater Association, of which I am the Chief Executive, has approximately 300 members. Of these only seven have done away with water metering. The outcome of this has with some exceptions not meant increased consumption over the major part of the year - this could probably be linked to great public awareness of water as a natural resource. There has, however, been an increase in water consumption, particularly during hot and dry summers, which of course is the most susceptible season.

The reason for this increased seasonal consumption has been investigated and it is quite clear, that this is due to garden irrigation. This has resulted in irrigation bans in such cases. In general, it would appear that total water consumption increases by some 5% if water metering is phased out.

There has been some analysis carried out in Sweden in order to evaluate price elasticity. It is quite clear, that this is low and that the picture differs a lot between different water utilities. There also seems to be many other circumstances that affect this fairly low correlation between price and consumption. I have already mentioned some of them.

There is quite clear evidence to prove, that water metering is usually an efficient aid to reducing water consumption. In Copenhagen, for instance, the consumption of water is now decreasing sharply, and they actually expect the consumption *per capita* to fall to 110 litres by the year 2001.

9   Summary

It would be wrong to hold a firm, general opinion on whether water should be metered or not. The most important thing which I think should be stressed is the fact that each individual water utility or water company should make their own decision because of the criteria which apply to each individual case.

Since discussions on water metering are in progress in many countries and some, like the United Kingdom, to a large extent are considering installing meters, it could perhaps be of some value to know that in a country like Sweden, where water resources are almost unlimited, water is still metered and will remain so even in the future. Metering is also an efficient way to keep control of the water flows in the network. The purpose for metering does in other words not necessarily be to keep down consumption.

In conclusion, it is much more important to regard water metering from an ecological point of view rather than in purely financial terms. In my opinion, the general public must always be given a clear message – that water is a natural resource that cannot be consumed in unlimited amounts. Metering is a simple and obvious way of broadcasting this message.

EFFECTIVE AND TRANSPARENT STRATEGIES FOR COMMUNITY WATER SUPPLY PROGRAMMES IN DEVELOPING COUNTRIES
Strategies for community water supply

R.C. CARTER, S.F. TYRREL and P. HOWSAM
Water Management Department, Silsoe College, Cranfield University, UK

Abstract
Community water supply (CWS) programmes in developing countries form an important part of the implementation of national water policies. Many CWS programmes fail to perform to their full potential, and are difficult to evaluate, because of a lack of clearly expressed, quantified, and user-centred objectives. The paper contributes to the development of effective programme strategy by proposing such a generalised framework of objectives as a model for any CWS programme. The paper goes on to show how adoption of such a framework of objectives can lead to the identification of a balanced set of programme activities and the corresponding staffing requirements. Clear thinking about programme strategy leads in turn to more effective achievement of intended impact, and more straightforward demonstration of programme performance through the process of evaluation.
Keywords: community water supply, evaluation, objectives, strategy.

1 Community water supply and national water policy

National water policies in developing countries usually put high priority on rural domestic water supply. Community water supply (CWS) programmes, which form part of the strategy to deliver this service, aim to reduce the time and energy expended in water collection, and to improve public health. In order for such programmes to bring about these beneficial impacts, three conditions must be fulfilled. First, new (more reliable, closer, cleaner) water sources must be <u>constructed</u> to high standards; second, these new sources must continue to <u>function</u>; and third, they must be <u>utilised</u> effectively.

Water Policy: Allocation and management in practice. Edited by P. Howsam and R.C. Carter. Published in 1996 by E & FN Spon. ISBN 0 419 21650 2

2   Evaluation of CWS programmes

Whether CWS programmes are implemented by Government, by international agencies, or by non-Governmental Organisations (NGOs), both Government and funding organisations need to evaluate the performance of such programmes.

Evaluation of the performance of CWS programmes should, ideally, attempt to measure the impact of cleaner, more accessible water on the public, directly. However, the methodological difficulties associated with impact evaluation are immense, and it is now generally recognised that less direct methods can be used. If clean, accessible, reliable, water supplies are both functioning and utilised as planned, then it may be assumed that the intended benefits (on time-saving and public health) will follow.

The functioning and utilisation of improved water sources form the focus of WHO's Minimum Evaluation Procedure [1] for water supply and sanitation projects. This procedure is meant to be used after the completion of construction, and applied to water supply, sanitation, and hygiene education elements of the project.

In the case of on-going programmes, there is frequently an over-emphasis by programme managers on new source construction. Consequently even WHO's minimum targets of source functioning and utilisation take second place to the programme's target construction rates. Moreover, it is often construction and capital expenditure rates which impress funding organisations and politicians, and so monitoring and evaluation which concentrate on these statistics are often felt to be highly relevant to donors and Government. In this context any evaluation study which tries to go further than reporting programme outputs (new sources constructed) and spending rates runs into difficulties.

3   Programme objectives are often unclear

Difficulties of programme evaluation are often symptomatic of more fundamental programme management weaknesses. In particular, this paper focuses on the inadequacy of programme objectives, encountered by the authors in a number of recent evaluation studies.

If a CWS programme's only objective is to construct new sources (at as rapid a rate as possible), then its entire strategy will be focused on this target. Programme activities, staffing, and expenditure will all be construction- or hardware-related. Functioning of constructed sources, utilisation of sources, and beneficial programme impact all take lower priority. If, however, functioning, utilisation and impact are given explicit and high priority, then programme strategy should reflect this. A much wider range of programme activities and staff will include both hardware and software (education, training and capacity building) elements, and, despite the additional time which will need to be devoted to software aspects, the programme is much more likely to achieve long-lasting and beneficial impact.

The paper sets out the argument for adopting a framework of verifiable objectives, as an essential strategic component of CWS programmes in developing countries. Such a framework of objectives underpins and justifies programme methodology and staffing, so leading to more effective programmes which can be readily evaluated.

4   Examples of inadequate objectives

Programme objectives may be inadequate in two ways:

- they may be insufficiently focused, and imply relative improvements rather than explicit, absolute, targets. CWS programmes commonly aim to "supply clean water", without stating the water quality parameters involved, or their target levels. Similarly, provision of "better access" is often promised, without quantification of time or distance targets. In the usual absence of pre-programme baseline studies, relative targets are both meaningless and impossible to evaluate later.
- there may be a focus on design levels and supply targets, rather than on utilisation. For example, a supply target of, say, 25 l/h/d may be stated or implied; it is far more important however to ensure that this amount of water is actually consumed. The supply target has implications for the design process and the capital cost of the scheme; whilst the same figure as a utilisation target has broader implications for community education, as well as for other related design aspects (for example the necessary proximity of source to user).

The lack of clearly stated and agreed objectives does not necessarily mean that programmes are making no useful impact on the communities with which they work. However, we would argue that programme strategy is far more likely to be effective, and impact as intended, if objectives are clear, quantified, verifiable, and user-centred. Moreover, programme performance and impact are more likely to be demonstrable, through the evaluation process.

5   Inadequate objectives result in incomplete methodologies

If objectives are unclear or incomplete, then programme methodologies (activities, staffing, and budgets) are also likely to be incomplete and ineffective. The most common expression of this is in relatively young programmes, where the priority is to establish a strong construction capability. It is understandable at this stage if community capacity-building, planning of cost-recovery, hygiene education, maintenance planning and training of caretakers, take second place to the construction of new sources. The problem emerges as the programme matures, and construction targets continue to take precedence over issues of sustainability and impact, ie. the functioning and utilisation of the new sources. Programmes in Eritrea, Ethiopia, and Uganda, recently evaluated by the first author, and ranging in age from less than one year to over ten years, all show this emphasis on construction targets at the expense of targets relating to long-term sustainability and impact, and all lack clearly stated programme objectives.

We would argue that a comprehensive and quantified set of user-centred objectives, such as those set out below, ensures that there is a correct balance between construction (hardware) and community aspects (software); and that this balance will be reflected in the programme activities, programme staffing, and expenditure.

6   Developing effective and transparent strategies

Assuming that the argument for clear, quantified, programme objectives is accepted, two further assertions follow. First, such sets of objectives are to some extent programme-specific; each programme needs to develop the detail in such a way as to reflect the peculiarities of its physical, social, and economic environment. Second, the set of programme objectives needs to be developed and agreed in consultation with the community involved.

This is not the place to rehearse the arguments for community participation (CP) in water supply programmes in developing countries. Whether or not CP is seen as desirable for wider social goals (capacity-building, community empowerment), the hard fact is that if the community does not own, operate, maintain and pay for its water supply, then no-one else will. In developing countries, Governments and most NGOs simply lack the financial resources and legal and regulatory frameworks to sustain services to growing populations. The World Bank's recent study [2] of 121 rural water supply projects, asked "to what degree does participation contribute to project effectiveness?", and concluded: "the results are clear: beneficiary participation contributed significantly to project effectiveness ....". Sustainability depends on community participation.

Nevertheless, we would argue that at some point consultation and negotiation with the community needs to be translated into an agreed strategy, in order to provide the basis on which the external support agency (ESA: Government, technical assistance, or NGO) can function effectively. We do not argue against the notions of flexibility and dialogue, but strongly believe that without clear strategies (consisting of objectives, activities, staffing, and budgeting), ESAs frequently fail to be as effective as they could be.

There is here a potential culture-clash. The community may know what it wants (although it is all too easy for outsiders naively to imagine that "the community" is a homogeneous body with clear channels of internal communication and effective means of resolving conflicts), but it will almost certainly not express those aspirations in quantified terms. On the other hand the ESA, to be an effectively managed organisation needs quantified objectives and a clear strategy for action. The results of dialogue with the community need to be translated into a form which the ESA can use in its strategic planning and effective organisational management.

The general model for which we would argue would be a formal agreement between the ESA and the community (to the extent of a written contract), setting out objectives and programme activities, and the responsibilities of both parties to the agreement. In the case of an ESA which is not part of Government (eg foreign technical assistance provided by a lender or donor, or an NGO), the programme objectives should of course be consistent with Government policy guidelines.

Recently, Carter et al [3] proposed that the preceding argument regarding programme objectives, activities, and staffing could be applied to well-handpump projects. The paper proposed a generalised set of verifiable objectives appropriate to such projects. It is argued that such objectives could be applied to any community water supply technology and as such they have been modified slightly here (Table 1).

It is not the intention that the values used in Table 1 should be considered to be fixed or applicable in all circumstances. If for example, local hydrogeological conditions meant that water quality could not realistically be expected to reach < 10 faecal coliforms / 100 ml, then a revised target should be used. Inflexible objectives would also preclude community inputs and this is clearly not desirable. Rather, the merit of the objectives is in their quantified and verifiable nature, not in the target values themselves.

Table 1   Proposed objectives of community water supply programmes in developing countries (after Carter et al [3])

Overall Aims
The aim of such projects and programmes is to bring about health improvements, and reductions in time and effort spent in water hauling. These benefits are to be achieved through increased consumption of water, of satisfactory quality, from sources close to the users' homes. These goals should be achieved at acceptable capital and recurrent costs.

Specifically, the objectives should be:

- to bring about per capita daily consumption of 15-25 litres, of which a minimum of 15 litres per head per day should be used in the home;
- to provide one water source for every 250 users;
- to reduce time spent in water-hauling to a maximum of one woman-hour per day;
- to bring about significant improvements in water-hauling technology;
- to achieve a water quality target of 10 faecal coliforms per 100ml at the point of use;
- to reduce periods of zero-supply to no more than 2% (7 days per year);
- to supply these services at a per capita capital cost of no more than £15;
- to supply these services at a per capita recurrent cost of no more than £1 per annum.

The objectives set out in Table 1 are deliberately user-centred. For example, in relation to water quantity, the target is a certain actual rate of use; the water quality target is at point of use, not point of supply only; and the time-saving target is expressed in terms of the consumer's maximum expenditure of time on water hauling.
    Because of this user focus, the appropriate strategy to meet the objectives requires far more than simply construction activity. For these objectives to be achieved, it is necessary that the programme includes not only high quality design and construction, but also the establishment of an effective maintenance system, hygiene education (among other things to encourage water usage and cleanliness of household water storage jars), and the development of an agreed cost-recovery system.
    In the case of well-handpump programmes described by Carter et al [3] , it is shown how clear programme objectives enable programme activities and staffing to be derived. To achieve the objectives listed in Table 1, programme activities and corresponding staffing are set out in Table 2 (for more detail see the paper by Carter et al).   Similar tables could be drawn up for programmes involving other

technologies. Staffing is probably the most programme-specific aspect of the entire argument in this paper, since, especially in small programmes, multiple tasks can be undertaken by multi-disciplinary staff.

Table 2   Programme activities and staffing requirements for well-handpump water supply programmes in developing countries

Programme Activities	Programme Staff
• Coordination, procurement, management and monitoring	Programme management and administration
• Health and hygiene education	Health team
• Community mobilisation and training, and implementation of cost-recovery system	Social work team
• Site selection	Hydrogeological team
• Drilling and well completion	Drilling team
• Implementation of maintenance system	Pump maintenance team

7   Conclusions

Developing country Governments rightly desire better health and living conditions for their rural populations. One expression of this aspiration is in national water policies which give high priority to improved rural water services. Community water supply programmes form part of the strategy for delivering such services.

For community water supply programmes in less developed countries to achieve maximum impact, three necessary conditions must be fulfilled: new sources must (a) be constructed to high standards, (b) continue to function, and (c) be utilised effectively.

Programmes which lack clearly stated and quantified objectives in relation to functioning and utilisation - such as the quantified, user-centred objectives set out in Table 1 - tend to judge themselves, and allow of evaluation by others, only in terms of construction and expenditure targets. Such programmes consequently fail to achieve the full possible beneficial impacts of the technology which they introduce.

Clear, quantified, user-centred objectives, developed for each programme, and in full dialogue with the community, allow the identification and inclusion of the correct mix of hardware and software activities and staffing, in order to achieve maximum programme impact (for example see Table 2).

Moreover, programmes with clear strategies, consisting of quantified, user-centred objectives, an appropriate mix of community-focused and construction activities, and the corresponding human resources, are readily evaluated, and their impact is therefore readily demonstrable to funding agencies and Government.

8   References

1.   WHO (1983) Minimum Evaluation Procedure for water supply and sanitation projects. World Health Organisation, Geneva.
2.   Narayan, D (1995) The Contribution of People's Participation: evidence from 121 rural water supply projects. Environmentally Sustainable Development Occasional Paper Series No 1, World Bank, Washington DC, USA.
3.   Carter, R..C., Tyrrel, S.F., and Howsam, P.H. (1996) Strategies for Handpump Water Supply Programmes in Less-Developed Countries. Journal of the Chartered Institution of Water and Environmental Management, Vol. 10, No. 2, pp130-136.

WATER USE EFFICIENCY IN DELTA EGYPT: THE MIS-MATCHED PATTERNS OF SUPPLY AND DEMAND

Water use efficiency in delta Egypt

L. RADWAN
School of Geography and Environmental Management, Middlesex University, UK

Abstract
Most experts agree that Egypt now faces a serious and worsening water deficit and that it is increasingly likely that it will not only have limited ability to expand the irrigated area but may have to consider reducing the overall area under irrigation. This study looks at the efficiency of irrigation water distribution and use at the village level. Through a quantitative analysis of the operation of the irrigation distribution system within a particular field study region it indicates how far present assumptions of water requirements are accurate and how far the existing mechanisms are effective in ensuring an adequate supply reaches individual farm canals (mesqa). The resultant patterns of supply are contrasted with farmers' actual use patterns to determine where wastage occurs.

On the basis of this analysis, an attempt is made to identify how far conflict has resulted from failings in technical specifications of the irrigation system and how far from failings in the administrative system governing its operation. It is argued that although the Egyptian Government exerts control over the operation of the irrigation system at the macro-level, it does not effectively exercise social control at the village level.

Keywords: irrigation efficiency, peasant/state relations, supply and demand patterns, water requirements.

1 Introduction: the regional setting

1.1 Macro-level characteristics

Following the completion of the Aswan High Dam in 1968 it was widely felt that man had finally overcome the destructive pattern of annual floods and created a

Water Policy: Allocation and management in practice. Edited by P. Howsam and R.C. Carter.
Published in 1996 by E & FN Spon. ISBN 0 419 21650 2

reliable storage capacity to overcome long-term fluctuations. However recent trends suggest the possibility of a significant decrease in the river's overall discharge, or a need to reassess the periodic cycles of surplus and deficit [1][2]. Indeed given Egypt's current population growth trends and the fact that the nation now imports more than half of its food requirements, one could argue that Egypt already faces a severe annual water shortage of around 20 billion cubic metres. In addition a combination of economic, political and environmental constraints have prevented the Sudan from fully exploiting its allocated quota and other riparians from making any significant use of the Nile waters (Fig. 1). Under the terms of the 1959 Nile waters agreement, Egypt was to receive 55.5 billion cubic metres and the Sudan 18.5 billion cubic metres, as measured at Aswan. It is not unreasonable to expect that, as population pressures and food requirements grow, so too will moves to develop agricultural potential along the Nile in many of the upstream riparian states. The threat posed by such possible reductions in available water, raises the possibility that Egypt may not now only have limited ability to expand its irrigated area but that it may, at some point in time, need to consider a reduction in the overall irrigated area.

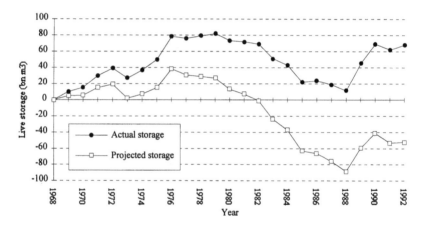

Fig. 1. Lake Nasser live storage given increased Sudanese utilisation

1.2 Scope of study

Given this backdrop of serious and worsening water deficit in Egypt it seems anomalous to find that a large %age of agricultural land is suffering from varying degrees of water logging and associated salinity problem [3]. At the same time it is not uncommon for farmers to complain of shortages either in specific regions or locations along canals, or at particular times within the irrigation cycle (seasonal or daily).

This paper seeks to illustrate that such a situation occurs primarily as a result of the inefficient use of the available water supply and the over application of water at the local level. Through a case study of one region I have sought to outline the causes and extent of wastage/inefficiencies in the distribution of irrigation water in rural Egypt. By studying water use as a simple supply/demand relationship, it was possible to locate where wastage and inefficiency were occurring. This was seen to be primarily on the supply side, although the inflexibility of farmer demand was also seen to be a significant factor in the mis-match of supply and demand patterns.

1.3 Location
The data for the analysis of irrigation supply and demand patterns are derived from the author's fieldwork in the administrative region of Fisha al-Sughra in the mid Delta [4]. The study mesqa, Um Aisha, can be regarded as representative of the majority of canals in the region and the area in general reflects the mixed cropping pattern common over much of the Delta. Measurements of flows along the principal distributary canals in the region indicated that the inflows to the majority of mesqa in the region were not dissimilar to the observed flows along Um Aisha. Other studies of water use efficiency have produced corroborative findings, indicating that many of the problems discussed here are common to other regions of the Delta [5][6].

2   Problems in the control and distribution of irrigation supplies

2.1 Assumptions and mechanisms governing irrigation requirements
This study highlights the lack of integration between the rigid patterns of supply administered by the irrigation ministry (MPWWR) and the informal farmer patterns of demand. Attention here is focused upon a quantification of supply and demand patterns to illustrate the extent of wastage and inefficiency within the present system and the constraints this places upon the co-operative communal scheduling of water use patterns. Problems associated with the patterns of supply can be divided into two categories. Firstly the fundamental assumptions upon which delta water distribution systems are based and secondly, failings in the allocative mechanisms governing supply.

   On the basis of data collected by the Ministry of Agriculture (MOA) assumptions are made concerning agricultural land area, cropping patterns and planting and harvesting dates. The nature of data collection, conducted primarily through the local co-operatives. introduces into these assumptions a number of errors. Firstly land area was observed to be overestimated to the order of 5% along most canals due to inadequate updating of land records either through negligence or, as was observed, due to corrupt practices governing the transferral of agricultural land to residential land, whereby illegal building was overlooked on payment of an appropriate fee. Secondly there was observed to be only a general recording of farmers cropping patterns, consisting of the principal crops (maize, wheat, berseem, cotton). This appeared to be a legacy of the enforced quota system which, although now of reduced importance, has led farmers to supply inaccurate data on their specific cropping patterns and encouraged co-operative officials to concentrate on recording areas for a narrow range of specified crops. Finally it was noted that the optimal planting and harvesting dates were assumed to be valid across the various regions, yet observations in the field indicated that actual planting and harvesting dates would often be delayed or put forward by anything up to one month as a result of institutional factors such as the late supply of seed and other inputs or various localised factors.

   Data collected in the manner described above is used by the MOA for national projections of cropped areas and patterns and by the MPWWR for calculating total crop water requirements and as such appears in published figures of national estimates. However at the same time officials at the MPWWR are aware that whilst in general terms such data might give an adequate picture of national water requirements, they accept that such figures mask a high degree of error. As a result the MPWWR has a policy of committing releases into main canals well in excess of the requirements which would be calculated from the available data. These releases are controlled through the maintenance of specific canal levels, ensuring that during any particular on-rotation water is available to a predetermined height. Thus whilst the ministry is aware in general terms of the water released into the main canals, it has no knowledge of particular releases into lower level canals and no measurements are made of how accurately water is divided between minor distributary canals nor of the quantity of through-flow passing from the system to the drains. Detailed knowledge of releases into lower level canals is further obscured due to the imprecision in recording of water levels. My own measurements of water levels indicated that the official levels recorded for both of the distributary canals within the study area (Shahabiya and Danduf) displayed a high degree of error.

3   Patterns of irrigation supply and demand

Given the above inaccuracies in the calculation of irrigation requirements it was necessary to observe the actual operation of the supply system at this level to determine how far this adequately met the pattern of required discharges. Measurements of actual inflow to mesqa Um Aisha were therefore compared to observed farmer use patterns and both contrasted with the total water requirements calculated from local data of cropping patterns, planting and harvesting dates and observed efficiencies (Fig. 2).

It is however important to note that there are a significant number of mesqa, or stretches of mesqa, where water supplies are less than adequate, often as a result of inadequate maintenance of structures and inaccurate monitoring of discharges. For

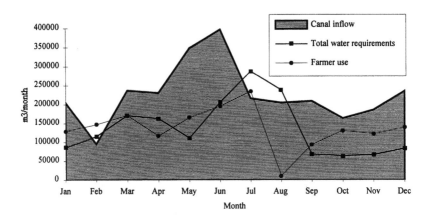

Fig. 2 Total water requirements, farmer use and canal inflow, 1991

the study region these were primarily mesqa associated with the Danduf distributary canal. This canal appeared to suffer problems due to mechanised dredging which had resulted in an uneven gradient along its course. Clearly it is the former which is more important at the national level, where water resources are becoming an increasingly scarce commodity, although it is the latter which has the most deleterious consequences for individual farm production. Attention below will concentrate on farmer use patterns along Um Aisha mesqa, to illustrate demand patterns under conditions of unconstrained supply.

3.1 Farmer use patterns

The common defence made by irrigation department officials for over supply is that individual farmers are over-using and wasting water (top-enders) and therefore additional water is supplied to ensure that sufficient water reaches all farmers (tail-enders). On the face of it, this argument cannot be applied to Um Aisha where tail-end water levels were generally high and few tail-enders indicated any serious occurrences of shortage. Indeed on most visits to the tail-end of the Shahabiya distributary canal during on-periods, high water levels were noted indicating that over supply was common to Shahabiya canal and all of its branches.

Given conditions of a continuous relative surplus, presenting farmers with an opportunity of unconstrained demand, it was possible to observe actual farmer use patterns and how far they accorded with patterns of optimal crop requirements. For the season September 1990-August 1991 records were kept of farmers' cropping patterns and irrigations along the study site. Were these to show patterns of farmer over-use then this could in part justify the existing regime of supply, if not then this could indicate a need to reassess the existing mechanisms for controlling water releases, to match more closely farmer patterns of demand. From the records a picture of the pattern of water use was established demonstrating not only the annual use patterns but also the seasonal, rotational and daily use patterns. The salient characteristics of these patterns are considered below before an overall impression of the annual water use pattern is established and the overall desirability of current farmer practices is assessed.

3.1.1 Seasonal use patterns

The most important seasonal discrepancies between supply and demand were as a result of the variance between the officially estimated cropping patterns and planting and harvesting dates and those actually observed. The most notable discrepancy occurred in late August (Fig. 3).

Most farmers at this time preferred to leave their maize crop to dry out for an extended period without irrigation, prior to harvest. This resulted in a period of 18 days (August 14-September 7) in which there were few irrigations within the study region. However this period coincided with two on-rotations resulting in high levels along Um-Aisha mesqa. As a result, only 7% of the available water was utilised during this period and most of the inflow passed through to the tail end drain without being utilised. Indeed at the head end of the mesqa, the high levels led to breaches of the embankment causing localised flooding. Similarly during April extra water releases were made along all canals in the region for the cotton requirements. However no cotton was grown along the Shahabiya or any of its mesqa. A small area towards the tail end of the Shahabiya mesqa was required to grow cotton under the compulsory cropping regulations. However, all farmers within this area had chosen not to grow cotton and instead were prepared to pay the fine, on the assumption that it would be covered by the income generated from growing alternative (vegetable) crops.

Most farmers were in fact growing wheat and this like maize required a pre-harvest drying-period. Therefore again little water was required during this time.

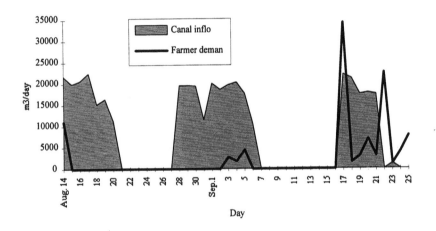

Fig. 3. Seasonal demand pattern Aug-Sep 1991

3.1.2 Rotational use patterns

The MPWWR generally maintain a constant pattern for releases during any particular on-period whereas the farmer demand pattern shows a predictable pattern of fluctuation (Fig. 4). The demand pattern at the start of an on-period is generally high, as farmers compete to irrigate their crops and where the time lapsed since the last but one irrigation (as farmers tend to irrigate every other period) is greatest, so too will be the demand.

During the high demand period there is a degree of enforced scheduling and farmers reliant upon the saqia (Egyptian water wheel), or tail end farmers, are at a disadvantage. By the middle of an on-rotation, demand has usually settled down and farmers are able to irrigate at times of preference. By the end of an on-period there is little demand, although it was noted that when an on-period extended significantly beyond the scheduled period there would be an increase in precautionary irrigations due to the farmers fear that the off-period may be similarly extended. Such a pattern of demand is clearly wasteful since competition during the first few days means that most of the inflow is utilised, this being followed by six or seven days when demand is slack and much of the water is unused. However it is clear that such a pattern of demand is shaped primarily by the nature of the supply system.

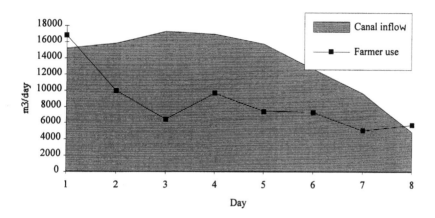

Fig. 4 Rotational supply and demand patterns. Average for all on-periods 1990-91

3.1.4 Diurnal use patterns

The supply pattern, as indicated above, is more or less constant throughout the on-period and therefore throughout 24 hours of any particular on-day. The demand pattern however shows a clear pattern of fluctuation with the majority of irrigations occurring from 5 to 11 am. As a result peak demand discharges are well in excess of average supply discharges (making use of canal storage capacity) (Fig. 5).

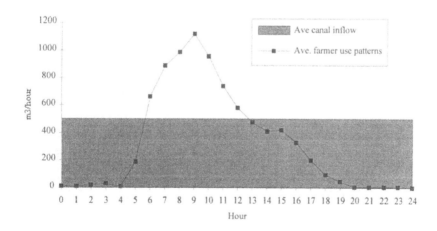

Fig. 5. Average diurnal demand and supply patterns 1990-91

During the period of peak use a number of farmers are prevented from irrigating, due to the form of lift technology employed or the location along the canal and are forced to postpone irrigations to a later time. Even where they are able to irrigate, all farmers will pay a greater price at peak periods due to the increased lift. Farmers at the tail end, or those using traditional water wheel technology in particular must pay a greater price in both time and money invested in irrigation.

If supply patterns matched more closely the demand patterns, canal levels would be constant. This would mean farmers would pay broadly similar costs to irrigate irrespective of time and location. Furthermore it would be possible to effect a reduction in total inflow and waste could be reduced. However it is unlikely that demand patterns (seasonal or daily) could be greatly modified and the change must therefore occur in the supply pattern. This can only be the case if farmers are involved in defining requirements and have some control over inflow.

4   Conclusion

In addition to the above modifications of irrigation practices there are many individual circumstances which could alter the normal patterns of irrigations. These could include local celebrations/anniversaries, market days and climatic factors such as increased rainfall or excessive heat. Thus patterns of irrigation along any specific canal will vary depending upon the particular physical and social circumstances of the community of irrigators. It can therefore be argued that the principal cause of wastage within the system is the variable nature of farmer use patterns. Indeed the standard response of many employees within the MPWWR when questioned on problems of oversupply and wastage within the system is to attribute this to unpredictable and excessive farmer use patterns. However the above analysis of patterns of demand has revealed that patterns of farmer use, although variable, were extremely close to the optimal water requirements and that they achieved high levels of efficiency in raising water from the mesqa to the field. The losses observed in the system were due to the lack of coordination between the supply and demand patterns for irrigation water. Losses were seen to occur as a result of seasonal factors, due to the lack of congruence between actual and official cropping patterns and planting and harvesting dates and due to the mis-match between the rotational and daily supply and demand patterns.

From the above we can see that it would be difficult to enforce a rigid structure of patterns of demand as these are variable in response to a wide range of social, physical and other factors. For greater efficiencies to be achieved it would therefore be necessary that the supply patterns be in some way modified to closer approximate to patterns of demand. There are various technical modifications which could be introduced to permit greater flexibility in patterns of supply, however for these to be effective in achieving greater efficiency of water use, they will need to promote increased participation of farmers in the processes of design, control and maintenance. The argument above has been that the principal problem of the present top-down system is that there is no such participation at lower levels and patterns of supply are therefore often un-responsive to actual farmers needs. Crop quotas and other agricultural policies as well as the behaviour of employees within the MOA at the cooperative level, ensure that the data collected is inaccurate and does not provide an accurate representation of water requirements. The technical aspects of the system are in a poor state of repair due to centralised financial control and the mechanisms for monitoring water releases are inadequate due to the apathy of poorly paid under motivated engineers. It has been suggested that change can best be effected by the formation at canal level of water user associations [7]. Indeed the present Government has adopted various measures to promote the formation of such associations, in the hope that this will permit a more flexible response to farmers needs within a short period (24 hours) [8]. There is certainly sufficient evidence of the success of water user associations in achieving greater water use efficiency and equity [9]. However for such water user associations to be successful they will need to be developed with reference to existing patterns of social organisation and must assume real control over financial resources, cropping patterns and local irrigation water supply.

5 References

1. Folland, C. K. et al. 1986. Sahel rainfall and world-wide sea temperatures, 1901-85, *Nature,* Vol. 320 17, London. April 1986.
2. Allan, J.A. and Howell, P. 1994. *The Nile: Sharing a scarce resource.* Cambridge University Press, Cambridge.
3. Macdonalds. 1988. *Rehabilitation of delivery systems in the old lands. (proj.Nr.EGY/85/012).* Mott Macdonald & Partners Ltd, Cambridge.
4. Radwan, L.S. 1994, *Unpublished D.Phil. Thesis,* Univ. of Oxford, Oxford.
5. Ruff, J. F. & Metawie, A. F. 1987. Interaction between supply of water and farmers demands for water. *Proceedings of Sixth Afro-Asian regional conference on water management in semi-arid areas.* ICID, Cairo.
6. Mehanna, S. 1981. Water allocation amongst Egyptian farmers. AUC, Cairo.
7. Mayfield, J.& Naguib, M. 1982. *Administering an interdisciplinary project: Some fundamental assumptions upon which to build.* EWUP, Cairo.
8. Hvidt, M. 1995. *Unpublished PhD Thesis.* Odense Univ. Denmark.
9. Hunt, E. & Hunt, R. 1976. Canal irrigation and local social organisation. *Current Anthropology.* Vol. 17 No.3 pp 76-90.

EVOLUTION OF WATER SUPPLY AND SANITATION IN FINLAND TENTATIVE IMPLICATIONS FOR ENVIRONMENTAL POLICIES

Water supply and sanitation in Finland

T.S. KATKO
Vaasa Institute of Technology, Finland
P.E. PIETILD
Tampere University of Technology, Finland

Abstract
The evolution of water supply and sanitation in Finland has been demand- rather than supply-driven especially in rural areas. Instead of being a facilitator, the Government has acted as a promoter through technical assistance, advice and financial support. After the oil crisis the specific water consumption has decreased continuously. The share of natural and artificial ground water has increased since the 1930s. The majority of municipal wastewater treatment plants were constructed in the 1960s and 1970s and today over 90% biological oxygen demand and phosphorus reduction is attained. Forest industries introduced efficient treatment some 10-15 years later. Treatment of point-sources is so efficient that it is high time to consider how to reduce loads from diffused sources and how to target environmental investments. Institutional experience favours private and public partnership.
Keywords: evolution, environment, Finland, policy, sanitation, water supply.

1 Introduction and background

The paper describes the on-going study on the development of long-term water supply and sanitation services in Finland, a northern country that today has a high level of water services, but that used to be a hinterland of Europe in the last century. The study has a wide approach including the development of technology as well as institutional issues such as organisations, legislation, financial issues, human resources development, research, enterprises, and future prospects [1]. One of the starting points is the hypothesis that sound management and planning of future water services will be possible only if the past evolution trends and the present situation is properly understood [2].

Water Policy: Allocation and management in practice. Edited by P. Howsam and R.C. Carter.
Published in 1996 by E & FN Spon. ISBN 0 419 21650 2

2   Finnish water resources and special features

The total area of Finland is 338 000 square kilometres and the population has recently reached 5 million. Just over a half of the land's area is covered by forests and 188 000 lakes and the rivers cover 9.9% of the surface area. The mean annual rainfall is about 660 mm, out of which one half is evaporated and another half is finally discharged to the ocean [3].

Most of the big lakes are situated in central and eastern parts of the country. A lot of humus is discharged from the forest and marsh-land areas causing the brown colour, taking up oxygen and making it more difficult for water treatment. The lakes are mostly shallow, either clean with low nutrient content, or slightly brown with a high humus content. In international geological books only the first and last pages are valid for Finland: the oldest formations, the Precambrian bedrock, and the youngest, the glacial formations. The bedrock contains hardly any limestone and, therefore, the buffering capacity of the waters is very low [4].

3   Methodology

In relation to the research programme the Master's theses on the evolution of water associations, wastewater treatment and water treatment were prepared. Moreover, a survey on the development of the sector enterprises was made.

Both quantitative and qualitative research methods were used. Statistical analyses on the diffusion of technology and an intensive literature review were carried out. The latter included also the "grey" literature. In addition, semistructured theme interviews of some 160 sector professionals with various backgrounds were conducted from 1989 to 1995.

4   Establishment of water and sewerage systems

The water supply and sewerage of cities developed for three reasons: clean drinking water and fire-fighting water had to be provided and hygiene had to be improved. Water works sprung up first in the largest cities and spread then gradually to towns. With a few exceptions, sewerage systems were established concurrently with water works.

Fact-finding missions were made abroad to seek knowledge to establish and develop water supply and sewerage already in the 19th century. C. Hausen, the city engineer of Helsinki, made a study trip to Continental Europe in 1889 and visited, among other places, the water works of 22 cities. He also prepared a report of several hundred pages on his trip [5].

The first common rural water pipes were laid a few years before Helsinki got its water works in the 1876. The first rural partnerships served only a few households, but expanded gradually. The first rural water supply networks were built in Ostrobothnia where the flat terrain allowed using wooden pipes. Outside the networks the primary source of rural water was the well. The amount of work done mainly by women was significant.

Around the year 1950 a so-called household rationalization committee, consisting of only women, was set up. Technical help was, however, provided bysector engineers. The work resulted in the 1951 Financing Act which was a tool the state used to support rural water supply and sewerage.

5   Selected innovation diffusions

5.1 Surface water vs. groundwater

A remarkable number of groundwater surveys were done early in this century, but the relatively rudimentary technology required limiting the research to the vicinity of cities. By the turn of the century one of the three biggest cities, Vyborg, used ground water. After the ground water exploration partly failed, the largest Finnish cities started using surface water and many towns followed suit. In 1930, groundwater accounted for only 8% of the total water supplied by public works but the share has increased continuously until this day (Fig. 1). Later estimates include also artificial recharge that started to evolve by 1970. The share of groundwater is expected to rise to 70% by 2010. Rural and small works have used groundwater almost exclusively.

5.2 Water treatment

There are several treatment methods that have been used once, abandoned and reintroduced. Slow sand filtration and activated carbon were used already in the last century, and reintroduced to supplement regular chemical treatment. Artificial groundwater recharge was planned and experimented with already early in this century while the 21 artificial-groundwater works in use in 1992 were constructed in the 1970s and 1980s.

5.3 Water consumption

Water consumption was quite small in the early days of water works compared to today, but consumption grew gradually as the networks expanded. In the 1960s people still believed strongly that cities would continue to grow constantly and specific water consumption would increase.

The specific water consumption of Finnish communities peaked in 1972 at about 335 litres - the year of a global energy crisis. In 1974, a sewage-fee act was enacted which more than doubled the water charges of consumers. Water works started systematic surveys to detect leakages in their networks. Industry connected to communal water works started conserving water and upgrading its processes. Improved fittings were introduced, e.g. the double-handle mixer was replaced by the single-lever mixer.. Construction methods and joints and sealings of piping materials improved also. Consumer attitudes and consumption patterns also changed. Specific water consumption has fallen since 1972 and was about 260 litres/person/day in 1993. The general trend is very similar to the three Finnish cities and one Swedish city shown in Fig. 2.

Water consumption is also affected significantly by metering arrangements. The Helsinki Water Works used water meters already in the last century and started to manufacture them in the 1930s. All in all, the use of meters has been wide-spread in Finland for a long time.

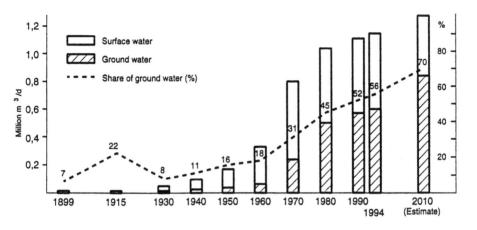

Fig. 1. Groundwater in public water works' supply in Finland, 1899-2010

5.4 Piping materials

Wooden pipes were used in the countryside until the late 1950s and early 1960s. At that time domestically manufactured plastic piping started gaining ground first in rural areas and later in urban areas. Nowadays, the share of plastic water pipes and sewers is about 70% and in new ones over 90%, which are probably the highest values in Europe.

5.5 Evolution of wastewater treatment

Fig. 3 shows the diffusion of wastewater treatment plants in Finland's urban areas. The first 50 years were spent "practising" and then most of the plants were built in less than two decades. The initial treatment plants were crushed rock trickling filters and Emscher tanks that were not as such suited to our conditions. Later stabilization ponds were followed by oxidation ditches and aerated ponds.

Around 1970, simultaneous precipitation with ferrous sulphate came into general use. Municipal wastewater treatment on the same general scale has probably only been implemented in Sweden and Switzerland. Many EU countries, such as Belgium, hardly treat their wastewaters at all.

A few biofilters were built specifically for treatment of food industry wastewater. Later on some communities have built two-stage treatment plants where the anaerobic and aerobic zones follow each other. Small plants have experimented with rootstock treatment plants and biorotors. Surface aerators and aerating brushes were used earlier, but later bottom aerators have been adopted.

The forest industry has built effective activated sludge plants for its wastewaters since the 1980s. The process, however, produces much sludge for which it is hard to find uses. The water pollution control measures of the forest industry are already apparent in downstream waters. Moreover, the forest industries are continuously

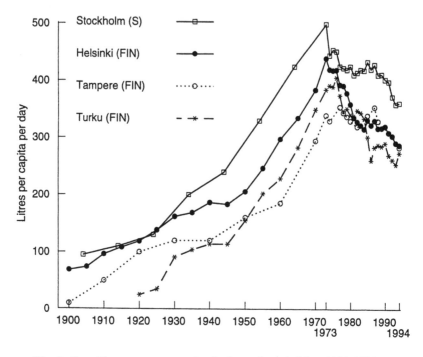

Fig. 2. Specific water consumption in four selected cities, 1900-1994

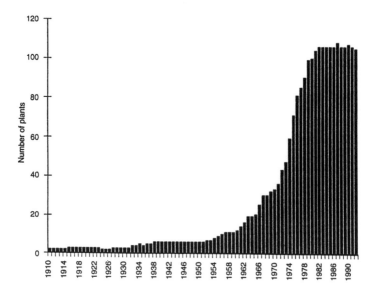

Fig. 3 Diffusion of wastewater treatment in Finnish urban centres, 1910-1990

developing cleaner processes while also trying to close their water circuits as much as possible.

6 Management and institutional aspects

6.1 Water supply and sewerage organisations

Cities have traditionally provided water supply and sewerage as a municipal service. Water charges have been collected from the beginning, but they did not, at least earlier, cover all related costs requiring allocation of tax revenues also for this purpose. In sewerage tax revenues were largely used earlier but nowadays the utilities have to operate on full cost recovery basis.

In rural areas and towns, especially in northern Finland, water supply is organised by water users' associations: partnerships, cooperatives or stock companies. The first two types are typically owned by private people whereas in the third category municipalities have often shares. There are presently a total of more than 1,000 water associations. The groundwork, implementation and running of a water association requires an enterprising and enthusiastic person, a "water nut" as they call themselves. Water associations have been established especially in dispersed settlements in recent years (Fig. 4).

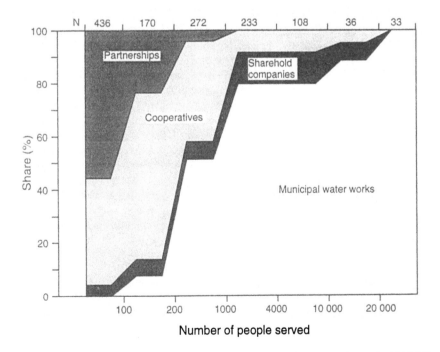

Fig. 4 Distribution of Finnish water supply organisations by size and type in 1988 [6]

In addition to water supply and sewerage works operating in only a single municipality, inter-municipal cooperation has also emerged since the 1960s. It may be contractual and of various degrees. Especially the river valleys of Ostrobothnia have seen the emergence of supra-municipal wholesale companies that sell water to local distributors. The Pdijdnne tunnel that serves the Greater Helsinki Area operates on the same principle. Areal projects have also been set up in the field of sewerage and wastewater treatment. Many municipal water and sewerage systems are presently being turned into autonomous utilities and incorporation is also planned in many cases.

As for human resources the duties of the professionals have changed a lot over the few decades: the first agricultural engineers moved to water supply and sanitary engineering and lately to environmental engineering. Professional associations acting as NGOs have retrained their members and promoted research and development. After importing various materials and supplies domestic manufacturing of pipes, pumps, chemicals and water fixtures started and later laid ground to several internationally oriented companies.

7   Discussion on policy implications

One of the key findings is that evolution of water services has been demanded instead of supply-driven. Government funding and support has been important but never more than just over 10% of sector investments.

Pricing of water services has been used since the beginning while full cost recovery has been reached just recently. Experience shows that people are willing and able to pay for water a price that they regard fair for operative service.

The qualitative requirements for domestic water have become increasingly stringent over time. Simultaneously, the quality of surface waters in many areas has deteriorated or they have been afflicted with new problems like algae. Groundwater quality is weakened by fluoride in addition to the traditional iron and manganese. Treatment techniques have certainly been developed, but many small works still need to do much more. In future, domestic water services including the institutional issues should be a focus As for wastewaters the average reduction of BOD and phosphorus, the limiting factor, is over 90%. It is high time to consider whether still to tighten the requirements further or to channel support to dispersed and similar sources.

Tentative findings suggest several lessons that could also be applied in other fields of environmental protection. In addition, there are several policy issues that could be relevant for economies in transition and developing countries.

8   Conclusions

Long-term experiences from water supply and sewerage in Finland allow drawing the following conclusions to be drawn:
- Old techniques are being reintroduced; everything does not have to be reinvested. More research focusing on the unique Finnish conditions should be conducted. Once problems are solved, new challenges tend to arrive. This seems to be universal.

- Experience and know-how from water supply and water pollution control should be utilised more effectively than so far in exports, environmental cooperation with neighbouring countries, development cooperation and other international activities.
- Environmentally sound development will take time: technology, financing, organisations, legislation, human resources, research and development, public affairs and sector entities are all to be developed simultaneously.
- In any society, technology selection should be related to the capacity of securing the services, especially their operation and maintenance. In many cases, the step-by-step approach to development is most feasible.

Acknowledgements: Financial support from the Economic Research Foundation and Maa-ja Vesitekniikan tukiry is gratefully acknowledged.

9   References

1.   Katko, T. (1996, forthcoming) *Water! - the history of water services in Finland,* (In Finnish, Summary in English).
2.   North, D.C. (1993) *Institutions, institutional change and economic performance,* Cambridge university press.
3.   Santala, E.(ed., 1990) Water services in Finland, Domestic water supply and sewerage, National Board of Waters and the Environment.
4.   Advisory board for water affairs. (1994) Water research programme by 2000, Ministry of the environment, report 3/1994 (In Finnish, Abstract in English).
5.   Hietala, M. (1987) The Nordic contribution to the discussion of water supply and sewerage, Development of various infrastructural services, The diffusion of innovations, Services and urbanisation at the turn of the century. *Studia historica* 23 . pp. 203-220.
6.   Katko, T. (1992) Evolution of consumer-managed water cooperatives in Finland with implications for developing countries. Water International. Vol. 17, No. 1. pp. 12-20.

UNDERSTANDING WATER SUPPLY CONTROL IN CANAL IRRIGATION SYSTEMS

Analysis of irrigation water control

B.A. LANKFORD
School of Development Studies, University of East Anglia, Norwich, UK
J. GOWING
Centre for Land Use and Water Resources Research, University of Newcastle upon Tyne, UK

Abstract
Water management on the extensive canal irrigation systems that supply the major parts of the world's irrigated acreage is difficult. This difficulty and the poor water-use efficiency arising from it can be shown to be caused by poor design practice. A method is presented which is intended to allow designers to evaluate the manageability of water supply stemming from their designs. Alternatively the method can be used by managers as part of a process of action research aimed at improving water control. Case studies on two irrigation systems in Swaziland are used to demonstrate the method of analysis.
Keywords: canal irrigation, design, operation, rehabilitation, water control.

1   Introduction

This paper is concerned with water supply control as a critical aspect of irrigation design. Water supply control is defined as the designed-in ability to regulate the supply of water over time over a canal or rotation command unit so that the irrigation need of the command unit at peak crop demand is met without excessive wastage. The term "designed-in" implies that the system is operated with an ease of management concomitant with performance aims and level of operator activity. Design architecture and operation is examined; a concept that embodies a combination of irrigation system infrastructure (gate/head control technology), system configuration (layouts, areas and groupings of fields into rotational units) and design operational procedures (e.g. allocation of supply within or between rotational units).

Interest in interactions between irrigation design and management has been growing since the mid 1980's when this topic was adopted by IIMI as one of its core

Water Policy: Allocation and management in practice. Edited by P. Howsam and R.C. Carter.
Published in 1996 by E & FN Spon. ISBN 0 419 21650 2

research themes [1][2]. During that time various researchers have highlighted the need and support for the diagnosis and action research of systems [3][4][5]. In the last few years the International Program for Technology Research in Irrigation and Drainage (IPTRID) [6] has been set up to promote such research. Other recent work has identified water control as being central to general irrigation performance [7][8]. Nevertheless, these initiatives have not gained the momentum that other reforms in irrigation practice have achieved, such as irrigation management transfer. The failure to pursue technological reform alongside management reform may be attributed to:

- An acceptance by operators of the "as-built" design as complete and unchangeable together with restricted knowledge about options for irrigation design stemming from a lack of suitable training or forum for exchange of "working" experience.
- The lack of funding/procedures/support for on-going diagnosis and action research of operation and water control design.
- A low number of suitable studies and/or publication of results and methods.
- A lack of experience in operating schemes by irrigation engineers involved in design feeding through to improved innovation of design.
- An institutional reliance on one particular school of design.
- The lack of inclusion of design criteria in bid/proposal and contract evaluation.
- Complex interference of other factors affecting performance such as field design.
- Difficulty of comparison between schemes by clients (farmers and operators).
- Conflicts within the irrigation profession regarding appropriate design.

2   Method of analysis of water supply control

Work on two irrigation schemes in Swaziland indicated that water supply control in rotational supply systems could be characterised on the basis of seven interrelated factors or categories. These are presented in Table 1. The first two, discharge-supply match (DSM) and gate discharge (GD) are measures of design sizing and may be used to investigate design approximations [2][9]. The next four head control (HC), discharge measurement (DM), discharge adjustment (DA) and feeder compatibility (FC), reflect technology choice, the type of design, the amount of manual operation and to some degree robustness of design. The last, rotation integrity (RI), is a reflection of both system design and design operational procedure. The characterisation method is applied to individual rotational units - termed here "leadstream groups" - at the tertiary level. A leadstream (or main d'eau) is the supply of water which cycles around the fields belonging to the rotational unit.

The proposed characterisation method does not attempt to quantify the design or its effect on performance. Neither does the method recommend that any one design is optimal. Rather, it allows operators to review water supply control and reflect on whether their activities and performance may be influenced by its design. It also should be noted that this method represents a conceptual framework for an extended research project, and that it is subject to further refinement.

2.1 Specific demand - supply match (DSM)

The demand-supply match (DSM) measures two aspects of design; a) the gate size which gives a discharge at its maximum setting and b) whether the canal is the correct

Table 1.   Characterisation of irrigation water supply control for rotated flow in tertiary canals.

Category number	Category of irrigation control	Category code	Classification of subtype	Subtype Code	Number Code
1	Specific demand - supply match (For whole group)	DSM	No subtypes. Demand hydromodule and specific supply are calculated. Specific supply is expressed as a fraction of demand hydromodule		
2	Gate discharge (Each gate is described)	GD	No subtypes. Gate discharges are expressed as a fraction of the maximum discharge found Max discharge = 1.0		
3	Head control (Each gate is described)	HC	Omitted	O	1
			Irregular	I	2
			Manual - active	MA	3
			Manual - passive	MP	4
			Automatic	A	5
4	Discharge measurement (Each gate is described)	DM	Omitted	O	1
			Irregular	I	2
			Manual - active	MA	3
			Manual - passive	MP	4
			Automatic	A	5
5	Discharge adjustment (Each gate is described)	DA	Irregular	I	1
			Manual - active	MA	2
			Manual - passive	MP	3
			Fixed	F	4
			Automatic	A	5
6	Feeder compatibility (For whole group)	FC	No subtypes. See separate method for scoring between 1 and 5 (Table 2)		
7	Rotation integrity (For whole group)	RI	Rotation integrity poor	P	1
			Rotation integrity medium	M	2
			Rotation integrity good	G	3

size to carry the required discharge. The terms specific demand and specific supply are used because crop water demand and canal supply can be more accurately compared when both are expressed in litres/second/hectare (l/sec/ha). Volume-based supply should be recalculated to a flow over time. DSM is calculated in three steps:

Step 1. Specific demand (which is also known as the hydromodule) is the irrigation need of the command area at peak demand expressed in l/sec/ha. The specific demand can be seen as the inverse of the water duty. A weighted average demand can be calculated if fields within the rotation unit have very different water requirements.

Step 2. Specific supply is calculated in l/sec/ha by dividing the maximum flow supplying the tertiary command unit in litres/second by its area in hectares. The flow is at the crop level by adjusting for tertiary canal and field losses. If the flow is not currently measured then flow measurement is necessary. If tertiary canal flows within a leadstream group are different, a weighted specific supply should be calculated.

Step 3. The demand-supply match is calculated by dividing the specific supply by the specific demand. If the specific supply matches the demand, the match is equal to or close to 1.0. An over- or under-supply gives a DSM greater or less than 1.0.

2.2 Gate discharge (GD)

This is a measure of the uniformity of flows in the canals supplying fields. Operators may wish to have uniform flows so as to not create bottlenecks, or to enhance visible equity of supply between leadstream groups. Gate discharge is expressed as a fraction of the maximum flow supplying fields in the group.

2.3 Head control (HC)

This is an expression of the **local** control of the level of water which regulates the discharge through the irrigation gate. Head control provides for a head difference between upstream and downstream water levels at the gate which gives stable flows. No distinction is made here between upstream and downstream level control in the conveyance canal (see feeder compatibility). Five main types have been identified:
1. Omitted (O, 1). Head control is effectively remote or absent in design.
2. Irregular (I, 2). The structure is faulty or broken, or water in the offtaking canal backs up and interferes with the upstream water level.
3. Manual-active (MA, 3). Manual adjustment is used. An example is the constant head orifice (CHO) gate which includes a head-controlling gate that needs frequent adjustment and is difficult to operate accurately [7].
4. Manual-passive (MP, 4). No manual input is required within certain flow limits otherwise input is minimal. Examples are composite-weir cross regulators [7].
5. Automatic (A, 5). No manual input is required over a wide range of flows. Two examples are optimally designed long-cilled weirs and electrically operated gates.

2.4 Discharge measurement (DM)

This is a measure with which the ease and accuracy of discharge measurement takes place. It can be characterised in one of the five following ways:
1. Omitted (O, 1). Absent in design.
2. Irregular (I, 2). Structure is broken, missing, incorrectly constructed or inaccurate.
3. Manual-active (MA, 3). Measurement requires manual recording. Examples include stick-gauged flumes, weirs and orifice gates.
4. Manual-passive (MP, 4). Measurement is designed-in and hidden from gate operator as in module gates (e.g. of the neyrpic or neyrtec design).
5. Automatic (A, 5). Flow measurement is recorded automatically (e.g. via float and sensor flow gauging and radio-telemetry).

2.5 Discharge adjustment (DA)

Discharge adjustment may not be necessary in all schemes depending on intended operation. Five classes have been identified. Note that there is no "absent or omitted" class since this would fall into the fixed class which requires no manual input.
1. Irregular (I, 2). The gate is broken, missing or incorrectly constructed.
2. Manual-active (MA, 2). Gates are adjusted manually but can be set at continuously variable openings. Examples are sluice gates and adjustable flow dividers.
3. Manual-passive (MP, 3). Gates are adjusted manually but have easily discernible settings such as on-off or two or three settings giving stepped flow rates. Examples are neyrpic gates with one or two shutters that are either on or off.

4. Fixed (F,4). Here manual input is reduced further as gates do not need opening at all. Examples are fixed flow dividers.
5. Automatic (A, 5). The gates are adjusted by automatic, hydraulic/electrical, or possibly computer controlled means.

2.6 Feeder compatibility (FC)

Feeder compatibility describes how well the upstream canal delivery system is designed so as to complement the tertiary turnout design and requirements. The objective of feeder compatibility is the accurate delivery of flow for the turnouts which is congruent with the cumulative and changing demands of the leadstream groups. Table 2 shows the scoring system based on four main aspects of feeder compatibility:

1. Measured flow may enhance the accuracy of supply of water in the secondary system for tertiary turnouts. There are three main subtypes; absent or broken; manually measured (e.g. a flume); or automatically measured (e.g. a modular gate).
2. Flow fluctuations at the head of secondary canals may lead to flow variations in offtaking turnouts. The degree to which these variations are dampened is scored accordingly; absent or broken technology; technology that gives non-steady flows (e.g. manually-operated sluice gates); and technology that gives steady flow such as long-cilled weirs in the main canal.
3. Responsiveness of supply refers to the design of the secondary canal gate to adjust to changing downstream demand. The three main types are absent, manual or automatic (e.g. hydraulically-operated gates sensitive to downstream water levels).
4. Accuracy of supply. Having investigated the flow or range of flows, it is then possible to check whether the supplying canal delivers the correct flow for the combined demand of the leadstream groups. This should be done at peak demand.

Table 2. Scoring system for feeder compatibility (starting score = 1)

Aspect of feeder compatibility	Classification of subtype	Score
Measured flow	Absent or broken	Add 0
	Manually measured	Add 0.5
	Automatically measured	Add 1.0
Flow fluctuation	Absent or broken	Add 0
	Non-steady	Add 0.5
	Steady	Add 1.0
Responsiveness of supply	Absent or broken	Add 0
	Manual	Add 0.5
	Automatic	Add 1.0
Accuracy of supply	>25% difference in required supply	Add 0
	10-25% difference in required supply	Add 0.5
	<10% difference in required supply	Add 1.0

2.7 Rotation integrity (RI)

This reflects the manner in which the cycling of the leadstream around the group's fields are adhered to. As it is not easy to calculate an accurate measure of the rotation integrity, three broad classes are suggested:

1. Poor (P, 1). Within the secondary command unit, fields are not aligned to individual tertiary leadstream groups. Water is cycled in no discernible pattern, frequently to fields on a driest-basis first. This type of operation makes the area and specific supply of the leadstream group extremely difficult to determine.
2. Medium (M, 2). Water often circulates in a discernible pattern but occasionally leadstreams are transferred between groups (due to driest-first irrigation) leading to a broken rotation. The area and thus specific supply are not known with certainty.
3. Good (G, 3). Leadstreams are circulated only within their respective groups. Irrigation is scheduled to fields within the leadstream group on driest-first basis, and a clear rotation of delivery is discernible. This allows the specific supply to be easily calculated since the area of the leadstream group is known.

Scoring of water supply control may be difficult in some schemes, and in cases may have to be omitted. Furthermore, scores could be estimated between whole numbers for systems that do not fall easily into the above named classes.

3   Characterisation of two irrigation systems - case studies from Swaziland

Two tertiary systems from neighbouring irrigation systems (MSCo and IYSIS) in Swaziland were analysed with the method. Table 3 gives the results of analysis and Figures 1 and 2 are the characterisation diagrams for MSCo and IYSIS respectively. The supply for the MSCo command area closely matches the irrigation demand (DSM = 96%) whereas the IYSIS rotation unit is oversupplied (135%). There is variability in gate discharge for MSCo (GD = 1 and 0.86) but uniformity for the IYSIS group. The score for all head control structures at IYSIS is 4 (all are long-cilled weirs) but broken and irregularly constructed weirs at MSCo scored 2. At MSCo, DM scored 3 in one canal (a cut-throat flume was present) but zero for the other. For IYSIS, DM = 4, reflecting the use of neyrpic modular gates. Discharge adjustment for MSCo scored 2, reflecting orifice gates, but DA = 3 at IYSIS since flows are chosen in three steps; 0, 60 and 120 l/sec. For both IYSIS and MSCo, feeder compatibility scored 4.25 which originated from a starting score of 1.0, + 1.0 for automatically measured flow at the head of the secondary canal (neyrpic gates and flow recorders), + 0.75 for flow fluctuation (corrections to gates on main canal required about three times a day), +0.5 for manual adjustment of neyrpic gates/orifice gate at head of secondary canal, and +1.0 for accuracy of supply since in both cases the secondary canal turnout was accurately sized within 10% of the maximum demand flow. For both systems, rotation integrity scored 2 because leadstreams were sometimes mixed between rotation units.

The analysis provides avenues of diagnosis of manageability of water supply, and of means by which water control may be improved. Thus, managers at IYSIS may wish to evaluate whether the medium-scored rotation integrity is a reflection of the large DSM in one group and the need to move water between leadstream groups on the S9 secondary canal due to a resulting imbalance of supply between the groups.

If necessary, it would be possible to re-size the nerypic gates to deliver the correct flow. Managers operating the example MSCo leadstream group may wish to investigate whether discrepancies in gate discharge between the two gates involved and the need for manual measurement of flow are leading to an unacceptable loss of water control. From there, managers may decide to correct the problem either via changes to gate technology or via more stringent gate-operator management.

Table 3. Analysis of water supply control within leadstream groups MSCo and IYSIS

Category number		1		2	3	4	5	6	7
Specific demand (l/s/ha)	Specific supply (l/s/ha)	DSM	Gate discharge (l/sec)	GD	HC	DM	DA	FC	RI
MSCo - Leadstream group, fields 201/2+3 & 201/4+5 (area = 30.3 ha)									
Gate 1	1.892	1.824	0.96	59	1.00	2	3	2	4.25	2
Gate 2	1.892	1.824	0.96	51	0.86	2	1	2	4.25	2
IYSIS - Leadstream group, fields S7/20-22 & S9/1+2 (area = 46.9 ha)									
Gate 1	1.892	2.558	1.35	120	1.00	4	4	3	4.25	2
Gate 2	1.892	2.558	1.35	120	1.00	4	4	3	4.25	2
Gate 3	1.892	2.558	1.35	120	1.00	4	4	3	4.25	2

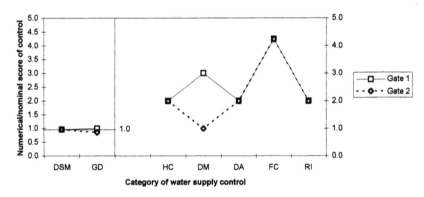

Fig. 1. Characterisation diagram of water supply control for MSCo leadstream group

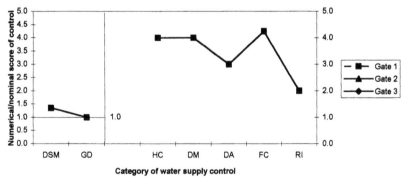

Fig. 2. Characterisation diagram of water supply control for IYSIS leadstream group

4   Conclusions - policy implications

Irrigated agriculture is the major category of demand for water in many countries and is widely criticised for its profligacy in water use. In any individual scheme therefore, the operational policy must be to deliver adequate supplies to all users at the highest attainable level of efficiency. However, irrigation managers are confronted by the trade-off that generally exists between equity and efficiency because of the inadequate level of control over water distribution that is designed into the system. Real progress with improving water control in irrigation will be achieved only if management reforms and technological reforms receive equal recognition and attention. Provision of manageable irrigation infrastructure requires a better understanding of the interactions between design and management. The policy of separating the process of "design" from the process of "operation" serves to exacerbate the problem. Objective methods of assessing both design and "manageability" of water supply control will contribute to closing the gap between policy and practice.

Acknowledgements: B.A. Lankford greatly appreciates the financial support provided by the Jack Wright Memorial Trust and would also like to thank staff at IYSIS and MSCo, particularly Ian More.

5   References

1. International Irrigation Management Institute. (1984) *The Research Framework.* Annual Report. IIMI, Sri Lanka.
2. Murray-Rust, D. H. and Snellen W. B. (1993) *Irrigation System Performance Assessment and Diagnosis.* IIMI, Sri Lanka.
3. Bottrall, A. (1981) Action research towards improved water distribution. *Irrigation Management Network* Paper 5c. Overseas Development Institute, London.
4. Horst, L. (1983) Irrigation systems - Alternative design concepts. *Irrigation Management Network* Paper 7c. Overseas Development Institute, London.
5. Abernethy, C. L. (1987) Diagnosing technical problems with existing systems. *Proceedings of Seminar on Rehabilitation of Irrigation Schemes.* ICID, London.
6. International Program for Technology Research in Irrigation and Drainage. (1995) *GRID Network Magazine of IPTRID.* HR Wallingford, UK.
7. Plusquellec, H., Burt, C. and Wolter, H. W. (1994) *Modern Water Control in Irrigation. Concepts, Issues, and Applications.* World Bank Technical Paper No. 246. Irrigation and Drainage Series. World Bank, Washington DC, USA.
8. Bolding, A., Mollinga, P.P. and Van Straaten, K. (1995) Modules for Modernisation: Colonial Irrigation in India and the Technological Dimension of Agrarian Change. *The Journal of Development Studies,* Vol. 31, No. 6. pp. 805-844.
9. Lankford, B.A. and Gowing, J. (1996) The impact of design approximations on the operational performance of an irrigation scheme: a case study in Malaysia. *Irrigation and Drainage Systems,* Vol. 10, No. 3. (Forthcoming).

SECTION 5

WATER ECONOMICS

THE VALUE OF WATER VALUATION
The value of water valuation

J.T. WINPENNY
Overseas Development Institute, London, UK

Abstract
In the context of treating water as an economic good, there is growing interest in estimating its economic values in different uses. The paper reviews the methods by which water values are estimated in different sectors and how these values are used in modelling the allocation of supplies. Evidence on empirical water values is presented from a range of countries. Conclusions are drawn about the potential use of water values for planning and management, including their relevance for pricing.
Keywords: economic values, modelling, netback, opportunity cost, pricing, water values, willingness-to-pay.

1 Introduction

It has become customary to refer to water as an economic commodity, the allocation of which should observe economic principles. The economic approach to the allocation of resources is to use prices and markets to ensure that the resource is applied to its most valuable uses [1]. Where the supply of water is not unlimited, and marginal units of supply have a positive cost, the value of water consumption is maximised when net marginal benefits are equal in all uses. In that case, it is impossible to raise total net value by reallocating water from one user to another.

This theoretical ideal conveys the important practical lesson that the allocation of limited water supplies should take into account what the water is worth to different kinds of users. If one group of users - sector A - is applying it to valuable purposes, while another - sector B - is using it wastefully or for low-value applications, by reallocating it from B to A the total consumption value of water may be increased. Although A has a higher **average** value of water use, increasing applications would

Water Policy: Allocation and management in practice. Edited by P. Howsam and R.C. Carter.
Published in 1996 by E & FN Spon. ISBN 0 419 21650 2

normally cause diminishing **marginal** values, while the same process would happen in reverse with B. If the process continued to the limit, **marginal** values of water would be the same in both sectors, and there would be no point in making any further reallocations.

It is important to note that in the above situation, the **average** value of water use would continue to be higher in A than in B, even though **marginal** units had the same value. Average values are of considerable interest for the purpose of reallocating water, and many empirical studies are concerned with average values. However, it is the equality of **marginal** values that would satisfy the so-called Pareto Criterion, where redistribution would make no-one better off without making someone else worse off.

The remainder of this paper has three sections. The first is concerned with methodology: it briefly reviews the methods by which water values are estimated in different sectors, and how these values are used in modelling the allocation of supplies. The second section reviews a number of empirical studies of water values conducted in a range of countries. Finally, the paper draws conclusions about the practical relevance of water valuation for planning and managing this sector.

2   Methodological considerations

2.1 Valuation methods

The methods of valuing water are highly eclectic, depending on the sector or type of use [2]. Because water is not, in general, priced as an economic good, actual prices are a poor guide to economic values. The largest body of evidence has been collected for urban household consumers. Surveys are made of households already receiving individual piped supplies, or where it is proposed to introduce such provision. The studies attempt to estimate users' willingness-to-pay (WTP) for their water, either from direct household surveys, or by inferences drawn from changes in consumption following a tariff change.

This information is used to construct a demand curve relating the quantities of water consumed at different values or prices. With the usual shape of such a curve, users will enjoy a "consumers' surplus" at any given price, indicating that they would be willing to pay higher sums than those actually charged for the most precious units of water. In principle, the total area under the demand curve measures the benefit, or value, of the water.

Different approaches are taken to valuing water used in agriculture. One method is to obtain estimates of the marginal productivity of water from crop-water trials, relating changes in crop yield to different doses of water, other inputs remaining constant. Economic values are then attached to the changes in yield using market prices of the commodity. A more common method (sometimes referred to as "netback") is to derive water values as a residual from farm budget data. Starting with the gross value per hectare of the crop, all costs apart from water are estimated and deducted. What remains is the maximum WTP for water. As a refinement, costs can be taken to include capital recovery, or even a "normal" profit margin.

Industrial water valuation poses more of a problem. Water is normally a tiny part of total costs, and it would be misleading to attribute the whole residual value to this factor. Much industrial water is also self-supplied, either from wells, direct abstraction from rivers, or from recycling. One device is to regard the cost of recycling (treatment and reuse) as the upper limit on industrial WTP - since for values higher than this the firm would be rational to re-use its own supplies rather than buy in from the mains.

A cruder short-cut to industrial water values, employed by several studies reviewed below, is to compute ratios of gross output or value added to the volume of water involved in the process. These are measures of the water-intensity of different industrial sub-sectors, and indicate the upper limit of WTP for water, but do not indicate the real productivity of water, nor do they give a realistic pointer to WTP.

Water also has in-stream value for waste assimilation, which can be estimated by comparing the cost of natural assimilation with the reduction of pollution by other means (e.g. reduction at source). In a similar fashion, the value of water for navigation can be regarded as the cost advantage of water-borne transport over the next cheapest mode (e.g. railway). This can be a negative item when water-borne transport is unprofitable, before subsidy.

Water used for generating hydroelectricity is normally valued according to the cost advantage of hydro over other, thermal, alternatives. In this, as in other, cases, values differ according to whether a short- or a long-term viewpoint is taken (which affects whether capital costs enter the computation).

There are two standard approaches to the valuation of water for recreation and tourism. The Travel Cost Method infers such values from the travel costs (including time) of visitors to the site in question, which are used to construct a hypothetical demand curve for the recreational or amenity benefit of water. Alternatively, or sometimes in parallel, the Contingent Valuation Method employs opinion surveys to uncover the values that visitors, or armchair observers, derive from the existence of the watery asset [3,4].

This does not exhaust the different uses of water. In some river basins, maintaining in-stream water flow is essential for flushing sediment out of river beds and channels. Its value for this purpose (rather than for other uses involving abstraction and consumptive use) is measured in relation to the extra cost of alternatives such as dredging [5].

2.2 Modelling the allocation of water

Possessing average and marginal values of water in different uses is the first step towards modelling its allocation. In the common situation where the demand for water in a particular hydrological area, at ruling prices, exceeds its supply, and where transfers between users is feasible, the maximisation of the use value of water, subject to constraints, is one possible aim of the exercise (the "objective function"). As we noted earlier, this would be achieved where marginal water values were equalised across all users. Because the marginal value of water to a specific user changes as more or less is consumed, a realistic model would incorporate demand functions for each sector.

For example, in agriculture the average value of water under a particular crop tells us very little about what marginal amounts of water would be worth to farmers - they might be willing to pay only very small sums for a little extra: conversely, taking marginal amounts away from them to supply some other user might deprive them of very little. But it is also true that the first units of water supplied to farmers are likely to be relatively valuable, even if the average value is low. As such farmers receive more water, its marginal value falls. This explains why water values observed in trades and auctions are often very much higher than we would expect average values to be. Optimisation models can allocate water to maximise the chosen objective function, subject to satisfying certain constraints (e.g. minimum flows, full provision of priority users). A linear programming structure is common, though non-linear functions may be used as a more realistic refinement. The Basin Level Model developed for the Yellow River in China [6] uses a constrained optimisation approach, assuming that the Chinese authorities wish to obtain maximum economic benefit from the operation of the system, as well as investments in it, subject to various hydrological, physical and agronomic constraints. In this case, a non-linear structure was chosen because of non-linearities in hydropower generation and in the link between crop water stress and crop yield. Municipal and industrial demand, being a relatively small and vital part of the total, is taken as a constraint, and is not therefore part of the quantity to be optimised.

Another optimisation model has been developed for the Nkomazi West district of South Africa [7], where water conflicts are arising between dryland crops, livestock, irrigated sugar, conservation, dams, and household consumption. Various constraints were set - e.g. household requirements, minimum flows for conservation purposes, and a minimum level in the dam - but thereafter other users (in practice, the various forms of agriculture) were allowed to compete for the water. The model produced allocations that would maximise value added.

One of the best-known models is that developed by the Harvard Middle East Water project [8], which has generated estimates of the value of water at stake between Israel and Palestine. Private demand curves for water are estimated for households, industry and agriculture. A special feature of this model is the attempt to ascribe a social value to water, meant to represent national aims as well as private demands.

3   Empirical water values: international evidence

This section briefly reviews empirical estimates of water values. It makes no claims to be comprehensive: the survey includes some well-known, as well as some lesser known, exercises. There are many estimates of water values in individual uses (e.g. specific crops, households in a particular town, values of a particular stretch of water for angling, etc), but the studies cited here all purport to compare water values between two or more sectors, crops, or uses. The evidence is grouped into regional categories: the USA, China, UK and Southern Africa.

3.1 USA
In the early 1970s the US National Water Commission carried out a systematic and comprehensive review of the economic value of water in all the main user sectors and environmental functions - agriculture, industry, domestic (municipal), hydroelectric generation, waste assimilation, navigation, recreation, and fisheries and wildlife habitat [9]. In 1986 an equally comprehensive study was published by a researcher at Resources for the Future, again drawing almost entirely on US data [2]. Between them, these studies represent the most comprehensive and systematic assembly of water values to date.

The two studies produce a similar ranking of water values between different sectors and absolute values that are broadly consistent. Updated to 1991 values (US cents per cubic meter) the lowest value uses include low-value farm crops (1-6), industrial cooling (0-1), waste assimilation (0-2), navigation (0, but up to 37 in specific stretches) and hydro-electric generation (0-4). The highest values were found in speciality crop production (10-80), industrial process use (18-80), in-house domestic consumption (2-26), and some recreational sites (1-40).

Almost all categories show a wide range of values, for sector-specific reasons. The result depends vitally on the methodology and conventions that are used, e.g.: whether a short- or long-run view is taken, which affects the treatment of capital costs; whether marginal or average values are taken; the season, region and crop; crop prices at the time of the study, etc. For these reasons, it is important to examine the fine print attached to each valuation exercise before using the values as representative of a sector, or in transferring the result for analytical purposes elsewhere [10].

3.2 China

The three studies reviewed here are all drawn from the Yellow River (Huang He) Basin in Northern China. The River is of vital importance to irrigated agriculture, which supplies food to the Basin's large population. There is also a sizeable municipal and industrial demand for water. It has the highest sediment load of any major river in the world. It also has extreme seasonal and year-to-year variability. Although flood control is the main preoccupation of the river basin managers, there are awkward trade-offs between flood prevention, sediment control, irrigation, and power generation.

The average value of water used in irrigation was found to be c. Y 0.24/cu.m. (3 US cents, at current rates) while its marginal value, at critical times and in the most productive regions, was c. Y0.80/cu.m.(9-10 cents). The marginal value of water for power production was estimated to be c. Y0.15/cu.m.(2 cents) [6]. A separate study of the benefits of reducing sedimentation estimated the value of water saved to lie in a range of Y.0-14 (0-2 cents) per ton of sediment prevented, depending on the use, location and time of year [5].

Values of water for industry and agriculture were also estimated for a region near Tianjin in the context of a study of the costs of over-exploiting the aquifer [11]. Using the value-added method (which over-estimates true values) they discovered a range of water values in different industrial sectors of Y 4-35 (US $0.5-4) per cu. m.   This compares with less than Y1 (12 cents) in agriculture.

3.3 United Kingdom

A recent study was done for the National Rivers Authority [12] of values for water in various uses. Using the residual value method, and the short term concept, it was estimated that agricultural values ranged from 15p (23 cents) per cu.m. for soft fruit, 5-9p (8-14 cents) for field vegetables, down to 0.5-2p (1-3 cents) for cereals and grass. The only other UK data appearing in the report are negligible values for fish-farming, heavily qualified because of the marginal and non-commercial nature of much of this enterprise.

A net-back analysis has also been done for irrigated crops grown in East Anglia. Hypothetical WTP is estimated for water used to grow winter wheat, barley, oilseed rape, potatoes and sugar beet. The method is to "net back" from gross margins by deducting various non-water costs, and to regard the residual amount as the maximum WTP for water. The main complication was the presence of sizeable subsidies, without which 4 of the 5 crops would have been unprofitable (a negative residual, implying negative WTP for water). The only positive WTP was for potatoes, implying a maximum value of water of £1.22 ($1.89) per cu.m. [13].

3.4 Southern Africa

The Nkomazi district model in South Africa generated the following marginal values for water: R0.35/cu.m. (10 cents) in dryland crops, practically zero under traditional livestock rearing, and R0.35 (10 cents) under irrigated sugar [7]. The negligible values for livestock water calls into question whether the output and services of animals (including non-quantifiable factors, e.g. social prestige, are adequately reflected).

In Zimbabwe, a study of Bulawayo's water sources (14) enabled rough values to be placed on agricultural, domestic and industrial consumption. The agricultural values (US 10-15 cents per cu.m.), were average figures obtained by rough residual imputation. Industrial values (for process water not less than 23 US cents/cu.m., less for cooling uses) were guesstimates based on a sample interview survey). In the absence of WTP data for household consumption, the prevailing (1993) flat rate tariff of 12 US cents/cu.m. is taken as the minimum estimate for urban use.

4   The value of values

The estimation of water values has several potential uses. Firstly, it can indicate the productivity or benefits of water in its different uses. This information is useful in planning and allocating water in a region or basin, where supplies are becoming scarce or where future provision is likely to be costly. For instance, the Yellow River model [6] demonstrated that the future overall water balance depends overwhelmingly on the amount of water needed for flushing sediment. The model helps to justify proposed public investment in the Xiaolangdi Dam, an efficient way of downstream sediment control, releasing large amounts of water with a high opportunity cost.

Secondly, it can enable the benefits (and opportunity costs) of water supply and conservation schemes to be determined more accurately. For example, Young & Gray's study provided evidence of overinvestment in American hydraulic schemes:

"..we do not find any apparent underinvestment in water resource developments at the present time. Evidence concerning costs of public developments for irrigation and navigation suggests, in fact, an overinvestment by the public for these purposes. Costs of interregional water transportation are typically large relative to water values at potential points of use." [9].

Thirdly, valuation provides information useful for the development of water markets and transfers. An active market in water will only develop where the use value of buyers exceeds that of sellers by a margin sufficient to offset transactions costs. The public interest is safeguarded where these net private benefits exceed costs imposed on third parties or the environment [15]. Valuation is useful for monitoring and regulating water exchanges.

Finally, valuation assists better water pricing, by providing evidence on WTP and elasticity of demand for different types of user, seasons, purposes, quality, reliability, and other determining factors. In theory, if the values of water in all its various uses and locations are known, opportunity cost pricing could be used to ensure its optimal

allocation. In practice, pricing based on resource costs seems to be much more practicable. As a recent study for the UK National Rivers authority concluded:
"In the theoretically optimal "opportunity cost" form the costs imposed by abstractors on all other water users, including the environment, would need to be calculated. Such costs vary enormously over space and time and would be virtually unique for each abstraction." [12, p. 65].

The potential of water values is clear, but whether they will be used more actively in water planning and management depends on practitioners developing more confidence in the robustness of the methodology and data sources. It is evident from the brief review in sections 2 and 3 that water values are currently obtained in a highly eclectic fashion. The sources of some data are controversial (e.g. those derived from WTP surveys). Values within the same sector or broad user types differ greatly, e.g. according to whether they are marginal or average, time of year, reliability of supply, access to water-saving techniques, type of crop or product, and other factors. In these circumstances, exaggerated claims for water valuation should be avoided, and excessive precision in such estimates is a cause for suspicion.

5   References

1. Winpenny, James (1994) *Managing water as an economic resource,* Routledge/ODI, London.
2. Gibbons, Diana C. (1986): *The economic value of water.* Resources for the Future, Washington, D.C.
3. Organisation for Economic Cooperation and Development (1995) *The economic appraisal of environmental projects and policies: a practical guide,* Paris.
4. Winpenny, J.T. (1991) *Values for the environment: a guide to economic appraisal,* HMSO, London.
5. Dixon, John A., Scura, Louise F., Carpenter, Richard, & Sherman, P.B. (1994), *Economic analysis of environmental impacts,* Earthscan Publications Ltd., London.
6. Kutcher, Gary; McGurk, Stephen; & Gunaratnam, Daniel J. (1992) *China: Yellow River Basin. Water investment planning study,* presented to a World Bank Irrigation & Drainage Seminar, December.
7. Hassan, R., Berns, J., Chapman, A., Smith, R., Scott, D., & Ntsaba, M. (1995) *Economic policies and the environment in South Africa: the case of water resources in Mpumalanga.* Division of Forest Science & Technology, CSIR, Pretoria.
8. The Harvard Middle East Water Project: Brief Summary (1994), (anonymous), J.F. Kennedy School of Government, Cambridge, Mass..
9. Young, Robert A. & Gray, S. Lee (1972), *Economic value of water: concepts and empirical estimates. Final Report to the National Water Commission.* Department of Economics, Colorado State University, Fort Collins, Co..
10. Winpenny, J.T. (1995) *Sustainable development in the water sector,* presented at Development Studies Association Conference, Dublin, September.
11. Adams, B., Grimble, R., Shearer, T.R., Kitching, R., Calow, R., Chen dong Jie, Cui Xiao Dong & Yu Zhong Ming (1994), *Aquifer Overexploitation in the Hangu*

Region of Tianjin, People's Republic of China. British Geological Survey, Nottingham, 1994.

12. Rees, J.A., Williams, S., Atkins, J.P., Hammond, C.J., Trotter, S.D.(1993), Economics of water resource management, R&D Note 128, National Rivers Authority, Bristol.

13. Bate, R.N. & Dubourg, W.R.(1994), *A netback analysis of water irrigation demand in East Anglia*, CSERGE Discussion Paper WM94, University College London.

14. Winpenny, J.T. (1993), Managing water as an economic resource: a case study of Bulawayo, Zimbabwe, unpublished paper, Overseas Development Institute, London

15. Saliba, Bonnie Colby & Bush, David B. (1987), *Water markets in theory and practice: market transfers, water values and public policy.* Westview Press, Boulder and London.

INSTITUTIONS IN WATER RESOURCE MANAGEMENT: INSIGHTS FROM NEW INSTITUTIONAL ECONOMICS

Insights from New Institutional Economics

I.D. CARRUTHERS and J.A. MORRISON
Wye College, University of London, Wye, UK

Abstract
Mainstream economists, in advocating policy for the water sector have tended to neglect the important institutional factors crucial to the success of their recommendations. This fact has long been recognised by the Institutional Economists, who for their part have been unable to develop a consistent analytical framework and consequently their observations have generally been overlooked. This paper explores the importance of institutional arrangements in the water sector and introduces some new schools of thought, falling under the broad banner of New Institutional Economics, which might at last allow insightful analysis of the interaction between policy and the complex institutional arrangements in the water sector.
Keywords: allocative mechanisms, collective action, Irrigation Management Transfer, New Institutional Economics, privatisation, transaction costs.

1   Introduction

The world of water is in many ways an inward looking world with a relatively small specialist group, generally technical in their orientation, dominating policy deliberations. Emerging ideas and new approaches to the common problems of development trickle down slowly from other sectors and disciplines. This may rapidly change because water problems are moving to centre stage as we quickly emerge from the era of 'cheap and plentiful' water to one where it is clearly 'scarce and valuable'.

In this paper we seek to promote trickle down from the world of economics to the multidisciplinary arena of water policy and to explore recent developments which we consider to be of great relevance to the rapidly changing policy environment.

Water Policy: Allocation and management in practice. Edited by P. Howsam and R.C. Carter.
Published in 1996 by E & FN Spon. ISBN 0 419 21650 2

2   Early Institutionalists

In the 1920's institutional economists such as T.B.Veblen, Gunnar Myrdal and W.C. Mitchell criticised conventional economists for ignoring the non-economic, institutional factors in their models and for distorting and oversimplifying the strictly economic phenomena [1]. They chastised their fellow economists for ignoring insights from other disciplines such as sociology, politics and law.

In effect two groups of institutionalists emerged in the post-war era. Those who stressed the economic elements and the more dominant group who emphasised the broader social and political elements. In the development economics literature those who stressed institutional or structural barriers to workings of markets were termed structuralists.

If we adopt a somewhat naive view of the structuralist position we can caricature them as lying politically between the right wing neoclassical economists stressing market forces and the left wing Marxists. Structuralists were not ideologically against using markets rather than administrative allocation to promote development but were depressingly obsessed by the attendant problems, and this hindered their ability to contribute to the development debate.

Development practice has been dominated for the last fifteen years by the neoclassical economists stressing the power of markets if you can 'get the prices right'. Any non-response to 'correct prices' was seen to be less a problem of structural barriers and more a farmer risk assessment process expressed as a lag in response. But as the lags have become longer, the necessity to assess structural impediments to market efficiency have grown.

Water sector policy has been far from immune to these economic influences, despite the dominance until the 1980's of engineers in planning, construction and water management. For example, there has scarcely been a World Bank water loan over the last 25 years without a legally binding commitment by the recipient Governments to raise water fees at least to cover operation and maintenance costs, to reduce or eliminate other input subsidies, export taxes or related macroeconomic adjustments such as reducing harmful overvalued foreign exchange rates. The fact that few, if any, of the water sector economic conditions have been met and yet rarely, if ever, have any long term sanctions been applied, can perhaps be regarded as an symptom of institutional problems at national and international levels.

Institutional innovation has been attempted. For example, the much heralded para-statal organisations were almost always a disappointment after the initial enthusiasm had dimmed and old bureaucratic culture reasserted itself. More recently impoverished Governments have discovered that farmers have apparently newly acquired engineering and management skills that enable them to run irrigation systems and many have been turned over to them. The most quoted instance of wide ranging reform is the Philippine National Irrigation Administration which is regarded as a success [3]. It is true to say that the positive impact of economic policy reform has been minimal in most countries but recently old problems of financial shortages and deficient maintenance have become prominent [4]. Now, at a time when economies and irrigation systems seem sluggish in their response to this pricist medicine, the structuralists have been reborn as 'new institutional economists' and have started to advocate novel solutions to the poor performance that is said to exist.

3   What are institutions?

The term institution, like the term sustainability, has a number of meanings and we each carry private understandings that can be so varied as to sow confusion. Elinor Ostrom, a writer who has had considerable influence on thinking about institutional reform through her work in irrigation, has alluded to the difficulty of defining exactly what we mean by institutional arrangements. She compromises by stating that 'an institution is the interaction of preferences, rules, individual strategies, customs and norms' [5]. In short, institutions set out the way things work.

At the very least this statement helps us to distinguish between an institution and an organisation, often a primary source of confusion. As Knight relates, an institution is a set of rules that structures the actions among actors whilst organisations are collective actors who might be subject to institutional constraints [6]. Thus a Subak in Bali, Indonesia is an organisation which has distinctive institutional arrangements for distributing water. Organisations like a Subak generally have an internal structure or an institutional framework governing the interactions of those persons who constitute the organisation.

4   Institutional arrangements in the water sector

The preceding paragraphs indicate the difficulty of attempting to rigorously define institutions, but also serve to highlight the many interacting factors that must be considered in their analysis. Perhaps a more useful way to proceed is to look for real life examples of institutional arrangements and then to determine how these might be usefully compared and analysed in a way that can inform policy making in the water sector.

In the water sector the core activities that need to be carried out include construction, collection and/or abstraction, water share allocation and resource mobilisation for maintenance of the collection and delivery systems. Each activity requires a set of decisions involving a group of interested parties. We can also state that the current institutional arrangements allow the decision to be made and the resulting activity to be completed, but not necessarily in due time, nor to satisfy a set of technical, economic or other relevant criteria.

If we restrict our discussion to the allocation of water it is possible to list three main types of institutions for the control of transactions between parties: the market; hierarchy or Government agency; commune or community [7]. There are of course many variations in between.

There has been much discussion recently as to which is the most appropriate mechanism for allocating what is in many regions an increasingly scarce resource. In many countries the privatisation or turnover of the management of irrigation systems has been deemed appropriate. The official rationale is that decentralising decision making to the beneficiaries will make more efficient use of all resources but the driving force has often been the shortage of public sector finance. For much the same reasons, water markets are being promoted in many parts of the world to allocate the locally managed resource.

However, water is not a typical good. A useful paper by Gray looks at the economic dimensions of water. In the paper the diversity of uses of water is seen as reflecting its various economic characteristics. These range from the characteristics of marketable "private type" goods sold like any other commodity to those of collective "public type" like flood control [8]. Gray states that a given water policy might need to reflect any or all of the six characteristics listed below rather than assuming that the first characteristic is all that matters. In doing so he hints that the relative importance of each element depends on the set of users, the location of use, and its timing. Without explicitly saying so, he recognises the importance of the institutional structure in determining the effectiveness and efficiency of the allocation of this atypical resource. Gray's characteristics of the water resource are listed as follows:

- marketable private good
- public or collective good
- common property resource (differing from the public good characteristic in that it is subject to right of capture, becoming private on capture)
- externality characteristics (including the effects of water transactions on third parties)
- public utility characteristics (the high fixed cost, lower per unit cost of output characteristic of the water sector)
- option values (this relates to the foreclosure of future options, for example as a result of interbasin transfers which are often irreversible.

Thus, even in the face of increasing pressure on Government recurrent resources, the evidence is growing that the drive to privatisation is too rapid and the model adopted too simplistic for the water resource.

The neo-classical paradigm would suggest that privatisation is rational. However, it has lately been criticised for ignoring the complicated working procedures that determine optimal resource use strategies and which are a direct result of the resource's varied characteristics. The neo-classical approach is essentially static, taking no account of the medium to long term implications of policy other than in efficiency terms. Platteau quotes Bardhan as stating that 'we often apply the simple laws of market supply and demand without being fully conscious of the complex of institutions on which contracts in actual markets crucially depend' [9].

If information was costless, it would, in principal at least, be easy to establish a market in water which would ensure that the resource would be used more efficiently. The fact that water markets are not widespread reflects the high costs of obtaining information and monitoring and enforcing rules, i.e. the costs of transacting. As a result, many of the rules established in the past can be understood as responses to limitations of information in an environment where water was in relatively plentiful supply. However, as scarcity value increases these traditional rules can become very inefficient [10]. The task facing policy makers now is how to formulate rules that will "work" in this new era.

Neo-classical economics' deficiency with regard to these transaction costs has long been recognised in the Institutional Economics school. However, the older generations of institutionalists failed to understand the origins of the institutions they discuss and therefore have not been in a position to predict how institutions might change in response to new economic conditions [10]. Livingston relates that a more pragmatic approach to policy making is offered by that school and that recommendations are not held as universal truths, but are seen as being the best overall structure or improvement given the factorial base of a particular situation and the associated possibilities and limitations [11]. They have therefore added little of use for the practical decision maker.

5   The NIE continuum

Lately however, a set of approaches falling under the generic term New Institutional Economics (NIE) has not only made promising inroads into the analysis of the determinants of institutions (i.e. the reasons for their existence and their evolution over time) but could also prove useful for evaluating their economic efficiency as well as their income distributional impacts [12]. This approach takes account of the institutional character but is essentially an adaptation of the neo-classical approach.

New Institutionalists have been defined as neo-classically oriented economists who have acquired an interest in the institutional phenomenon [7]. Certainly, its proponents do not discard the insights given by the neo-classical approach. Their aim is to build on the traditional approach whilst attempting to add value to the insights from that theory by incorporating the important institutional dimension.

NIE is a complex of complementary strands of analysis. We therefore use a typology based on Nabli and Nugent's listing of the most visible lines of investigation [12] These lines are depicted as a continuum between the institutionalist school and the neo-classical school.

There are two broad approaches relevant to analysing water development problems using NIE, the Transaction Cost school and the Collective Action school.

5.1   The Transaction Cost school
Within this school there are three related emphases: contractual choice; information choice; and property rights. The school argues that institutions are transaction cost minimising arrangements which may change and evolve with changes in the nature and sources of transaction costs and the means for minimising them. It is costly to transact in the water sector primarily because of the scattered nature across the country of the main actors and hence the costliness of measurement and of enforcement of the transaction. It takes scarce resources to define, measure and monitor any rights that are transferred in economic activity. Even if all exchanging individuals had the same goals there would still be transaction costs involved in acquiring the necessary information about the level of attributes of each exchange unit, for example the quality and/or reliability of supply of a given quantity of water, the location of buyers and so forth.

In practice, there are asymmetries of information among the economic players. This contributes to the varied behaviour of individuals acting in combination, and has radical implications for economic theory and for the study of institutions. Not only does one party know more about some valued attribute than the other party, he or she may stand to gain by concealing that information. In addition there are costs of enforcement which cause no problem when it is in the interest of the other party to live up to the agreements, but without institutional constraints, self-interested behaviour could preclude optimal interaction and exchange. The most dramatic example of enforcement failure known to the writers comes from Pakistan where a special deep silt clearance from a canal was reversed overnight with bulldozers when the headenders found their water supply fell with the silt removal.

Institutions therefore provide the structure for exchange that determines the cost of transacting and the cost of transformation, the latter being influenced by technology employed, which we traditionally perceive to be the critical variable. However, a situation of insecure property rights can for example result in the use of technology that employs little fixed capital and doesn't entail long term agreements. By ignoring the transaction costs and, more importantly, their sources, decision makers could end up imposing the "wrong" type of technology.

Institutions also determine potential returns on opportunism, cheating and so forth that arise in complex societies, especially those with a wide geographic spread such as irrigation. An effective institutional arrangement overcomes the cost of formulating and enforcing stringent rules by creating a simpler set of rules that then make a variety of informal constraints effective [13]. Unfortunately, in countries where there is a decline in respect for law and order, or a loss of either Government or traditional local authority, the effectiveness of activities such as irrigation which must rely heavily on local consensus, may be eroded by the same factors that have weakened Government.

Many of the new research efforts proceed from a legal perspective and emphasis rights and rules [7]. They discuss economic yield as a function of property rights and define institutions as rules that establish economic relationships between individuals. Hence the inappropriate technology employed as a result of insecure property rights could be replaced by the "appropriate" technology introduced by the decision maker if the right institutions were in place.

5.2 The Collective Action school

This school focuses on the individual's motivation. Again there are three main emphases in writings: behavioural norms; common property resource management; and rent seeking, all of which aim at the elimination of free riding, such as the non-payer of water fees or the non-participant in drain cleaning. The approach is concerned with explaining the way in which interest pressure groups succeed or fail to develop and how and why the relative strengths vary over time [12]. Practitioners show how to tackle the free rider problem and how to identify the main conditions for successful collective action. The school is a combination of theoretical developments e.g. Olson, Runge, Ostrom, Wade, Nabli and Nugent.

There are of course links between the transaction cost and the collective action schools. For example, transaction costs are often incurred in order to decrease the free rider problem. Indeed, it is a crucial assumption of the transaction cost approach that the economic agent can behave in a strategic or opportunistic manner.

6   Policy in practice

To conclude, we look briefly at the types of insights that NIE can give to the water sector and then at avenues for future research :

- in the water sector there is overemphasis on privatisation, or turnover, with little recognition of the cultural and institutional constraints nor of self interested behaviour;
- where there is a recognition that traditional institutions maybe best, little thought has been given to the future effects of changes in external pressures on the resource such as increased demands for water from urban use and tourism; or increased pollution from industry and in the ability of the existing institutions to evolve in response;
- in the past the overriding efficiency criteria adopted by economists has resulted in the introduction of technologies and policies that are inappropriate given the institutional structure.

Analysts must probe this key concept in particular and ensure that it takes full account of stability, resiliency and equitability. Failing this, separate criteria will have to be applied.

Future research must address the problem of how to put policy on a transaction cost minimising path. North has emphasised that not all institutional arrangements lower transaction costs. Some, for example rules that require useless inspections, raise information costs or make property rights less secure, will in fact raise transaction costs. There can therefore be too much as well as too little regulation.

By affecting transaction costs and co-ordination possibilities, institutions can have dramatic effects by enhancing or retarding growth [12]. By affecting resource mobilisation and incentives for accumulation and innovation they may induce or hinder economic efficiency in allocation.

Twenty five years ago Schmid concluded that the dynamic complexity of institutional interactions makes empirical work difficult. The external environment is fluid and people learn and change and that to make empirical progress a relevant set of concepts and linkages is needed [14]. NIE could provide the framework that allows us at last to incorporate some of the central concerns of the structuralists that bear directly upon water policy deliberations.

7 References

1. Myrdal, G. (1984) in *Pioneers in Development.* (eds G..Meier and D.Seers) Oxford: Oxford University Press for The World Bank.
2. Little, I. (1982) *Economic Development: Theory, Policy and International Relations* Twentieth Century Fund, Basic Books, New York
3. Johnson, S., Vermillion, D. and Sagardoy, J. (1995) *Irrigation Management Transfer* Rome, IIMI/FAO.
4. de los Rayes (1995) Personal communication
5. Ostrom, E. (1986). An agenda for the study of institutions. *Public Choice*, Vol.48, pp. 3-25.
6. Knight, J. (1992). *Institutions and Social Conflict* Cambridge University Press

7. Sjostrand, S.E. (1992). On the Rationale behind 'Irrational' Institutions. *Journal of Economic* Issues, Vol. XXVI, No.4, pp. 1007-1040.

8. Gray (1983) Water: A resource like any other? *Agriculture and Forestry Bulletin,* Vol.6 No.4. pp.47-49. University of Alberta.

9. Platteau, J.P. (1992). The Emergence of the New Institutional Economics. *Land Reform and Structural Adjustment in Sub-Saharan Africa: Controversies and Guidelines.* Rome, FAO pp.21-46

10. Hoff, K., Braverman A., et al. (1994). Introduction. *The Economics of Rural* Organisation *theory, practice and policy.* (eds K. Hoff, A. Braverman and J. Stiglitz) World Bank

11. Livingston, M. L. (1993). Normative and Positive Aspects of Institutional Economics: The Implications for Water Policy. *Water Resources Research* 29(4): 815-821.

12. Nabli, M.K. and Nugent J.B. (1989). The New Institutional Economics and its Applicability to Development. *World Development* , Vol.17, No.9. pp. 1333-1347

13. North, D. (1990). *Institutions, Institutional Change and Economic Performance,* Cambridge University Press.

14. Schmid, A. (1972). "Analytical Institutional Economics: Challenging Problems in the Economics of Resources for a New Environment." *American Journal of Agricultural Economics* , Vol. 54, pp. 893-901.

WATER AND ECONOMICS - WHAT DOES EXPERIENCE TEACH US SO FAR?

Water and economics - lessons learned

C.H. GREEN
Flood Hazard Research Centre, Middlesex University, UK

Abstract
Economic analysis has now been applied extensively to issues of water policy and has been found to be a useful tool, but, in the predominant form of economic analysis, is an incomplete and inadequate tool.   Since progress results from learning from our mistakes, this paper concentrates on what we have learnt about the limitations and inadequacies of current economic methods.

   In particular, making choices necessarily involves ethical questions and strong ethical assumptions are often incorporated into the form of economic analysis adopted. Consequently, the predominant form of economic analysis, 'neoclassical economics' is, I shall, argue a very parochial form of economics, and one which might be better termed an 'Anglo-Saxon economics'. It is also one which is narrowly focused upon the supply and demand for goods which are supplied in a competitive market.   There are consequently major problems when we seek to apply it to water issues, which typically involve public goods.   Finally, the neoclassical economic tradition is very hermetic and consequently economic theory tends to embody naive theories and methodologies which ignore the results of research from other disciplines.
Keywords: benefit-cost analysis, choice, economics, environment, ethics, markets, supply

1   The application of economic analysis to water policies

Any form of analysis is useful to the extent that it enables us to make slightly better decisions than we would otherwise make. In spite of its limitations, economic analysis has already contributed significantly to the analysis of decisions concerning the water environment.   Irrigation works have long been the subject of economists' interest,

Water Policy: Allocation and management in practice. Edited by P. Howsam and R.C. Carter.
Published in 1996 by E & FN Spon. ISBN 0 419 21650 2

mainly because of the belief that they were often inefficient [1]. Benefit-cost analysis is now routinely used to evaluate flood alleviation and coast protection works [2] and a methodology has been developed to allow the routine assessment of the benefits of river water quality improvements [3]. The benefits of hydrometric networks have been assessed [4] as have the benefits of alleviating low flows in rivers [5]. More recently, studies have been undertaken to determine whether the control of pesticide usage at source is more or less efficient than treatment to remove pesticide residues before putting water into the potable supply [6]. The value of water put into supply [7], of improvements to the standards of service of water and sewerage services [8], the economics of demand management [9] and the issues of drought management [10] have all been subject of economic analysis.

A number of studies have been undertaken of the use of economic instruments to control water abstraction or waste discharges [11][12].

2   What economics has achieved so far

Thus, economic analysis has been extensively applied to water; has there been any benefit from all that activity?

Economists are not creative in the same way that engineers or landscape architects are; economics can only be used to evaluate options which have been identified or invented by others. Economics, therefore, typically serves to stop mistakes rather than to identify new and better solutions. In particular, economics helps us to avoid falling into that pervasive trap described in the aphorism: 'having lost sight of our objectives, we redoubled our efforts'. Projects not infrequently take on a life of their own, the objectives of the project coming to be whatever it is the project does rather than the original identified need. What benefit-cost analysis consistently demonstrates is that good intentions are not enough; that if you simply focus on the good intentions, better methods of achieving those ends are ignored [13].

3   Practical lessons

Two kinds of lessons can also be drawn from all this activity. In general, since applying economics in practice is different from the text books, there are some practical lessons. Secondly, what should not be done is almost as important as what can be; what are the major outstanding theoretical and methodological issues which limit the applicability of economic analysis?

3.1 Benefit-cost analysis (BCA)
The principle of benefit-cost analysis should be applied to BCA: it should be undertaken as an iterative process of refinement, where the costs of further refining the analysis are compared to the gains in improvements to the decision from such further refinement. The first stage should be a quick and dirty pre-feasibility assessment using readily available data; this can then be refined if it appears that any option is likely to be economically justified.

The results of a BCA are no better than the options evaluated; there may be some far better options which were not included in the assessment. Therefore, to guard against this risk, it is useful to define some set of options which should normally be included in the options to be compared [14].

A BCA is a process of option identification and selection and not a product; the best guide to assessing the adequacy of a BCA is thus whether it is was undertaken as a process. Thus, key criteria to judge a BCA are who was consulted and when, and what options were identified [14].

It is common to confuse uncertainty about what to do with uncertainty about outcomes. Sensitivity analyses in BCAs tell us what we already know; unless a decision is sensitive to a variable then there is no reason to include that variable in the analysis. Instead techniques can be used which explore how robust the decision is to the necessary uncertainty about the outcomes of that decision [15].

Discounting is an incomplete procedure for comparing streams of benefits and costs over time. Whilst it allows the comparison of the opportunities foregone by investing capital in a scheme, the assumptions it embodies about preferences for the distribution of consumption over time are false [16]. It is therefore necessary to supplement conventional discounting with other comparisons in order to select the preferred option [17].

3.2 Markets
Markets are always imperfect and market prices always need some degree of adjustment before they approximate to the opportunity cost of the production.

There is usually market failure in water; it seems to be an almost universal truth that 25% of water consumed could be saved with a net gain to the consumer [10]. More generally, price elasticity of demand often seems to measure little more than the extent of market failure.

The priced economy only covers part of the flows of resources and consumption; the prices paid for those goods are thus distorted to the extent that an individual depends upon unpriced resources and consumption.

3.3 The environment
Because neoclassical economics is limited to individually given values, it is necessary to apply the concepts of critical and constant natural capital [18] in order to accommodate the other forms of value which some environmental resources have.

In many decisions, particularly those involving coastal erosion, there is no option which offers environmental benefits without any environmental disbenefits. In these circumstances, environmental mediation [17] is likely to be more appropriate than attempting to articulate, in economic terms, the trade-off between different forms of environmental gains and losses.

The Hedonic Price Method [20], as a method of evaluating the different characteristics which make up a good, should probably work for anything for which there is a market. Unfortunately, this excludes the UK housing market; where one person has to decide to move before a house is released to the market. The reasons why someone chooses to move appears to be quite different from the characteristics they look for when buying a house [21]. Furthermore, the market is heterogeneous and the evidence from studies of housing is that the utility function contains lexicographic and multiplicative components [22], as well as highly subjective variables, which make the identification of the required equation problematic.

The Travel Cost Method is the economists' reinvention of the geographers' [23] Gravity Theory model to explain spatial interactions. The basic assumptions of the Travel Cost Method have been shown not always to be satisfied in the UK [24] where, moreover, an additional problem is the high proportion of recreational visits which are made on foot.

Conjoint Analysis, or the Stated Preference Method, is a well-established market research technique [26] to value non-priced goods. It yields good results if respondents pay attention and respond in a simple-minded way. However, they tend to find the task they are asked to do very boring and respond in complex ways.

Contingent Valuation [27] is a second social survey method. Economists either have a strong faith in it or anathematise it. A good Contingent Valuation study will provide understanding of what people want and why they want it; it is this understanding which gives value to the results and without this understanding the results have no meaning. Few Contingent Valuation studies however satisfy the norms of good social survey research practice.

4   Theoretical lessons

Economics can be described as the application of reason to choice where a choice is defined as selecting between two or more alternatives by comparing their performance against one or more objectives. Since the selection of the objectives is outside of economics, the choice of the objectives, and hence the rate at which consequences of the alternatives are to be traded one against another, are ethical or moral questions and not technical questions. However, the neoclassical economic model makes strong assumptions about what those assumptions should be and why choices are necessary.

Since choices are made by individuals and society, economics cannot help but either compete with, or draw upon, the other social sciences, especially with psychology and sociology. Unfortunately, rather than draw upon the research results and methodologies from those other disciplines, neoclassical economics simply invents psychological and other theories, and methodologies, as it goes along.

4.1 Axioms
Neoclassical economics is based upon three axioms: that choice is necessary because of scarcity of resources, that value is determined by individual preference; and that individuals are rational. The first is only a partial explanation since choices may also be necessary because the options are mutually exclusive in time or space, famously one cannot be in two different places at once. Since deep ecologists [27] argue that species have an inherent value by right of existence, the axiomatic claim of the second axiom automatically falls. As Sen [28] noted, the axiom of rationality, the application of reason to choice, has tended to become arbitrarily redefined to objective, selfishness, which the individual seeks to achieve through reason.

4.2 Supply side limitations
Whilst the distinction is conventionally made between private and public goods, this is essentially only a distinction on the demand side of the equation. It may be argued that

an equivalent distinction needs also to be made on the supply side of the equation between those goods which an individual or company can provide and those which can only be provided through a collective group or society [29]. In the past, such collective goods were often cooperatively constructed and managed as Common Property Resources [30].

4.3 Theories of choice
Anglo-Saxon economics developed around the analysis of the supply and demand for private goods, broadly those which can be bought and sold in a market. This theoretical structure has then been assumed to be a general theory of choice which can be applied to all choices. Thus it is assumed that choices about public goods are structurally similar to those about private goods: that Blue Whales are no more than very large cups of coffee in terms of the way in which choices are taken about their provision. That the theory of demand for private goods is a general theory of choice is a sweeping presumption [29].

4.4 Time
Economics has so far almost totally failed to incorporate any of the characteristics of time. The recognition that time is a constraint on production, just as much as the factors of production, resulted in the development of Operational Research and it is towards Operational Researchers rather than economists that production managers turn for advice on how to optimise production. Equally, time might be argued to act as a constraint on consumption, just as much as income [30][31].

4.5 Implicit theories of psychology and sociology
Whilst Mills sought to distinguish the domain of economics from those of the sciences, in reality economics competes with the social sciences and embodies implicit psychological and sociological theories. These implicit theories often conflict with the knowledge gained from the social sciences and are always untested; economists generally tend to ignore research from other disciplines.

For example, economic analyses, particularly CVM studies, embody implicit cognitive models as to what people want and therefore value. Economists tend to assume that people can state a willingness to pay for whatever it is that the economist wants to value, defined in whatever terms are convenient to the economist. Often, the implicit cognitive models assumed by the economists are in contradiction to what is known about cognitive structures [32].

Learning is a fundamental human trait but it is not incorporated into the neoclassical economic model. Consequently, the neoclassical assumption that we attempt to apply reason to choice should not carry with it the assumption that we are always successful in optimising our behavioural choices. The evidence is rather that we make rather a lot of mistakes, in purchasing as in other decisions. The important question is under what conditions do we make the fewest mistakes; is this, for instance, when we have the most experience of that form of purchasing? The psychologist will also want to ask how the individual learns those preferences as well as how good is the individual's performance.

4.6 Ethics
Conventionally, the economic value of a resource is thought to consist of two

components, use value and nonuse value. Unfortunately, economists have first speculated as what these motives might be and then simply assumed that their speculations provide an adequate theoretical framework to account for these motives. Instead, there is emerging evidence that the reasons why people value environmental resources are essentially moral reasons, beliefs that we have duties to other people, other generations and other species or that we ought not to pollute [24][33].

The honest answer is that, at the moment, economists don't know why people value the environment for more than the use we can make of it. When we don't know what it is that people value or why they value it, it is foolhardy to attempt to attach a monetary value to it; economic evaluation is thus limited to use value. Any number is not better than no number unless we know what the number means.

There are some reasons for believing that when confronted with a choice about the provision of a public, collective good then individuals respond in terms of the social desirability of the good, and what they perceive as their obligation to contribute towards the cost of providing for that good, rather than solely in terms of their personal preference [34].

5   Conclusions

We have to choose how to make choices; to decide what are the objectives which we seek to satisfy both in selecting between the options and in the process itself. Reason is not itself an objective in the same way that fairness, equity and efficiency may be; it is a servant of decision making. Moreover, choices nearly always involve ethical or moral decisions which cannot be reduced to technical issues. Having chosen how to make choices, reason is a way of reducing the complexity of decision making to a level where we can better understand the choice we have to make. Economic analysis can then help us by routinising the trivial so as to both create consistency between decisions, which is itself a form of fairness, and leave more time to take the more difficult decisions. By structuring those more difficult choices, it also helps us to manage their complexity. In turn, we have to choose our economics, otherwise our economics will choose us; we will allow an abstract system of analysis to choose our societal objectives and the ethical choices we wish to make.

This new economics is likely to be more like a social science using experimental methods, and focused upon gaining understanding about what people want and why they want it. It will plagiarise other disciplines for insights and methodologies. A demand for public, collective goods may form the basis of a general theory of choice and demand for private goods the trivial case of this general theory since it is desirable to keep those parts of existing theory which work. At the same time, Islamic and other forms of economics, built upon the moral and ethical principles of non Anglo-Saxon societies, may also emerge.

However, we cannot stop making decisions about water policy whilst we develop such an economics. Consequently, we have to continue to apply reason to choice but to concentrate on gaining understanding as to the nature of the choice rather than simply applying text book analyses by rote. We have learnt more about the nature of these choices from applying economics to water policy so helping make better choices. At the same time, we learn about the form of the economics which we require to develop for the future.

6   References

1.   Herrington, P. (1987) *Pricing Water Services*, OECD, Paris.
2.   Ministry of Agriculture, Fisheries and Food (1993) *Flood and Coastal Defence: Project Appraisal Guidance Notes*, HMSO, London.
3.   WRc/OXERA/FHRC (1994) *Assessing the benefits of river water quality improvements: Interim Manual*, Foundation for Water Research, Marlow
4.   CNS Scientific and Engineering Services (1991*) The Benefit-Cost of Hydrometric Data - river flow gauging*, Foundation for Water Research, Marlow.
5.   House, M. A., Tunstall, S. M., Green, C. H., Portou, J. and Clarke, L. (1994*) The Evaluation of the Recreational Benefits and Other Use Values from Alleviating Low Flows*, R & D Note 258, National Rivers Authority, Bristol
6.   Heinz, I., Flessau, A., Zullei-Seibert, N., Kuhlmann, B., Schulte-Ebbert, U., Michels, M., Simbrey, J. and Fleischer, G. (1995) *Economic Efficiency Calculations in Conjunction with the Drinking Water Directive (Directive 80/778/EEC); Part III: The Parameter for Pesticides and Related Products*, Report to the European Commission, INFU, Dortmund
7.   Gibbons, D. C. (1986) *The Economic Value of Water*, Resources for the Future, Washington D.C
8.   Tunstall, S. M., Green, C. H., Sawyer, J. and Herring, M. (1993) *Customer preference and willingness to pay for selected water and sewerage services*, OFWAT, Birmingham
9.   National Rivers Authority (1995) *Saving Water: the NRA's approach to demand management*, Demand Management Centre, Worthing
10. Green, C. H. and Tapsell S. M. (1996*) Loss functions for variations in potable water supply*, Report to the Office of Water Services, Flood Hazard Research Centre, Enfield
11. ERL/OXERA (1992) *The Use of Market Mechanisms for the Water Environment*, ERL, London
12. Silsoe College/FHRC (1996) *The Use of Tradable Permits for Irrigation Waters*, Report to the Royal Society for the Protection of Birds, Silsoe College, Silsoe
13. Surr, M., Starmer, A., Watson, D., Young, D., Green, C. and Potts, E. (1993) *Cairo Wastewater Project, Egypt: Interim Evaluation*, Overseas Development Administration, London
14. Green, C. H. (1994) *Stinking Fish: a Sceptic's guide to the assessment of the quality of a benefit-cost analysis*, report to English Nature, Flood Hazard Research Centre, Enfield
15. Green, C. H. (1995) Sources of uncertainty in the appraisal of flood alleviation schemes, paper given at the EUROFLOOD Workshop on Uncertainty, Paris
16. Green, C. H. (1991) The value bases of ecological and economic evaluation, in (eds.) *Valuing the environment*, (eds. A. Coker and C. Richards), Belhaven, London

17. Penning-Rowsell, E. C., Green, C. H., Thompson, P. M., Coker, A. C., Tunstall, S. M., Richards, C. and Parker, D. J. (1992) *The benefits of coast protection and sea defence: a manual of assessment techniques*, Bellhaven, London

18. Gillespie, J. and Shepard, P. (1995) *Establishing Criteria for Identifying Critical Natural Capital in the Terrestrial Environment*, Discussion Paper 141, English Nature, Peterborough

19. Parker, D. J. (1995) *Hengistbury Head: Warren Hill Coast Protection Scheme Proposal Benefit-Cost Appraisal*, Interim Report to Bournemouth Development Services, Flood Hazard Research Centre, Enfield

20. Rosen, S. (1974) Hedonic prices and implicit markets: product differentiation in Pure Competition. *Journal of Political Economy*, Vol. 82, pp. 34-55

21. McAuley, W. J. and Nutty, C. L. (1982) Residential preferences and moving behaviour: a family life-cycle analysis. *Journal of Marriage and the Family*, pp. 300-309

22. Veldhuisen, K. J. and Timmermans, H. J. P. (1984) Specification of individual residential utility functions: a comparative analysis of three measurement procedures. *Environment and Planning A*, Vol. 16, pp.1573-1582

23. Olsson (1965) *Distance and Human Interaction: A review and bibliography,* Regional Science Research Institute, Uppsala

24. Green, C. H., Tunstall, S. M., N'Jai, A. and Rogers, A. (1990) The economic evaluation of environmental goods. *Project Appraisal*, Vol. 5, No. 2, pp.70-82

25. Louviere, J. L. (1988) *Analyzing Decision Making: Metric Conjoint Analysis*, Quantitative Applications in the Social Sciences 67, Sage, Newbury Park

26. Mitchell, R. C. and Carson, R. T. (1989*) Using Surveys to Value Public Goods: The Contingent Valuation Method*, Resources for the Future, Washington D.C.

27. Naess, A. (1993) The Deep Ecological Movement: Some Philosophical Aspects, in *Environmental Ethics - Divergence and Convergence*, (eds. S. J. Armstrong and R.G. Botzler), McGraw-Hill, New York

28. Sen, A. K. (1977) Rational fools: a critique of the behavioural foundations of economic theory, *Philosophy and Public Affairs*, Vol. 6, pp. 317-344

29. Green, C. H., van der Veen, A., Reitano, B., Wierstra, E., Ketteridge, A-M., Otter, H., Rivilla, M. (1996) *The use of economic instruments in catchment management*, EUROFLOOD Technical Annex, Report to the European Commission, Flood Hazard Research Centre, Enfield

30. Ostrom, E. (1990) *Governing the Commons: the Evolution of Institutions for Collective Action*, Cambridge University Press, Cambridge

31. Carlstein, T. *Time, Resources, Ecology and Society*, Allen and Unwin, London

32. Soule, G. (1955) *Time for Living*, Viking, New York

33. Green, C. H. and Tunstall, S. M. (1996) Contingent Valuation: a psychological perspective, in *Contingent Valuation*, (eds. I. Bateman and K.G. Willis), Oxford University Press, Oxford

34. Green, C. H. and Tunstall, S. M. (1993) The environmental value and attractiveness of river corridors, paper given at *Les Paysages de l'eau aux portes de la ville; mise en valeur ecologique et integration sociale*, Lyons

SUSTAINABLE IRRIGATION MANAGEMENT THROUGH COST RECOVERY SYSTEM
Sustainable irrigation management

M. ASAD UZ ZAMAN
Executive Director, Barind Multipurpose Development
Authority, Rajshahi, Bangladesh.

Abstract
Barind Multipurpose Development Authority (BMDA) deals with the multiple development of three districts of Bangladesh, within 0.775 million hectare of land. The objectives of BMDA are to bring 0.162 million hectare of land under controlled irrigation, to augment surface water resources, electrification of irrigation equipment and small scale rural industries, partial mechanization, crop diversification programme (CDP), afforestation and construction of rural feeder roads.

Irrigation from deep tubewells (DTW) is the vital source of small scale irrigation for the project area. The farmers utilise water from these wells, operated either by group management or by the project, called departmental management system. An integrated irrigation and agricultural management system with the linkage of the community involved in the project activities, has been developed.

Upon completion of the project with required infrastructure and providing all facilities, the project aims at a financially self driven project by generating income through cost recovery from water conveyance for irrigation and meeting all cost for O & M. On the basis of encouraging performance and achievement in the past, the very objectives of self financing activities of the project are considered sustainable.

Keywords: credit, cost recovery, irrigation management, objectives, sustainability, training.

1 Introduction

To improve the living condition of 5.616 million people of a comparatively depressed and backward area covering 0.775 million hectare of land, the Barind integrated area development project was undertaken in 1985. Initially, the Bangladesh Agricultural

Water Policy: Allocation and management in practice. Edited by P. Howsam and R.C. Carter.
Published in 1996 by E & FN Spon. ISBN 0 419 21650 2

Development Corporation (BADC), an autonomous body was assigned with the task of implementing the project. Over the passage of time, having observed the potential of the project, its geographical area increased to include 25 thanas in 1992 under phase II of the project. In view of the national importance of the project, "Barind Multipurpose Development Authority" (BMDA) was created to implement the project under the direct supervision of the Ministry of Agriculture.

2   Objectives

In order to facilitate income generation and improve the quality of life of the people in the project area, as well as to support and sustain agricultural growth and ecological balance, the following activities have been undertaken :

- Bringing 0.162 million hectares of land under year round cultivation through the existing and programmed deep tube well.
- Augmenting surface water resources through re-excavation of derelict ponds and canals (locally known as khari) and also constructing the cross dams.
- Partial mechanization through introduction of power tiller.
- Electrification of irrigation equipment and agro-based industries in the project area.
- Large scale afforestation and expansion of nurseries to achieve an ecological balance.
- Construction of 110 Km rural feeder road, linking production areas to important growth centres.

3   Small scale irrigation

Investigations show that the area has an appropriate system providing scope for ground water extraction to the extent of utilizing about 8,728 number of deep tubewells in 17 thanas as per study conducted by Master Plan Organisation (MPO) and Ground Water Circle-Bangladesh Water Development Board (GWC-BWDB).
Presently around 5,000 deep tubewell, 37,200 shallow tubewells and 1,400 low lift pumps are being operated. The total area brought under controlled irrigation through the above equipment is around 0.234 million hectare which is 34.72% of the total cultivable land of 0.583 million hectare. Barind authority is responsible only for DTW irrigation management.

3.1 Management of deep tubewell irrigation
Deep tubewell irrigation management system is broadly of two types   (I) group management and (II) Departmental (BMDA) management system.

3.2   Group management system
Under this system farmers organise themselves into groups called water users association (WUA) that enter into a lease-agreement with BMDA in matters of

operation of deep tubewells and manages irrigation in the command area. The principal features of such lease agreements and arrangements are as follows.

- All the water users are members of the WUA. These committee-members are elected from the general members forming a working committee consisting of one group leader or manager, one chairperson, one vice president and some members. They sign the lease agreement with BMDA and make necessary arrangements for payment.
- Upon receipt of the request for lease agreement from the WUA, BMDA verifies the details of the application and, if all stipulations are found to be complied with grant permission to the association and conclude the lease agreement.
- Before sinking the tubewell in a particular command area, BMDA engineers inspect the site and select a spot that is typically at the higher altitude. The owner of the spot requires to transfer the ownership of an area equal to 6 m by 6 m. After the tubewell is sunk, BMDA staff take away the handle and the drive shaft of the machine and deposit those in the stores so that the tubewells can not be made operational until the irrigation charge is paid by the groups.

The irrigation charges are levied at the following rates for payment in due time.

Table 1. Irrigation cost for group managed well

Discharge of Tubewell (cusec)	Minimum Command Area	Irrigation charge Without Rebate (Tk.)	Irrigation charge paid before 31st January (20% rebate)	Irrigation charge Paid between 1st Feb. to 15 Feb.(10% rebate)	Irrigation charge paid between 16 Feb. to 31st March
1.20-1.49	18 ha.	10,135	8,100	9,129	10,135
1.50-1.74	23 ha.	12,150	9,720	10,935	12,150
1.75-2.00	25 ha.	13,500	10,800	12,150	13,500

* Tk. 40 = $1

If the irrigation charges are not paid by 1st April, penalty at the rate of 15% (Tk. 7.50 per ha.) per month or part thereof is charged in additional to the principal amount.

- BMDA bears the cost of repair and spares up to one-third of the full irrigation charges realised. If the cost exceeds the limit, the additional costs are to be borne by the WUA. In both the cases, departmental or group management operating system, mechanic services are free of cost. Trained personnel are ever-ready to support mechanic services when and where required.
- All the operating costs other than explained above are borne by the WUA.

3.3 Departmental (BMDA) management system

In the following cases the irrigation system comes under BMDA management system.

- The schemes that remain non-functional for two consecutive irrigation seasons due to factional quarrel.
- The schemes which have not fully paid their dues over the last two years.

- The schemes whose engines are non-functional for a long time due to severe damage to the machine.
- All the deep tubewells that are not in use, and
- The tubewells which have been electrified
- If the water users association prefers departmental management system due to its operational suitability to group management system and willingly hand over to BMDA.

In this method of operation BMDA undertakes the responsibility of operating the wells and the farmers get irrigation facilities on payment of irrigation charges.

3.4 Mode of payment of cost recovery from BMDA managed wells.

- Farmers are to pay the irrigation charge before taking irrigation water in advance at the rate fixed in the system given below.

Table 2. Irrigation costs for BMDA managed wells

Crop : Irri/Boro paddy.							
Diesel operated						Electrically operated	
System-1		System-2		System-3		System-4	
Irrigation charge per hour (TK.)		Expected irrigated area (ha)	Irrigation charge per ha (TK.)	Expected irrigated area (ha)	Irrigation charge per ha (TK.)	Irrigation charge per hour (TK.)	
upto 1.2 cusec	above1.2 cusec					upto1.2 cusec	above 1.2 cusec
35	40	8.23-13.5	2223.00	8.23-13.5	5928.00	60	75
35	40	13.6-27	1852.50	13.6-27	5557.50	60	75
35	40	above-27	1667.25	above-27	5187.00	60	75
Crop : Wheat /Potato/Mustard and other							
35	40	8.23-13.5	1259.70	8.23-13.5	2778.75	60	75
35	40	13.6-27	1185.60	13.6-27	2593.50	60	75
35	40	above-27	1111.50	above-27	2223.00	60	75
Crop : Aus paddy							
35	40	8.23-13.5	1259.70	8.23-13.5	2964.00	60	75
35	40	13.6-27	1185.60	13.6-27	2778.75	60	75
35	40	Above-27	1111.50	Above-27	2593.50	60	75
Crop : Transplanted Aman paddy							
35	40					60	75

System-1 : The farmers are to bear the cost of fuel only. All other costs are borne by BMDA,
System-2 : As system-1. System-3 : All operation cost are borne by BMDA including fuel.
System-4 : All costs are borne by BMDA

- For all the wells under departmental management system the irrigation charge is realised in form of coupons sold by BMDA. To avoid cash transaction in payment of irrigation charge for possible complexity in keeping proper account in the field, missing and pilferage of money, coupons of different denominations like- Tk. 500, Tk.100, Tk.75, Tk. 50, Tk.10, Tk.5 & Tk.1 are printed in the Government security printing press. (Tk. 40 = $ 1).

- The coupons have three perforated parts. The 1st part remains as the office copy. The operator keeps the 2nd part and the 3rd part is refunded to the farmer. The operators record the coupon number and necessary information.
- These irrigation charge coupons are readily available in all offices of BMDA and any person can purchase the coupons of any amount and use those in any departmentally operated wells under the jurisdiction of BMDA.
- A commission at the rate of 5% is provided to a purchaser who purchases the coupons for a minimum amount of Tk. 1000 at a time in cash from the office
- To reward the water users lottery is drawn on the 15th July each year. Several attractive prizes of Tk. 750 to 10,000 are distributed among the winners possessing the coupons of the same number of the farmer`s foil.

With the introduction of coupon system the water-lord business has been abolished. Under this system the farmers can purchase water frequently at the lower price as needed. Unlike the group management system they are not bound to pay the full amount of water charge at a time. This, in turn, encourages the farmers to irrigate a greater area and reduces any sort of harassment by the so-called middlemen or water-lords. The provision of incentive or penalty is also remaining with BMDA to impose upon the BMDA staff for their success or failure to realise irrigation charges. The amount of incentive ranges from 2% to 10% of the realised irrigation charge and for the default cases 10% to 30% of the travelling allowances are held up which is gradually paid to the staff when the default amount is realised.

4   Training

BMDA provides training to operators, the mechanic assistants and the power tiller operators. Moreover, the farmers are also trained on water use and crop cultivation. Nearly 3000 operators, 500 mechanic assistants and 500 power tiller operators have been trained. A policy of positive discrimination in favour of women has led to a situation where 90% of all plant watchers and 100% of the electrified deep tubewell operators are women. Male operators are still largely employed for diesel engine operated tubewells.

The main principle of this employment is based on the payment from income e.g. "No income No payment," basis. The minimum monthly remuneration is Tk.750 but it may be increased up to Tk.1200 depending on the amount of irrigation charges realised from a particular command area.

5   Supervised credit facility

A supervised credit programme has been launched with National Bank Ltd., a private Bank. The bank provides credit to the farmers only in kind not in cash. The bank and BMDA staff complete all the required formalities in the DTW field. No farmers are allowed or required to come to the bank office. All these activities are performed through credit slips. BMDA receives payment for irrigation water and seeds, and private dealers receive payment against fertiliser and insecticides from the banks, by debit to borrowers account.

Already the 8th crop season's loan programme has been completed with 100% realization of the disbursed amount. Under the model landless share-croppers are also getting loans without collateral. The financing model is gaining popularity day by day among the farmers.

6 Crop diversification programme (CDP)

To divert the farmers from traditional cultivation of paddy-paddy-and paddy for all the three crop seasons in a year and to attract less water consumptive crops such as mustard, wheat, potato and vegetables, BMDA has set up a programme. BMDA purchases the seeds from BADC district seed office and gets a rebate of around 7%. The rebate amount is divided into four equal parts. The 1st one-fourth goes to field offices as incentive, the 2nd one-fourth goes to farmers as commission during purchase of the seeds, and the remaining one-half remains with BMDA to meet the carrying and handling charges. This programme seems to be an effective one.

7   Monitoring and evaluation

The Assistant Engineer holding the prime responsibilities for irrigation activities in a particular thana assigns and distributes tasks among his subordinate officers and field staff such as Senior Sub-Assistant Engineer, Sub-Assistant Engineer, Mechanic and Assistant Mechanic normally in the months of October-November (just before the irrigation season starts).

All sub-ordinate officers and field staff are given responsibilities individually for maintaining a number of wells of some particular location. The Assistant Engineer constantly supervises and monitors the progress of activities and activities of the individual sub-ordinate staff on a daily and weekly basis.

The Executive Engineer (district level officer) monitors and evaluates the progress of thana level irrigation activities weekly, fortnightly and monthly. The Executive Director does it at least thrice a year in a joint meeting of all concerned officers and field staff.

Individual evaluation is done based on number of wells allotted and operated, area irrigated, accrued irrigation charges and realization.

Not only the irrigation and water management activities are monitored by the project people, other components that are generated for the social and environmental benefits are also monitored and evaluated with due care.

8   Sustainable irrigation system

To achieve the sustainable irrigation system it is necessary to ensure judicious lifting and careful use of water, construction of appropriate water distribution systems, electrification of irrigation equipment, mechanised farming system and imparting training to the concerned field officers and staff for acquiring appropriate knowledge on requirement of water use and fertiliser doses for different crops at different growing stages and also knowledge on seeds of appropriate varieties, pest control and crop diversification.

BMDA is quite aware of these requirements and trying to proceed slowly but steadily to achieve the target of optimum utilisation of irrigation wells. The main strategies of Barind irrigation management system are to make BMDA self financed in respect of meeting the O & M cost, salaries of total engaged manpower with the participation of local farmers for smooth functioning of the system.

Although the cost recovery from irrigation is the key to self financing the authority, other components of the project are also contributing to self sustainability. The effect of the components with irrigation and water management programme to sustainability was evaluated by P. Howsam & D. Sutherland on their visit to the project area as "An efficient operation and maintenance scheme has been set up, together with a cost recovery scheme which has proved to be highly effective, with close to 100% recovery. A coupon system for irrigation water, which is administered with a firm but fair approach, together with incentive schemes at a variety of levels, are the keys to its success". They also commented that- "These measures can easily be quantified but what is less easy to define but is nevertheless very evident is the excellent level of commitment and motivation of both the BMPDA [BMDA] staff and the farmers and communities involved. In general the philosophy is one of proceeding slowly but surely, with an emphasis on achieving sustainable development rather than on achieving ambitious numerical targets". Thus it can be summarized and concluded that:

- With due participation of the community involved in the project activities with its infrastructural consolidation it is close to the target of its self financing.
- An appropriate cost recovery system for distribution of irrigation water from dependable irrigation units can enable the project itself to be sustainable one.

9   Bibliography

1. Rahman, M.M.S. (1994) An Economic Analysis of Deep Tubewells under Barind Integrated Area Development Project in an Area of Rajshahi District, Bangladesh, A thesis.
2. Ghafur, A. & Latif, A. (1995) Barind Integrated Area Development Project : An Evaluation, pp 19-46
3. Peoples Republic of Bangladesh, Ministry of Agriculture. (1995) Project Proforma for Barind Integrated Area Development Project- Phase-II.

WATER POLICY: ECONOMIC THEORY AND POLITICAL REALITY

J. MORRIS
Management and Marketing Department, Silsoe College, Cranfield University, UK

Abstract
Rising demand, supply deficit and a deteriorating environment have forced water onto the political agenda. Water policy attempts to meet the demands for water whilst simultaneously protecting and, where possible, enhancing water resources and the aquatic environment. Regarding water as an economic commodity in order to guide water resource decisions and achieve water use efficiency is currently a favoured policy instrument. In practice, however, economic principles and market processes are unlikely in themselves to deliver sustainable water management, without regulation and direct action by Government and its agents. Water policy can benefit from the discipline of economics, but it is no substitute for capability in political systems.
Keywords: commodity, economics, policy, pricing, water management

1   Introduction

Water is quickly superseding land as the world's most limiting resource. 70% of the globe is water but most of it is not directly usable. Less than 3% of all water is freshwater, and of this, 80% is locked up in the ice caps.

In its natural form, the hydrological cycle describes water as a renewable, recyclable resource. Like other natural resources, water is a source of income and wealth generation: a key determinant and indicator of the quality of life. It provides an input to economic activity, a sink for waste, and supports living systems, including humans. Unfortunately, as far as human needs are concerned, there is often a mismatch between points of source and use, both temporarily and spatially. Resources are committed to overcoming this imbalance. Furthermore, many uses

Water Policy: Allocation and management in practice. Edited by P. Howsam and R.C. Carter.
Published in 1996 by E & FN Spon. ISBN 0 419 21650 2

result in degradation of water quality and in some cases virtual loss, with negative consequences for welfare and the performance of economic systems themselves.

2   Water policy objectives and methods

Rising demand, supply deficit and deteriorating water environments have forced water on to the political agenda.   In the main, water policy attempts to resolve conflicts between pressure for social and economic development and protection or enhancement of water resources and the water environment: achieving economic growth whilst simultaneously controlling resource use and pollution [1][2].   The terminology of water policy indicates the underlying principles and concerns, namely: sustainable development, environmental appraisal, precautionary approach, polluter pays, and to varying degrees, the disclosure of information regarding proposed development and potential risks.

   The main methods or instruments by which Governments can seek to achieve water and related environmental policy objectives can be classified as regulation and command, economic instruments, and direct action.   Regulation through legislation, licensing and enforcement is used to guarantee minimum standards of service and environmental quality.   Regulation can be expensive and inflexible.   Economic instruments use market principles to achieve policy objectives.   This involves pricing water in ways which reflect value in use and/or cost of supply, and, by means of judicious use of taxes and subsidies, shaping decisions on water resource development and allocation in order to achieve maximum economic efficiency.   In practice the use of economic instruments is hampered by their unreliability, especially given lack of information on how market participants might react.   Direct action may involve public provision of water services, education for water users, scientific research to formulate and implement water policy, and the administration of policy itself..

3   Water as an economic commodity

Traditionally, water in its natural state has been regarded as a 'free' good of unlimited supply with zero cost at the point of supply.   Users pay for transfer costs relating to: transport, treatment to meet quality requirement, and disposal of used water (including materials in solution).   Opportunity costs of water are generally ignored. As a consequence, users have little incentive to ensure water is put to best use or used efficiently.
Economic efficiency requires that:
- Marginal (extra) Benefit of Use > or = Marginal Cost of Supply,
- Marginal Benefit per unit of Resource is equal across all uses

In theory it is possible to derive demand and supply curves which show:
- the marginal benefit obtained from consumption (and the willingness to pay)
- the marginal cost of supply and the willingness to supply at given prices.

and, where the two intersect, a theoretical price which maximises economic efficiency and welfare. In theory it is possible, given sufficient information, to formulate prices in the various segments of the water market which use water as a final consumer good, an input to production, or as a medium for waste disposal [3][4]. This approach applies equally to the removal of excess water associated with land drainage and flood defence. In this case the marginal benefit of drainage is the avoidance of losses associated with excess water. Flood defence is justified if benefits at least recover the costs of alleviation [5].

In practice, of course, applying market principles to water management is much more complicated because water has a number of characteristics which make it difficult to fit the economists' model of a normal commodity and a perfect market. Water is:

- a 'fugitive', re-usable good
- a common property/public good
- a climatically dependent stochastically supplied resource
- subject to economies of scale in provision or disposal
- is an essential, life supporting commodity with no substitute
- is associated with many non-market, environmental qualities

Given the characteristics of the demand for, and supply of, water and the failure of markets to adequately accommodate social and environmental factors, it is unlikely that economics alone can provide a sufficiently comprehensive and reliable framework for policy. This view is enforced by the observation that within the time frame of many politicians and corporate organisations, economic performance excludes and may be at odds with maintaining the integrity of natural and social resources and systems.

4   Water policy and sustainable development

Following the Rio Summit in 1992, water resources policy is emerging as that part of a strategy for Sustainable Development (SD) which relates to freshwater resources and the water environment [6]. SD has emerged as one that most people can agree with: that is, take a long term view, do not compromise the future in pursuit of present gain, involve people and emphasise the quality of life and living systems in the definition of development.. SD involves a switch in emphasis from supply management (which attempts to meet rising demands by withdrawing more water from a depleted resource base) to demand management (which attempts to reduce consumption by increasing efficiency in use). Furthermore, this switch encourages both suppliers and users to think of water as an economic commodity, and policy makers to use of economic instruments to achieve water use efficiency.

5   The political economy of water

At present there often appears to be a gap between the theory and the practice. Where stated, water policy objectives seem reasonable, but the real challenge is to translate these into targets and actions (such standards of service in water supply or objective water quality indicators). There must be a commitment to implementation and the methods of chosen must be appropriate and effective. These are essentially political issues. Commitment depends on the extent to which water is on the political agenda. Implementation strategy depends on the dominant political ideology. At present, and for the foreseeable future, this is one of economic liberalisation and the market.

Economics can help to promote the concept of resource costs and benefits, raise the quality of the debate about sustainable futures, and help to assess the implications of alternative policies and strategies. Its main technique, cost:benefit analysis, can help. But like any predictive, judgmental and single-discipline method, is not necessarily reliable and complete, and is liable to all kinds of bias.   There are particular difficulties handling distributional impacts, unforeseen environmental effects and the social consequences of things going wrong.   There are especial problems during periods of economic adjustments and rapidly changing economic circumstances, such as for economies in transition.

The question of how to put values on untraded, especially non-user benefits of the aquatic environment present a particular challenge. Economists have responded by developing methods to place values on the social and environmental impacts of water resource development which can be incorporated in the economic decision making process [7][8]. These methods are confounded by many theoretical and practical difficulties.   Many argue that, whilst these techniques confirm that there are significant welfare impacts associated with environmental change, it is misleading to pretend that they can be precise. Principles of environmental policy, especially regarding precaution and sustainability, might be better served by using economics to determine efficient ways of delivering politically and legally defined standards of service and quality (e.g. river water quality, urban flood defence), rather than defining these in the first place.

Thus, economics cannot handle these issues of water management alone. There is a need for strong political stewardship which embraces regulation and direct action, and an institutional capability to support this.

6   Water pricing

Central to the concept of water as an economic commodity, is that it commands prices which reflect costs of provision and benefits in use, and it can, at least in theory, be traded between buyers and sellers like any other marketable item. In this case, water prices will reflect opportunity value in the best alternative use plus any costs of transferring it into the sector application. Where water use leads to environmental degradation, the economic value of these impacts or their mitigation, should also be included in the water price. Charging for water is an emotive issue, not least because it falls from heaven. Charging raises all kinds of social and ethical questions, especially regarding the income distribution effects of charging for an essential, zero substitute good, and the social risks of failing to meet basic living standards. The same issues arise with respect to charging for drainage and flood defence, especially when flood water originates elsewhere.

The theoretical boundary for pricing ranges between the cost of supply and the benefits in use. The consensus is that charges should at least recover the operation and maintenance costs of a water supply system, and that part of capital costs which is compatible with ability of users to pay. In practice, it is the latter which determines the upper limit. There is also agreement that where possible charging systems should be volumetrically based, both to make the link with marginal costs and to encourage economy in use. This has implications for the design and operation of water delivery and use systems (and underlying legislation), especially water measurement technologies and, in some cases, the management of water distribution by user associations. In the case of drainage, charges within a defined hydrological area can be reasonably levied per ha given that potential benefits are equally distributed.

7   A water market

The concept of water as an economic good also implies that property rights, either held collectively or individually, define ownership, use and responsibilities. There is general agreement that access to water must be regulated through licensed quota to serve the public interest. It is possible that creating a market in tradeable licences, however, could achieve allocative efficiency by moving water to the highest bidder and most beneficial use. Lots of questions arise as to who should hold the initial rights and who should be allowed to buy and sell. Original holders stand to gain substantially in water deficit situations, although trading licences may do little to alleviate the basic problem of shortage of supply. They may even lead to greater take up of licensed quantities, thus exacerbating the supply problem.

Particular care is needed to define the hydrological boundaries over which water can be traded and the priorities to safeguard environmental standards. Tradable licences could allow water to move across sectors. Licences could, for instance, be bought for the purpose of environmental enhancements. This pre-supposes that each sector is internally efficient, for example that the prices received by farmers for irrigated crops are not clouded by Government subsidies or taxes, or that water supply companies are able to pay high prices because they can easily pass these to domestic users in an uncontested monopolistic market. (Hence the need for OFWAT and the K factor) [9]. In England and Wales, new licence applicants must demonstrate reasonable need. Thus, water supply companies for example must show that they are not using new water to replace that lost in a leaky delivery system. The market is not left to its own devices.

8   Economic incentives

Economic incentives and voluntary participation are perceived as the most cost effective ways of meeting water policy objectives within a politically defined regulated framework. For example, it is possible to determine the financial losses to farmers of changing farming practices to comply with water quality standards. The question then becomes whether the polluter should pay for polluting, or be compensated for not doing so. The present situation is complicated by the use of supported commodity prices (and therefore incentives to pollute) to protect farm incomes such that financial benefits to farmers exceed the benefits to society as a whole. In future, however, we're likely to see a de-coupling of the two. Policies in the agricultural/water sector are likely to involve a mixture of compulsion (limits on polluting inputs or outputs), incentives (such as wetland management agreements) or cross compliance conditions (e.g. farmers get guaranteed prices if they install buffer zones to limit emissions to water).

9 Participation in water management

In accordance with the criteria for sustainability, there is will be a call for greater participation of stakeholders in all aspects of water resources management, with more devolution of powers and responsibility at catchment and user group level. This process, by promoting the principles of local management and financing by beneficiaries themselves, is also intended to delivering the potential benefits of demand management. Some cautions are required however.

The process of transfer of ownership and operation of water supply systems including domestic and irrigation systems to private companies or user groups has proved popular to Development Agencies and in some cases Governments themselves. The rationale includes: substitute local management and discipline for poor or even corrupt governance, inculcate the ethos of buyer first in supply organisations, reduce costs, achieve greater transparency, and immunise provision of public services from Government interference and budgets, or frequent change in political administration.

Privatisation and asset transfer may suit some politicians because they can distance themselves from contentious issues, like inadequacy of funding and supply failure, and environmental damage. Governance is handed over to appointed regulators whose role is to safeguard the public interest. The result is sometimes more regulation and control by expensive non elected quasi-Governmental organisations. In other cases, transfer can only be achieved by Governments

These are controversial issues in countries undergoing economic reform and transition. Full cost recovery, beneficiaries must pay and asset transfer are the language of conditionality for development assistance. But the practice needs to be tempered to suit the circumstances, especially when much of the physical infrastructure is dilapidated, user ability to pay is severely constrained by macro-economic factors, market concepts and institutions are absent or in their infancy, water law and property rights are inadequately defined, capability in both management and regulation is limited and the social and environmental risks of getting it wrong are considerable. Under these conditions, user groups are reluctant to take on the responsibilities and liabilities of management transfer without considerable help, both financial and institutional. By necessity, Governments remain as guarantors, in many cases retaining the liabilities which private operators will not accept, and responsibility for service elements which serve the public interest. The reality is that most water resource projects are at least part funded by the public purse, either directly or through income support to users. Most agencies offering credits to countries in transition come from countries where this is common practice

Greater emphasis must be placed on achieving improved efficiency in distribution and use. Economic pricing of water and volumetric charging systems will encourage water saving technologies and practices on the part of users themselves. Monopolistic supply companies must be subject to performance review as a condition of price setting. Simultaneously, economic water pricing can provide funds for research and development, extension, advice, technical assistance and possibly financial incentives for initiatives which conserve water. Information on water consumption rates, costs and benefits is particularly important to guide user decisions. Access to water may be conditional on water saving technologies and improved practices.

10 Conclusion

Much of the recent debate on natural resource and environmental management is tied up with that of public and private ownership of resources and the provision of services. The prevailing political persuasion favours privatisation, liberalisation and deregulation where possible, compulsory competitive tendering, internal markets, service level agreements, beneficiary and polluter pay, and market pricing. This tends to emphasise water as an economic commodity and the use of market principles to guide resource use. In itself, however, the market is unlikely to be a reliable agent of sustainable water resource development and all that this implies. Regulation and direct action in the public interest are needed to ensure the integrity of water resources and the water environment. Economics can help in so much as it conforms to the prevailing ideology, but water resource management is fundamentally a political product.

11 References

1. National Rivers Authority (1993) *Water Resources Strategy*, NRA, Bristol
2. Environment Agency (1996) *The environment of England and Wales*, Environment Agency, Bristol
3. Gibbons, D.C. (1986) *The economic value of water*. Johns Hopkins University Press
4. Rees, J.A, Williams, S., Atkins, J.P., Hammond, C.J. and Trotter, S.D. (1993). *Economics of water resource management*. R&D Note 128, National Rivers Authority, Bristol
5. Ministry of Agriculture, Fisheries and Food (1993) *Flood Defence Project* Appraisal Guidance Notes, HMSO, London
6. Department of the Environment (1994) *Sustainable development: the UK strategy*. Cmnd 2426 HMSO, London
7. Field, B. (1994) *Environmental economics*. Mcgraw Hill International.
8. Winpenny, J.T. (1991) *Values for the environment*. HMSO, London
9. Office of Water Services (1995) *Report on tariff structure and charges*, 1995-6, OFWAT Birmingham

PAYING FOR WATER

Paying for water

H. JACKSON, MP
Member of Parliament, Sheffield, UK

Abstract
"It droppeth as the gentle rain from Heaven upon the earth below". The argument in this paper is that *managing Water* means *managing the whole water environment*, and is properly regarded as an essential 'Public Service'. The comments are obviously drawn from the history and development of the service in the United Kingdom, but many of the principles around how the service should be paid for are generally applicable. Customers have no choice of supplier of sewerage or water, but simply want a *safe*, *efficient* and *reliable* service. They cannot shop around for the best deal, and therefore want a simple, fairly constant, and affordable charge. The private/public debate is a diversion. A fair and simple charging system is required whoever manages the operation.
Keywords: domestic metering, environment, leakage, paying for water, tax, water supply.

1 Introduction

Water is a free and natural resource, part of the planet's atmosphere on which all life depends. It has no substitute, and its plentiful use is the foundation of good health. Indeed, as War on Want' has publicised, poor water or sewerage account for 80% of the world's disease.

Human activity, has left the air and soil polluted, so that water courses are no longer fit to drink. The concentration of huge numbers of people living in urban areas also brings a concentration of their waste and excrement. Industrial processes need coolants and turn to water as the most convenient substance. New agricultural techniques soak the land with pesticides which poison the water as it drains into rivers.

Water Policy: Allocation and management in practice. Edited by P. Howsam and R.C. Carter.
Published in 1996 by E & FN Spon. ISBN 0 419 21650 2

The cost therefore of providing a clean water supply is not simply the treatment of water and its delivery to homes and industry; it also involves the best management of the total water environment, involving sewage treatment, drainage from roads and fields, and pollution control.

Britain has one of the oldest and most thorough water and sewerage systems in the world, primarily because the rapid urbanisation in the 19th century forced on public authorities the need to develop sewage and clean water treatment in order to stem disease.

It became one of the first 'public services' to be financed by local authorities, and was usually, though not always, run by the authorities themselves.

2   Principles and options of payment methods

The total overall charge to customers, together with any element of state subsidy, must be sufficient to cover both the current operating costs of a water and sewerage service, and the finance necessary to maintain an infrastructure and system which meets future resource demands and standards of pollution control.

What are the options?

- Should any charging system bear least hard on those with less, at the expense of richer households ?
- Should it be State financed through national taxation or should it be financed through local taxation ?
- Should the drinking water element be metered and be paid for as it is used, leaving the drainage and sewerage on a taxation base ?
- Should the whole Bill be levied on the basis of the volume of drinking water used ?
- Should the charge be paid separately and direct to the operator, but based on household income as an income tax ?
- Should the charge be based on property value ?
- Should the charge vary according to the difficulty of the operation in a particular area, or should it be kept more or less uniform across any one country, or indeed any one district or water catchment area ?
- How should charges for industry be determined ?
- How and by whom should the charging system, and indeed the level of the charges, be determined ?

These questions need political answers.

They arise whether the industry is run by public or private companies.

Governments either national or local are best placed to make such decisions.

2.1 Breaking down the costs
In any country or system it is useful to break down the costs of the operation, in order to arrive at the best charging and financing mechanism. In Britain, where costs have been analysed, allowing for regional variations, the split works out approximately:

- Sewerage and Highway drainage (including the carriage,
  sewage treatment and pollution control)   55%
- Drinking Water - storage, treatment and delivery   45%

Since the raw material is virtually free, Industry has a hugely capital intensive financial structure. Within the drinking water element, the ratio of costs relating to the volume consumed as against the fixed costs of maintaining the plant and infrastructure averages 15%:85%, although it will become even more capitalised if significant investment in new reservoirs or boreholes is required.

In Britain therefore so long as demand stays roughly constant 90% of the cost of the whole operation relates to the fixed capital costs of the infrastructure, pipes and treatment plants, and a mere 10% to the volume of water running through. In this situation a measured basis of charge goes against the reality of the pattern of costs.

In 1995 we had a very hot dry summer, and water shortages. One issue which emerged was the degree of leakage from pipes which was 'wasting away' - 830,000,000 gallons per day (enough to provide water for half the population).

The lack of enthusiasm with which the water companies have tackled leakage in Britain is actually a symptom of the industry's financial structure. If the volume lost had affected the cost of the operation in a significant way, we can be sure that greater effort would have been put into leakage reduction. It is only when the sufficiency of the resource is threatened that companies were driven to put extra resources into leakage reduction.

2.2 The history of charging in Britain

In most of Britain although the costs of drinking water, and sewerage, are separately listed, and in some areas delivered to the consumer by different Companies, the charge to the customer is combined. In Scotland drainage and sewerage is paid for direct through local taxation, whilst water is a separate charge levied on the same taxation base.

Property values have formed the historical tax base for water and sewerage in Britain - the same as for taxes levied by local authorities, for activities such as waste disposal, highway maintenance, planning, police, fire, and importantly, education. Each property in the country had a rateable value attached to it for this purpose.

However at the point at which the water industry in Britain was privatised, the Government was also intending to shift the basis of local taxation from the traditional property value base to a 'Poll Tax' - levied on each and every adult. It was assumed therefore in the legislation that the Water Industry would also have to find a new charging basis, and the one which fitted best with the Poll tax was a metered charge, providing a link to the usage and number of people in the household.

The Poll tax however met with huge popular opposition, as it dramatically shifted the burden of taxation away from the wealthy in large houses and big gardens, to poorer large families in smaller properties. The Government was then forced in 1991 to switch back to a simplified property banded base for local taxes, now called the 'Council Tax'.

With the exception of Scotland however, both the Regulator and Government have continued to assume that a metered charge will in the long run prevail, despite the similar way in which it shifts the burden of payments onto lower income households.

2.3   The way forward for Britain

In Britain the Regulator, Ian Byatt, set out his principles governing 'Paying for Water' in the OFWAT document of that name published in 1991.

"A customer's Bill should, as far as practicable, reflect the costs which that customer imposes on the waste and sewerage systems for a supply of clean water, disposal of dirty water and draining surface water from the property and the highway."

This badly needs refining in a number of ways.

First, whereas the principle of balancing cost to the customer with cost of delivering the service is valid if 'Customer' means the totality of customers, it is inappropriate if applied to individual households or businesses. Without clarification, it means that customers in rural areas at the end of pipelines, or those where the infrastructure is in a bad state are unfairly penalised.

Second, it makes no mention or allowance for the possibility of an element of state subsidy: for example, for exceptional capital investment on new resources or to meet a particular environmental disaster or unforeseen threat.

Third, it does not allow for state help towards meeting the charges of those on very low incomes. In Britain again, although there is an element of state support for water charges within the amount allowed for the essential needs of households living on state benefit, it is a fraction of their real cost, and has not kept pace with the steep rise in water prices since privatisation.

Fourth, it does not address the public health requirement that the service should aim to be one which is guaranteed by statute to every household regardless of their means.

There is some concern in Britain at the growing use of prepayment devices which have a timing device within them and which cut off the drinking water element of the service after a certain length of time unless the 'Water key' card is recharged. It may be that this breaches the statutory duty of Companies to deliver a constant service to every households, since a house without a supply of running drinking water 'statutorily unfit' to live in.

2.4   Water conservation

Supporters of metering, as with the Poll Tax, first justified it on grounds of fairness. Now however in the face of considerable opposition they use the 'conservation' argument instead. Indeed this argument carries with it much better logic.

It is certainly right for industry, where every incentive needs to be used to encourage large users NOT to use drinking water for industrial processes, but rather to find ways in which rain or river water can be utilised and recycled to minimise the cost for everyone.

It is equally right to measure more carefully exactly where drinking water is going.

In Britain the hot summer of 1995 brought serious water shortages. It exposed the water Companies themselves as being the main waster of drinking water in the 830 million gallons a day which leaked from their pipes. The call to consumers to save water fell on deaf ears when it was not combined with equally loud demands on the Companies to reduce the amount of water lost through leaks.

An opinion poll conducted by MORI for the Royal Society for the Protection of Birds, asked respondents to identify which of the following they believed to be most efficient with regards to saving water.

The results showed :

Banning the use of garden hosepipes and sprinklers in certain areas for certain periods	31%
Compulsory water metering for all customers	15%
Government to set enforceable targets for water companies to report leakage from their own pipes	69%
Promoting and encouraging households to have water meters installed	21%
Making grants available to help households save water, eg by installing smaller toilet cisterns or controlling leaks on their property	41%
None of these	3%
Don't Know	3%

3   Conclusions

Customers have no choice of supplier of sewerage or water, but simply want a *safe*, *efficient* and *reliable* service. They cannot shop around for the best deal, and therefore want a simple, fairly constant, and affordable charge.

It is the task of the public authority to set both the charge and quality standards, covering drinking water quality; water wastage and resource management; pollution control; safe sewage treatment; and environmental protection of rivers and beaches. Government must also decide the proportion of subsidy they are prepared to put in from general taxation.

A property banded charge is simple, and cheap to administer. It is also flexible. It offers an easy way of introducing rebates (possibly for single occupants), or extras (possibly for evident waste or mis-use), or incentives for water efficient purchases in the home or garden.

Domestic metering helps to raise awareness about conservation.

But it has disadvantages:

* it puts no pressure on the operators not to waste their own supply;
* as a conservation measure it is a crude way of getting the domestic sector to cut down on usage.
* poorer consumers will cut back on essential uses, for example sharing baths, flushing the toilet less often, and which could have public health risks.
* those in large properties with big gardens pay at the top rate on a property base and would probably see a saving if they switch to metering thus forcing up the costs for the rest.
* the costs of installation, maintenance, reading and billing by meter are estimated to be about £25 on every Bill - about 13% of the average Bill in Britain.

A distinction should be made between drinking water and other sources since excessive use of tap water being used to water gardens causes peak levels of demand a bit like the rush hour congestion, which became extremely difficult to manage.

The private/public debate is a diversion. A fair and simple charging system is required whoever manages the operation.

SECTION 6

WATER POLITICS

THE POLITICS OF WATER DISTRIBUTION
Negotiating resource use in a South Indian canal irrigation system

P.P. MOLLINGA and C.J.M. VAN STRAATEN
Department of Irrigation and Soil and Water Conservation, Wageningen Agricultural University, Wageningen, The Netherlands

Abstract
This paper argues that water distribution in jointly-managed canal irrigation systems is an inherently political activity. Examples of the political contestation of water use are given for a South Indian canal irrigation system. At tertiary (outlet) level the social power of large farmers over input supply and employment structures water distribution practices. At secondary (distributary) level conflicts between different categories of farmers and Irrigation Department officials are mediated by local politicians. The policy implication of this analysis is that fostering change in irrigation management is not only a question of `getting the incentives right', financial or otherwise, but requires addressing the issues of social power and empowerment as well.
Keywords: irrigation management, politics, water distribution.

1   Introduction

The performance problems of jointly-managed large-scale canal irrigation systems have been one of the most vexing issues in the international irrigation management debate. One particularly persistent theme is the organisation of farmers/water users in Water Users Organisations (WAU) at the level of the tertiary unit. "The perceived reason the problem [of inefficient use of water and capital] exists is that farmers are not organised, and the perceived solution to the problem is appropriate social organisation of farmers." [1]

Hunt notes that the interest in WUA solutions is to an important extent based on an analogy between examples of successful management practices in Irrigation Communities (that control traditional or communal or farmer managed irrigation

Water Policy: Allocation and management in practice. Edited by P. Howsam and R.C. Carter.
Published in 1996 by E & FN Spon. ISBN 0 419 21650 2

systems) and groups of farmers in the local hydraulic units of large canal systems. He concludes that the analogy is false. "A point-by-point comparison of WUAs with Irrigation Communities shows that they share only a few features, and, importantly, do not share the major ones, which are access to specific benefits, the systematic relationship among the various kinds of work, a clear charter for the authority of the leaders, and articulated responsibility from farmer to headgate for allocation of water." [1]. The conditions for successful `self-governance' of irrigation systems have been spelt out in detail by Elinor Ostrom [2][3]. Her `design principles' for irrigation organisation are based on the study of a large number of farmer managed irrigation systems, particularly in Nepal. These principles are increasingly used to draw up designs for management improvement in jointly managed canal systems.[4]

The next logical step has been to argue for making jointly-managed systems more like Irrigation Communities. In a comparative study of different types of jointly managed canal systems Merrey concludes that "single irrigation systems managed be system-specific organisations that are both financially and organisationally autonomous and accountable to their customers generally perform better and are more sustainable over the long term." [5] Autonomous single systems are the type of jointly-managed systems that come closest to self-governing Irrigation Communities. The key parallel is the fully internal organisation of accountability.

The idea of autonomy-with-accountability is the core of current irrigation management turnover policy formulations [6]. It is early days, but so far the results of turnover initiatives are mixed. More remarkable is the fact that the irrigation studies and policy community has recently been taken by surprise by dramatic and reportedly successful turnover processes in Mexico. Mexico has been declared the model, and people from all over the world -including engineers from the system discussed in this paper- are invited to visit Mexico with the hope that they will reproduce the experience at home.

Blueprint approaches may be psychologically reassuring for professionals with an instrumental view of development, but are generally unsuccessful and need to be demythologised [7]. This paper argues for the context-specific approaches, and more particularly for recognition of the *political* nature of existing irrigation practices and efforts to change them. By 'political' we mean that the process of contesting and negotiating water use is governed by social relationships of power. In the particular case discussed it also has the narrower meaning that politicians are involved in water distribution, but this is not the central point. Usually the politics of water distribution and other irrigation management tasks are conceptualised as undesirable interference and the mixing up of issues. The prevalent idea is that politics is better kept out of irrigation management. When one accepts the argument that water distribution, and irrigation management in general, is *inherently* political, this has important consequences for how one goes about changing it. In addition to creating the appropriate incentive structures for institutional change [2][3], the issues of social power and empowerment need to be addressed. To show that water distribution is inherently political, this paper discusses actual water distribution practices in a South Indian large-scale canal system. After a brief introduction to the system in section 2, we discuss in section 3 distribution practices at the tertiary (outlet) level, and in section 4 at the secondary canal (distributary) level. In the concluding section 5 we return to the implications of the main argument of the paper.

2   The Karnap irrigation system

The case studied is a 240,000 ha canal irrigation system in South India that we have named the Karnap System. It is a so-called protective irrigation system, which means that water is scarce by design and water allocation policy is to spread water thinly over a large number of users [8]. This is done through 'localization' policy, a form of land use planning which stipulates that specific crops should be grown in certain areas. In reality water is appropriated by a limited number of farmers: water distribution is highly unequal in a classical head-tail pattern.

The history of the Karnap system starts with a situation of abundant water, resulting from the gradual construction of the infrastructure after the completion of the reservoir in 1953 up to the opening of the last distributary in 1968. For a long time the whole reservoir was available for part of the command area. Irrigation developed slowly, because land had to be levelled and bunded to make it suitable for irrigated cropping. As a result of the steady increase of water-intensive rice and sugarcane cultivation, water scarcity occurred in the first distributaries in the mid-1960s and was system-wide around 1980. A relatively stable head-tail pattern of distribution established itself. The evolution and stabilisation of the distribution pattern did not go uncontested. We discuss an example at tertiary (outlet) and secondary (distributary) level.

Data were collected during one year on three different distributaries, of which the head end distributary discussed here was one.

3   Managing scarcity at outlet level

The institutional response to scarcity at this level has by and large been the design of detailed schedules for rotational water distribution by farmers themselves. As a side remark it can be noted that this finding contradicts the assumption that farmers are generally unorganised at the outlet level. Irrigation personnel does not move downstream of the pipe outlet structure that leads the distributary canal water into these 50-200 acre units. One such a rotation schedule is in operation in the Niiru pipe outlet. Farmers claim it has been in operation for more than 15 years. Its features are given in Fig. 1. The rotation is on a time per acre basis and the outlet command is divided in not fully contiguous but regularly sized blocks. The rotation interval is 6 days. The subdistributary from which the outlet draws water is closed for one day per week.

This rotation schedule is equitable in principle, but actual water distribution in the outlet command is highly unequal. Water use is concentrated in the head end, where rice and sugarcane are grown. Without exception, farmers want to grow the most water intensive crops, rice and sugarcane, as these are commercially the must remunerative crops. The cropping pattern is thus a good indicator of water distribution. Rules for equitable distribution co-exist with a pattern of unequal distribution without leading to public conflicts. This somewhat surprising finding can be explained by looking at the wider context in which the distribution of water takes place.

In the older parts of the Karnap system there is a reasonably regular pattern of holdings of larger farmers being in the head reaches while those of smaller farmers are in the tail. Over a period of 30-40 years larger farmers managed to get their land located in the head reaches. But large landholdings do not in themselves explain unequal water

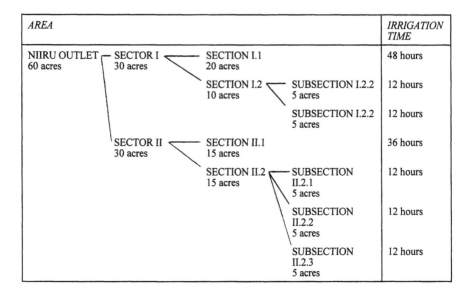

AREA				IRRIGATION TIME
NIIRU OUTLET 60 acres	SECTOR I 30 acres	SECTION I.1 20 acres		48 hours
		SECTION I.2 10 acres	SUBSECTION I.2.2 5 acres	12 hours
			SUBSECTION I.2.2 5 acres	12 hours
	SECTOR II 30 acres	SECTION II.1 15 acres		36 hours
		SECTION II.2 15 acres	SUBSECTION II.2.1 5 acres	12 hours
			SUBSECTION II.2.2 5 acres	12 hours
			SUBSECTION II.2.3 5 acres	12 hours

Rules:- Sectors I and II irrigate every other day; every week a different sector starts.
- The irrigation of Section I.1 should not always be on the same days of the week; Section I.2 should be allowed to irrigate on weekdays with good water supply as well.
- In Section II.1 the order of irrigation of plots is alternated after every sequence (head/tail, tail/head).
- In Subsections II.2.1, II.2.2 and II.2.3 day and night irrigation are alternated.

Fig. 1. Rotation schedule Niiru outlet

distribution. Although they are a basis of wielding social power, the exact mechanisms of exerting that power still need to be identified. In this case, the most prominent mechanism is credit relations, and secondly employment relations. The Niiru pipe outlet is dominated by two large farmers owning between 20 and 30 acres each. Through them other farmers have access to several inputs on credit: fertiliser, pesticides, seeds and traction. At least 6 farmers in the outlet command had such relations with these two in 1991-92. Those farmers who have less than 10 acres are considered here as small farmers. They number 20 in the Niiru outlet. The figures regarding the credit relations are probably on the low side, considering the volume of trade of the two large farmers. Moreover they only consider the 1991-92 year, not those arrangements made in previous years.

In addition the two large farmers are employers of some small farmers in the outlet. More importantly, they employ their wives and daughters, who go out to work as daily wage labourers to add to the household income.

There is no direct evidence of the strategic use of the above relations in water distribution in 1991-2. The overall picture is that of anticipation of, consent to and no conflicts on unequal water distribution. Tail enders anticipate unequal distribution by their choice of crop: they cultivate `dry' crops such as sorghum, cotton and millet which demand less water. The implicit bargain is that the large farmers are allowed sufficient water for their rice and sugarcane, but that the tailenders will get sufficient water for the maturation of their dry crops. This becomes clear in periods of extreme water scarcity. In these periods the rotation schedule is rigorously implemented and water equitably distributed on a time/acre basis. In these periods tail enders do make claims and head enders do keep to the schedule. Another indication of the existence of this implicit bargain is that one of the two large farmers has extensified his land use by growing trees on part of his holding. This crop is only irrigated when water is unwanted by everyone else.

To conclude, the water distribution pattern at outlet level can only be understood when the socio-economic relations among different categories of users are taken into account. These relations have to do with large farmers' power over input supply and employment.

4   Managing scarcity at distributary level

The main response of the Irrigation Department to the advent of water scarcity in the late 1960s has been the introduction of rotation schedules at distributary level. In this case a schedule was introduced which involved the daily closure of one or more subdistributaries plus pipe outlets taking water directly from the distributary, starting in the head on Sunday and ending with the tail subdistributaries on Saturday. More than twenty years later this system is still in use. It is, however, not a rigorously implemented schedule, but a continuously negotiated settlement between different groups of farmers and the Irrigation Department. It can be interpreted as the maximum redistribution of water to tail enders that head enders allow. Attempts to introduce more rigorous schedules have systematically failed.

The daily business of water distribution at distributary level is intervention in and negotiation of gate-settings along and obstructions in the canal. Farmers use all the strategies identified by Chambers [9] for intervening in water distribution above the outlet: fact-finding, lobbying, appropriation, guarding, and construction, capture and maintenance. Irrigation Department officials work on the basis of different management strategies. We identified four: management by force, management by bribe, management by default, and management by strategic manoeuvre. The first strategy involves using all available human, legal and material resources to enforce a pattern of water distribution as close as possible to the localization pattern. This involves closely supervising field staff, being on the canal a lot, confronting interfering farmers, mobilising law, legal procedures and the police. It will be clear that this will demand strong motivation and dynamism of the irrigation official involved. The second management strategy, management by bribe, is the most commented on. There is no doubt that there are many cases in which irrigation officials demand or are offered payment in cash or kind in return for supplying water. It is not clear that it is also the dominant pattern. The third strategy, management by default, involves disengagement from management. Field staff are left to their own devices, because the irrigation official takes no interest whatsoever in the water management. The last strategy, management by strategic manoeuvre, was used by the irrigation official in charge of the distributary discussed here. The central element of his approach was to consequently enforce rotation, but to be accommodating towards farmers who really wanted extra water at particular moments. He let these farmers take extra water for a limited period when this could not be avoided, and at the same time reduced the supply into outlets or subdistributaries where he knew water was not short at that moment. In the 1991-92 season this strategy worked out well, except for one occasion when the supply to the distributary was very low. He then decided to raise the gate of the distributary inlet, to get extra water from the main canal. Essentially this is an extension of the same approach to a higher level. This style of management requires detailed knowledge of the distributary, as well as insight in the local socio-economic and political situation.

The main actors in distributary management besides farmers and Irrigation Department officials, are politicians. In this distributary of the Karnap system the MLA, the Member of Legislative Assembly, the state parliament is of particular importance. In India's constituency-based parliamentary system each member of parliament has a clearly defined base area, for which he/she for all practical purposes functions as a resource broker. If the constituency overlaps with parts of an irrigation system, the MLA will most likely involve him/herself in water distribution. The mechanism enabling MLA's to influence the behaviour of Irrigation Department officials is his/her influence on the transfers of Government officials. Chief Ministers and Ministers delegate their local decision making with regard to transfers to MLAs in return for their support to the Cabinet.[10] (See for a more elaborate description [11].)

From the perspective of the farmer, influencing water supply through the MLA or another politician is a deviation. Putting pressure on employees of the Irrigation Department directly is a much shorter institutional route. These methods come into existence because virtually no formal accountability mechanisms exist between farmers and Irrigation Department officials. The absence of such mechanisms makes exerting direct pressure a cumbersome affair, one reason being that it has to be repeated all the time. Farmers explained that lobbying with their MLA gave a bigger chance of longer lasting success, and was cheaper. Through lobbying, farmers exchange their electoral support for the MLA's influence on Irrigation Department officials. The exertion of this influence allows the MLA to reproduce his/her base for re-election. Irrigation Department officials have very few resources to act as equal partners in this triangle, though they are not as helpless, and as innocent as they often portray themselves to be. To illustrate these arrangements we will give one example.

Example
One of the head end subdistributaries was localised for the irrigation of dry crops, but instead a lot of rice was grown in the head end of the subdistributary, consequently creating a considerable water scarcity in the tail end of this canal. Furthermore, the intake of the subdistributary was situated in a bend of the canal in a very unfavourable position. The drop downstream of the offtake had been destroyed by downstream farmers, which had further reduced the discharge into the subdistributary. One night the tail end farmers of the subdistributary destroyed the gate of the offtake, thereby increasing its discharge. The Irrigation Department booked a case against the farmers for damaging Government property, but the police took no action. The Irrigation Department tried to partially close the gate, but farmers guarding the offtake chased the officials away by throwing stones. The Irrigation Department official realised that he would not be able to change the situation on his own, and thought of another plan. He decided to approach the

leaders of the distributary tail-end farmers, who were suffering because of lower supplies, and to ask them to go to the MLA to complain about lack of water, and ask the MLA to put pressure on the farmers of the head end subdistributary. 'When the Irrigation Department calls a meeting the farmers won't listen, but when the MLA calls it, it is different.' is how he explained his strategy. The tail end farmers went to the MLA to complain about the water shortage, and explained its cause. The MLA realised the seriousness of the situation, and, after collecting additional information from the Irrigation Department official, took immediate action. A number of people belonging to the head end subdistributary were arrested by the police and put behind bars. The MLA then left to the State capital for two days on other business. The families of the arrested persons became very nervous, and on the return of the MLA prayed him to release their kin. The village to which the arrested persons belonged was actually just outside his constituency, but he commanded some respect there. Besides being an MLA he was also the owner of a ricemill and a fertiliser shop, where villagers took fertiliser on credit and borrowed money from. In the meeting the MLA promised to release the people from the police cells, if the village promised to allow the Irrigation Department to repair the gate. The villagers accepted this and the MLA instructed the Irrigation Department to take the necessary action.

This discussion shows that water distribution at distributary level is a process of constant negotiation around a set of rules that expresses the overall balance of power. The negotiation process is a political process not just because it involves politicians, but mainly because it is governed by the economic and institutional power relations among those involved.

5   Conclusion

The examples discussed show that water distribution must be understood as a case of politically contested resource use. Irrigation management cannot be approached as a black box which will automatically work well when the incentive structure is right. The processes going on within the box need to be understood in relation to the wider relationships of socio-economic and institutional power. We suggest that analysis of water use from a 'political contestation' perspective is relevant for all levels and regions, though the exact form that politics takes may vary greatly. At policy and watershed level this is easily recognised. Reference can be made to many national and international disputes over water allocation among sectors and systems, the Middle East probably being the most intensely studied and debated region. At lower levels the perspective equally applies, but is much more sparsely documented (for other canal irrigation examples in South Asia see [12], [13] and [14]). The policy implications of such a perspective are threefold.

- Water management policy and its implementation needs to be location-specific, based on thorough understanding of local processes, and recognise that fostering change implies becoming an actor in the existing networks of social power.
- Institutional change in water management is likely to be slow (though there may be very specific circumstances under which it is quick), needs long time horizons and long-lasting commitment.

- The present emphasis on financial incentive structures as an instrument for achieving institutional change has strong limitations. The irrigation debate needs a more serious discussion of the issues of social power and empowerment. This theme is prominent in other domains of development policy (for example around gender issues), but in irrigation it still needs to find a place on the agenda.

6   References

1.   Hunt, Robert C. (1989) Appropriate social organisation? Water user associations in bureaucratic canal irrigation systems. *Human Organisation*, Vol. 48, No. 1, pp, 79-90.
2.   Ostrom, Elinor (1990) *Governing the commons. The evolution of institutions for collective action.* Cambridge University Press, Cambridge.
3.   Ostrom, Elinor (1992) *Crafting institutions for self-governing irrigation systems.* ICS Press, San Francisco.
4.   Meinzen-Dick, R., Mendoza, M., Sadoulet, L., Abiad-Shields, G.   and Subramanian, A. (1994) *Sustainable Water Users Associations: Lessons from a Literature Review*, Washington, D.C.: World Bank.
5.   Merrey, Douglas J. (1995) *Institutional design principles for accountability on large irrigation systems.*   Paper prepared for presentation at a seminar at Wageningen Agricultural University 27 October 1995.
6.   Kloezen, Wim H. and M. Samad (1995) *Synthesis of issues discussed at the international conference on irrigation management transfer, Wuhan, China, 20-24 September 1994.*   Short Report Series on Locally Managed Irrigation. International Irrigation Management Institute, Colombo.
7.   Long, Norman and Jan Douwe van der Ploeg (1989) Demythologizing planned intervention: an actor perspective. *Sociologia Ruralis*, Vol. 29, No. 3/4, pp. 226-249.
8.   Jurriëns, Rien, Peter P. Mollinga and Philippus Wester (1996) *Scarcity by design. Protective irrigation in India and Pakistan.* Liquid Gold Special Report No. 1. ILRI and DISWC, Wageningen.
9.   Chambers, R. (1988) *Managing Canal Irrigation: Practical Analysis from South India*, Oxford University Press and IBH, New Delhi.
10.   Zwart, F. de (1992) *Mobiele Bureaucratie: Manipulaties met Overplaatsingen van Ambtenaren in India*, Amsterdam.   (Mobile bureaucracy.   Manipulations with transfers of civil servants in India; Ph.D. thesis in Dutch.)
11.   Wade, Robert (1982) The system of administrative and political corruption: canal irrigation in South India. *Journal of Development Studies*, Vol. 18, No. 3, pp. 287-328.
12.   Merrey, Douglas J. and James M. Wolf (1986) *Irrigation Management in Pakistan: Four Papers.* IIMI Research Paper No. 4, IIMI, Sri Lanka.
13.   Gorter, Pieter (n.d.) *The politics of canal irrigation. An analysis of the water distribution in a canal irrigation system in Gujarat, India.* CASA Working Paper No.5, Centre for Asia Studies Amsterdam.
14.   Wade, Robert (1988) *Village Republics. Economic Conditions for Collective Action in South India*, Cambridge University Press, Cambridge.

POLITICAL DECENTRALISATION AND RIVER BASIN MANAGEMENT
River basins and decentralisation policies

A. NICOL
Departments of Politics and Geography
School of Oriental and African Studies
University of London, London, UK

Abstract
Decentralisation policies can be broken down into an administrative and a political component, of which the latter appears to be most significant. Frequently decentralisation has been included as a part of 'liberalization' and 'good governance'. The affect on river basin management is likely to be significant particularly when international basin development is an issue. It is important to begin to develop a new way of 'modelling' socioeconomic relationships within river basins. A 'Virtual Basin Model' is suggested in order to facilitate clearer basin planning and to assess the impact of decentralisation. Ethiopia exemplifies certain social and political implications of decentralisation policy and highlights some of the conflicts which can develop. 'Good' water resources development could, conversely, become an indicator of 'good governance'.
Keywords: decentralisation, development, Ethiopia river basin, virtual basin,

1 Introduction

River basin management involves two simultaneous processes: technocratic scientific and managerial decision making and socioeconomic decision making which is often less transparent and frequently represents individual, group and regional interests. In the latter case resources of power, be they structured according to a democratic or undemocratic system, are gained, stored, transferred and exchanged for individual or collective interest and material gain. The significance of decentralisation for river basin management lies primarily in its political impact on the technocratic function. Overall, in sub-Saharan Africa, for example, this may have important consequences for national and regional development.

Water Policy: Allocation and management in practice. Edited by P. Howsam and R.C. Carter. Published in 1996 by E & FN Spon. ISBN 0 419 21650 2

2   What is decentralisation?

Decentralisation, as a policy, is often linked to 'democracy' and 'good governance'. It is something 'recommended' as a policy tool in a variety of socioeconomic circumstances by many international donors, without its meaning being clear. Certainly, its practical application may not benefit water resources management.

The principal problem with the idea has been precisely the range of meaning attached. Frequently, it is taken to convey a great variety of ideas from the 'empowerment' of local people to 'devolution of Government', or the subdivision of regional administrative units. Invariably, however, decentralisation also means 'more democratic 'Government, multipartyism, and the 'liberalisation' of the economy.

This paper, however, divides 'decentralisation' into two principal processes and one emergent process: on the one hand an administrative-bureaucratic process which may be termed *deconcentration* [1] and on the other the essentially political-legislative process of *devolution*. Both are effectively political in their outcome if not in their application. Rondinelli and Nellis [2] define administrative decentralisation as 'the transfer of responsibility for **planning,** management, and the raising and allocation of resources from the central Government and its agencies to field units of Government agencies, subordinate units or levels of Government, semi-autonomous public authorities or corporations...'. The extent to which this bureaucratic-administrative deconcentration is political will depend on how it is attached to the interests of particular elite groups, ethnic interests, or other actors with a stake in the 'transfer' of decision-making capacity. Devolution, the more explicitly political process, ,...requires that local Governments be given autonomy and independence, and be clearly perceived as a separate level over which central authorities exercise little or no direct control.' [3].

A third type of decentralisation is now emerging which might be termed *segmentation*. This incorporates both devolution and deconcentration, and is a fundamental restructuring of the internal political boundaries of a country -and its constitutional provisions-to accord with real or perceived social boundaries (usually ethnic or religious). Where segmentation involves the geographic division of river basins, as we shall see in the case of Ethiopia, the implications for water resources policy are particularly striking.

In all three processes other political ends-including the co-option of local groups, the coercion of the local administration via these elites and the eventual development of effective 'hands-off central Government control-may exist. Indeed decentralization itself depends on political factors including the 'will' to steer the transfer of authority from the centre to local institutions; frequently this 'will' requires perceived benefits on the part of individuals within the authorities concerned. The assumption that 'decentralisation' as such, even in the form of *deconcentration,* is a benign process can be dangerous for planning purposes .

In analysing decentralisation Rondinelli [2] cites two main schools of thought: public choice, which is based on neo-classical economic theories of rational, interest maximising behaviour and optimal decision-making when left free of Government control; and policy analysis, which takes a broader brush approach and includes political, behavioural and administrative factors affecting the implementation of policy. The latter is essentially a descriptive approach. Rondinelli argues that it is necessary to employ a political-economic analysis of decentralisation policy in order to identify the interests of the various actors involved in decentralisation. Reports produced for the World Bank have shown that economic criteria are often insufficient to analyse decentralisation policies '...because they were initiated primarily for political reasons' [2]. This approach, however, for the purposes of decentralisation within river basins, has to include an international dimension when the basins cross one or more state boundaries. There is, in effect, an international political economic aspect to decentralisation within river basins as well (see below). Nonetheless a political economy approach which identifies the economic interests of groups within a state, arranged according to their relationship to the state apparatus, provides insights into the problems of 'decentralisation' by helping to reveal the aspects of policy which are conditioned by these relationships and the probable political impact of policy on non-stakeholder communities.

The main problems with decentralisation policies have been identified as problems of scale whereby the creation of smaller management units leads to management problems; the attitudes of central authorities where decentralisation is seen to weaken entrenched elite privileges; a reduction in quality of governance may occur as the overall quality of decision making is reduced (mainly through lack of technical capacity and information); the problem of co-ordination where duplication of actions may waste resources; and the problem of reallocation of resources from relatively rich to relatively poor areas [3]. In this last case the state has abrogated its responsibility to act as 'honest broker' in the reallocation of resources, which, in river basin management, would seem to be one of the key roles a state should maintain.

3   What does it mean in Africa?

The African context holds three principal areas of interest for a study of decentralisation and river basin management. In a wider sense it is significant too because of the apparently vast appetite of international donors for the implementation of 'decentralisation' policy linked to the notion of 'good governance'-or, as Rothchild puts it, 'to promote an enabling environment for economic and political development' [4].

The first area of interest is the centralisation of the post-colonial African state. Where decentralisation has occurred in some cases it has been simply an attempt to 'penetrate' the periphery of society politically and administratively whilst reducing the burden (particularly financial) on the political centre. Part of this apparently paradoxical policy often involved the decentralisation of costly developmental expenditure items, such being the case in Sudan in the recent round of decentralisation [5].

Secondly, particularly where pastoral groups are concerned, the African experience has frequently raised questions of forms of ownership over natural resources. Either the resources themselves were deemed to be 'open access' to all-whereby people could not easily be excluded and use by one group did not preclude use or consumption by another [2] including the state itself, or the state took over the management of the resource as a means of asserting control over the different user groups. The nature and management of common property resources is therefore an important aspect of 'decentralisation policy' where decentralisation involves the devolution of Government functions to particular regions: 'Many of the problems of providing and maintaining services and of dealing with over consumption or overuse of public resources in developing countries arise from the failure of Governments to detect common property institutions and to assume that a resource is unowned and therefore in need of Government regulation' [2].

Lastly, in terms of 'river basins, sub-Saharan Africa has recently experienced a number of serious droughts and the prospect of future structural supply deficits developing at a national level. More effective river basin management of both water supply and demand is essential, including, where necessary, supranational management.

4   What does this mean for river basins?

The management of river basins, *prima facie,* should work better under a policy of decentralisation where the basin units are small and more numerous, and less well where they are larger and fewer. The former case allows more basins to be covered either wholly or in part by a single administrative unit (assuming this is indeed better for planning purposes), whereas the latter could cause more subdivisions of basins between administrative units, leading to potential bureaucratic confusion.

The principle expounded by the World Bank that, 'nothing should be done at a higher level of Government that can be done satisfactorily at a lower level' [6] relates mainly to the question of service provision of water resources, and less to the overall planning of river basins. 'Where provincial or municipal capabilities are inadequate to manage a complex system of water resources' the Bank states that it will support training and capacity building '...to improve local management so that decentralisation can eventually be achieved' [6]. In this sense, therefore, capacity building has to precede decentralisation. If the hydrological unit of the river basin is taken to be the most logical planning unit from a technical and engineering standpoint then anything which 'can be done' at the local level has to be measured against the yardstick of real or potential hydrobasin-level management capacity.

Political-geographic division or redivision can disrupt international management of river basins, if decentralisation at the national level changes the political character of the basin area lying within a country. Where, for example, downstream riparians rely on the water resources of one principal water course (Egypt and the Nile river are a case in point), the upstream disruption of centralised management may add considerably to the complexity of establishing a supranational management body and renegotiating existing treaties on water use. For this reason an overall national management body drafting broad policy guidelines should also be delegated to liaise with any international basin-wide organisation.

Decentralisation must, therefore, be a dual process of deconcentration and devolution (leading to technical capacity-building and participation) on the one hand, and on the other, the delegation of negotiating rights and responsibility for broad policy formation from the regional to the central, or national level. Without this 'duality' it is likely that decentralisation could cause tension where international rights and allocations are concerned.

As water becomes a scarcer commodity and a 'closed access' as opposed to an open access' good, supplies may be limited by purchasing power or by the inability of groups and individuals to secure the material resources necessary for ensuring access. The types of socioeconomic relationships found amongst and between groups within river basins (or within areas covering subterranean water resources) will change profoundly requiring that future successful basin management involves some mapping of these changes. The 'Virtual Basin' Model (VBM) represents 'political space' inhabited by groups and water uses (the two are usually, but not necessarily synonymous) and may complement the geographical space depicted in conventional maps, approximating to a kind of political hydrology, representing flows and reservoirs of power.

Although portrayal of the river basin's political dynamics might be qualitative and simply provide a 'representation' of power relations it could contribute to the development of a more multidisciplinary and, eventually, quantitative modelling of socioeconomic and political river basin characteristics in the longer term.

5 What are the implications for Ethiopia?

Ethiopia contains an abundance of surface water and is the source of one of the most strategically important rivers on the continent-the *Abbay* (Blue Nile) which contributes over 75% of the mean annual flow of the main Nile as measured at Aswan. However, in spite of its huge annual surface water supply the seasonal nature of the flow and the landscape through which it travels make the harnessing of the resource for irrigation and hydropower both difficult and costly. In addition to the natural and financial constraints, politically much of the surface water cannot be readily exploited without an accommodation with downstream riparians. (An estimated 97% of the total mean annual flow crosses the country's borders to neighbouring states). Endemic civil conflict within the country between the central state and peripheral nationalist forces has also prevented overall development. Although some two million hectares (ha) of land are estimated to he irrigable, fewer than 100,000 ha were being irrigated (as large-scale schemes) in the late 1980s; significantly, too, most of the remaining potential is in the major river valleys which cut through several regions and contain the richest alluvial soils [7]. Furthermore, much of this land lies in the lowlands where land-use conflict with pastoralists could be generated. Such large-scale resource development could also generate up to 7,000 MW of hydroelectricity according to the estimates made in the 1960s [8].

The position as a supplier of water places the Ethiopian Government in a dilemma, however. In a world of water markets Ethiopia could have a potentially powerful position as a 'rentier water economy'. Where political factors govern, however, such as in the Nile valley where established downstream rights are an obstacle to development, the Government has a huge resource, much of which it cannot use at present. Prior to the secession of Eritrea in 1993 Ethiopia comprised 14 river basins (10 perennial and 4 seasonal), together accounting for a mean annual flow of an estimated 1 1 1. 25 billion cu m, of the which the *Abbay* contributed some 52.6 billion cu m. Just over this amount-about 54.4 billion eu m are considered to be exploitable [9]. At present only some 2.5 billion cu m are consumed each year. The country desperately needs to develop its hydropower potential to enable the rehabilitation and conservation of its non-renewable forestry resources, much of which have been destroyed for fuel wood in the last two decades leading to severe watershed erosion. Partly as a result of this wood-fuel use land degradation in the highlands has contributed to the country's structural agricultural deficit. The key issue now is what further impact will the current political changes in the country have directly on future river basin management, and indirectly on the ability of the country to harness its water resources for developmental purposes. Ethiopia's current situation may he summarized as:

- holding a strategic position as 'water tower' to surrounding states
- developing a federal system based on ethnic affiliation within geographical areas
- weak regional institutions
- strong central control of regional politics in spite of devolution
- long legacy of centralised state power

The present Government has sought to retain the territorial integrity of the Ethiopian state - excepting the secession of Eritrea in 1993 - through a policy of federalisation based on the recognition of 14 ethnically defined regions within the country (many of which share parts of the same river basins). In addition the central Government has also sought to realign the development policies of the state with the prevailing notions of development held by most of the major international donors. Decentralising Government to the 'ethnic regions' has both served to assert the Government's 'democratic credentials' and to reduce the pressure on the centre from peripheral nationalist forces. It has functioned as a containment policy in which the state has been segmented socially, but central power has been ensured through the manipulation of regional politics.

The implications for river basin management are considerable when area, group and socioeconomic cleavages coincide. Given the strong identification-at least on paper-of geographical area with ethnic group affiliation, if a river basin is divided up between two or more regions the Government (itself largely dominated by one group, from Tigray) has the difficult task of deciding on how the resource is to be shared between regions, according to the provisions of the constitution. Article 51 of the 1994 Constitution, under Powers of the Federal State says the federal state '...shall determine and administer the utilisation of the waters of lakes linking two or more States or of rivers crossing the boundaries of two or more states'. [10]. Given the weak nature of the bureaucratic-administrative deconcentration, which in many areas is virtually non-existent, the policy of federal decentralisation in Ethiopian has, in effect, assumed wholly political characteristics.

The country's most managed river basin - the Awash - has witnessed the potential impact of the new policy almost from its inception. Covering some 120,000 sq.km the Awash valley forms part of the Ethiopian rift system and includes some 70,(X)O ha out of the total (large-scale) irrigated area of 100,000 ha in Ethiopia, made possible after the seasonal flow of the Awash was controlled through the construction of the Koka dam in 1960. The dam subsequently supplied hydropower to the capital, Addis Ababa. The valley is in an extreme rainfall deficit area where key grazing resources of the Afar pastoralists are located. Private farms were established in the 1960s and cotton and bananas were cultivated; these farms latterly became state farms under the socialist Government in the 1970s. Afar pastoralists in whose region (now the new

Region 2) they stood were physically excluded from their most fertile grazing lands. The fertile alluvial soils along the river were a 'key resource' for the Afar pastoralists providing grazing for their livestock, particularly in drought years. Having been granted political autonomy in 1993 in common with the other new regions the Afar claimed back what they regarded as theirs, regardless of the consequences for the farms themselves, echoing Article 44 of the Constitution promulgated in 1994 which states: 'All persons who have been displaced or whose livelihoods have been adversely affected as a result of State programmes have the right to commensurate monetary or alternative means of compensation...' [10]. Often the conflict with state farm officials was serious and involved direct threats. In recognition of the possible resource use conflicts between Ethiopia's sizeable lowlands pastoral community-the pastoral habitat of Ethiopia covers about a half of the country's total land area-and other resource users the constitution stipulates that their livelihoods should be protected: 'Ethiopian pastoralists have a right to free land for grazing and cultivation as well as a right not to be displaced from their own lands' [10]. Thus the Government has sought to defuse future conflict with pastoralists over the resource issue.

It is unlikely that words in the Constitution, however, will suffice. The articulation of resource use with the needs of the state and the needs of the region's population may well conflict again and require that legislative provision balances state and community needs, and the needs of the environment. In much the same way as technical knowledge of a whole basin can benefit one state in that basin over other states, the same may be said to be true of regions within a country if they are in competition. This leads to the conclusion that the decentralisation of knowledge and the capacity to acquire it may be one of the most essential elements of sustaining any future decentralisation programme, although the political hurdle of knowledge-sharing is likely to be the hardest to overcome.

6   What conclusion can be drawn?

Perhaps the most positive conclusion to be drawn from the preceding discussion is that the articulation of regional needs within central bodies responsible for water policy development will be the litmus test of the Government's sensitivity to the efficient management of national water resources. Indeed, the positive hypothesis that decentralisation is not simply a politically expedient policy of control over the potential and real challenges from so-called 'peripheral' regions may itself be tested through looking at the success or not of the efficient and sustainable development of water resources in a country's river basin(s). Perhaps, conversely, water resources development may provide a useful indicator of political development in the long run, and of the general efficacy of policies of decentralisation.

7   References

1.   Mawhood, P. (ed) (1993) Local Government in the Third World-Experience o Decentralisation in Tropical Africa, Africa Institute of South Africa, pp. 1-7.

2. Rondinelli, D.A., McCullough, J.S. and Johnson, R.W. (1989) Analysing decentralisation policies in developing countries: a political economy framework. *Development and Change,* Vol. 20, pp. 57-87.

3. Carey, D. (1995) Management and supply in agriculture and resources: is decentralisation the answer? *Natural Resources Perspectives,* No. 4, June, Overseas Development Institute, London.

4. Rothchild, D (ed) (1994) Strengthening African Local Initiative: Local Self Governance, Decentralisation and Accountability, Hamburg African Studies, No. 3, pp.1-11.

5. Economist Intelligence Unit (1996) *Sudan Country Report,* lst Quarter.

6. 'Water Resources Management - A World Bank Policy Paper'(1995) The World Bank, Washington D.C., p. 17.

7. Kebbede, G. (1992) The State and Development in Ethiopia. Humanities Pres International, Inc, New Jersey, p.65.

8. Beschorner, N. *(1993) Water and instability in the Middle East,* IISS Adelphi Paper No. 273.

9. Abate, Z. (1994) *Water resources development in Ethiopia, - an evaluation of present experience and future planning concepts,* London.

10. Constitution of the Federal Democratic Republic of Ethiopia (1994) (Unofficial English translation from the Amharic original), 8 December 1994, Addis Ababa, p.27.

Appendix I

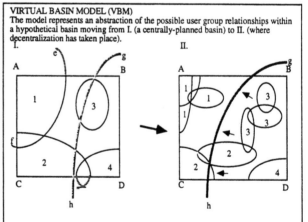

VIRTUAL BASIN MODEL (VBM)
The model represents an abstraction of the possible user group relationships within a hypothetical basin moving from I. (a centrally-planned basin) to II. (where decentralization has taken place).

ABCD=the socio-economic boundaries of a river basin where: A=interests represented by agricultural production (which may incorporate a number of different interest groups, varying according to type of production); B=potential or actual hydropower production; C=industrial users; D=domestic users: within the g-h 'elipse' are the interests of another state downstream, cutting through hydropower, domestic use and some agricultural use in I.: in completing 'elipse' e-f one visualizes the water which comes from outside of the basin in the form of 'virtual water' (after Professor Tony Allan, SOAS).

Moving from I. to II. one conceptualizes what might happen to the 'political space' within the basin, whereby decentralization has multiplied the interests in spheres 1, 2 and 3 and has allied the interests of 2 and 3 in the case of, perhaps, one particular region. The international interest itself has expanded outwards as a result and, if one assumes that the new but smaller interests might still all have to be accommodated in a future agreement with the downstream state then the political picture appears to have become more complicated. Areas not included within the 'elipses' might be called 'free' political space'; where there is more space the political environment is potentially more dynamic.

MANAGING WATER RESOURCE DEVELOPMENT IN THE CUNENE RIVER BASIN

Bilateral cooperation on the Cunene

P.S. HEYNS
Department of Water Affairs, Windhoek, Namibia

Abstract
In view of the international status of the Cunene River, the implementation of water infrastructure development has been carried out within the framework of a number of international agreements and appropriate institutional arrangements. This paper provides an overview of the Cunene catchment, the agreements and arrangements, how the work has been implemented, what major development constraints were experienced and what the future holds for the development of the Cunene Basin.
Keywords: agreement, commission, cooperation, Cunene River Basin, hydropower, irrigation, steering committee, water resource

1 Introduction

Namibia and Angola, sharing a common border over a distance of 340 kilometres (km) from the Ruacana Falls in the east to the Atlantic Ocean in the west along the Cunene River, are situated on the western seaboard of the southern African subcontinent. Refer to Fig. 1 for orientation.

The hydroclimate in Namibia is typically arid and as a result, the rivers in the interior of the country are all ephemeral. Their runoff is erratic and unreliable. The only remaining alternative to augment these scarce water resources is to utilise the potential of the international perennial rivers on the borders of the country to supply water for domestic, industrial, agricultural and hydropower uses to a growing young nation.

The perennial Cunene River is therefore of critical importance to Namibia in view of its hydropower potential which is in excess of 2300 MW, and the availability water which can be utilised to support socio-economic development in northern Namibia.

Water Policy: Allocation and management in practice. Edited by P. Howsam and R.C. Carter.
Published in 1996 by E & FN Spon. ISBN 0 419 21650 2

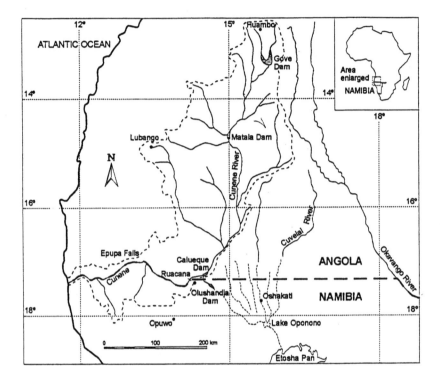

Fig. 1. Location of the Cunene River Basin

2   Characteristics of the Cunene River

The Cunene originates at 1 500 metres (m) above mean sea level in the central Angolan highlands near Huambo and has a total length of approximately 1 050 km. The catchment covers 106 500 square kilometres (km²) of which 92 400 km² (86,8%) is situated in Angola. The balance of 14 100 km² (13,2%) is in Namibia.

The rainfall in the Cunene catchment decreases from 1 300 millimetres per annum (mm/a) in the headwaters to practically zero at the mouth of the river. More than 90% of the rainfall in the catchment occurs in the summer months from November to April in the form of convective thunderstorms. The mean annual runoff at the mouth of the Cunene is 5 500 million cubic metres (Mm³). The net evaporation in the catchment varies between 300 mm/a in the upper reaches and 2 500 mm/a near the coast.

In spite of the fact that the Cunene is a perennial river, the runoff is seasonal and subject to considerable variation. The average flow is 174 cubic metres per second (m³/s), but the peak flow can be as high as 1 500 m³/s while the winter base flow has been as low as 1,0 m³/s and this illustrates the need to regulate the flow of the Cunene River to optimise its utilisation.

The Cunene River Basin is characterized by three distinct drainage patterns due to the topography of the catchment. The upper part is hilly and mountainous where the water flowing in the tributaries of the Cunene is perennial and confined to well defined channels with rapids. The high rainfall and low evaporation make the area ideal for the location of a regulating dam. The central part of the catchment comprises very flat areas where the tributaries are no longer perennial due to the lower rainfall. The runoff contribution to the Cunene by these rivers is reduced by additional factors such as evaporation and seepage losses in the extensive floodplains. These plains are suitable for irrigation and elevated enough to allow the diversion of water from the Cunene to the Cuvelai Basin in northern Namibia. The lower part of the catchment between Ruacana and the coast cuts a steep, narrow gorge through a very mountainous area on its way to the sea. Impressive rapids and magnificent waterfalls like those at Ruacana (140 m) and Epupa add to the wonderful scenery that meets the eye. Most of the lower portion of the catchment is in Namibia, but contributes very little to the total runoff.

The hydropower potential of a river is proportional to the flow and the available head. The steep canyon below the Ruacana Falls drops more than 1 000 m to the coast and this makes the Cunene the most suitable perennial river accessible to Namibia for the generation of hydro-electric power.

3   Existing and future infrastructure development on the Cunene

The most important existing water infrastructure facilities on the Cunene River are the Gove Dam, the Matala Dam, the Calueque Dam, the Ruacana Weir and the Ruacana Power Station.

Between 1952 and 1958 a multi-purpose power supply and irrigation scheme was established at Matala in Angola. The dam had an installed hydropower capacity of 27 million watt (MW) and supplied irrigation water through a system of canals to some 5 000 hectares (ha) of land. The hydropower capacity was recently upgraded to 39 MW, but the present mode of operation and utilisation of the irrigation project is not clear.

The Gove Dam, which has a capacity of 2 574 Mm³, located in the upper reaches of the Cunene, was completed in 1973. The purpose of the dam is to regulate the flow of the Cunene River and to facilitate the optimum utilisation of the Ruacana Power Station. This dam is not operated due to various political and technical reasons.

Construction on the Calueque Dam to further regulate the Cunene and to divert water to Namibia, commenced in 1973, but the dam has never been completed due to the war in Angola. The dam is located on floodplains, upstream of the Ruacana Falls, about 18 km north of the border between Angola and Namibia. The pumpstation which supplies water southwards to the Olushandja Balancing Dam in northern Namibia, is housed in the partially completed concrete section on the southern side of the river and is fully operational.

The Ruacana Diversion Weir, situated about 800 m upstream of the Ruacana Falls in Angola, diverts the flow of the Cunene to three hydropower turbines in the Ruacana Power Station on Namibian Soil. The power station has an installed generating capacity of 240 MW. The efficiency of this facility is reduced because the Gove Dam cannot be used to regulate the flow in the river optimally.

The power demand in Namibia increased so much since the Ruacana hydropower plant was completed in 1978 that additional sources of power are presently under investigation. One alternative is to construct a dam with an installed hydropower capacity of 400 MW at the Epupa Falls on the lower Cunene River. This hydropower source will contain the cost of electricity in Namibia to acceptable levels and enhance the possibilities for industrial, mining and socio-economic development in the country.

Detailed feasibility studies are presently being done, including a comprehensive environmental assessment. The main aim of the feasibility study is to optimise all the hydropower alternatives and to make a cost estimate of the preferred alternative. This result will then be compared to the cost to develop other alternative sources of power like a thermal power station, a gas field and the importation of power from a country like Angola or South Africa.

The purpose of the environmental assessment is to investigate all the impacts of the proposed alternative hydropower options on the lower Cunene, in order to facilitate decision making and to propose an integrated environmental management plan.

4   Constitutional development of the Cunene Basin States

Constitutional changes in Germany, Portugal, South Africa and Angola had some remarkable influence on the development of water infrastructure in the Cunene Basin.

Three major colonial powers, the British, the Germans and the Portuguese had an interest in the area to the north of the Orange River in the Cape Colony, also known as *territorium nilus* or no man's land. In 1878 the British annexed a small stretch of the dismal and desolate west coast around the Bahia das Baleas - bay of the whales, or better known as Walvis Bay. The Portuguese laid claim to the west coast from Cabinda to the 18 degrees south latitude. The Imperial German Government ignored the Portuguese claim of the land between the 18°S latitude and the Cunene River when Bismarck annexed the west coast, excluding Walvis Bay, between *Angra das Voltas* (the Orange River), and the Cunene River as a German *Schutzgebiet* (Protectorate) in 1884.

The Union of South Africa was established in 1910 after the bitter Boer War at the turn of the century. During the First World War South African troops occupied German South West Africa in support of the British. This effectively ended German rule on 9 July 1915, but a Military Government remained in place until 1925 when an Administration for South West Africa was established by South Africa.

In terms of Article 22 of the Peace Treaty of Versailles of 1919 German South West Africa was classified as a Class C Mandate. At the inception of the League of Nations in 1920, the Union of South Africa became the Mandatory for the Territory. This meant that South West Africa could be administrated as an integral part of the Union of South Africa. In terms of this Mandate, the Government of the Union of South Africa had sovereignty over the Territory and therefore the authority to enter into negotiations with the Government of the Republic of Portugal on the development of the Cunene River Basin.

In 1961 South Africa became a Republic, left the British Commonwealth and again started to negotiate with the Portuguese Authorities on the Cunene.

In 1974 the Caetano-regime in Portugal came to a fall. This opened the door for the independence of Angola on 11 November 1974, after more than 500 years of Portuguese colonial rule.

The struggle for the independence of Namibia commenced in 1959 under the leadership of SWAPO. Between 1966, when the armed conflict started, and 1989 when the United Nations Transitional Assistance Group arrived in Namibia to oversee the democratic election, a process of gradual change in the attitude of the South African Government eventually led to the independence of Namibia on 21 March 1990. This made it for the first time possible for Namibia to negotiate with Angola on the Cunene as a sovereign state.

5   International agreements on the Cunene

The development of water and power supply schemes in the Cunene River Basin has always been done within the framework of international agreements and cooperation between the two basin states.

At the Berlin Conference in February 1885 the Portuguese relinquished their claim of the land between the Cunene River and the 18°S latitude and the northern border of Namibia was confirmed in a Declaration, also referred to as the First Border Agreement, signed in Lisbon on 30 December 1886. Portugal admitted its acceptance of Germany's fixation of the northern border and agreed that the border between the Portuguese Province of Angola and the German Protectorate of South West Africa shall be the Cunene River up to the waterfall where it breaks through the Serra Canna, and further eastwards in a straight line to the Cubango River, and further eastwards etc.

In June 1926 an Agreement, also referred to as the Second Border Agreement, was reached between the Governments of Portugal and the Union of South Africa to remove the ambiguities of the First Border Agreement. The Ruacana Falls was identified as the waterfall referred to in the first Border Agreement and it was confirmed that the middle of the Cunene will be the border along the river. This border was demarcated and firmly established the Cunene River as an international watercourse.

The South African Government realised the importance of the Cunene as a perennial water source for the supply of water into northern South West Africa and wanted to reach agreement on utilizing its share of the water for hydropower generation and the supply of water for domestic and agricultural uses.

In July 1926 Portugal and South Africa entered into an Agreement on the use of the water of the Cunene. This agreement, which granted South Africa the right to use one half of the flood water of the Cunene, is referred to as the First Water Use Agreement. The agreement made provision for the diversion of water from Angolan territory to generate hydropower at Ruacana and for the transfer of water from Calueque, across the watershed from the perennial Cunene Basin to the ephemeral Cuvelai Drainage Basin in northern Namibia.

In April 1964 the South African Government approved in principle the report of a Commission of Enquiry into South West African Affairs. This report proposed a five-year development plan which included the development of the envisaged Cunene

River Scheme at an estimated cost of ZAR 49 million (1964 values).

In October 1964 the Governments of the Republics of South Africa and Portugal entered into an Agreement, also referred to as the Second Water Use Agreement, regarding rivers of mutual interest in general and to determine the feasibility of the Cunene River Scheme. Between 1964 and 1968 most of the required investigations and feasibility studies for this project were carried out.

In 1969 Portugal and South Africa concluded a Third Water Use Agreement on the actual development of the Cunene River Scheme. At that time provision was made to construct the Gove Dam, the Calueque Dam and pumpstation, the hydro-electric power station at the Ruacana Falls and the Ruacana Diversion Weir.

The construction of the Cunene River Scheme commenced in 1970, but the conflict between the three rival political factions in Angola (the MPLA, UNITA, and the FNLA), as well as the armed interventions by South Africa in Angola to protect its interests in Namibia, against the liberation army (PLAN) of SWAPO, severely affected the development and operation of the Cunene River Scheme between 1974 and 1988.

In September 1990, shortly after the independence of Namibia, a further agreement on the development and utilisation of the potential of the Cunene River was reached between the Governments of the Peoples Republic of Angola and the Republic of Namibia. This Agreement not only recognised, endorsed and affirmed the previous three Water Use Agreements on the Cunene River, but it was also agreed to evaluate the possible development of further schemes on the Cunene which will accommodate the future water and power needs in both Angola and Namibia

In view of the provisions in the 1990 Agreement, a Protocol of Agreement was signed in October 1991 between Angola and Namibia to commence with the development of a new hydropower scheme on the Cunene. Since then, a pre-feasibility study was done on the proposed Epupa Dam and due to the positive results of this study, it has been decided to continue with a full feasibility study on a number of alternatives to establish a new hydropower plant on the Cunene. This work is still in progress.

6   Institutional arrangements to develop the Cunene

The First Water Use Agreement made provision for the creation of a Joint Technical Commission to investigate, design, construct and operate the envisaged facilities to be established on the Cunene. This Commission had to be instituted by 1927, but this idea never realised and between 1926 and 1964 virtually no further cooperation took place between South Africa and Portugal on the Cunene. However, in spite of this, the Portuguese Authorities developed the Matala irrigation and power scheme within Angolan territory between 1952 and 1958.

In terms of the Third Water Use Agreement of 1969, a Permanent Joint Technical Commission (the PJTC) was established to advise the Governments about the Project, as well as to guide and monitor the development of the Cunene River Scheme. A Joint Operating Authority would also be established to operate the scheme. However, between 1974 and 1989 this Commission could not function due to the hostilities between Angola and South Africa and the works were never completed to such an extent that the Operating Authority could start functioning. In the 1990 Agreement between Angola and Namibia, the PJTC was re-instated and is very active. Provision was also made for a Joint Operating Authority to regulate the flow of the Cunene River for hydropower generation and the diversion of water.

In view of the technical nature of the present feasibility study, the PJTC appointed a Steering Committee for the Feasibility Study (the SCFS) to monitor the activities of the consortium of Angolan, Namibian, Norwegian and Swedish consultants. In order to complete the unfinished Calueque Dam, the PJTC appointed a Task Force for Calueque (the TFC) to execute the necessary studies and construction activities.

7   Management aspects under consideration

Although the water use agreements on the Cunene make provision for dispute resolution, the basis for negotiation about the equitable and reasonable sharing of water has never been established in spite of the fact that the 1966 Helsinki Rules of the International Law Association on the Uses of the Waters of International Rivers had been available at the time of the 1969 water use agreement. The consideration of the Helsinki Rules, as well as the Draft Articles of the International Law Commission on the Law of the Non-Navigational Uses of International Water seems inevitable in view of the recent insistence by the Angolans that especially the 1969 agreement on the Cunene should be reviewed.

The Water Use Agreements not only dealt with institutional arrangements, water allocation and proposed infrastructure development, but also practical matters such as granting access to Angolan territory for investigations and construction, the laws that would apply, the sharing of costs, economic feasibility, the cost of water utilised, the operation of future infrastructure and dispute resolution. It even made provision for reducing the adverse impacts of construction works by requiring the cleaning up of the construction sites. These requirements embody studies on most of the environments that need to be evaluated in modern environmental assessments, for example the biophysical, social, economic, historical and political environments.

The newly proposed hydropower development of the Cunene has evoked considerable resistance from environmentalists, but a comprehensive environmental study is being done according to the guidelines of the Namibian Environmental Assessment Policy.

8   Conclusion

It is not only the conceptualization, development and acceptance of international water agreements that are instrumental to sound, implementable water policy or water infrastructure development with regard to international rivers, but the evaluation of those agreements in a changing environment as a result of more information and a better understanding of the functioning of river basin system that enhance the sustainability of such development. Disruption by political issues, including wars or the threat of wars, can seriously delay the implementation of projects outlined in international agreements, while hostile acts can cause damage to existing infrastructure.

In spite of all the border and water use agreements on the Cunene River, it took nearly 88 years before the first joint infrastructure, development the Gove Dam, was completed in 1973. This shows that basin states should start at the earliest possible time to enter into agreements to investigate the potential for sustainable future development of international water sources.

The delay in the establishment of the Joint Technical Commission on the Cunene in 1927 was a major handicap in cooperation and joint planning between the basin states. The need for an organisation which brings a group of competent academics and technicians from the basin states together, is clear. Such a technical must direct investigations and advise their respective Governments on the potential to realise the expectation of each basin state as far as the sustainable development of international waters is concerned.

The civil war in Angola and the Namibian struggle for freedom not only delayed further development on the Cunene, but caused damage to the existing infrastructure and left some components uncompleted. The South Africans were denied access to the pumpstation at Calueque in Angola after 1976 and an unnecessary water scheme had to be built from a point below the Ruacana Falls where Namibia had direct access to the Cunene. The pumping head increased from 18 m to 450 m and the supply capacity had to be reduced from 2 m^3/s to 0,6 m^3/s. The capital cost implications of contingency infrastructure development and the uneconomical operating costs of an inappropriate interim water supply scheme, as well as the cost to repair damaged facilities, place an unwanted burden on the economies of the affected basin states and should be avoided in the interest of all parties concerned.

The agreement between Angola and Namibia to accept the old agreements between the colonial powers (Contrary to the Nyerere Doctrine where Tanzania rejected the Nile Agreement) immediately led to further cooperation on the development of the Cunene and gave Namibia access to Angolan territory to operate the Calueque Pumpstation. However, although provision has been made for dispute resolution through arbitration, one of the perceived constraints in the existing institutional arrangements on the Cunene, is the absence of an understanding about a set of rules which can be used as a basis for negotiations and consensus on the equitable and reasonable allocation of water resources. The Helsinki Rules of the International Law Association or the proposed Draft Articles by the International Law Commission may be considered for that purpose.

The new dispensation in managing the Cunene Basin is working well and is making it possible for the basin states to meet five major obligations when it comes to sharing international waters, namely to cooperate, to exchange information, to plan jointly and to apportion water equitably to efficient and reasonable water uses in such a way that it will not cause appreciable harm to each other.

9   References

1.   SWA Annual 1977, pp 170 - 172
2.   Border and Water Use Agreements, Namibian Government

WATER CONFLICTS IN THE MIDDLE EAST
Middle East water conflicts

A. MEDZINI
Department of Geography, "ORANIM" School of Education, Haifa, Israel

Abstract
In a world where the amount of resources is constant and unchanging but where their use and exploitation is growing because of the rapid population growth, a rise in standards of living and the development of industrialisation, the resource of water has become a critical issue in the foreign relations between different states. As a result of this many research scholars claim that, today, we are facing the beginning of the "Geopolitical era of water".

The danger of conflict of water is especially severe in the Middle East which is characterised by the low level of precipitation and high temperatures. The Middle Eastern countries have been involved in a constant state of political tension and the gap between the growing number of inhabitants and the fixed supply of water and land has been a factor in contributing to this tension. The destabilisation of the balance between the quantity of water, the quantity of land and the number of residents, in addition to disagreements between the states of the area about economic, political and ideological questions have caused a number of researchers to develop theories which attempt to predict future armed conflict.

This article examines the limitations of theories grounded in economic, political, ideological and military factors which are intended to predict a future war between the co-riparian states in the region.
Keywords: conflict, economy, geopolitics, ideology, international relations, Middle-East, models, water policy,

1   Introduction: the role of water in the Middle East

Man's use of water is an important issue everywhere, but in the Middle East it

Water Policy: Allocation and management in practice. Edited by P. Howsam and R.C. Carter.
Published in 1996 by E & FN Spon. ISBN 0 419 21650 2

constitutes a major problem.
Three main factors are responsible for the situation:

a)   The physical geography and the climate of the area
b)   The development of agriculture which constitutes the main consumer of water in
     the area
c)   Rapid population growth.

a)   Water shortage is undoubtedly one of the main features of the Middle East. The
area is chiefly arid or semi-arid, precipitation is seasonal and limited to winter, whilst
droughts are frequent. All these factors add to the dependence on imported food in
the countries of the area [1].

Rainfall, which occurs mainly in the mountainous regions of the Middle East, is
hardly ever used by farmers, because gradients are steep and temperatures low in the
mountains, whilst rivers flow for hundreds of kilometres before reaching the arid
zones of the area with its wide plains suitable for agriculture.

As a result of the political division of the area, the rivers cross international borders
(except the River Litani). Consequently, over half the population in the area is
dependent on water from rivers which cross international borders. Moreover, two
thirds of the Arabic speaking population of the area is dependent on water carried by
rivers originating in non-Arabic speaking countries (in addition to populations
residing in arid areas). This adds acute political sensitivity regarding the sharing of
resources of water [2].

b)   Traditionally, agriculture and livestock were the foundation on which the local
economy rested. Today, approximately 30% of the working population still subsist
on agriculture, and another sector of the population is dependent on agricultural
produce as agricultural raw material, although the contribution of agriculture to the
G.N.P. in the Middle East is declining steadily and the number of persons employed
in agriculture is equally becoming smaller. Despite the agricultural revolution in the
Middle East in the past fifty years which found expression in the transition from
traditional to modern agriculture, the irrigated areas in the countries of the Middle
East are smaller than 10%, and 60% of the area is used for dry farming, chiefly grain
[3]. Many countries wishing to, but being currently unable to add to the areas under
irrigation will require large quantities of water and financial resources.

c)   Rapid population growth in the area has led to increased consumption of water
resources. In 1950 the population of the area amounted to 130 million residents, in
1985 it had risen to 265 million, and by the year 2000 it will reach 420 million, and
will have doubled in twenty-five years' time. The ratio between water, land resources
and population size has been de-stabilised. Accelerated urbanisation, rising living
standards, industrialisation and the wish to produce their own food supplies contribute
to the pressure on water resources whilst adversely affecting their quality. The
countries mainly affected are the ones located downstream. The limited quantity of
water available can no longer meet the agricultural, industrial and domestic needs of
the countries of the area.

The quantity of water available from the several resources in the area is estimated at 163 billion m^3 annually. This quantity is only approx. half of the 305 million m^3 required annually by the countries in the area to produce their own food [4].

A study of water resources done by INWARD estimates the basic needs for water at approximately 55 m^3 per person for domestic purposes in addition to a further 1150 m^3 required to produce basic foodstuffs. According to the study, the minimum requirement per person is therefore 1205 m^3 In 1985 only 9 member countries of the Arab League were able to meet this need, whereas another 12 countries were unable to do so. Rapid population growth in the area increases the number of countries falling into the category of countries with water resources in short supply, and very few countries will be able to meet their own needs in the future [5].

Destabilization of the balance between available land, size of population and water resources has turned the Middle East into an area more dependent than any other area in the world on other countries to supply its food requirements. In 1960, the area was still able to produce its own food and even export certain quantities of surplus produce. In 1973, countries in the area imported food in the amount of $40 million. The figure rose to $200 million in 1980 and to $230 million in 1989 [3,6]. More and more countries have become totally dependent on imported food; attempts to deal with the situation involve development programs. As the need to import food means not only economic dependence on other countries, but political dependence as well, the countries involved are stepping up their development programs which are based on the use of increasingly large quantities of water. This in turn will in future impact political conflict with regard to the distribution of water resources obtained from joint rivers. Bulloch & Darwish writes: "While water is becoming scarce in other places, leading to conflict of national interests, it is only in the Middle East that aggrieved countries have vast financial reserves, huge standing armies, air forces, bombs, rockets and, in some cases, nuclear capability. They also have a modern history of being willing to settle disputes by military means, a history of conflict, a common acceptance of the use of force to end quarrels" [8].

2   The impact of water shortage on relations between countries in the Middle East

It has been shown that physical, agricultural and demographic factors produce a situation in which increased exploitation of water resources has become vital for the development of the area. Another characteristic of the area are the complex relations between the several countries. The low level of mutual trust impedes or prevents cooperation and joint water resources cannot be developed; when this issue is added to other areas of severe conflict between the countries in the Middle East, e.g. social, political, economic and ideological tensions as well as personal aversion to heads of state felt by some political leaders in the area, the struggle for water resources becomes more acute, and chances for cooperation are slim.

Water shortage has become a subject of great importance in Middle-Eastern regional politics, both on the covert and the overt level. Overt politics can be watched and evaluated when agreements are signed to share water resources (e.g. the agreement with Egypt regarding the use of the River Nile, the Israel-Jordan Peace

Treaty), when complaints are lodged with the UN. (e.g. regarding development of the Euphrates by Turkey), or in the event of a military threat (e.g. Syria's attempt to divert the Jordan River in the 60s). Covert politics finds expression in power struggles (the case of Iraq and Syria), in strategic threats to deny access to water resources (e.g. Turkey and Syria), and apprehension regarding future water shortages (which among other things impact the chances for peace between Syria and Israel). It is difficult to evaluate the importance of the impact of covert factors involving water on relations between countries, but covert politics undoubtedly impact significantly the relations between the different countries in the area.

Recognition of the increasing severity of the problem of shortage of water in the area has led many researchers and politicians to the assumption that the future of the area is linked to the issue of water, and they believe that water will be the main cause of a future regional armed conflict. Joyce Starr writes for instance: "Water security will soon rank with military security in the war rooms of the defence ministers." [7]. Bulloch & Darwish writes "Unlike the region's traditional border, ethnic or ideological disputes, which are normally defused with little or no military conflict or put on ice by brides and pressure from external powers, the existing and coming water disputes make a large-scale military conflict very likely...In the Middle East, potential trouble spots are not confined to the three great rivers systems of the area, the Nile, the Tigris-Euphrates and the Jordan. Conflicts can also arise in places where people and countries are dependent on the sparser quantities of water stored in rock and sandstone aquifers" [8]. Peter Gleick writes: "Water has already been a source of conflict among nations. We fight for access to water as a tool and weapon in battle, and we target the water facilities of our enemies. While water resources have rarely been the sole cause of conflict, fresh water resources are becoming more valuable in many regions, and the likelihood of water-induced conflict is changing over time. In arid and semi-arid areas of the world, where water is already a vital resource, conflicts over access and possession are likely to worsen" [9].

This is certainly correct to argue that water reservoirs and dams have been military targets since World War II through the Gulf War, the examples adduced by researchers do not substantiate their argument that those wars were actually fought over resources of water. The 1967 war between Israel and Syria is the only case in which the water resources of a river were occupied. However, this is an exceptional example adduced by researchers to substantiate their stance. It is a fact that in large areas in the world where the residents were starving (due either to internal strife or successive years of famine), no attempts were made to conquer resources of water in neighbouring countries. It will appear that the theory of military conflict was mainly developed by academics connected with Strategic and International Relations Research Institutes, it being important to these researchers to warn of the possibility of future armed conflict to justify their existence.

Another contribution to the atmosphere of conflict has been made by researchers who regard the shortage of water as an unsolvable problem. Thus Frey & Naff argue as follows: "The shortage of water is the heart of the problem and the shortage of water is a zero-sum security issue and thus creates a constant potential for conflict" [10]. Actually, they do not realise that, taking the economic approach, water is not a zero-sum, because it is expendable when food is imported, and armed conflict is thus prevented. The import of food from the world market is the most effective means of compensation for water shortage. At the same time it must be conceded that wealthy countries, such as the Gulf States and industrialised countries such as Israel are equipped to handle food imports with ease, whereas poorer countries, such as Syria and Egypt regard industrialisation as the ultimate answer to their problems and have difficulties handling imports from other countries which to them are no more than an interim solution.

Many politicians use the sensitive issue of water shortage to create a favourable climate of opinion for themselves, it being easy to show the direct link between quantities of water available and food production, a higher standard of living, the quality of life etc. It will appear that politicians make use of this issue mainly for internal political purposes.

Not only politicians, but also journalists frequently use headlines, such as "the water bomb", "water wars", "water crises", water conflicts", "rivers of fire", and it is clear that such captions are meant to stress the conflict and attract the attentions of their readership. The stand taken by economists who are aware of the problem of water shortage is mainly economy-oriented and deterministic: they do not give security subjects, and ideological, political and social question connected with them the emphasis they deserve. For example, articles have been published suggesting that the location of dams should be chosen according to considerations of low levels of evaporation only, or crops be planned only according to economic considerations and not in the context of the real needs of the state [11,12]. To meet the needs of the state, they propose that the co-riparian states should trade water or agriculture produce with each other. This utopian approach to economic thinking, cannot work in the political climate prevailing in the Middle East region.

The central question is whether the conflict over the right to certain quantities of water and the struggle for its quality is impacted by ideological, political, economic and security factors, and whether a political struggle between countries sharing resources of water was created, or whether the controversy over water resources created economic, political, ideological and military conflict between the countries involved.

The present paper focuses on models serving a) to analyse conflicts arising from these factors and b) to predict the likelihood of a future war, fought to gain control of the ever dwindling water resources in the area.

3   Theoretical constraints on the military conflict

To explain the "water policy" of Middle Eastern states and assess the level of likelihood of another war against this background, several researchers have tried to develop theories ranking the above factors in their order of importance.

Frey & Naff developed a cognitive mapping model to study the several approaches taken by the co-riparian states towards water resources and the degree of importance each of these states attaches to the factors listed above. This would be the basis for a 'mental map' showing the ranking order of the relative importance of each of these factors from the point of view of the co-riparian states themselves. The authors claim that the map would be a tool to identify the significant differences between the ranking of the factors by the different states and could moreover be used to distinguish between real and imaginary conflicts. They claim that the closer the connection between the factors the higher their level of importance [13,14].

Admittedly, this cognitive 'map' contributes to a better understanding of the factors likely to decide the water policy of a given state. However, it does not gauge the level of importance of each individual factor relative to the others, and it cannot be used to make a quantitative assessment of the sum total of all the factors in a given state relative to such sum total in one or more other states. Another model which attempts to make a quantitative assessment of the several factors determining the "water policy" of a given Middle East state was developed by Gleick. His argument is the following: as water shortage causes economic and political tension which may reach a level which would justify war, he suggests that the traditional tools should be used to analyse security crises such as, for instance, a shortage of crude oil.

Gleick analyses five factors which determine the water policy of a state:

1. the degree of water scarcity
2. the extent to which the water supply is shared by more than one region or state
3. the relative power of the co-riparian states
4. the ease of access to alternative fresh water sources
5. the ease of access to substitutes for water [9]

To distinguish between significant and marginal factors, the numerical sum total of the factors establishes the level of importance of the water shortage in a given state: this level would determine its water policy.

The problematics of this model derives from the subjectivity of the data and the similarity of numerical grades assigned to dissimilar factors. For example, the importance of foodstuffs self-sufficiency is assigned the same numerical grade as hydro-electric power self-sufficiency of the number of states having access to a riparian drainage basin, regardless of the fact that each of these factors is different in significance and weight.

Naff developed the power matrix model to attempt the identification of the possibility of another war over water resources. Naff's criteria are grounded in a number of basic factors:

1. riparian position within the drainage basin;
2. projectable strategic power;
3. economic interests;
4. external and internal politics [14].

Each factor is assigned a subjective numerical value indicating its level of importance.

If this model is used, the level of probability of armed conflict is highest when a state situated downstream has the strongest defence forces, riparian development interests, and is most likely in the future to face a lack of water. On the other hand, the level of probability of armed conflict is lowest when the state is situated upstream and has the strongest army, or when chances are small that it will be faced with water shortages.

The factor of the balance of military power is developed by Mandel, who argues it is made up of three components:

1. the state's overall political/ military/ economic power level;
2. the states technological power to disrupt or alter the river basin;
3. the states geographical power reflected in a more or less advantageous downstream position with respect to the river [15].

The shortcomings of this model are the same as those pointed out when Gleick's model was discussed: the main difficulty results from the subjectivity of the data and the allocation of similar numerical values to different variables although in reality the factor of level of economic interests need not be identical to the factor of projectable strategic power or the factor of internal politics in a given state.

4   Conclusions

It is true that the geography of the Middle Eastern states is conducive to lack of water exacerbated by modernisation, population growth, the development of agriculture, industrialisation and urbanisation processes, as well as by rising standards of living. Equally, it is true that the shortage of water impacts relations between the Middle Eastern states - in particular covert relations which, in this area, find expression in mutual suspicion against the background of religious, national, ideological, economic and political tensions, as well as personal relations which are equally fraught with suspicion. On the other hand, the increased demand of water may be also an impetus to peace, as it has between Israel and Jordan in 1995.

This background served as the basis of opinions voiced by newspapermen, political leaders and researchers who attempted to develop theories of armed conflict which are mainly grounded in research methods used by students of international relations which are not currently suited to the forecast of behaviour of individual states, or possibilities of conflicts of states sharing a drainage basin. It should be borne in mind that the level of interests of states changes over time, and interests which were regarded as vital at a certain time are not necessarily valid at another time. Developing theories does undoubtedly contribute to the understanding of relations between different states in the Middle East and the factors linked with the issue of water, but theories might usefully be re-worked and enhanced to neutralise the level of researcher subjectivity still attaching to them as well as the tools to determine the level of relative importance of the factors.

5   References

1.   Richards, A. and Waterbury, J. (1990) *A political economy of the Middle East: state, class, and economic development,* Westview Press, Inc.
2.   Kolars, J. (1990) "The course of water in the Arab Middle East", *American-Arab affairs,* No. 33, Summer, pp. 56-68.
3.   Underwood, A.K. (1981) "Gulf faces a growing food crisis", *8 Days, International Middle East Business,* Vol. 3, No. 51, 26 December, p. 53.

4. Fahmi, I.J. (1988) "The problem of food security in the Arab world", *Dinar,* Vol. 1, No. 9, pp. 7-10.
5. Clarke, R. (1991) *Water: the international crisis,* Earth scan Publications LTD, London.
6. Comet (1992) "Agriculture in the Middle East", *Comet,* No. 35, January, pp. 24-40.
7. Starr, J.R. (1991) "Water wars", *Foreign Policy,* Vol. 70, No. 2, Spring, pp. 17-36.
8. Bulloch, J. and Darwish, A. (1996) *Water Wars - Coming Conflicts in the Middle East,* Gollancz Victor, London, pp. 15-32
9. Gleick, P. H. (1992) "Water and conflict", *Environmental change and acute conflict,* No. 1, September, pp. 1-27.
10. Arlosoroff, S. (1994) *Water resources management: intra-regional cooperation,* paper prepared for presentation for the Conference, "Regional Cooperation in the Middle East, Vouliagmeni, Greece, November 4-7.
11. Waterbury, J (1994) *"Transboundary Water and the Challenge of International Cooperation in the Middle East",* in Rogers, P & Lydon, P (Eds.) Water in the Arab World, Perspective and Prognoses, Harvard, pp. 39-64.
12. Frey, F.W. and Naff, T. (1985) "Water: an emerging issue in the Middle East, Annals, *AAPSS,* No. 482, November, pp. 65-84.
13. Naff, T. and Matson, R.C. (Eds.) (1984) *Water in the Middle East: conflict or cooperation?* Westview press, Boulder.
14. Naff, T. (1994) *"Conflict and Water Use in the Middle East",* in Rogers, P & Lydon, P (Eds.) Water in the Arab World, Perspective and Prognoses, Harvard, pp. 253-284.
15. Mandel, R. (1991) *Sources of International river basin disputes,* Paper prepared for presentation at the annual meeting of the International studies association, Vancouver, B.C., March, p. 6.

TRANS-BOUNDARY WATER POLICY COORDINATION UNDER UNCERTAINTY
The Israeli-Palestinian Mountain Aquifer

S. NETANYAHU
Agricultural and Resource Economics Department,
University of Maryland, College Park, Maryland, USA

Abstract
Efficient use of trans-boundary natural resources requires coordination of resource related policies among the entities involved. Coordination is typically considered valuable when there exist public goods, externalities, heterogeneous players, and time lags and discontinuities in the decision making process. However, the environment under which potential for coordination of policies exists is likely to be characterized by uncertainties. Uncertainties are associated with *technical* elements such as players' perception of the economic outlook, objectives targeted by the policy makers and their relative weights, a mechanism to deal with those objectives and their impact, and with *strategic* elements such as players' sincerity in revealing true preferences, acting in good faith, and disclosing all "private" information. Unilateral policy design under uncertainty may result in a welfare loss for each of the entities involved. On the other hand, coordinated policies under certain types of uncertainties improve entities' welfare.
Keywords: Mountain aquifer, policy coordination, trans-boundary water resources, uncertainty.

1 Introduction

Resources common to two or more political entities can be managed with various degrees of cooperation such as full harmonization of policies, joint expenditures, rule based framework, continuous exchange of information, and continuous joint decision-making (policy coordination). Cooper [1] identifies four reasons for coordination among Governments. Three of these reasons are associated with standard microeconomic "market failure" analysis: existence of public goods, presence of externalities, and

Water Policy: Allocation and management in practice. Edited by P. Howsam and R.C. Carter.
Published in 1996 by E & FN Spon. ISBN 0 419 21650 2

existence of a limited number of heterogeneous Governments in size and influence. The fourth argument is associated with time lags and discontinuities in the process of decision making. In the case of trans-boundary water resources, the degree of cooperation is influenced by hydrogeological, technological, economic, and political factors. Incentives to cooperate and the magnitude of cooperation are also enhanced by definition of property rights in the aquifer, externalities experienced in the absence of joint management, and external water resource opportunities. Other factors such as political stability and international image can also encourage cooperation.

The problem of water scarcity has become more acute for Israelis and Palestinians because of economic and population growth and because of degradation of historic sources. New sources and more efficient use of old ones are needed. These require large investments and effective institutions for allocating water, monitoring its use, and ensuring its quality. Coordination and cooperation between the entities are required for implementing each of these measures. However, coordination is not free of difficulties. The sources of many of the difficulties are intra- and inter-Governmental disagreements on issues such as the initial position of the economy, the economic outlook, the appropriate objectives and their proper weights, and the best mechanism to deal with a certain policy and its objectives. In addition, due to potential strategic behaviour, Governments must develop trust in each other. All those sources of difficulties arise due to the uncertainty attached to them. To reduce the risks associated with water resources, Governments should consider coordinating their water policies.

The purpose of this paper is to examine the effect of uncertainty on the incentives of Governments to coordinate trans-boundary water resource policies. The analytical framework is based on the work of Ghosh and Masson [2]. In their work on international macroeconomic policy coordination, Ghosh and Masson consider several aspects of uncertainty. First, they consider technological (additive and multiplier) uncertainties, such as the initial position of the economy, the proper weights to give objectives such as unemployment and inflation, the relevant policy multiplier, etc. Second, they consider strategic uncertainties related to the behaviour of Governments who engage in bargaining over monetary policies. Strategic uncertainties are attributed to issues such as true beliefs and preferences, trustworthiness, and private information. Ghosh and Masson's main conclusion is that macroeconomic uncertainty, far from reducing the incentives to coordinate policies, can increase the benefits from international coordination.

This study is motivated by the increasing concerns regarding demand and supply of common fresh water resources. Domestic concerns exacerbate when water resources are common to two countries or more. The consequences of water policies in one country affects the water resources available to the neighbouring country. The magnitude of the externalities can be reduced if Governments decide to coordinate their water policies. Policy coordination is valued not just for its impact on reducing externalities but also for its potential to reduce certain sources of uncertainty. Coordination under an uncertain environment can potentially create welfare gains for the countries involved. Efficient exploitation of trans-boundary natural resources requires multilateral basin-wide cooperation [3]. However, accurate knowledge with respect to the state of the resources and social expectation with respect to Governments' strategic behaviour are limited. These limitations imply that the exploitation of trans-boundary water resource involves various aspects of uncertainty.

Technological uncertainties exist with respect to quantities of water available, alternative water sources, interaction between water resources, initial position of the agricultural sector, the proper weight to give to objectives such as agricultural output and water reserves, and the level of renewable water resources. In addition to technological uncertainties, strategic uncertainties in Governments' behaviours can be identified. Governments sincerity in revealing true preferences, committing to an agreement, and disclosing all "private" information are questioned. The presence of these arguments that underline some of the reasons for uncertainty in trans-boundary natural resources and the potential of policy coordination to reduce their impact on nations' welfare motivate this study.

2 The Mountain Aquifer

2.1 Israeli and Palestinian water issues

The sources of the dispute between Israel and the Palestinians over the rights to use the MA are related to the climatic-hydrologic characteristics of the region. Israel pumps water that emerges in the Yarkon-Taninnim (YT) Aquifer of the coastal plain but which originates in the rain that falls over the Judea and Samaria mountains. Due to the urgency of water problems, an Israeli-Palestinian cooperation over the use of the MA should not be postponed. Externalities resulting from current use patterns and from Israeli and Palestinian urban development in the area call for coordination and cooperation. That is, because the Aquifer is a common property, neither party bears the cost it imposes on the other by lack of proper management. In the absence of cooperation, the Aquifer can be depleted by over-pumping and its quality degraded by lack of effluent management. A solution to these problems must be reached by coordinating water related policies. Increasing opportunities for voluntary water cooperation between Israel and the Palestinians have surfaced as a result of recent peace talks and agreements.

2.2 Hydrological overview

The MA lies under the mountains of Judea and Samaria. More than one-third of Israel's average total water production of 1,892 million cubic meters per year (mm^3/yr) originates in the MA. It consists of two major hydrologically disconnected basins, the YT Basin (or the Western Aquifer) and the Eastern Mountain (EM) Basin.

A large portion of the water collected in the Judea and Samaria Mountains emerges in springs or is pumped from groundwater in the YT Basin. Maximum sustainable yield of the YT Basin is 350 mm^3/yr, which is about one-fifth of Israel's total water production. The EM Basin consists of seven sub-aquifers. The Western border of the EM Basin serves as the divide between the hydrological systems of the EM and YT Basins.

In recent years, an average of 382 mm^3/yr has been removed from the YT Basin including both spring water and pumping. Only 20 mm^3/yr of this amount have been consumed by Palestinians. Average Israeli pumping in the YT Basin has exceeded the maximum sustainable yield. In the EM Basin, production (springs and pumping) in the years 1987/88 through 1992/93 averaged 378 mm^3/yr. Water quality is not uniform. The EM water resources are exploited by Palestinians (110 mm^3/yr), Jewish settlers

(40-60 mm^3/yr), and Israeli local water associations. (For additional discussion see for example [4] and references there.) The connections among sub-aquifers are crucial for water policy coordination because they affect each party's ability to pump, the quality of the water, and the cost of pumping. In order for Israelis and Palestinians to reach a sustainable agreement over allocation and management of the aquifer, an understanding of the hydrogeology of the Aquifer is needed.

3   The need for policy coordination

In the past several years there has been an increase in the understanding of the vitality of multilateral cooperation over trans-boundary natural resources and the environment. Areas where international cooperation over the management of trans-boundary natural resources takes place include water resources, fisheries, and air pollution. Inefficiencies in the use of natural resources are present when one country's resource exploitation policies result in externalities on the resource exploitation targets of neighbouring countries. The exploitation of trans-boundary water resources when targeting only national water related policies while ignoring neighbouring countries' targets illustrates this point. To overcome the externality effect that is created by a unilateral action, externalities should be internalized. This requires passing the authority to a central planner. However, due to sovereignty issues, it is unlikely that trans-boundary water exploitation policies will be determined by a central authority. Internalizing externalities can be overcome by policy coordination. Hence, countries which share the resource should jointly design policies which reduce the trade-offs faced by an individual country in such a way that each country is led to choose a policy which corresponds to the regional socially optimal policy.

Both positive and negative externalities provide an incentive to coordinate. Coordination does not eliminate those externalities or the trade-offs among various targets but it changes them so that the maximum possible level of welfare can be obtained. When Governments choose water related policies, they face a trade-off between the environmental and inter-generational benefits of pumping a lower quantity of water against current economic losses, especially in the agricultural sector. If policies are not coordinated, then neither Government takes account of the externalities of its policies onto the other country. For example, if certain levels of water quality-quantity are desirable, a country may introduce stringent water policies. As water use restrictions are introduced by one country, there will be an increase in the marginal value of the water in that country relative to the other country's marginal value of water. The increase in water prices in one country leads to an increase in the price of its agricultural products and a reduced domestic and foreign demand for domestic agricultural products. If water intensive goods are traded between the entities that share water resources, then an increase in agricultural prices will increase inflation in the importing country. Alternatively, the importing country's desire to fight inflation can result in a policy that increases its domestic agricultural output and hence in increased water pumping, in which case additional extraction costs are incurred. Also, increased pumping often results in a decline of water tables and in a deterioration of the quality of water. When water resources are common, both countries are likely to be worse off. Therefore, with an uncoordinated regime, Governments may set water related policies while ignoring the externalities such policies can impose on a neighbouring country. However, in the coordinated environment, each Government pursues regionally optimal policies and all Governments attain a higher level of welfare.

We saw that uncoordinated use of trans-boundary water resources may lead to irrational or myopic Government action. Alternatively, uncoordinated regimes may be due to an inability of a sovereign nation to pre-commit itself to a particular water policy (e.g., due to domestic pressure). Even if the Government of one country commits to consider its neighbouring country's welfare when choosing its domestic water policy, and the neighbouring country believes that the other Government is trustworthy and chooses its own water policy to maximize both countries' welfare, then the neighbouring country has no incentive to stick by a similar commitment and it is likely to choose policies which maximize only its own welfare. Hence, policies tailored to an uncoordinated regime tend to occur and result in inefficiencies due to the inability of Governments to pre-commit themselves to a coordinated regime. This is the classic prisoner's dilemma problem. However, this uncoordinated framework does not include (1) the interdependency of individual's choices on their expectation of others' choices and (2) uncertainty that each person has regarding the actions of others. Once these elements are considered, the environment fits Sen's assurance problem where players coordinate their action through some rule which assures the sustainability of the agreement.

4   Policy coordination

4.1 Overview

We first analyse the effects of coordinating water policies internationally in a deterministic case. In each country, water is mainly being allocated to the agricultural sector. Policy makers target conflicting objectives: agricultural production and water reserves. By increasing the level of water that remains in an aquifer, policy makers achieve several purposes: (1) leaving water for future generations, (2) reducing the agricultural welfare loss in case of bad weather, and (3) reducing contamination/salination levels of that source. Government chooses the quantity of water supply. Each Government's welfare depends on water table level (i.e., the stock of water) and the value of agricultural output. The welfare function of each Government is quadratic and separable in water reserves and agricultural output. This implies that the utility from water remaining in the aquifer and from the value of agricultural production increases at a decreasing rate if the utility function is concave. The equations for the value of agricultural output and the water reserves are derived from a model that includes four sets of home and foreign equations: agricultural output, water demand, water cost, and stock of water [5].

In the absence of any shocks, policy makers would not experience unexpected trade-offs between agricultural output and water reserves. In a stochastic environment, Governments face a conflict between achieving the two competing targets of high level of water reserves and high value of agricultural output.

If water reserves decline unexpectedly and Governments do not adjust water policies, then the country's water resources will experience an increasing positive rate of deterioration, lowering the country's welfare. Alternatively, Governments can tighten their water supply to achieve a lower rate of degradation or avoid it all together. Such a step will buy Government a large welfare gain from controlling degradation and must be measured against a welfare loss from reducing agricultural output. This result depends on the comparative advantage each Government has in 'producing' either high water reserve or high agricultural output. If a Government has a comparative advantage in 'producing' high water reserve, then its welfare gain from tight water policy ought to exceed its welfare loss from a reduction in agricultural production.

However, when an individual country attempts to improve its own welfare, it reduces the welfare of the other country via the transmission effect. Tightening water policy by lowering the water supply level at home can affect the marginal users, farmers, and increase in the cost of agricultural products, which in turn can increase inflation in the foreign country which trades agricultural products with the home country. The foreign country, in an attempt to avoid such consequences, will try to reduce its food dependency on the other country and hence supply its farmers more water quantities, regardless of the magnitude of the shock. This would yield a deterioration of the quality of the water resources common to both countries.

4.2 Conflict and coordination in deterministic environment

The example in the previous section demonstrates how the consequences of Government actions transmit across boundaries and affect the welfare of other countries. Government actions can be coordinated or un-coordinated. In the un-coordinated regime, an individual country sets policies by maximizing its own welfare, taking the actions of the other Government as given, and hence ignoring the consequences of its actions on the other country. In this section we assume that policy makers choose their optimal targets in a deterministic setting. Since no economic disturbances are present, policy makers do not face trade-offs between agricultural output and water reserves. We can derive the optimality conditions for both Governments and find the reaction functions. Solving the two reaction functions simultaneously yields the un-coordinated (Nash) equilibrium.

Due to the symmetry of the structure of the model and the identical parameters, the water policies setting of the home and foreign countries will be the same. At the (Nash) equilibrium neither country can unilaterally improve its welfare. However, it is possible for at least one country to improve its welfare level by a joint change in water policy given there exists a Pareto improving set of water policies (i.e. a set of policies that improve the welfare of at least one country and leave the other indifferent relative to their uncoordinated equilibrium setting).

4.3 Additive (model) uncertainty and the gains from coordination

By adding additive uncertainty to the model we introduce disturbances which affect the level of the agricultural output or water reserves but do not change the policy multipliers. Common sources of such uncertainty are lag in data collection and policy implementation, imperfect knowledge about the structure of the economy, and other exogenous shocks. The impact of the uncertainty regarding additive disturbances on welfare gains from coordination is studied in this section.

Since the results should not be attributed to the specific linear-quadratic framework, we consider a general functional form. We find that because additive uncertainty does not change the nature of the policy spill-overs from one country to the other, it has little effect on the gains from coordination.

4.4 Coordination under multiplier (parameter) uncertainty

Structural parameters of a model cannot be estimated with complete accuracy. The uncertainty regarding these parameters will be reflected in uncertainty in the policy multipliers and therefore are assumed random variables. In this section we examine the effect of multiplier uncertainty on the gains from coordination. In the model, each utility function has two domestic multipliers and two transmission multipliers, such that each pair is associated with the agricultural output function and the water reserve function.

The coordinated and the un-coordinated solutions do differ. Since the coordinated equilibrium is the unique symmetric Pareto efficient outcome, it must be welfare superior to the un-coordinated equilibrium. This is in sharp contrast to the certainty case where there is no incentive to coordinate policies when Governments operate in a deterministic setting. We conclude, therefore, that the multiplier uncertainty itself leads to welfare benefits from coordination. Obviously, gains from coordination can be influenced by the degree of uncertainty about domestic or transmission multipliers.

5   Strategic uncertainty and enforcement

So far, it has been shown that international coordination yields gains under structural uncertainties. We now turn to strategic uncertainty. When Governments negotiate over international matters, they may either intentionally misrepresent their views and objectives during the negotiation process or deviate from the principles agreed upon once the agreement is signed.

Do Governments deliberately renege on agreements? It has been argued that, in general, Governments view the political cost of losing credibility as outweighing potential economic benefits. Based on game theory literature it has been argued that international monetary cooperative agreements may be sustainable because far-sighted Governments recognise the costs of cheating. Some believe that the greater the visibility of the agreement the greater the political cost of reneging [2]. Others refute this assumption showing that most targets specified in the G-7 summit meeting were not achieved.

If coordinated water policies are to be advantageous relative to uncoordinated policies, Governments must trust their partners. Mutual trust becomes crucial when monitoring and compliance verification are costly or technologically impossible. Under such conditions, there is a possibility of cheating or at least for biased interpretation of the agreement so that the outcome is more favourable towards one of the parties than the other. On the other hand, specifying an agreement in detail regarding the actual instrument setting not only damages the sovereignty of a country but also is likely to be unacceptable as an exogenous decision by each country's politicians who may want to design instrument settings based on information available to them.

A coordinated regime is particularly susceptible to defection. The uncoordinated regime is a Nash equilibrium and by definition represents each country's best response, given the actions of the other Government. Therefore, once the un-coordinated equilibrium is attained, it is stable, and no Government will unilaterally deviate from it. However, coordinated equilibrium is not stable because, once a Government believes that its partner will stick by the agreement, it has an incentive to deviate, at least under a static framework.

Sustaining cooperation requires an institutional enforcement mechanism or trigger mechanism. An institutional enforcement mechanism refers to a policy whereby rules are written to cover every contingency. This necessarily implies that the institutional enforcement mechanism can support very simple policies (e.g. the Bretton-Woods agreement). A trigger mechanism refers to a situation where punishment follows defection, which means a non-cooperative regime is pursued for a specified length of time. Hence, Governments trade benefits of cheating on the cooperative agreement against the cost of triggering a punishment period in which it will only attain the level of welfare associated with the non-cooperative equilibrium. This notion is supported by the "folk theorem" of repeated games, where it is claimed that trigger mechanisms can sustain the cooperative regime without any explicit enforcement penalties between Governments. However, executing the punishment results in a loss to all players. Therefore, it is essential that the punishment be credible and Governments can commit not to coordinate for several periods once either Government is caught deviating from the agreement. To be able to commit not to coordinate, entities must be able to absorb the cost of an un-coordinated regime. Strategic uncertainty and the viability of trigger strategy as an enforcement mechanism when the analytical framework itself governed by model and parameter uncertainties ought to be studied in more details [5].

6   References

1. Cooper, R. N.   (1985) The Prospects for International Economic Policy Coordination, in *International Economic Policy Coordination* (eds. W. H. Buiter and R. C. Marston), Cambridge University Press, Cambridge, pp. 366-72.
2. Ghosh, A. R. and P. R. Masson. (1994) *Economic Cooperation in an Uncertain World*, Blackwell, Oxford.
3. Biswas, A. K.   (1993) Management of international waters: problems and perspective. *Water Resources Development*, Vol. 9, No. 2. pp. 167-188.
4. Netanyahu, S., R. E. Just, and J. K. Horowitz. (1995) Possibilities and limitations in sharing the Mountain Aquifer between Israel and the Palestinians, in *Joint Management of Shared Aquifers: The Second Workshop* (eds. M. Haddad and E. Feitelson), Truman Institute and the Palestine Consultancy Group, Jerusalem, pp. 169-199.
5. Netanyahu, S. (1995) *Trans-boundary water resources: Policy coordination, enforcement, and bargaining under uncertainty.* Department of Agricultural and Resource Economics, University of Maryland at College Park.

LEGAL AND INSTITUTIONAL ASPECTS OF GROUNDWATER DEVELOPMENT IN THE PHILIPPINES

Philippine groundwater law and institutions

A.S. TOLENTINO, JR
IUCN Commission on Environmental Law
Quezon City, Philippines

Abstract

This paper presents an overview of Philippine legislations, policies, regulations and controls regarding the appropriation, development, extraction and control of groundwater, especially the acquisition of water permits therefore. Specifically, it discusses the organisation of Government agencies dealing with groundwater, their responsibilities, tasks and capacity-building programs, the organisation, development and capacity-building of water users' associations, the interrelationships among the agencies including problems encountered while carrying out agency programs and tasks related to groundwater.

Key words: Control areas, groundwater resources, institutions, legislations, Philippines, water permit

1 Introduction

The Philippines is a country of more than 7,000 large and small islands. Many of its provincial centres, as well as Metro Manila, are coastal and naturally depend either wholly or partly on groundwater for water supply. Community water supplies with motorised pumping are growing in number in some of the larger centres and problems with groundwater salinity is increasing.

2 Groundwater Resources Development Legislation

The hierarchy of Philippine legislation on water resources development begins with the 1987 Philippine Constitution. It provides, in particular, that all waters are owned

Water Policy: Allocation and management in practice. Edited by P. Howsam and R.C. Carter.
Published in 1996 by E & FN Spon. ISBN 0 419 21650 2

by the State from which emanates the authority of an entity to appropriate, distribute and utilise the waters of the State. For the definition of the present institutional arrangements concerning groundwater resources appropriation, the Philippine Water Code (1976) requires a water permit from the National Water Resources Board (NWRB) as evidence of a water right, except when the purpose is for domestic use. Thus, without a water permit, an institution engaged in municipal water supply or irrigation has no legal basis to appropriate groundwater and distribute the same to its customers. Implementation of the Water Code rests with the NWRB.

The Water Code allows the owner of the land where water is found to use the same for domestic purposes without the necessity for a water permit provided such use is registered when required by NWRB. For all other purposes, the Code, through its Implementing Rules and Regulations, sets forth the process to secure a water permit.

An application form furnished by the NWRB is filed in any of the following offices designated as agents of the NWRB in the province where the point of appropriation is situated: Department of Public Works and Highways (DPWH) District Engineer's Office; National Irrigation Administration (NIA) Provincial Irrigation Engineer; or local Water District General Manager.

If the application is in Metro Manila it is filed directly with the NWRB. A number of documents, depending on the use for which the water is to be appropriated, has to accompany the application. Among others, the usual requirements are: location and spacing of well drilling sites; purpose of the appropriation; brief description of the project; articles of incorporation if applicant is a private corporation; a layout map of the area that will be served by the groundwater; amount of water to be used and duration of water use. A filing fee from every applicant is collected except for Government agencies, water districts and duly organised associations or cooperatives for irrigation or rural water supply.

The Office where the application is filed will then undertake a field investigation to find out whether the application will have an adverse effect on public or private interest. If the application meets the requirements, it is transmitted, with the appropriate recommendation, to the DPWH Regional Director who is authorised to issue a permit to drill. This permit is in the nature of a temporary water permit valid for six (6) months subject to conditions stipulated in the permit.

Within the six-month validity period of the permit to drill, a report on the result of the drilling operations is submitted to the investigating office. The latter, upon receipt of the report on drilling, studies the same and considers the application for withdrawal of groundwater in regard to safe yield, pumping lift, adverse effects, beneficial use, and adequacy of proposed well, and submits its recommendations to NWRB through the DPWH Regional Director for final action. In cases of applications for irrigation or water generation, the applications are also coursed through the Regional Directors of the NIA and the National Power Corporation respectively.

If the application is for industrial use, or where waters may become polluted, the NWRB refers the application to the Department of Environment and Natural Resources (DENR) for comment and recommendation. Otherwise, the NWRB approves or disapproves the application within sixty (60) days after receipt thereof from DPWH Regional Director.

Upon approval of the application, the NWRB issues a water permit subject to the condition that the groundwater well shall conform with the NWRB requirements and that the permittee shall submit to NWRB the plans and specification of the well for approval.

When the construction of the well is completed, the permitee reports to NWRB with information on depth and diameter of the well, drilling log, specifications and location of casings, cementing, screens and perforations and results of tests of capacity, flow, drawdown and shut-in pressures. When satisfied that the well is in accordance with the requirements of the permit, the NWRB issues a certificate of compliance.

Other implementing rules and regulations of the Water Code with implications on groundwater are as follows:

1. Groundwater mining may be allowed provided that the life of the groundwater system is maintained for at least 50 years,
2. No person shall recharge groundwater without a permit from NWRB. The grant of this permit has been delegated by NWRB to exercise the same whenever necessary, and
3. As between two or more appropriators of water from the same source of supply, priority in time of appropriation gives the better right. However, when the priority in time cannot be determined, the order of preference in the use of water is:
   a) domestic and municipal use;
   b) irrigation;
   c) power generation
   d) fisheries;
   e) livestock raising;
   f) industrial use;
   g) other uses.

3   Government agencies with groundwater resources development function

The institutional aspect of water resources development in the Philippines is a complex one. Some fifty (50) existing Government institutions are directly or indirectly involved with water resources development. During their operations, whether independently or in cooperation with other agencies, overlaps in effort and conflicts in jurisdiction are naturally expected. These often arise from poor communication or co-ordination between and among agencies. Below are brief descriptions of the functions / activities of some groundwater related Government institutions.

3.1 National Water Resources Board (NWRB)
The NWRB is composed of heads of department and agencies most concerned with water resources. It coordinates the water resource activities of the various agencies within the framework of the national development plan and policies. It makes recommendations on matters pertaining to water resources to the President through the National Economic and Development Authority (NEDA). It has nine (9) members, namely, the Secretary of Public Works and Highways, Chairman, The

Secretaries of Agriculture, Economic Planning, Environment and Natural Resources, Energy and the Heads of the Metropolitan Waterworks and Sewerage System (MWSS), National Irrigation Administration (INIA), the National Power Corporation (NPC).

3.2 Metropolitan Waterworks and Sewerage System (MWSS)

The MWSS is a Government corporation created under Republic Act No 6234. It owns or has jurisdiction, supervision and control over all waterworks and sewerage systems in the cities comprising Metro Manila and a number of contiguous municipalities in the provinces of Rizal and Cavite. MWSS has the power to approve, regulate, and supervise the establishment, operation and maintenance of waterworks and deep wells within its jurisdiction operated for commercial, industrial and Governmental purposes and to fix just and equitable rates or fees that may be charged to its customers.

3.3 Local Water Utilities Administration (LWUA)

LWUA is a Government corporation operating as a specialised lending institution for the promotion, development and financing of local water utilities. Its power and duties include making loans to qualified local water utilities, establishing technical and managerial standards for local water utilities, providing technical assistance and establishing training programs and seminars for personnel of local water utilities especially in the areas of utility management, operation, maintenance and customer service.

3.4 Rural Water Development Corporation (RWDC)

RWDC encourages self-help and self-reliant water supply projects and promotes the organisation of non-profit, non-stock rural waterworks associations now called Rural Waterworks and Sanitation Associations (RWSA) primarily for the purpose of providing water supply services in the rural areas.

3.5 Barangay Water Program (BWP)

BWP is a component of the Provincial Development Assistance Project of the Department of Interior and Local Government under an agreement between the Philippine Government and USAID. It is a rural water supply program designed to develop national and local Government capacity to plan, design and implement small water supply systems that will be owned, maintained and managed by the water users through water service co-operatives.

3.6 Local Water Districts (LWD)

LWDs are quasi-public corporations organised under the Local Water District Law (Presidential Decree 198) for the purpose of acquiring, installing and operating water supply and distribution systems for domestic, industrial, municipal and agricultural uses.

3.7 Bureau of Construction (BOC) of the Department of Public Works and Highways (DPWH)

BOC is a staff bureau of the DPWH which has functional supervision over the construction of projects of the DPWH not assigned to special Project Management Offices. In regard to water supply projects, this function is handled by the Division of Water Supply of the BOC but is limited only to projects financed purely by Philippine Government funds.

3.8 Local Government Units
The Rural Waterworks Development Corporation (RWDC) and the Barangay Water Program (BWP) depend on local Governments to undertake the field implementation of their rural water supply projects.

3.9 National Irrigation Administration (NIA)
The NIA is another agency concerned with groundwater. However, due to high costs of energy and agricultural inputs and comparatively low prices of agricultural products, it has suspended the implementation of groundwater irrigation projects which are not economically viable under the present situation. The resumption of NIAs groundwater irrigation program, however, is a possibility in the future if the cost of energy comes down and the prices of agricultural produce go up.

4   Problems and issues

Several problems and issues were observed which impede the optimum development and control of groundwater resources in the Philippines. These are described below.

4.1 Control of well drilling and abstractions
There is a requirement to secure a water permit from the NWRB before drilling a well or abstracting groundwater in situations other than single family domestic use. This requirement is often disregarded except in Metro Manila. Drilling and abstractions may take place without any permit at all.

The reasons for non-compliance with the permit requirement include lack of public awareness of the need for controlling abstractions, the consequences of uncontrolled overdrawing of the aquifer and lack of awareness of the value of taking expert advice. Above all, the main deterrent to a potential applicant is the time taken to process an application. This is due to the lack of expertise in the agencies deputised by the NWRB to evaluate the drilling reports which are pre-requisites for the grant of drilling and water permits.

4.2 Multiplicity of agencies
At the national level there are four agencies handling rural water supply projects, namely: The Rural Waterworks Development Corporation (RWDC); Barangay Water Program (BWP) in the Department of Interior and Local Government and Project Management Office for Rural Water Supply and Bureau of Construction, both in the Department of Public Works and Highways. For field implementation, both RWDC and the BWP depend on the local Government units while the PMO-RWS and the BOC both depend on the District Engineers of the DPWH. This situation resulted in overlapping capability-building programs at the provincial level and made institutional work more difficult to the field implementers.

4.3 Inconsistency in financing policies

Policies of the different agencies differ as to the recovery of construction cost. Applications may then be delayed and possible resentments generated when neighbouring Rural Waterworks and Sanitation Associations are given different terms.

5   Prospects for the Future

Consideration of the existing agencies and legislations related to groundwater development and of the problems of control in areas susceptible to salinity intrusion lead to the following recommendations:

5.1 Training

There is a need to strengthen the program for training technical staff in agencies involved with groundwater, especially at the local levels. Special emphasis should be given to proper siting, design, drilling and testing of pilot and production wells, and optimum pumping rates. The objective would be to improve the standard of water supplies, protect the aquifers, and develop a capacity for appropriate action on applications for groundwater permits. Philippine-based courses will be necessary to develop the required expertise in the agencies, and fellowship programs should emphasise hydrology courses.

5.2 Co-ordination of policies and training

Various agencies are often working in parallel in assisting the planning activities and in the training programs on rural water supply development. Coordination of those activities would have advantages as it would make the best use of training manpower, facilitate the reconciliation of varying policies and avoid duplication of activities in developing capabilities of local Government units.

5.3 Decentralisation of permit system

To enable faster action on application for water permits, the grant of drilling permits should be further delegated by the National Water Resources Board to the Metropolitan Waterworks and Sewerage Resources Board and to the District Engineer's Office as soon as the capability for doing this is established at that level. Likewise, the registration of well drillers in the provinces should be delegated to the District Engineers, subject to qualification requirements.

5.4 Designation of control areas

Where salinity intrusion is of such nature that it is essential to impose regulations and to develop alternative sources for safeguarding the aquifers, then a Control Area may be designated in accordance with Article 32 of the Philippine Water Code.

5.5 Tariffs as a means of control

Tariffs may be used not only for financing the existing supply but also for developing alternative sources, particularly where sources are at risk from saline intrusion. Incremental scales may be introduced to discourage wastage and private owners in control areas may be subject to a resource or sewage levy to encourage a switch to public supplies.

5.6 Establishment of priority uses

Establishment in the Control Areas of the order of preference in the Philippine Water Code, which provides that domestic and municipal uses are superior in right to all other users when priority in time can not be established. In this regard, limited fresh groundwater supplies should be protected from very large abstractions. For example, in control areas, a water permit for irrigation, if it is to be granted, should be temporary and revocable in favour of domestic and municipal use.

5.7 Public information

This requires a program on groundwater conservation. Designation of Waterworks Extension Officers at the local levels who will oversee the program and provide advice on prospective groundwater appropriations should be done. Likewise, training of personnel from other agencies should also be considered.

6 Bibliography

1. Alejandrino, A. (1985) Philippine Water Resources Policies - An Appraisal, National Water Resources Council, Quezon City.
2. Environmental Management Bureau (1989) Groundwater Salinity Intrusion Control in the Philippines, Quezon City.
3. de Leon, J. (1995) Allocating Water Rights - Philippine Context, National Water Resources Board, Quezon City.
4. Rojas, D. et.al. (1981) Water Quality Management, Philippine Environmental Law, Vol. 1, Quezon City.

SECTION 7

INSTITUTIONAL ISSUES

PRIVATE SECTOR PARTICIPATION IN WATER PROJECTS
Private sector participation in water

L. MARTIN
Anglian Water International, Huntingdon, UK

Abstract
This paper examines the lessons being learned by the Private Sector when they embark upon participation in water projects in emerging and developing countries. There is a real need to ensure that the private sector can be encouraged to participate in such schemes, in a way which allows their involvement to the mutual benefit of not only these players and the client organisations, but also, crucially, the customers and end users of the services provided. However, implementing such participation successfully is far more difficult in practice than it might appear in theory. By utilizing a series of case studies in key territories, the paper makes a series of recommendations to clients, funding agencies and to the private sector players themselves, for ways in which successful, viable, long-term Private Sector Participation schemes can be created, engineered, financed and then operated.
Keywords: BOT/BOOT schemes, operating concessions, private sector, privatisation, project finance, waste water projects, water supply projects.

1 Introduction

The capital requirements of the global water and waste water markets are colossal: conservatively estimated at between US$ 600 billion and US$ 1,000 billion over the next 10 years. With an annual capital spend of at least $ 60 million, it is therefore not surprising that private utilities-based industry has recognised the water sector to be one of the key growth areas for its activities. Established players are extending their countries of interest and portfolios, and new companies are aggressively entering this increasing competitive market.

Whilst the addressable market is clearly less than this total figure (when schemes

Water Policy: Allocation and management in practice. Edited by P. Howsam and R.C. Carter.
Published in 1996 by E & FN Spon. ISBN 0 419 21650 2

locked into either Governments or local players are excluded, the remaining market size may average US$ 40 billion per annum over the next decade), it is still enormous. Today, the private sector funds approximately US$ 15 billion of water and waste water capital schemes world-wide annually, but this is predicted to increase over the next 10 years to at least US$ 45 billion by 2005.

The growing need for the involvement of the private sector in the water and waste water industry stems from two separate factors:-

- *Size of the market*: As shown above, the overall requirements of the water sector are huge, and growing. The traditional view of water as being in the public sector cannot be sustained with this level of demand for expenditure.

- *Market requirements*: The requirements of the water sector are changing, from a time in the 1960s and 70s when large-scale water supply or waste water treatment schemes were seen to be the answer to urban water needs, to today's increasing view that improved management of existing infrastructural assets (water networks, sewerage systems, etc.) is a prerequisite for effective water supply and sewage disposal.

Many water supply and waste water treatment schemes are still truly capital-intensive, requiring massive investment in resource management projects, dam construction, trunk mains and urban sewerage systems. However, pure civil works is likely to account for only 25-30% of the total water capital expenditure. The remaining monies will be expended on Mechanical and Electrical Plant (M&E), Process Design, etc, of course, but, increasingly, on capital improvements to distribution and collection systems and for operational efficiencies in areas such as telemetry, pump scheduling and network management.

Over the last decade, a clear trend has emerged in the world water industry towards the willingness of Governments to accept and indeed encourage increased involvement of the private sector, both to finance and to manage the industry's infrastructure and services. There are three principal socio-economic developments which drive this trend:-

- *Perceived investment needs*: This is subtly different from actual capital needs. Firstly, there is now a growing awareness of environmental issues by the general public. This drives the wastewater/effluent treatment element of the water sector. Secondly, increased legislation, e.g., tighter worldwide standards for potable water quality is increasing the need for water treatment distribution investment. Thirdly, the rise of middle-income population in many emerging countries is forcing improvements in water supply and sanitation as more people aspire to improvements in standards of living. The customer's voice and opinions are becoming a far more important issue to address, both in developed and emerging water markets.

- *Capital efficiency needs:* At the same time as the water sector is perceived by Governments and individuals to require greater investment, so too are many other parts of the utility spectrum, e.g., transportation, communications and power. These demands place additional constrains upon already stretched fiscal resources. There is therefore a great need to use limited capital efficiently and the public sector are accepted as being expert in this area.

- *Asset management:* The water industry is one of the most capital intensive utilities and there is a growing political consensus that the private sector is more able than its public counterparts to manage existing (and new) assets efficiently. This may be carried out in parts, e.g., privatising the revenue collection aspect of operations, or as an entire system concession (with or without asset ownership).

Responding to these trends, a number of models have evolved, both to encourage private sector finance and to increase the involvement of that element in the operation and maintenance of water infrastructure. These are illustrated in Fig. 1.

The emergence of the variants of 'BOT'/'BOOT', etc, whereby the private sector finance the project (at least in part) and then operate the scheme for a period of, say, 25 years, before transferring the asset back to the client, has been a key development over the last 5 years. The advantages for the recipient are that many of the financial risks are transferred to a commercial company, better equipped to resource and to deal with them. A complete 'turnkey' solution is provided for the initial problem, supplied efficiently, at a competitive price.

Implementation of truly successful and mutually beneficial private sector projects is, however, less straightforward in practice than it might appear theoretically. Whilst there are celebrated success stories in the water sector, there are also many schemes which have proved problematic, either to the private sector company or in terms of customer service. There is therefore a real need to ensure that Private Sector Participation (PSP) projects continue to be as beneficial and successful as possible and that more such viable schemes are introduced. Without sustained participation by the private sector, the burgeoning demands for water and waste water described above will not be able to be met. In order to encourage such PSP schemes, a number of issues need to be addressed, stemming from lessons already learned in other projects. This paper examines a number of those lessons, using specific examples of PSP projects, and makes a series of recommendations to clients, funding agencies, investors and the private sector players themselves, describing ways in which successful, beneficial and profitable projects can be created and operated.

	Contracts for Public Sector	Public/Private hybrids	Full Privatisation	
Specific sites, (e.g. WTW or WWTW) or elements of system	Design and build (D&B)	DBO BOT BOOT	BOO Privatisation of a function	Increasing scale and complexity
Entire water utility system	Operation and Management (O&M)	Concession	Full system privatisation	

Increasing Private sector involvement

Key: DBO: Design, build, operate   BOT: Build, operate, transfer
BOOT: Build, own, operate, transfer   BOO: Build, own, operate

Fig. 1. The Spectrum of Private Sector Participation

2 Lessons Learned

A number of lessons can be learned from existing projects. These can be summarized into five major headings as follows, and these will be examined in turn:-

- *understand clients' needs*
- *appreciate clients' strengths*
- *understand the projects' risks*
- *appreciate operational implications*
- *maximise training and development opportunities.*

2.1 Understand clients' needs

Understanding the clients' needs are vital to the success of a project. Each project is different; requirements are unique. Proponents should not embark upon a scheme with preconceptions of the needs of the client. Moreover, it is important to ensure that the true *needs*, rather than *wants* of the client are met. Aid-funded projects in particular may include an extensive 'wish-list' of desires rather than real requirements to meet water needs, and the true needs may be able to be met with less sophisticated solutions, more appropriately.

Each solution has to be similarly bespoke, and tailored to these needs (not wants). A standard, 'off-the-shelf' World Bank (for example) Terms of Reference, driving a project, will produce a standardised proposal, but by definition this will almost always provide sub-optimal solutions to the problem. The needs of the client also have to be understood before the contract is signed. This may appear obvious, but in one recent aid-funded project in India, the client's representative who was managing the project had never seen the Terms of Reference to which he was committed, and therefore was unaware of the scope of work to which the company was working.

Finally, the solutions provided to meet the clients' needs must be *appropriate*. In other words, they need to match the requirements of the environment, the financial circumstances for implementation and the prevailing expertise of the recipient. An inappropriate solution can be more harm than no solution at all. For example, programmes to reduce levels of non-revenue water frequently include the procurement of electronic leak detection equipment, but may not accompany this with appropriate operative training. Unopened packing cases containing leak noise correlators, costing many thousands of dollars, are not an uncommon sight in certain countries; not through lack of will, but because of a lack of appropriate follow-up support and training.

2.2 Appreciate clients' strengths

The strengths and abilities of the client are often underestimated. There is a danger that too little will be assumed of the client's workforce, whereas without doubt the only first hand source and knowledge of the underlying problem lies therein. In waterworks' refurbishment projects, for example, inherent ingenuity in keeping virtually derelict plant operating frequently with sophisticated software solutions should not be overlooked. Successful PSP schemes need to build on the partnership between existing expertise and external inputs to maximise benefits to customers and returns to investors; this development has to be able to recognise and nurture existing talents.

2.3 Understand projects' risks

From an investment perspective, it is essential to understand, evaluate and apportion project risks. Without this, schemes are unlikely to develop, let alone succeed in future, as so many potential PSP projects have foundered on this one issue. It is vital that risks are shared exclusively *and* exhaustively by those agencies and players who can afford to bear the risks. Everyone needs to know who is bearing what element, and to understand why. Risks have to be defined unambiguously and explicitly quantified over the whole life of the project, and all of this must take place before the project has started.

The private sector can be instrumental in assisting in these processes, but it needs to be stressed that private investment is not a panacea for the avoidance of risk by public or Governmental bodies in the water industry. In other words, the private sector is not in a position to take on risks which remain the responsibility of others. Water supply BOT projects will continue to require a 'minimum supply' or 'take-or-pay' agreement if they are to be financially viable. Central Government sovereign guarantees are frequently required to support undertakings from state-based water organisations to enable long term debt finance to be raised at commercial rates.

2.4 Appreciate operational implications

Activity in water and waste water PSP schemes is understandably front-end loaded, meaning that the initial years of design, construction and commissioning of projects are critical ones. However, there is no point producing a technically excellent works if it cannot be maintained effectively and efficiently. The project therefore needs to be bankable over the whole-life of the scheme, so longer term operational issues must be addressed from the start. Examples of such issues include assessing downstream network performance in a water supply BOT, to ensure that the ultimate customers can receive (and therefore be willing to pay for) the water produced, or evaluating the long-term storm water retention characteristics of an expanding sewerage system, to determine the hydrological performance of a waste water treatment plant over the life time of the contract.

2.5 Maximise training and development opportunities

Anglian Water International is proud to regard itself as a leading organisation and sees every PSP scheme as an opportunity to learn more. Effective local training is certainly an integral part of the operational implications outlined above; it will be highly cost-effective and, when successfully implemented, ensures that the private sector's solution is appropriate to the local skills environment. Short term benefits are that the scheme rapidly moves to a position of investment payback, and long-term training enables the project to become and remain autonomous and self sufficient. Feedback from training and development enables the proponent to determine whether concepts and skills have been retained and understood. In brief, appropriate and progressive training represent the secret of many projects' success.

3 Country specifics

Many of the above lessons can be illustrated by reference to three countries at different stages in their development of private sector participation (PSP) in water projects: India, the Philippines and Malaysia. Space only permits the briefest of appraisals, however, in this review.

3.1 India

India has undergone profound economic reforms in the 1990s. The new liberalisation has reduced Governmental (GOI) involvement in economic activities and private ownership of utilities is increasing. Through these reforms the GOI has recognised that infrastructure desperately needs private sector funds. In the water industry especially, assets dating from the colonial era now require significant rehabilitation, in addition to the new plant and networks needed to meet a growing population and an expanding middle-income group with expectations of improved water services.

As in most emerging countries the power sector leads the water industry in terms of PSP. Private power plants continue to have a chequered history of development, particularly in terms of central (federal-level) guarantees. The influence of State (and Metropolitan) level control and autonomy of water undertakings in India may make similar water BOT/BOOT projects uncertain for the same reasons for some time to come.

Water PSP projects in India are still largely Design and Build (D&B) in nature (see Fig. 1) and many private investors remain to be convinced that a satisfactory revenue income stream can be created from the municipal market and maintained over the lifetime of the scheme in order to support the required investment in BOT/BOOT projects. However, the size and growth of the market is such that these issues will have to be addressed and overcome if the development of the economy is to be supported by adequate water supplies and waste water services.

3.2 The Philippines

The provision of reliable water supplies and, to a lesser extent, adequate sanitation facilities, are the foremost issues of both socio-economic development and public consciousness in the Philippines at present. The Government of the Philippines (GOP) has seized the initiative to encourage PSP in water, following the success of the privatisation of power production in 1993 and 1994. President Fidel Ramos has promulgated legislation (The Water Crisis Act, 1995) which will fast-track PSP projects and overcome many of the barriers to water privatisation schemes. As such, the Philippines is further along the route to active privatisation in water and the Act allows a window of opportunity for private investors.

At the time of writing however (February 1996), and after 6 months of the Act's twelve-month duration, only one relatively minor water concession has been let. Why? There are probably two major reasons. Firstly, country risk is high and cannot be overlooked. Long-term investment projects require long-term bank support and many bankers, with memories of the Philippines' recent political past, are still wary of entering into agreements of over 5 years duration. The Philippines is also subject to more natural risks than many other territories: droughts, typhoons, earthquakes, volcanic eruptions and associated disasters, such as lahar flows. All these risks need not only to be apportioned between the project proponents, but also factored into the subsequent tariff structures for schemes. Secondly, water privatisation is far more complex than power privatisation and it would be myopic to believe otherwise. For water supply BOTs to be successful, the dynamics of the existing distribution (delivery) system need to be adequately understood. Far too little is known of the performance of water assets in the Philippines for this to be possible at this stage.

The privatisation of Metro Manila's extensive water and waste water system (MWSS) is rightly being delayed, pending the resolution of this (and other) key issues by a team working under the auspices of the IFC. In other cities' Water Districts, privatisation of the utility has been proposed, but little if any Asset Management Planning has yet been done to facilitate this. The Philippines presents an outstanding opportunity for PSP in water at the moment. The GOP has demonstrated a real commitment to address many of the bureaucratic issues which can confront privatisation projects, but without adequate data on system dynamics and performance, there is little chance of many 'quick' solutions to the Water Crisis being forthcoming during the lifetime of the Act.

3.3 Malaysia
Malaysia represents an example of a country where PSP in water has been effective over a number of years. Extensive projects, notably for rural water supplies and country-wide waste water privatisation have taken place, and many elements of water operations are already in private hands. Malaysia is able to fund its own water privatisation projects without recourse to either aid money or foreign investment, however it still acknowledges that overseas expertise is required in key areas of water management.

Over the course of the next 2-3 years, Malaysia will see each State moving independently towards either corporatisation or full privatisation of its water supply function. From experiences to date, these will be successful only if the change produces improved customer service and demonstrable value for money from the investment.

Malaysians are correctly viewing third-country water PSP elsewhere in the ASEAN region as a future venture, in cooperation with established international water companies. The success of its own State water privatisations may determine how well these ventures are received in those countries.

4   Recommendations

In order to encourage the most effective involvement of the private sector in water projects, three main recommendations are proposed:-
* *ensure greater involvement in the processes of PSP*
* *ensure value-engineering solutions are adopted*
* *allow maximum dialogue between participants.*

4.1 Ensuring greater involvement
The private sector need to be involved at the earliest possible stage in privatisation processes. Advising on Terms of Reference for projects will allow customised programmes, suited to individual clients' needs, appropriate to those circumstances. Aid agencies should also become more involved in shortlisting and the tender assessment processes for their projects. Both the client and the aid agency (if

appropriate) should be actively involved in technical, financial and economic low risks to be appreciated and apportioned more equitably, and involvement in the provision of necessary technical information by the client (rather than a third party consultant) would improve the long-term success of the venture.

4.2 Adopt a 'value-engineering' approach

This recommendation means working towards a clients' needs, not wants, ensuring that solutions are appropriate to the level of local skills and level of training and avoiding over-engineered solutions. If the true, underlying problems are understood, an optimum solution can result. As an example, the answer to a supply shortfall may lie in improvements to the water distribution system and billing methods, thereby reducing non-revenue water, rather than in the construction of a new BOT water treatment works. It may be both, of course, but only a full understanding of the management of the whole system will allow that question to be answered. The value engineering solution is, by definition a long-term successful one, and represents the best value for money to all parties over the lifetime of the project.

4.3 Maximise dialogue

Firstly, involve the major players: there are not many international water operators. If involved earlier, they can focus on economically viable solutions more effectively. Secondly, involve the client in this dialogue; improve his experience at the same time. This discussion needs to address the requirements of the whole system (both production and delivery) and the requirements of investors, operators and third parties (i.e. municipal authorities and customers). Only if all these requirements can be met, and ideally exceeded, can long-term, financially-viable PSP projects be assured of success.

Acknowledgement: The author wishes to thank Anglian Water International for permission to publish this paper. The opinions expressed within it are personal ones and do not in any way purport to represent the views of AWI.

TOWARDS SUSTAINABLE WATER RESOURCES MANAGEMENT: SHARING EXTERNAL SUPPORT AGENCY POLICIES AND PRACTICES
ESA support for integrated WRM

D. SAUNDERS, E. DE LANGE, AND J.T. VISSCHER
IRC, International Water and Sanitation Centre, The Hague, The Netherlands.

Abstract
This paper discusses the water resources management (WRM) policies and practices of selected major external support agencies (ESAs). It draws particularly on a review prepared for the May 1994 OECD/DAC meeting in Paris. Important findings include that whereas all agencies have endorsed the principles of Rio and Dublin, there is a tendency to support sustainable WRM on an 'ad hoc' project basis. Different ESAs have supported strategies and practices which together provide valuable experience that may be used to help realise sustainable WRM. The paper presents a selection of approaches to WRM highlighted by ESAs as promising and supports the call from the Noordwijk Ministerial Conference and the OECD/DAC meeting on WRM to promote capacity building, the integrated management of water at the lowest appropriate levels and to overcome the lack of reliable information on policies and approaches in WRM. Keywords: capacity building, community participation, external support agencies, information collection, water policy, water resources management.

1   Introduction

Continued mismanagement of natural resources is threatening human health and sustainable development, from both an economic and environmental perspective. In response to international recognition of this problem external support agencies (ESAs) endorsed the principles espoused at the United Nations Conference on Environment and Development (UNCED) in Rio de Janeiro and the International Conference on Water and the Environment in Dublin, both in 1992. These conferences specifically emphasised the need for urgent action and gave an indication of programme areas needing greater attention. In a comprehensive response the

Water Policy: Allocation and management in practice. Edited by P. Howsam and R.C. Carter.
Published in 1996 by E & FN Spon. ISBN 0 419 21650 2

Noordwijk Ministerial Conference for Drinking Water and Environmental Sanitation (1994) endorsed a detailed Action Programme for Governments to tackle key issues raised in UNCED Agenda 21. Similarly at the Development Assistance Committee (DAC) meeting of the OECD on Water Resources Management (Paris, 1994), all OECD member countries reaffirmed their countries' commitment to this new policy consensus (see box).

Until recently the World Bank has been the only agency with a specific WRM policy [1], although developments suggest that several and perhaps most ESAs are developing more comprehensive policies and taking integrated approaches into account. For example, the Dutch Directorate General for International Cooperation (DGIS) is preparing a water resources management policy for their international development cooperation. Similarly, the Swedish International Development Agency (SIDA) is in the process of developing a detailed policy for the promotion of integrated WRM practice, and is currently actively engaged in South Africa on a number of multi-faceted water resource development and management projects. They are also actively supporting the formation of the Global Water Partnership through the secretariat located at SIDA. Which aims to consolidate existing UNDP and World Bank sponsored programmes and bring together key partners from all sectors involved in water resource development and use. With particular emphasis on sustainable investment in integrated programmes incorporating capacity building, it is estimated the initiative will influence the allocation of US$ 30 to 40 billion through World Bank loans [2].

Major principles of water resource development

- Integrated management of water, allowing for the implications on health, socio-economic and environmental costs of poor management.

- Involvement of all stakeholders, reflecting the different needs of men and women and involving public, private and other organisations in developing an efficient and accountable sector.

- Capacity building to develop an enabling institutional environment which optimises use of available resources and helps to establish responsibility for management at the lowest appropriate levels.

- Dealing with water resources as a social and economic commodity, in order to ensure efficient allocation and use of water.

- Development of reliable information on policies, programmes, projects and innovative solutions, to facilitate water resources management in the future.

Adapted from the Noordwijk Conference and the OECD/DAC meeting [3].

2 ESA support for WRM to date

In preparation for the OECD/DAC meeting on water resources management in Paris 1994 a review was compiled of the approaches in water resources management of 17 OECD member countries and 9 international external support agencies. Prepared through a process of consultation with staff members from contributing ESAs, the review is comprised of profiles of each ESA including their support for the water sector and their WRM policies, and draws general trends through comparison. Furthermore, ESAs were specifically requested to present projects or approaches they considered particularly promising for water resources management, as related to the key points raised in the Dublin Statement.

2.1 General Conclusions
Some general conclusions regarding support for water resources management can be drawn from the review of ESA profiles [4].

Although ESAs are publicly committed to integrated water resource development and management, WRM receives no financial allocations and has not been distinguished as a separate issue in budget lines. There is no readily available information regarding investment in WRM and it appears that no foreseeable increase is likely under the current policies of most ESAs, however some do plan to reallocate existing budgets to emphasise integrated resource development

Although official development assistance increased from US\$ 23 billion to US\$ 57 billion between 1982 and 1991, the relative share of water supply and sanitation commitments decreased from 8.1% in 1982 to 5.1% in 1991, (see Fig. 1). Statistics from the Creditor Reporting System suggest a similar pattern for the funding of irrigation projects [4]. However national Government investment in the water sector appears to be improving, information from the World Bank's World Development Report for 1994 on infrastructure indicates this actually increased from 0.3% to 0.45%, of GDP between 1982 and 1991 [5].

The dominant share of financial support in the water sector targets Africa, followed by Asia and Latin America. Financial support from OECD member countries varies dramatically from \$100,000 to \$100 million per year per country, though over half of the ESAs provide roughly \$160,000 per year to a large number of countries while each imposing their own policy and administrative procedures. Most assisted countries receive support from more than one ESA, in some cases forcing them to fulfil the different requirements of up to 15 ESAs. Between 1986 and 1991 OECD member countries assisted between 7 to 52 countries each, averaging 25, but this number will drop as ESAs plan to concentrate their assistance more in the future. International ESAs assisted water projects in 26 to 127 countries, averaging 68.

In most ESAs staff numbers have been reduced in recent years as a result of increased involvement from specialised staff from assisted countries and the private sector, and reduced budget allocations. Very few employ specialised staff who focus on WRM, rather it is generally added onto the tasks of water supply and irrigation specialists. In training and research several ESAs are starting to promote institutions from assisted countries, particularly involving them to support capacity building. In research however emphasis is still more on utilizing ESA institutions to implement the research activities with support for local partners.

Although all ESAs recognise the need for active collaboration, in practice it too often takes the form of consultation. Rarely do ESAs genuinely join hands with a national Government to develop effective strategies on WRM and avoid the overlap and duplication of efforts.

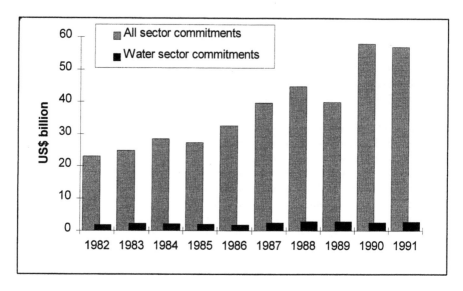

Fig. 1. Official development statistics and water sector commitments, 1982-1991 [4]

2.2 Promising approaches as presented by the ESAs

The 26 ESA profiles together presented a total of 88 approaches to water resources management which the ESAs suggested might be considered promising. Covering a range of issues these have been grouped into seven broad categories, (see Fig. 2 and Table 1). It should be noted that there is a degree of bias inherent within the selection since a disproportionate amount of contacts used for the review were from within the drinking water supply and sanitation sector.

Nearly 30% of the promising approaches are concerned with the development of **national plans** for continued water resource development, and water policies and legal frameworks to control water resource exploitation. Though developed for use by national ministries, such documents rarely touch on the inter-relationship of Governmental bodies involved in water abstraction, provision and use. As a result they rarely promote the integrated management of water resources between different controlling bodies and users with contrasting needs. Although a number of ESAs have been involved in the development of national water policy and plans, few indicate that they utilise this as a capacity building exercise, utilizing national expertise and limiting ESA involvement to technical backstopping and financial support. The Uganda Action Plan, supported by Danish International Development Assistance (DANIDA), is an interesting example which attempts to pre-empt this issue by emphasising the need for ministerial collaboration and setting out mechanisms for this process. Between both departments directly involved in the development, delivery and use of water and other stakeholders. Similarly it stresses the importance of creating an enabling environment and actively promotes capacity building at a national, district and community level to plan development, monitor use and manage water resources.

The promotion of integrated *catchment management* or river basin development projects account for over 15% of suggested approaches. These programmes by their very nature require a progressive change in inter-ministerial attitudes and collaboration, quite apart from needing closer and more realistic relationships between authorities and water users of all stripes. A watershed management and protection programme in Nicaragua, (SIDA funded), supports the development of methods for the conservation of surface and groundwater. With an emphasis on capacity building to develop the effective management of water resources, the programme aims to strengthen institutions responsible for research and regulation.

Nearly 16% of the promising approaches in WRM identified by ESAs can be categorised as conventional *technical assistance* to the irrigation or water supply sectors, although several included promising elements such as promoting efficiency of water use, water conservation, or aspects of demand management. A demonstration and training farm carrying out applied research is being implemented by the Syrian Ministry of Agriculture with Spanish technical assistance. As well as giving practical training to farmers it aims to research the efficiency of different irrigation systems and methods with a view to optimise water use.

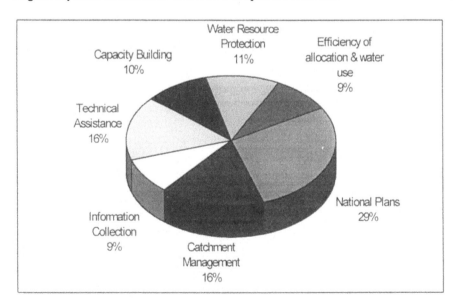

Fig. 2. Breakdown of promising projects and approaches in WRM

Table 1.   Summary of the main issues covered by the promising approaches as
presented by ESAs.

Promising Projects & Approaches Identified	Number
National water policy, master plans and legal frameworks	21 (4)
Catchment management, river basin development projects and integrated environmental programmes	14
Technical assistance	
drinking water supply systems	8
irrigation projects	4 (2)
Information collection	
water resource assessment and database development	4 (4)
Capacity building	
national and regional Government	2 (3)
community participation and water user	2
associations decentralisation of water utilities	2
Water resource protection	
monitoring and catchment protection	3
pollution control and waste management	7
Efficiency of allocation and water use	
conservation	3
water re-use	2
public awareness raising	2
developing economical tools for WRM	1

N.B.   figures in brackets are regional encompassing over five countries.

Roughly 10% of promising approaches fell under each of the last four groupings. Firstly, *information collection*, including various projects tackling national water resources assessment or regional database development for hydrological, hydrogeological, meteorological or catchment-wide data. Surprisingly there was no mention of supported projects utilizing GIS systems, despite their proven value in the assessment, planning and the management of water. Initiated in 1982 the National Water Resources Information Centre in Yemen, sponsored by DGIS, primarily focused on institutional development of the General Department of Hydrogeology.

With a strong emphasis on professional skills development, and building on national capacity in water resources assessment and management. Today the centre boasts self-sustained programmes with experienced nationals working in programming and database management, installation and operation of automatic monitoring networks and water resources assessment studies.

Of those promoting *capacity building*, roughly half imply a focus on formal institutional development in water resources development and management at a national and regional level. The remainder focus on the decentralisation and privatisation of water utilities, and on facilitating community involvement in the development and management of their own water resources through local user associations and direct involvement in decision making. In Lombok, Indonesia, an Australian Government funded rural water supply and sanitation project focuses on capacity building within the community. A community based process of self-survey and management enabled communities to conceptualise problems and affordable solutions in issues related directly to their family and community welfare. The project has successfully avoided adverse environmental impacts and is stimulating appropriate local development.

Of those tackling *water resource protection* most focused on waste management, often within urban municipalities, and the improvement of pollution control on major water courses. For example, in Tunisia the German development bank Kreditanstalt für Wiederaufbau, (KfW), financed project activities that concentrate on the improvement of sewage networks and treatment plants, as well as opening controlled dumps to ensure proper waste disposal, in order to protect the Medjara catchment area and contribute to the conservation of limited water resources. Other tackled issues concern catchment protection through modifying land use practices, and regular monitoring as an aid to water management. In one case, a fully integrated approach for protection of small steep catchment areas in Bolivia, financed by the Swiss Development Corporation (SDC), utilised an integrated natural resource approach incorporating bio-engineering methods and modifying land use practices.

Finally the last grouping, *efficiency of allocation and water use*, covers a diverse range of issues such as general public awareness raising in respect to water conservation through the encouragement of re-use by industry and agriculture, and development of economic tools to assist in effective water allocation, use and management. In Mexico an Overseas Development Administration (British Government) funded project takes a three pronged approach to promote re-use of water by major users. Firstly it minimises wastage of treated water by limiting leakage and unaccounted for losses. Secondly by modifying water use in industrial processing and cooling it aims to reduce industrial discharges and improve their quality. Thirdly it promotes the re-use of industrial wastewater by agriculture.

3   Conclusions and recommendations

There are signs that since the Noordwijk Ministerial Conference and the OECD/DAC meeting less than two years ago, and despite both limited financial resources and staff, a number of ESAs are developing specific policies in water resources management and are increasingly promoting the practice of integrated water management.

In the past many ESAs have assisted countries in establishing their own water master plans. Today there is a shift in emphasis from this narrow concept towards establishing policy frameworks for integrated water resources management.

Further efforts are required to put these policies into practice. Awareness needs to be raised within national Governments concerning the importance of integrated water resources management, to create a shared feeling of responsibility. This will require not only the documentation and dissemination of past experiences with water resources management, but will also require ESAs to re-evaluate their own sectoral division of water issues and approach counterpart organisations as genuine partners.

Capacity building appears to be an inherent component of many of the strongest approaches. This suggests that an increased emphasis on learning as opposed to technology transfer is a key factor in successful water resources management. To ensure sustained water resource development it is important this should not only focus on national Government, but also at lower appropriate levels within the community and amongst all stakeholders with a vested interest in the short or long term use of water resources.

A number of ESAs have already started to place increased emphasis on issues raised by the conferences, such as promotion of integrated WRM, capacity building, involvement of stakeholders, tackling water as a social and economic commodity, and establishing sources of information. It is important that this momentum for change is not lost and increased attention is now given to the practical challenges involved in ensuring sustained integrated water resources management.

4   References

1. World Bank (1993) Water Resources Management: A World Bank Policy Paper, Washington D.C.; World Bank (1995) Towards Sustainable Management of Water Resources, Washington D.C.

2. Environmental Bulletin. (1995) vol.7, no.3, p.5; Water and Environmental International. (1995) vol.4, no.36, p.4.

3. Noordwijk Ministerial Conference On Drinking Water and Environmental Sanitation 22-23 March (1995), Noordwijk; OECD/DAC Meeting on Water Resources Management 10-11 May (1995), Paris.

4. Visscher, J.T. and Sorensson, M. (1994) Towards Better Water Resources Management: A Catalogue of Policies and Strategies of External Support Agencies, Reference Series 10, IRC Water and Sanitation Centre, The Hague.

5. World Bank (1994) The World Development Report 1994: Infrastructure for Development, Washington.

SUPPORT TO WATER RESOURCE MANAGEMENT IN DEVELOPING COUNTRIES
SIDA's experiences and policies

B. JOHANSSON
Department for Natural Resources and the Environment, Swedish International Development Cooperation Agency, Stockholm, Sweden

Summary
The Swedish International Development Cooperation Agency, Sida, has been supporting water related projects since its establishment. A strategy for Sida's support to rural water supply projects has been developed, emphasising simple affordable technology, user participation and integration of health and gender aspects (1987, 1991).

Sida participated actively in the Nordic Initiative on freshwater resources which was one important input in the development of the Dublin principles and Agenda 21 in 1992. Based on the Dublin principles and, amongst other things, the experiences of support to household water supply projects, support to land and water management in east and southern Africa, Sida has decided to support:

- sustainable management of water resources in southern Africa with emphasis on awareness and capacity building and support to integrated management of international water resources; and
- the Global Water Partnership, as one way of consensus building and putting the Dublin principles in practice, given the urgent need for coordinated actions to safeguard and make better use of available water resources.

Considering the Dublin Principles, some of the overall lessons learned in Sida's support to water resource management projects could be summarized as follows:-

- The awareness of water as a limited and vulnerable resource, especially in the arid and semi-arid parts of the world, is crucial for the efficient management of water. Without such an awareness, from the highest political level to the level of consumers, there will probably be resistance towards necessary measures to save

Water Policy: Allocation and management in practice. Edited by P. Howsam and R.C. Carter. Published in 1996 by E & FN Spon. ISBN 0 419 21650 2

water resources.

- One such important measure is an adequate pricing of water reflecting the alternative cost of water as well as the environmental cost but with proper consideration of the necessity of supplying a minimum amount of domestic water to poor households at an affordable price.
- True stakeholders' participation is essential in the planning, implementation and monitoring of water resource management projects, including relevant ministries and other public authorities, private sector, non-Governmental organisations and other interest groups.
- Integrated water resource planning is complex and time consuming. The responsibility of rural water supply, urban water supply, agricultural use, hydropower and industrial use of water often rests within different ministries. If the water resource is shared with one or more countries, the integrated planning is even more complex.
- It is, at least in the short term, much easier to support investment projects aiming at increased supply of water than to support projects aiming at improved water use and efficient management of water.
- It is necessary to include a gender perspective in the planning, implementation and operation of water resource projects.

Based on the above experience, Sida will develop an integrated water resource management policy during 1996 to further coordinate and strengthen its support to water resource management projects in the future.

Keywords: Dublin principles, Global Water Partnership, Sida's water policy, water resource management.

PRIVATE GROUNDWATER DEVELOPMENT IN THE LOWER INDUS: POLICY ISSUES

Private groundwater development, Lower Indus

L.E.D. SMITH and P.A. PATHAN
Department of Agricultural Economics, Wye College, University of London, Wye, UK

Abstract
In the Lower Indus it is vital to exploit the full potential of conjunctive use of surface and groundwater as a solution to the problems of inflexible canal supply, waterlogging and stagnating production. Investment in public deep tubewell schemes over 25 years has failed to achieve this, and policy now focuses on the farmer led expansion of use of private shallow tubewells. The emerging pattern of groundwater development is sub-optimal in terms of efficiency, equity and sustainability, with private tubewells concentrated in the "periphery" of the command area because they are installed primarily as a response to inadequate canal supplies. The potential gains from conjunctive use are not being achieved and "secondary salinisation" is occurring. The policy of transition from public to private tubewells in Pakistan is necessary but implementation could be improved through attention to the pattern of tubewell development, promotion of water markets and reform of traditional methods of water allocation. It is argued that this would lead to increased and higher value output, better salinity control and improved equity of access to water resources.
Keywords: conjunctive use, Lower Indus, private tubewells, public tubewells, SCARPs, SCARP transition, water markets.

1 Introduction

In the Indus Basin seepage from canals, inefficient basin irrigation and poor drainage have combined to cause a rise in the watertable that has generated widespread salinisation and waterlogging. This restricts both yields and cultivated area, but in areas of fresh groundwater (around two thirds of the basin, [1]) also provides the opportunity for conjunctive use of canal supplies and groundwater. Given the scale of

Water Policy: Allocation and management in practice. Edited by P. Howsam and R.C. Carter.
Published in 1996 by E & FN Spon. ISBN 0 419 21650 2

the system and scarcity of capital for investment it is vital to develop conjunctive use as a relatively low cost solution to the problems of inflexible water supply and waterlogging in fresh groundwater areas.   Other investments such as channel improvements to reduce seepage, on farm improvements and drainage water disposal can then be concentrated in the saline groundwater zones [2, 3].

Internationally, conjunctive use has been inadequately researched [4]. Information on the performance of groundwater development in Pakistan, plus insights into future improvements are also lacking [5]. Using secondary sources this paper reports the preliminary findings of research that aims to assess the characteristics and performance of the emerging pattern of private groundwater development in the Lower Indus.   It focuses on the SCARP North Rohri (Salinity Control and Reclamation Project) area in the cotton-wheat zone of the Left Bank of the Indus.

2   The potential gains from conjunctive use and equity considerations

Conjunctive use is the combined and integrated management of surface and groundwater for optimal productive and allocative efficiency [6]. It has the potential to contribute to improved agricultural performance, sustainability and equity in a variety of ways. For the farmer pumped groundwater provides an increased and more controllable water supply that should facilitate the irrigation of additional land and permit increased irrigation intensities. Dilution with surface water can also enable relatively saline groundwater to provide this additional resource. Increased supply can also support shifts in cropping pattern towards water intensive, higher value crops or crops requiring improved timeliness and control of application. Less uncertainty of supply should reduce risk averse behaviour by farmers in relation to input use or investment in land improvements and water intensive crops.   At the basin level conjunctive use could help optimise the distribution and use of water resources.   In drought years a greater proportion of surface flows could be directed to those parts of an alluvial basin with a saline or inaccessible aquifer, while areas with good groundwater depend more heavily on tubewells.   Potential gains of 17-20% in agricultural production and 14-16% in employment have been projected for the Indus Basin given more efficient management of surface and groundwater [7]. A further benefit is control of watertable depth which, as in the Indus, often provides the initial motivation for groundwater development.

The impact of conjunctive use on equity is likely to be location specific. Usually, groundwater is until captured an open access resource that can be exploited by anyone able to make the relatively modest investment in a lifting device, but once captured becomes private property. Tubewell owners pump water from beneath their own land and that of their neighbours, and hence tend to appropriate non-tubewell owners' share of the resource [8]. Where extraction exceeds recharge, over pumping by some farmers will impose an external diseconomy on their neighbours through the extra investment and operating costs of deeper wells. Conversely, where positive recharge leads to waterlogging, pumping may benefit neighbours if their watertable is lowered. It is likely that resource-rich farmers will tend to gain access to groundwater before those who are resource-poor. For example, in India tubewell ownership has been found to be positively correlated with holding size [8].

3 The failure of public tubewells and transition to landowners

From 1960 the Government response to rising watertables was implementation of a series of tubewell drainage schemes (SCARPs). The tubewells ranged from 56-142 litres per second capacity and 40-120 metres depth, and were primarily located at the head of watercourse commands in fresh groundwater zones. While initially successful in regulating the watertable and providing a supplementary source of irrigation water their performance rapidly declined [9][10]. Causes included poor operation and maintenance and a lack of farmer participation in design and implementation [10].

Some increase in cropping intensity, a shift to higher value crops and control of the watertable can be attributed to the SCARPs, but their most significant impact has been to trigger sustained investment in private tubewells [1] with over 250,000 installed since 1960 [9]. These are low capacity (7-28 litres per second) and 6-10 metres deep, with the advantages of improved care and maintenance under private operation, less salinity build up through tapping only the upper layers of the aquifer, and complete control over water use for owners. Control of waterlogging and reclamation of salt-affected land achieved since 1960 has largely resulted from private tubewells rather than the SCARPs [9]. Since 1980 in response to this and the increasing fiscal burden of SCARPs fresh groundwater development has been left to landowners. Pilot Transition Projects have also sought to replace SCARP tubewells in SCARP-I in Punjab and SCARP North Rohri in Sindh, through termination and replacement with private wells of equivalent capacity or transfer to private or community ownership.

4 Characteristics and performance of private tubewells in SCARP North Rohri

Assessing the performance of irrigation systems requires a wide range of indicators given the inherent complexity and the multiple objectives of interest groups [11]. Assertions here are based on only three indicators: the pattern of tubewell location, the output of tubewell using farmers, and equity of access to groundwater for landowners.

4.1 The pattern of private tubewell development in SCARP North Rohri
Data for 150 SCARP tubewell commands on 12 distributaries shows that private tubewells have been heavily concentrated on tail reach watercourses. Little data is available, but field observations and discussion with farmers confirm that the pattern on watercourse commands is similar. SCARP tubewells were located at the head of watercourses, but deficient operation means their existence was only a limited disincentive to head or middle watercourse reach landowners investing in a tubewell. Private tubewell development has thus been concentrated in tail reaches of both watercourses and the canal network, or in *"peripheral"* rather than *"core command"* [13]. Evidence from India [13] and from Punjab in Pakistan [14] also shows this concentration in tail reaches where farmers have been primarily motivated by the need to substitute for deficient canal supplies. This pattern is the opposite of that

expected to maximise benefits from conjunctive use, and may lead to excessive withdrawals and deteriorating groundwater quality in tail areas. Head reaches receive the greatest recharge to the aquifer, tend to have a higher watertable and most need vertical drainage. Groundwater can be used for irrigation with less risk of salinisation, while at the tail it is more limited and quality often deteriorates. Vertical drainage, though sometimes still necessary at the tail, is of less priority while surface supplies are important to recharge the aquifer and to provide for adequate leaching of salt.

In Punjab studies reveal increasing reliance on private tubewells at the tail in response to poor SCARP well performance, and inadequate canal supplies caused by deferred maintenance and institutionalised corruption that favours head end farms. Private tubewells have alleviated initial waterlogging and salinity, but watertables at the tail are still falling. Pumping costs increase while soil salinisation dissociated from waterlogging has returned in tail, and even middle reaches, caused by reliance on groundwater of marginal quality. This *"secondary salinity"* [14, 15] depresses yields, threatens sustainability, and restricts crop diversification. These problems are also emerging in North Rohri where tubewell water samples have been classified as useable to marginal (500-1660 ppm total dissolved salts, [12]).

SCARPs have been described as the first large scale vertical drainage and true conjunctive use systems of water management [5]. Tubewells were installed to regulate watertables, concentrated in high recharge areas and the water was usually added at the head of watercourses. This beneficial pattern of conjunctive use is not being sustained as SCARP wells are closed and replaced by private tubewells. The emerging system is better described as merely *"joint use"* [6], with groundwater exploited to compensate for failures in the canal system and little account taken of the dangers of "secondary salinity".

4.2 Output from conjunctive use in SCARP North Rohri

It appears [12] [16] that there is no significant difference in cropping intensity on farms with private tubewells compared to those without. Cropping intensity primarily depends on water supply indicating that the tubewells are mainly used to make good shortfalls in surface supplies without gaining the full benefits of conjunctive use. Moreover there may also be little difference in crop choice between farms with and without private tubewells. This is certainly the case for the small samples used for the transition project baseline survey. Results from the larger sample, do suggest that more sugar cane and Kharif vegetables are grown with private tubewell compared to farms without. Data from the same sources on crop yields is also inconclusive. In the baseline survey only cotton yields were significantly higher on farms with private tubewells, while sugar cane yields were lower. The other survey of farms with private tubewells does show higher yields for the three main crops, but the difference is disappointing, and yields are still well below the potential achievable in the region.

A few case study farms monitored before and after tubewell installation have shown increases in cropping intensity and a shift to more water intensive crops [16], but these have tended to be located in tail reaches with very poor canal supply. The observed improvement has only brought these farms back on to a par with others more favourably located.

From this data it appears that private tubewells largely substitute for canal supplies and only a small proportion of potential conjunctive use benefits are achieved. This poor performance may also be due to under-irrigation by around 10-20% of requirements to save fuel expenses [16], (the majority of tubewells recently installed are diesel powered, [12]). As most private tubewells are located in tail reaches many owners experience comparatively high pumping costs because of the greater depth to the watertable.

4.3 Conjunctive use and equity in SCARP North Rohri
There is a tendency [16] for tubewells to be installed by resource-rich landowners given that these have greater access to the capital required for installation and running costs. Land ownership in Sindh is highly skewed, but the extent of this is obscured by fragmentation, phantom ownership, and widespread litigation. Exclusion of resource-poor landowners from the gains from conjunctive use will have direct implications for the distribution of benefits from any policy that promotes groundwater development. The central question is how to ensure resource-poor landowners can gain access to groundwater. Though in principle this could be done with public tubewells, in practice their operation and management has been too ineffective. Collective ownership of tubewells is an option, but conjunctive use systems do not inherently require collective action. Social conditions in Sindh are also not conducive to the establishment of new community organisations unless these are based on the extended family or clan. Government is not good at developing such organisations but it will be difficult and costly to set up and replicate NGOs to achieve this over the SCARP areas.

The feasible option in the short term is to develop water markets to provide access to groundwater for landowners without tubewells. There is an urgent need to establish the extent to which water markets exist, the potential for their development and whether conditions are conducive. This requires study of the existing system of water rights and institutions.

5   Water rights and water markets

Under the warabandi system farmers can supplement canal water with private tubewell water only if they have an uninterrupted right to the total flow in the watercourse, the stretch of watercourse between their fields and the tubewell is unused, or they have direct access. This rigidity affects the economics of tubewell installation because of fewer potential purchasers of the water [17]. Capital costs cannot be easily spread over a wider area and other water users. Landowners who can afford installation will tend to buy low capacity wells just sufficient for their needs and not to provide groundwater to others even at a monopoly premium rate. The rigidity implicit in the warabandi system prevents maximisation of the private and social benefits from conjunctive use, while restricting access to groundwater largely to those who can afford tubewells.

Poor farmers can benefit from groundwater development by the rich if they gain access through water trading [18]. Fully functioning water markets will enhance this, particularly if competition to supply reduces monopoly prices. Five major benefits from groundwater markets are claimed [18]: non tubewell owners gain higher, lower risk income through buying water; an increase in the land value of both tubewell and non-tubewell owners; tubewell owners can spread overhead costs thus increasing the technology's adoption; increased wages and employment for the landless, as a result of increased area and/or production by both tubewell owners and non-owners; incentives for efficiency as lost sales are the opportunity cost of over-irrigation.

According to Shah's classification [18] Sindh has a *"high potential, low utilisation"* profile for water markets. There are large and easily accessible groundwater reserves, but highly underdeveloped water markets (only 8% of landowners in the North Rohri area bought water from private tubewell operators in 1994 [12]). Factors influencing competitiveness of groundwater markets in Sindh are considered in Table 1.

Table 1.   Potential Determinants of Monopoly Power For Groundwater Sellers on the Left Bank of the Indus in Sindh (adapted from Shah [8].

	Enhancing competition	*Enhancing monopoly power*
Physical and climatic factors	• Abundant aquifer close to surface • Cropping pattern dominated by less water intensive crops(wheat and cotton) • Flat topography • Access to canal supplies as an alternative irrigation source	• Low and erratic rainfall
Institutional and economic factors	• Relatively low cost of lift irrigation systems • No spacing or licensing regulation of installation • No other barriers to entry, ready availability of technology and technical support for operation and maintenance from the private sector	• Lack of competing efficient public tubewells charging low water prices • Predominant use of unlined field channels by water sellers, raises effective water prices through seepage losses • Relatively low density of tubewells. • Unreliable rural electricity supplies • Lack of electricity supply or bureaucratic and licensing constraints to securing supply • Rigidities of the warabandi system, restricting choice of water seller for buyers

While there are few physical constraints to competition there is a formidable number of economic and institutional constraints, but these at least suggest an agenda for policy reform or public investment.

Flat rate charging for electricity may increase pumping and create incentives for water selling because the marginal cost of pumping is zero [18]. This may be the most effective means of providing poor farmers with access to groundwater, but establishing competition between suppliers is vital to control monopoly pricing. The possibility for over exploitation of the aquifer needs to be monitored and again the pattern of tubewell development in relation to recharge is vital. It is clear in Sindh that whilst landowners express a preference for electric wells, the unreliability of supply and corruption associated with connection are leading to the majority opting for diesel units [12]. This may increase competition by increasing tubewell density, but diesel pumping costs that increase pro-rata with usage may inhibit development of water trading. Performance of the power sector may improve in future given increasing foreign investment and possible privatisations.

6 Conclusions

The emerging, unregulated, pattern of private tubewell development in North Rohri is not optimal in terms of water use and salinity management. Because groundwater substitutes for, rather than complements canal supplies it appears to have had relatively little impact on output in terms of yields or cropped area; though there is some evidence of a shift towards more diverse cropping patterns. Sustainability is threatened by secondary salinity and access to groundwater for resource-poor landowners and dependent share tenants or labourers is not equitable.

Improvements could be achieved by encouraging more head reach landowners to install tubewells, preferably electrically driven with power tariffs charged at a flat rate, who should then choose to use and sell more groundwater. Part subsidies for installation of higher capacity wells (or scavenger wells or interceptor drains) might be justified if supported by farm level investment analysis. Head-enders would gain from more control over water and from water sales but have to accept restricted access to surface supply. The implicit energy subsidy may be justified by the positive externalities of vertical drainage and improvements in equity of distribution. Middle and tail reach farmers would receive improved surface flows, increased recharge for shallow tubewells and the opportunity to buy groundwater of good quality. Reforms to the warabandi system and modifications to field channels would be needed, and participation of all affected parties in the design and implementation process.

More research is needed to fully assess the performance of the emerging pattern of conjunctive use in Sindh and to formulate detailed means for improvement. The current policy of transition from public to private tubewells is necessary but implementation could be improved through attention to the pattern of tubewell development, promotion of water markets and reform of the warabandi system. Given the socio-political environment change will not be easy, but this also applies to other reforms already being implemented. The options identified here are at least based firmly on landowners' self interest.

7 References

1. O'Mara, G.T. (1988) The Efficient Use of Surface Water and Groundwater in

Irrigation: An Overview of the Issues, in *Efficiency in Irrigation: The Conjunctive Use of Surface and Groundwater Resources*, O'Mara, G.T., (ed.), World Bank: Washington, D.C. pp. 1-17.

2. Lamb, R. (1991) Decision Decade. *International Irrigation Management Institute Review*, 5(1): pp. 17-19.

3. Ahmad, M.A. and Kutcher, G.P. (1992) *Irrigation Planning with Environmental Considerations: A Case Study of Pakistan's Indus Basin.* Washington D.C.: The World Bank.

4. Colmey, J. (1990) Groundwater and the Rural Poor. *International Irrigation Management Institute Review.* 4(1): pp. 7-9.

5. Smedema, B. and Zimmer, D. (1994) Vertical Drainage and Conjunctive Use, in *GRID, IPTRID Network Magazine.* pp. 7-8.

6. Vincent, L. and Dempsey, P. (1991) *Conjunctive Water Use for Irrigation: Good Theory, Poor Practice*, Overseas Development Institute: London.

7. O'Mara, G.T. and Duloy, J.H. (1988) Modeling Efficient Conjunctive Use of Water in the Indus Basin., in *Efficiency in Irrigation: The Conjunctive Use of Surface and Groundwater Resources*, O'Mara, G.T., (ed.), World Bank: Washington, D.C. pp. 128-138.

8. Shah, T. (1988) External and Equity Implications of Private Exploitation of Ground-Water Resources. *Agricultural Systems.* 28: pp. 119-139.

9. World Bank. (1991) *Second SCARP Transition Project, Pakistan, Staff Appraisal Report.* The World Bank: Washington D.C.

10. Johnson III, S.H. (1988) Large-Scale Irrigation and Drainage Schemes in Pakistan, in *Efficiency in Irrigation: The Conjunctive Use of Surface and Groundwater Resources*, O'Mara, G.T., (ed.), World Bank: Washington, D.C. pp. 58-76.

11. Smith, L.E.D. (1990) An Economist's Perspective on Irrigation Performance Assessment: With Examples from Large Scale Irrigation in Morocco. *Irrigation and Drainage Systems.* 4: pp. 329-343.

12. SDSC. (1995) *Baseline Report: Impact Evaluation Study, SCARP Transition North Rohri Pilot Project.* Sindh Development Studies Centre: Hyderabad.

13. Shah, T. (1991) Water Markets and Irrigation Development in India, *Indian Journal of Agricultural Economics.* 46(3): pp. 335-348.

14. Kijne, J.W. and Velde, E.J.V. (1991) Secondary Salinity in Pakistan - Harvest of Neglect. *International Irrigation Management Institute Review*, 5(1): pp. 15-24.

15. No Stranger to Salt. (1991) *International Irrigation Management Institute Review.* 5(1): pp. 25,30.

16. Irrigation and Power Department, Government of Sindh.(1994) *Annual Report: SCARP Transition North Rohri Pilot Project.* Project Implementation Assistance Consultants: ACE, ZCL, HEC and NESPAK.

17. Bhatti, M.A. & Kijne, J.W. (1990) *Irrigation Allocation Problems at Tertiary Level in Pakistan.* Overseas Development Institute: London.

18. Shah, T. (1993) Efficiency and Equity Impacts of Groundwater Markets: A Review of Issues, Evidence and Policies, in *Groundwater Irrigation and the Rural Poor: Options for Development in the Gangetic Basin*, Kahnert, F. & Levine, G., (editors) The World Bank: Washington D.C. pp. 145-161.

TOWARDS THE 21ST CENTURY - BUILDING INSTITUTIONS FOR IMPROVED MANAGEMENT OF IRRIGATION WATER
Institution building for irrigation

M HVIDT
Centre for Contemporary Middle East Studies, Odense University, Denmark

Summary
Access to adequate and reliable sources of water is essential for sustaining and developing societies in arid or semi arid locations. Due to limited possibilities of expanding the water resources, increasing population pressure, more modern life styles, urbanisation and industrialisation, the water resource has come under considerable strain over the last half century.

Often, water needs for irrigation alone consumes between 80 and 90% of the available water in these countries. Thus, with increasing pressure on the resource, Governments (and donors) have had to find ways to optimise the use of the scarce resource - or phrased differently 'to do their best with what they have.'

At the overall level, three distinct strategies or focuses have been, or is being applied, by Governments in order to develop and utilise water resources. Firstly, the 'construction' focus, in which engineers seek to capture new or additional water resources by erecting structures , eg, dams, weirs, canals. Secondly, the operation and maintenance (O & M) focus, which became the emphasis in the 1980s. It stresses rehabilitation and improvements of already established systems, adequate O & M procedures, decentralisation and farmer participation, financial sustainability and environmental concern. Finally, the new and emerged focus called 'Water Resources Management' which aims to place water supply and demand for all purposes (including irrigation) under the far broader umbrella termed water management. It adopts a comprehensive analytical approach to water resources planning, focus on the productivity of water, water conservation, demand management through attention to water economics, innovative financing, accountability for services, user participation, and appropriate technology.

The centrepiece of the two latter strategies is 'good' management. And a precondition for good management are strong and viable institutions.

Water Policy: Allocation and management in practice. Edited by P. Howsam and R.C. Carter. Published in 1996 by E & FN Spon. ISBN 0 419 21650 2

Of particular significance are the changes in demands placed on institutions charged with the task of managing irrigation water from society at large, and the lessons learned about changes in the institutional capacity to meet these demands.

Of importance is the current state of thinking concerning institutional change as it relates to optimising the use of irrigation water and providing sustainable systems performance. The neo-liberal economic strategy has come into dominance among donors in the latter part of the 1980s. It stresses decentralisation, deregulation, and privatisation as a means to optimise institutional performance.

At a more practical level, the process of implementing the key elements of the O & M focus should be analysed. This includes working at changes in system rehabilitation, O & M procedures, financial concerns (cost-recovery), decentralisation, and the effort to create and sustain Water Use Associations.

The analyses are based on data collected for two research projects undertaken by the author:

1. An extensive field survey of the first experiences resulting from the shift from state control to farmer control over the allocation and distribution of irrigation water in Egypt.
2. A cross-country study dealing with institutional change in large scale irrigation systems in Pakistan, Philippines, Indonesia, Morocco and Mexico.

THE SELECTION OF AN ORGANISATIONAL STRUCTURE FOR THE MINISTRY OF WATER AND IRRIGATION IN JORDAN
Irrigation organisation in Jordan

B.A. AL-KLOUB and T.T. AL-SHEMMERI
School of Engineering, Staffordshire University, Stafford, UK

Abstract
The selection of a potential organisational structure for the Ministry of Water and Irrigation in Jordan was carried out using a Multi-Criteria Decision Aid software. The structure selected will allow the Government to manage efficiently the national infrastructure, and direct control over the functions of planning, regulating and control. Distribution and collection system to be operated on a decentralised basis that could eventually be transferred to the private sector.
Keywords: multi-criteria decision aid analysis, organisational structure.

1   Introduction

In Jordan, there is a need to strengthen the institutional responsibilities for water strategic planning, management and delivery to meet future challenges. The current per capita consumption of renewable water resources is the lowest in the Middle East [1] resulting in water quality and environmental problems.

There is an urgent need to utilise the water resources efficiently, preserve the water quality, and develop the local capability to plan and implement a long term national water strategy. The current organisational structure of the Ministry of Water and Irrigation (MWI) is unsatisfactory and there is a need for institutional restructuring to build stronger organisation to achieve capability for :
* Planning, designing, building, operating, and maintaining major water projects.
* Understanding water quality impacts, and managing successful programmes to sustain water quality.
* Effective water distribution, cost efficiency and recovery.
* Water policy formulation and commitment to water demand management.

Water Policy: Allocation and management in practice. Edited by P. Howsam and R.C. Carter.
Published in 1996 by E & FN Spon. ISBN 0 419 21650 2

2   Organisational structures

There are various types of organisational structures which can be found in literature [2,3]: simple, functional, geographic, decentralised, strategic business units, divisional, informal, and matrix forms, each having it's own advantages and disadvantages.

The current structures for organisations responsible for running the water sector in many countries can be grouped into three categories:

- *The first*: where all significant water sector functions are concentrated in one Ministry or Authority and this has the advantages of: efficient use of staff if the culture/ work environment defines responsibilities, encourage communication, and motivation, better decision making if the work environment inhibit the true delegation of the authority and responsibility, visibility, because of the size and budget of the organisation the voices of other ministries will be weakened; and the water will have a strong voice in sectoral allocation of financial and staff resources. Possible disadvantages include competition for financial and staff resources within the ministry which may weaken the planning functions and enforcement of decisions.
- *The second*: where there is a separation between planning and services. This has the advantages of increasing responsibility for the development of sound national water policies, strategies, and excellence in the services, and disadvantages of over-staffing and the relatively higher resources needed for support services. The success would depend upon a high degree of cooperation between the different units. In addition, there may be an overlap in responsibility and programs if the cultural and work environment does not encourage cooperation.
- *The third*: the fragmented one, where institutions are created on an ad hoc basis to deal with problems as they arise. This has advantages of being action focused, less competition between the different units, and disadvantages of not favouring the development of a coherent national water strategy, inefficient use of people, and the need for higher degree of co-ordination of many units.

Within each of the above three structures there can be various degrees of decentralisation. In addition, privatisation could be applied as a device to lower costs through efficient use of staff and resources, and the potential for attracting new capital to the sector and less Government investment and subsidy. Moreover, local public participation and public awareness are essential features of any successful institutional structure to implement programs for water conservation.

3   Current organisational analysis

The primary Governmental organisations which are responsible for running the water sector in Jordan are: Ministry of Water and Irrigation (MWI), Water Authority of Jordan (WAJ) and Jordan Valley Authority (JVA) (the last two authorities are incorporated within MWI).

The current organisational structure for the MWI is shown in Fig. 1. In order to view the series of activities that are carried out in the sector, the value chain concept as developed by Porter [4] is utilised. The sector is a collection of value activities that are performed to design, produce, deliver, and support. This logical grouping of functions can address linkages among functions. Reviewing this concept would highlight three areas of concern, namely: sector planning, service delivery and support. Comparing these areas of concern with the existing functions of the water sector, and reviewing the current structure revealed the following :

- *Sector planning*:
  - Many functions are fragmented with many Governmental agencies involved in the sector having overlapping interests.
  - Within the three key water sector entities (WAJ, JVA, MWI), there is fragmentation of functions.
  - No explicit water policy exists.
  - Only a few policy development and planning activities exist, and these are under-resourced.
  - There is minimal activity in public participation functions.
- *Sector service delivery*:
  - Planning for service delivery is fragmented among organisations.
  - The preventative maintenance function is under resourced.
  - The need for technical support/skills is weak.
  - There is no specific function for co-ordination of donors activity in the water sector institutions.
  -

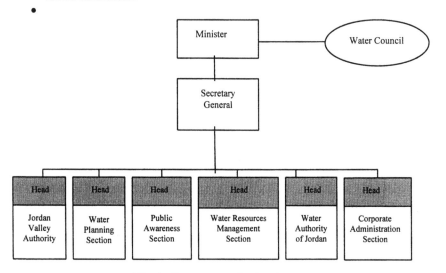

Fig. 1. Current organisational structure.

- *Sector support*:
  - There is a lack of management information and information systems capability.
  - Administrative support is found in almost every activity and the function appears to be over resourced.
  - The human resources management function lacks the required capabilities and organisational focus.

4   Possible future organisational structures

The following four options are now under consideration by the Jordan Government [5]. Each option is described briefly in this section, whereas an analytical evaluation of these options will be discussed in section 5 and thereafter.

4.1 Option 1: Status quo (rationalised organisation)

This option preserves as far as possible the present functions and administrative structures of JVA and WAJ under separate organisations (Fig. 1). However, where overlapping functions are identified, they need to be allocated to the organisation that is best to perform that function.

- Strengths
  The least disruptive to the existing system of all options, and the most familiar structure to existing employees and customers.
- Weaknesses
  The national infrastructure would be fragmented, detracting from the ability to demonstrate efficient operations. The local distribution and collection functions would be split between the two organisations. Therefore, the financial viability of the individual organisations would not be as clearly demonstrated. This might effect the ability to attract private sector involvement and investment.

4.2 Option 2: National/local organisation

The main theme of this option is the clear and distinct separation of the national infrastructure function (the wholesale system), from the local distribution and collection function (the retail system) (Fig. 2).

- Strengths
  Delineates the main aspects of the water sector in Jordan: planning, regulating control functions, national infrastructure, and local distribution and collection. In addition, it allows the Government direct control over planning, regulating, and control functions to manage the national infrastructure as a national resource while allowing it to be run in a demonstrably efficient manner, with direct accountability to the Government.

  The local distribution and collection systems could be run on a decentralised basis with appropriate geographic divisions (governorates) that could move towards individual financial viability. Eventually, these could move towards encouraging private sector investment and involvement when required.

4.3 Option 3: End-Use organisation

Under this option, the national infrastructure construction function is centralised and the local water and wastewater functions are split (Fig 3). The local functions can be further decentralised on a geographic basis (governorates).

  This option allows clear identification of the water and wastewater functions with the users of those services.

- Strengths
  One national organisation plans, manages, and develops national water sources.
  Planning, regulating and control functions would be centralised under the direct control of the Government which provides a higher profile for the wastewater

treatment function.

- Weaknesses

    The operation and maintenance functions would be split between water and wastewater, thereby detracting from the unitary nature of the national resource. Clear establishment of the costs of the national infrastructure would be difficult to identify, as would be the levels and points of subsidisation. The local systems would be split so that geographically-based organisations might be duplicated or more centralised.

    Although water and wastewater can be decentralised, many functions would have to be re-combined at the governorate level in order to make efficient use of staff.

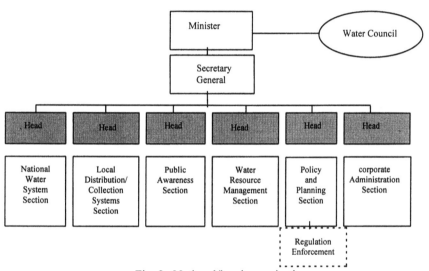

Fig. 2. National/local organisation.

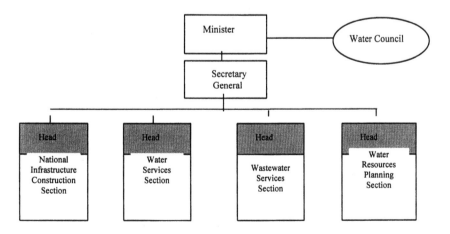

Fig. 3. End use organisation.

Financial viability would be less easy to establish at the local level. This would make the individual organisations (governorates) less attractive for private investment or involvement. This structure will require significant changes in legislation, consequently, implementation may be slower which may increases the risk that the benefits of full implementation will not be achieved. Long term implications include privatising the infrastructure construction unit, and possible splitting of planning, and regulatory activities in the future.

4.4 Option 4: Functional organisation

The construction function of both national infrastructure and local distribution collection systems is integrated in this option as a separate structure (Fig. 4). The operation and maintenance functions for the national infrastructure, the local distribution and collection systems are integrated as a separate structure but could be further decentralised on a geographic basis (governorates).

- Strengths

    The planning, regulating and control functions would be centralised under direct Government control and there would be efficiencies in having construction managed by one administrative unit.

- Weaknesses

    The centralised national and local systems would make it very difficult to identify the true costs of the national infrastructure, and the clear points of subsidy.

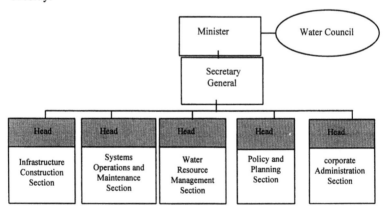

Fig. 4. Functional organisation.

Similarly, the costs of the local distribution and collection systems would not be readily identified. Consequently, the ability to assign authority and responsibility to specific organisations would be significantly reduced. This would detract from the ability to attract private sector investment and involvement.

5   Multi-criteria analysis

The use of multi-criteria decision-aiding methods is a must where there is limited investment resources and where an effective investment decision must satisfy the broad objectives defined by socio-political conditions which are sometimes non-commensurable and conflicting in nature. A user-friendly method in this category is the PROMETHEE Method (Preference Ranking Organisation METHod for Enrichment Evaluation) [6] implemented in three steps:
- *Enrichment of the preference structure* by introducing generalised criteria to remove scaling effect.
- *Enrichment of the dominance relation* by building:
  - A multi-criteria preference index to express to which degree an option is facing the other options together (strength and weakness of the option).
  - An associated outranking graph and outranking flow to express how each option is facing the other options together (strength and weakness of the option).
- *Exploitation for decision aid.* PROMETHEE I provides a partial ranking, including possible incomparable options, PROMETHEE II shows complete ranking of options. , and PROMETHEE V extends the application of PROMETHEE II method to the problem of selection of several options given a set of constraints.

6   Identification of the evaluation criteria

Two relevant studies were carried out recently to identify the necessary criteria for evaluation in the water sector in Jordan. The first, to rank water projects according to elicited multiple objectives [7] and the second, a joint study between Ministry of Planning and Canadian International Development Agency (CIDA) to identify the necessary information for water sector restructuring in Jordan [5]. Criteria developed in the second study were selected as basis of comparison in this study since most of the values of the first study are embedded in the second.   Each of the structural options was measured against the criteria to assess whether the structure fully, partially, or failed to meet the criteria based on a subjective scale. Five sets of objectives/criteria, comprised of seventy two criteria were developed:
- *Government national goals and objectives*: objectives extracted from the Government's economic and social development plan (1993-1997) and directly related to water as well as privatisation, decentralisation and restructuring.
- *Future vision*: design elements which provide a framework for the development of a future vision covering areas of:
  - Arrangement with external organisations.
  - National water strategy/public policy.
  - Management processes and practices.
  - Infrastructure development and management.
  - Human resource management.
  - Management of service delivery operations, and information management
- *Financial criteria*: accountability, financial feasibility, transparency, and commercialisation.

- *Organisational principles/criteria*: baseline requirements from previous experience and studies in Jordan and neighbouring countries.
- *World Bank recommendations*: recommendations which are identified by the World Bank for better sector institutional arrangements.

7   Results

The spreadsheet of PROMETHEE was built for the four structures. Inputs include: the generalised criteria, their types and parameters, associated weights, organisational structures, evaluation of options, the problem type (maximisation or minimisation). Output include: ranking, and general sensitivity analysis.   Equal weights were given for all criteria and later sensitivity analysis was carried out to judge stability of results for different weights.   Option 2   (National/Local Organisation) was the highest ranked option followed by options 3,4, and 1.

8   References:

1. Al-Kloub, B., and Al-Shemmeri, T.(1994) Looking for Alternative Sources of Water. *The Resource Journal*, Vol. 2, No. 2, pp. 8-11.
2. Pearce, J., and Robinson, R.(1991) *Strategic Management, Formalities Implementation and Control*, John Wiley.
3. Certo, S. and Peter, J.(1988) *Strategic Management, Concepts and Applications.* McGraw-Hill Inc., New York.
4. Porter, M.(1985) *Competitive Advantage: Creating and Sustaining Superior Performance*, Free Press, New York.
5. Debitte and Touche Consultants (1994) *Jordan Water Sector, Structural Adjustment and Policy Support Project*. Ministry of Planning, Jordan.
6. Brans, J., Vincke, Ph. and Mareschal, B.(1986) How to select and how to rank projects: the PROMETHEE method. *European Journal of Operational Research*, Vol. 24, pp. 228-238.
7. Al-Kloub, B.(1995) Application of Multi-Criteria Decision Analysis and Evaluation of Water Development Projects, in *Critical issues in Systems Theory and Practice*, (ed. by Ellis, K. , Gregory, A., Mears, B. and Ragsdell, G.), Plenum Publishing Corporation, pp. 89-94.

IRRIGATION MANAGEMENT TRANSFER: PRESSURES FOR! CONSTRAINTS AGAINST!

Irrigation management transfer

D.C. MARSHALL
Management and Marketing Department, Silsoe College, Cranfield University, UK.

Abstract
One of the major issues that faces the implementation of water policy is who manages the vital resource. In the case of the use of water for irrigation purposes, the transfer of it's management from Government to farmers and other non-Governmental organisations has become a prominent part of national agricultural policy in many countries. The policy supports the broader objectives of many states to :- reduce costs; improve transparency; encourage people's participation; share financial responsibility with users and use resources more efficiently. These objectives are particularly pertinent in the former centrally planned economies that are in transition towards a market economy. This paper uses a case study of a technical assistance programme in Bulgaria to identify some of the constraints and delays to the Irrigation Management Transfer (IMT) process.
Keywords: centrally planned economies, force field analysis, implementation of water policies, irrigation management transfer, rapid rural appraisal,

1 Introduction

The world-wide movement towards privatisation in many sectors of the economy is gaining momentum. This movement is never more obvious than in the former centrally planned economies of Eastern Europe. Seen as an integral part of the process of political independence and democracy it appears inevitable. The management of water in these economies is not immune from the same pressures. Who implements the water policies, and how the balance of control can be shifted from Government to private becomes key questions for policy makers. The difficulties that these questions raise are addressed by examining the transfer of the

Water Policy: Allocation and management in practice. Edited by P. Howsam and R.C. Carter.
Published in 1996 by E & FN Spon. ISBN 0 419 21650 2

management of water allocated for irrigation purposes.

The transfer of the management of irrigation (IMT) from Government to farmers and other non-Governmental organisations has become a prominent part of domestic agricultural policy in many countries. The movement has been in operation for a number of years and has been fuelled by the need for Governments to address the broader objectives of: cost reduction by the state; increased transparency and participation in Government and more efficient use of agricultural resources. Many of the approaches to the transfer of management have been based upon the technical and hydrological perspective. This has created a rather naive perception that the process of transfer is almost a mechanical, instrumental operation. Experience has taught that this approach is not always effective. It has become necessary to address, in more detail, the reasons for a slow uptake of management by users of irrigation systems. The following case study, which features the proposed transfer of management of irrigation in Bulgaria, is used to highlight some of the constraints and delays experienced in the process and to attempt to extrapolate some basic lessons that have to be learned. A model of analysis was constructed using the force field analysis of Lewin [1] together with a survey method based upon the rapid rural appraisal techniques collected and promoted by the International Institute for the Environment and Development (IIED) [2]

2   The case study

2.1 Irrigation in Bulgaria

Irrigation in Bulgaria began in the 15th century with the development of areas of the Maritza valley for rice growing. From 1920s onwards 35,000 hectares of land was irrigated under the Water Syndicate Laws which allowed the Ministry of Agriculture to grant the right to use public waters to Water Syndicates. In the 1940s with the advent of nationalisation and collectivisation of the economy agricultural cooperatives were formed in each village. By 1989 29% of agricultural land, approximately 1,230,000 ha, was under irrigation. Over the next four years a fall in the area under irrigation to around 110,000 ha. was attributed to several factors including:- the introduction of the market economy; the beginning of the restitution of land to private ownership; the collapse of the protected Russian market; the deterioration of irrigation infrastructure; the cost of water in high lift areas; no identified owners of the infrastructure and equipment previously owned by the cooperatives and vandalism caused by a high land tax levied upon farms with irrigation infrastructure.

The Ministry of Agriculture created a commercial company - the Irrigation Systems Company - (ISC) charged with the responsibility for the management operation and maintenance of the irrigation infrastructure. Some of the former state collectives are still operating, often with the same personnel, but in a more democratic way. In addition individual private farmers have formed their own cooperative form of management. A number of commercial opportunities have been seized upon by some businessmen who have bought out small farmers to create larger economic units. Nevertheless the majority of the farmers are operating small one or two hectare units.

2.2 The project

The European Union were providing technical assistance to the Bulgarian Government to assist in the definition and implementation of an adequate strategy for the development of Bulgarian agriculture. Assistance in the irrigation sub-sector included development and implementation of water management training programmes and support to the establishment of pilot Water User Associations (WUAs)

It was anticipated, by the EU PHARE team, that the setting up of water user associations was not going to be a straight forward task. It was currently assumed, both by Government and previous FAO/World Bank review missions, that with the irrigation infrastructure in place and a relatively compliant farming population it would be a simple matter to transfer the management of the irrigation systems to the users. If the right legislation was in place then control of the water resources was assured. With the opportunity to provide water to groups of users rather than individuals a more efficient and effective distribution would be achieved. The result would be a large reduction in state financing of this sector of the economy. On the basis of these assumptions, the Ministry of Agriculture adopted the policy of the rapid formation of WUAs as the preferred process for the transfer of irrigation management. This policy reflected the strong polarized view that it was either full transfer of management to these associations or the status quo. A conceptual model was needed to test these assumptions.

At the International Conference on Irrigation Management Transfer held at Wuhan, China in September 1994 Turral [3] reported that:-

"A strong consensus of participant opinion concluded that there is no one model for IMT, and that the problem of developing programmes is highly context-specific"

An acceptable model of the dynamics of management transfer strategies emerged when a continuum reproduced by Turral was superimposed on the Force Field Analysis of Kurt Lewin

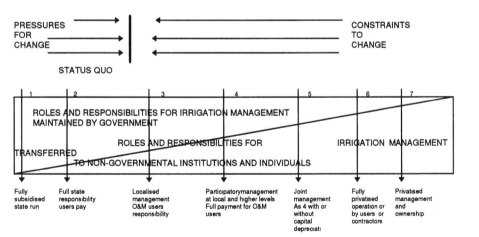

Fig. 1. Irrigation management transfer strategies

The reformulated task of the project team that evolved from a consideration of the model was to identify the pressures for and against the move towards IMT. The strong political and economic pressures for rapid transfer discussed above were already articulated, but the pressures resisting the movement were not so clearly understood. Turral [3] indicated that the various contexts in which transfer would take place would include climate, political economy, culture and religion, size or population of agrarian sector, education, resource base and competition for scarce resources, and scale of the irrigation system. Those who argue for a privatisation model of IMT point out that there are policy and institutional precursors that need to be in place for success. By exploring the constraints to the transfer of irrigation management the practicalities of adopting IMT policy in certain situations can be questioned. This identifies and minimises the effects of these constraints on the formation of Water User Associations.

2.3 The survey
Resource constraints reduced the survey to four sites across the country.   The Rapid Rural Appraisal (RRA) method of data collection was used because of limited time. The features are that it is iterative, innovative, interactive, informal and in the community. The researcher is required to keep to the minimum the amount and detail of information required to formulate useful hypotheses. The danger of subjectivity is reduced by the use of several different sources and means of gathering information. A number of RRA techniques have been developed. Direct observation; semi-structured interviews and secondary data review were used to collect information. Maps, flow diagrams and tables presented the data collected for analysis. The team randomly travelled the area talking to as many people as possible. The information, collected by observation and informal interviews, was recorded by means of a series of flow maps superimposed over the hydrological map of the site. Six information maps were prepared the first recorded the physical state of the irrigation system. The second represented the agricultural map of the area and registered total agricultural hectarage, areas of irrigated agriculture, cash and subsistence crops, and the data required to carry out an economic analysis of the area. The remaining four included the social and psychological forces that are likely to influence the transfer or lack of transfer of the system:- the social groupings of the inhabitants of the system e.g. by village or ethnic origin etc.; the feelings of the mayors, the farmers and any other relevant social group; the demographic features of the area; the ownership of the land and the major concerns of the people. The beliefs and values expressed or implied also formed part of this record. The orientation of the people towards the market economy and their adherence to a collectivist mentality were seen to be important perceptions that would influence their desire to manage the system. The traditional adherence to a rural lifestyle and to the locality was seen to affect the support given to local activities. The mobility map represented the movement of physical, human, informational and managerial resources both into and out of the area.

From this data recorded on the flow maps the team were able to interpret and identify a number of prominent factors that appeared to be constraints on the transfer of irrigation management. Agricultural constraints included ownership or tenancy of land, outlets and markets for their crops, the ability of the farmers to diversify their crops, the availability of credit, their willingness and or the need to irrigate, and their perception of both agricultural and irrigation policies as promoted by Government. The social factors were centred on the issues of community spirit, presence of strong community leadership and the commitment to the locality and the rural lifestyle. Constraints and delays related to the management of irrigation included the system constraints which featured the design and construction of the system, the acquisition, allocation and distribution of water in terms of its source and availability, the operation of the system in terms of its simplicity or complexity and the present level of maintenance of the system. The financial factors were identified as issues concerning the amortisation of design and construction, the cost of acquisition, allocation and distribution, the cost of operation and maintenance, the water charges and taxation levels and the economic viability of cash crops. Thirdly the cultural and psychological constraints and delays were seen to include a climate of accountability, commitment (motivation), cooperation, entrepreneurship, self-control (autonomy as well as adherence to rules) and managing or organising abilities present in the community. Finally agreement needed to be reached concerning the communities ability to manage formal institutions such as WUAs. This included decision-making, resource mobilisation, communications and conflict resolution within and between organisations, the presence of technical, financial and managerial experts in the system and the acceptance of the allocation of roles and responsibilities.

2.4 The findings

The discussions of the team were summarized on a table. An example of a "resistance" profile developed from the data, where 1 represents weak resistance to the transfer and 5 indicates very strong constraints, is illustrated below.

The area summarized below is a municipality that is served by an 8 million cubic metre dam with a pumping station that lifts the water to two gravity systems. Although the systems are in reasonable state of repair no irrigation has been used in the area for the last three years. The community had developed a strong need for leadership over the years of collectivisation and when absent a vacuum has been created. The cash crop was oriental tobacco but some maize and vegetables were grown for local consumption. Farmers had not been paid for last year's tobacco crop and so production had dropped from 6,500 tonnes to 1,200 tonnes. Although alternative crops could be grown there has been a move towards more animal production as a result of the loss of the tobacco market. The overall response to the situation appears to be that a large number of families are emigrating to Turkey. In one settlement 40 families remain out of the original 400. Agriculture is supported by the income from employment outside the region, for employment opportunities within the region are negligible.

In the analysis of this system the constraints to the transfer of management do not lie with the availability, acquisition, allocation, operation and maintenance of the irrigation system but with the economic, marketing, agricultural, social and cultural factors present in the context. It was found that each site visited yielded a different "resistance" profile thus strongly supporting the context specificity view expressed at the Wuhan conference. The team concluded from the visit to the four sites that the delays and constraints are so large that it could not recommend the transfer of irrigation management. It was seen that there needed to be major changes in the state of agriculture, it's policies, markets and input prices, land ownership, and in the desire and need to irrigate before there will be any possibility of the formation of sustainable water user associations.

		5	4	3	2	1	
A1i	Ownership / tenancy					■	Land restitution
ii	Outlets / markets		■				Not paid for 1994 tobacco
iii	Ability to diversify			■			Move to potatoes / animals
iv	Availability of credit			■			Outside work / families
v	Willingness / need to irrigate		■				None for 3 years [0/20,000]
vi	Agricultural policy			■			
vii	Irrigation policy		■				GOB should support
A2i	Community spirit			■			By family
ii	Commitment to locality			■			Weak Emigration to Turkey
iii	Community leadership		■				Mayors fill vacuum
B1i	Design / construction					■	Gravity
ii	Source / availability of water					■	Benkvski reserv. 8million cub
iii	System simple / complex					■	Simple
iv	Present efficiency level					■	90% efficient
B2i	Amortisation		■				
ii	Cost of acqu. alloc and distr.		■				High price 2.95 lv
iii	Cost of O and M		■				High cost
iv	Fee / tax collection	■					
v	Crop economic viability		■				No viable replacement crop
B3i	Accountability		■				
ii	Commitment (motivation)			■			
iii	Co-operation		■				
iv	Entrepreneurship			■			Fixed on one crop
v	Autonomy				■		By family
vi	Rule adherence			■			By family/religion
vii	Organising culture			■			
B4i	Decision making			■			
ii	Resource mobilisation			■			
iii	Communications			■			
iv	Conflict management				■		By family
v	Expertise		■				
vi	Role / responsibility allocation		■				1 WUA / no general exp.

Fig. 2. The findings summarized in a "resistance" profile

The rising costs of farm inputs and a reduction in prices for outputs created a reluctance on the part of farmers to use their limited cash flow for these inputs including irrigation even when this is readily available.

The reasons for the reluctance of farmers to participate in IMT were identified as :- an expectation that the state will provide the water as they have in the past; a leadership vacuum (which is occasionally filled by a mayor, the chairman or official of a former co-operative or some other influential person); a deficit of organising or managing ability; a lack of motivation to form associations and communities (a carry over from the time of collective farming) and a general lack of commitment to the agricultural lifestyle and to the localities particularly by the young. It was recognised that some farmers are not only unwilling but also incapable, at this stage, of managing large, complex and technical systems.

2.5 The recommendations

The team recommended in it's final report that because of the many varying situations present within Bulgaria that a range of transfer models could be identified:-

* Type I No transfer - the status quo remains with full Government control through the ISC in which the farmer is required to pay (Nos 1 and 2 of Fig. 1)
* Type II Limited transfer - some localised management in isolated examples (No. 3 of Fig. 1.)
* Type III Partial transfer - Participatory management at local and higher levels (No 4 in Fig. 1)
* Type IV Shared transfer - Joint management (No 5 in Fig. 1.)
* Type V Full transfer - Privatised management by users or contractors (No 6 in Fig. 1) with the possibility in the distant future of privatised ownership (No 7 of Fig. 1.)

The transfer strategy selected would be dependent upon the strength of the constraints and the extent of the delays to the transfer process identified in any survey of a selected site. The survey team identified a possible progression through the different strategies. In the context of Bulgaria a possible scenario would be

i.   ISC maintains management (Type I transfer)
ii.   Provision of infrastructural support to encourage irrigated agriculture by providing a favourable agricultural policy favourable markets and pricing policy, improvements to the internal farm network and completed land restitution
iii. Increase in the use of water (May be some Type II Limited transfer)
iv.   Promotion of Water User Associations
v.   Formation of Water User Associations
vi.   Take over by farmers of the allocation, distribution, repairs and maintenance of the system (Types II and III Limited and Partial transfer)
vii. Joint-management of total system (Type IV Shared transfer)
viii. Full privatisation of the whole system (Type V Full transfer)

In the process of the survey the team encountered many informal groups of farmers who had set up their own organisations to use the water from rivers, wells and boreholes.   These groups were not involved in the transfer from the existing Government infrastructure.   Nevertheless the experience indicated that when the conditions were right the Bulgarian farmers were able and willing to run their own system.

3   The learning

Currently organisational theorists are exploring ways of developing flexible adaptive ways of organising work.   The case study identifies that in the process of the transfer of irrigation management consideration of the context, environment into which the transfer will occur is as, if not more, important than the urgency usually exhibited to transfer out of the public domain.   The variability that is indicated in the case requires that more attention be given to the variety of transfer strategies that may be available if a flexible adaptive approach is adopted.   The implementation of policies to transfer irrigation from the public to private sector cannot and should not, be rushed.   This exploration raises the hypothesis that in general political pressures tend to force water policies and strategies to hurry implementation processes to their long term detriment.

4   References

1.   Lewin, K. (1951) *Field Theory in Social Science,* Harper.
2.   Pretty, J.N.; Guijt, I.; Scoones, I. and Thompson, J. (1995) *A Trainers Guide for Participatory Learning and Action,* IIED, London
3.   Turral, H (1995) *Devolution of Management in Public Irrigation Systems: Cost shedding, empowerment and performance,* Overseas Development Institute, London.

SECTION 8

WATER USERS

KEY ISSUES IN IMPROVING PEOPLE'S HEALTH THROUGH WATER AND SANITATION

Water and sanitation for health

J. LANE
Water Aid, London, UK

Abstract
The paper raises a number of current issues concerning water, sanitation and health in order to stimulate debate. A brief overview of diseases transmitted through water and poor sanitation is followed by a discussion of the links between water, sanitation, and community health. The paper ends by mentioning some of the key issues that face us all.
Keywords: environmental sanitation, excreta disposal, health, water supply

1 Diseases associated with water and sanitation

In public health engineering, water-related diseases are categorised by their transmission mechanisms [1]. Transmission can occur both in the domestic (within the home) and public (water delivery systems) domains.

There are four mechanisms of transmission of water-related infectious diseases:

1. Water-borne: transmitted through drinking water containing pathogens. Water which is contaminated with human faecal waste carries the risk of direct ingestion of, for example cholera and typhoid bacteria. All water-borne diseases can also be transmitted by any means which allows faecal material to enter the mouth (the faecal-oral route).
2. Water-washed: diseases whose transmission will be reduced by use of greater quantities of water (almost regardless of quality) for personal hygiene. These include diarrhoeal diseases transmitted by a faecal-oral route (in the absence of good hygiene), bacterial and fungal skin and eye diseases, and lice- or mite-carried infections.

Water Policy: Allocation and management in practice. Edited by P. Howsam and R.C. Carter.
Published in 1996 by E & FN Spon. ISBN 0 419 21650 2

3. Water-based: worm infections in which the pathogen spends part of its life cycle in an aquatic host organism, and which are contracted by physical contact with, or ingestion of, contaminated water. Examples include schistosomiasis, in which the intermediate host snail produces skin-penetrating cercariae; and guinea worm, in which the pathogen is passed on by ingestion of an infected water flea.
4. Water-related insect vector: transmitted by insects that breed or bite near water. These include malaria. Water projects can contribute to the spread of these diseases by increasing the favourable living conditions for the insects.

Diseases associated with poor excreta disposal may be transmitted by faecal-oral routes (eg. various intestinal viruses, bacteria, and protozoa, which cause diarrhoeas, as well as the more life-threatening cholera and typhoid), by ingestion or skin penetration via the soil (roundworm and hookworm), through eating contaminated meat (beef and pork tapeworms), and via water-based and insect vector routes (schistosomiasis and filariasis respectively).

Water-related and excreta-related disease categories overlap to a significant extent, but these classifications are both helpful to engineers who are trying to understand the causes of disease transmission, and so match their interventions to the existing public health situation.

Flies which breed in rubbish heaps and unprotected latrine sites also spread infectious diseases. A separate group of diseases (including plague and typhus) is transmitted by insects such as rats' fleas. Rats flourish in places with poor environmental sanitation.

Non-infectious diseases may also be caused by contaminants entering drinking water. Some contaminants occur naturally, such as arsenic and fluoride, while others such as nitrates and pesticides enter water from agricultural and industrial activities.

2   Reducing the risk of diseases related to water and sanitation

If we understand how a particular disease is transmitted, we can design specific measures to reduce or prevent it. Intervention can focus on:-

1. Interrupting the life cycle of pathogens. For example, guinea worm is prevented by stopping the consumer entering the water supply or by treating the water supply (eg. by filtration) to remove the infected intermediate host water flea.
2. Promoting safer hygiene behaviour practices to control faecal-oral infections.
3. Reducing the levels of chemical contaminants in water, by ensuring that industrial and agricultural waste does not enter into the drinking water system.

3   Impact of water and sanitation of community health

The impact of water-related diseases on the health of poor communities extends far beyond the medical effects of individual diseases. Water and sanitation have complex links with health, nutrition and poverty.

Drinking dirty water can make people of any age sick, but is particularly serious for bottle-fed babies. Contaminated water used to make powdered milk causes diarrhoea and vomiting. The loss of body fluids quickly leads to dehydration, one of the main causes of infant death in developing countries. Babies are often bottle-fed because of their mothers' heavy workload outside the home, which includes the time spent fetching water. High infant mortality rates are responsible for frequent pregnancies which have serious consequences both for women's health and for the health of other children.

Shortage of water is a major threat to community health. Water use in developing countries can be as low as 5-10 litres per person per day. This amount is just enough for drinking and cooking with little to spare for personal bathing or washing clothes and utensils. Recent studies have shown that poor personal and domestic hygiene from lack of water cause more sickness than dirty drinking water. Frequent infections are particularly dangerous for babies and infants who easily fall into the malnutrition - infection trap. Shortages of water also affect nutritional status by reducing the amount of food families can grow.

The labour involved in collecting water for domestic use is an enormous physical burden. This is mainly borne by women and children, who often have little access to beasts of burden or forms of transport. Carrying heavy loads of water over long distances causes chronic backache, joint pains and physical exhaustion. In extreme cases, deformities of the spine and pelvis occur.

The time involved in collecting water also has serious health implications. For children, it reduces their time for play, increasingly recognised as essential for healthy development. School attendance can also suffer, especially among girls, thus protracting the cycle of women's low literacy which in turn affects child survival rates.

There is a well documented link between poverty and poor health. Improving water and sanitation helps break this link in a number of significant ways:-
1. A water supply can provide a source of income through activities such as making and selling beverages, laundry work, growing vegetables and making bricks.
2. Less sickness amongst adults means more days spent in productive work.
3. Less sickness amongst children, and less energy expended collecting water, gives women more time for themselves and for agriculture for self-sufficiency and income-generating activities.
4. A cleaner environment promotes healthier living and awareness of the importance of hygiene practices which enhance the quality of life of women and men.

4 Key issues facing us now

Theses are some of the issues relating to water and health, intended to promote thought and debate. I do not claim that there are right and wrong answers to these questions.

4.1 Managing water supply
- How are we allocating water between the conflicting demands of the agricultural, industrial and domestic sectors? Do we appreciate the health consequences of our

failures to safeguard domestic supplies?

- In planning irrigation projects, do we incorporate health measures (such as controlling the habitat of insects) from the very beginning? Do we counter schistosomiasis by the full range of measures, or just to one or two of them? Do irrigation planners consult public health specialists to establish the epidemiology of diseases associated with planned projects?
- Do we monitor contaminants entering the drinking water supply, either directly from waste discharge or indirectly from aquifer intrusions? Are we doing enough to explain these problems to politicians?

4.2 Water and sanitation delivery

- Do we plan our public health work to cover both the public and domestic domains? How do we influence householders to carry out improvements within their domestic domain? Are we responsive to gender roles in the households we work with?
- Do we consult the users and beneficiaries of our projects? How do we know that our plans concerning safe water supply and sanitation correspond to their needs and wishes? Are the services we offer sustainable and relevant? Can they be replicated by other communities?
- Who are the best service providers for water, sanitation and health? What factors influence the choice of Governments, NGOs or private sector companies as the best organisations to provide these services?

4.3 Sanitation and health

- Do we look at sanitation as a marketing exercise, or a technological issue? Given the general failure of subsidy as an incentive, are we getting our messages through to motivate people to want latrines? Do we appreciate how long the process of behaviour change can take - usually much longer than water supply construction?
- Are we addressing the technological problems of developing low cost urban sanitation?

4.4 Hygiene promotion

- Does our fieldwork actually reflect our understanding that health is improved by the combination of sanitation and hygiene education with water supply? Or do we continue to concentrate on water supply alone?
- Have we acknowledged that didactic hygiene education is less effective than participatory, experiential learning? Do we build on people's existing beliefs and knowledge? How can we encourage people to spread hygiene education messages to each other?

5   References

1.   Cairncross, S. and Feachem, R.G. (1983) Environmental Health Engineering in the Tropics. John Wiley and Sons.

IMPROVING WATER DISTRIBUTION AND MANAGEMENT IN COMMUNITY SUPPLY SYSTEMS
Improving water distribution and management

E. QUIROGA, G. GALVIS, C.J. GARAVITO, E. PINTO
CINARA, Centro Inter-Regional de Abastecimiento y
Remoción de Agua,Universidad del Valle,
Facultad de Ingeniería, Cali, Colombia
J. T. VISSCHER
IRC, International Water and Sanitation Centre,
The Hague, The Netherlands

Abstract
This paper discusses main water distribution and water utilisation problems in community managed water supply schemes in Colombia and Ecuador. Distribution networks represent a considerable part of the investment cost of water supply systems but often receive little attention giving cause to many conflicts between users and low willingness to pay. The problems include high leakage, uneven distribution and high wastage. These problems have been addressed in different inter-institutional and interdisciplinary 'learning' projects in which institutions and individual communities joined forces in problem identification and solving. Together they were able to identify the underlying causes including design limitations, poor quality materials, uncontrolled extension of distribution networks, poor water use control, insufficient relation between payment and water use and perhaps most important poor understanding of these causes at the local level. Together they were able to capitalise on the better understanding of the problems and could lower water consumption and improve water distribution through the introduction of flow restrictors, water meters and through social pressure to repair taps in the households. The results clearly demonstrate the importance of participatory institutional support and validate the systematic approach which has been followed in the projects. This has a great potential to improve water distribution and reduce water loss in existing schemes which in turn has great impact on the production and treatment cost.
Keywords: community management, Latin America, participatory approach, water resources, water supply.

Water Policy: Allocation and management in practice. Edited by P. Howsam and R.C. Carter.
Published in 1996 by E & FN Spon. ISBN 0 419 21650 2

1   Introduction

The lessons learned in the International Water Supply and Sanitation Decade have shown that a water supply service can only be maintained with a minimum of external support if it satisfies the expectations of the users. These expectations concern major issues including good coverage, sufficient quantity, continuity of supply, acceptable quality and cost.   Other crucial factors for system sustainability are management requirements and the water culture in the community.   Many systems have been constructed which do not satisfy these requirements providing intermittent water supply with long service interruptions, thus putting in jeopardy the high investments and efforts made in their development.

In Colombia the theoretical water supply coverage is 76.4 per cent [1], but in reality only part of the water supply system provide good quality water on a continuous basis.   In the majority of Colombia's 1000 small municipalities, with less than 10,000 population representing 95 per cent of all municipalities, water supply is only provided for six or less hours per day [2].   This is also the case for part of the larger municipalities and departmental centres, implying a continuous rationing of the service. In the Department of Tolima, for example, in the municipality of Chaparral with a 20,000 population, almost 50 per cent of the community receive eight hours of water supply on three days of the week, a situation which does not even meet prevailing water quality norms [3].   In Ecuador 522 out of 941 systems were classified as providing a discontinuous service [4]. A recent participatory evaluation of 40 systems in eight provinces confirmed these data as users complained about the discontinuity of the service in 55 per cent of the systems [5].

Most of the systems in the communities in both countries have been established by Government institutions often with involvement of the users in their construction. Water supply construction has also been a popular item for politicians, but management of established facilities is mostly neglected.   In Colombia between 1970 and 1985, some 55 per cent of the strikes resulted from civil protests over lack of adequate water supply [6].   The poor functioning of water supply schemes is now starting to backfire as people no longer trust the politicians and the Government institutions as too many systems do not perform adequately.

2   Important causes of water supply problems

The cause of water quantity, quality and continuity problems include:

- The deterioration of micro-catchments as a result of deforestation, inadequate land management, detrimental agricultural practices and poor disposal of liquid and solid waste.   The problems are aggravated by the absence of a policy which stimulates the conservation of catchment areas with active participation of the communities concerned.   It is estimated that 600,000 hectares of forest is removed annually in Colombia and only 4 per cent of the municipalities have waste water treatment facilities [7].   In Ecuador it is estimated that 40 per cent of the surface area of the country is being affected by active or passive erosion processes, which have a negative influence on water availability [8].

• The poor quality of transport mains and distribution networks, which may represent some 70 per cent of the total cost of the water supply system. This results from inadequate design and construction of the systems and their unplanned extension. Pipes are over or under designed, do not include pressure break boxes or pressure or flow control valves, are poorly located and of poor quality material. This results in pipe ruptures and high water consumption in the lower areas with higher water pressure, whereas in the high areas of the network water does not reach the consumers because of the low pressure. In a recent evaluation in Ecuador low pressure zones were very common in 75 per cent of the 40 communities involved in the review, and in five communities interruptions occurred on average on more than five days per month [4]. After initial construction of the systems, new house connections are being made without analysis, advice or technical support resulting in poor water distribution. In the water supply system of El Tambo municipality in Colombia with 3600 inhabitants, the raw water supply has been almost entirely interrupted because of over 100 poorly constructed illegal connections to the transport main [9]. Pipelines are also deteriorating because of insufficient maintenance and poor repairs, resulting in a major water loss which in Colombia on average is over 50 per cent [1]. In a recent evaluation of 40 systems in Ecuador water loss ranged between 0 and 81 per cent with an average of 44 per cent in systems transporting on average 195 lpcd (50 - 600 lpcd) [4].

• Inefficient water use and water wastage, leading to high consumption levels, often well over prevailing design norms. In the south of Ecuador supply levels were found of 224 to 980 lpcd [10]. It appears however that these figures includes leakages in the distribution network because a recent evaluation in the same country found consumption levels in 16 communities with metered systems between 32 and 296 lpcd with an average of 80 lpcd. In Colombia supply levels often are higher than the norm which ranges between 120 and 230 lpcd [11].

3   A problem solving approach

The problems indicated above have been identified in Colombia in different learning projects established with support form CINARA and IRC. These projects promote the approach that communities are the owners of their own development. Partnership between agencies and communities is then required, to jointly establish programmes in which the communities become responsible for decision making and actively participate in programme implementation. This is stimulated by an approach which enables the community to jointly identify and clarify problems. This helps them to find adequate solutions together with the agencies involved. The learning project approach which is being followed comprises the following phases:

• An inventory of organisations intervening in water related issues in the community concerned and collection and review of information they have available about the community;

• A participatory evaluation together with community members to identify the water related problems. This includes the use of different participatory techniques such as mapping, household surveys, interviews and sanitary inspections. This evaluation enables the community to recover constructive water culture and habits, a renewed appreciation of their role in water supply management and identification of the problems in the existing infrastructure. This phase is the start of the discussion with the community about the problems they have with their water supply.

- Priority setting and clarification of the improvements to be established and the responsibilities and technical and financial commitments involved both for the community and the agencies. This is completed with the development of the design which is asserted with the community.
- Organisation of the construction or improvements to be made, which includes the establishment of a community monitoring committee. This committee reviews the progress of the works and the utilisation of materials and equipment. In this phase community members are also trained in management and maintenance of the facilities.
- Putting the system to work and completion of the training. This includes also the organisation of water surveillance and control and management of the catchment area.

4   Promising examples

The methodology and particularly the participatory evaluation of the water supply system has made it possible to improve the supply service in terms of continuity and distribution and to reduce water wastage through community action. Support elements which have been used include the installation of flow restrictors designed by CINARA, installation of water meters and social pressure to ensure repair of leaking taps and sanitary facilities in the households. The following examples may serve as an illustration.

4.1 The case of Inzá

In the municipality of Inzá with 2100 population, situated in the indigenous zone of the Cauca Department in the south of Colombia a strong influx of refugees occurred after a natural disaster in the area. To supply water to the community and the refugees, the water system was forced to provide 14 l/s by-passing the water treatment.

The community then received only 6 hours of water per day on average and the high parts only received water during the night when some valves in the lower parts were closed. CINARA with financial support from UNICEF developed an emergency project to improve the water supply system, which included the installation of 9 flow restrictors in the distribution system. This reduced water loss enormously bringing the demand down to 7 l/s allowing all water to be treated again and being distributed with a 24 hours service to all households in the communities [12].

4.2 The case of San Felipe

In the rural community San Felipe in the Department of Tolima in the central zone of Colombia, with 700 population, the water supply was improved by including treatment through multi-stage filtration, a combination of gravel roughing filtration and slow sand filtration. Initially the project was supported by the British Red Cross through the Centre for Environmental Health Engineering, University of Surrey, and thereafter by the Government of The Netherlands through IRC and the Colombian Ministry of Health through CINARA as part of a technology transfer project. Once the system was in place using the existing distribution network, water demand was well in excess of the treatment plant design which was based on a supply of 200 lpcd. An inspection of the distribution network with the water committee, showed that over 90 per cent of the users had leaking taps, pipes and sanitary facilities. To solve the problem the community assembled in a meeting and decided on their own initiative to establish a period of some weeks, within which all users should repair the defects that had been identified and purchase water meters. These meters were installed in January 1992 with technical assistance of the Departmental Health Secretariat. A five months period followed of meter reading, without tariff implications. This showed that Consumption levels in many households surpassed 350 lpcd and in some cases even reached up to over 1000 lpcd. With these data the water committee with agreement of the community has established new tariffs, which favoured a basic service level of less than 40 m^3 per household per month and discouraged higher consumption through incremental tariffs. This approach helped to bring down the average consumption of 90 per cent of the users to 200 lpcd (range 60 - 500 lpcd). On average 70 users (61 per cent of the total), used less than 40 m^3 per month (Fig. 1) but their total share in water consumption is only 25 per cent.

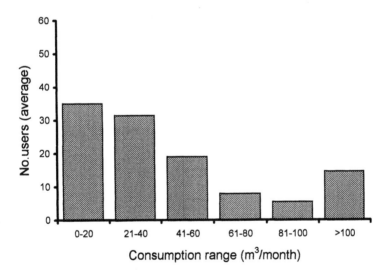

Fig. 1. Distribution of consumers according to consumption level in San Felipe [13].

The high water consumers, with consumption over 81 m^3 per month representing 10 per cent of the users consumed 50 per cent of the total water supply. (Fig. 2).

These large users included a small hotel and some cattle, chicken and dairy farms.

The smaller users maintained their service level after the installation of the meters and the consumers with lowest consumption levels, below 20 m^3 per month even somewhat increased consumption. The users with high consumption however initially reduced consumption as a result of the incremental tariffs. Gradually this effect was somewhat reduced as tariffs have not been raised since 1992 and consumption increased again, but not to the initial level. The theoretical coverage of the system was 98 per cent, but in practice because of discontinuous supply only 60 per cent of the users obtained the service. After meter installation true coverage reached 98 per cent. A very important point was that users because of their involvement in decision making accepted a 600 per cent increase in the basic tariff from US$ 0.25 to US$ 1.50 per month. Tariff collection now generates a monthly surplus of US$ 50, which enables the water committee to finance repairs of the system [13].

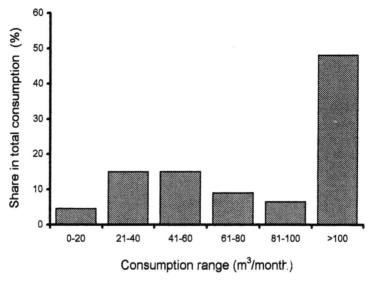

Fig. 2. Share of total consumption for users in different consumption ranges in San Felipe [13].

4.3 The case of El Hormiguero

In El Hormiguero, a small low income urban community of 2360 population in the suburbs of Cali, the second city in Colombia, CINARA in collaboration with the Municipal Public Service (EMCALI) and ten other organisations have developed a joint learning project focused on the improvement of the community water supply system, which received ground water from a well in the community with a high iron and manganese content. In the participatory review of the situation problems were identified related to the continuity and quality of the service, the quality of the distribution system, the poor conditions of taps and sanitary facilities and the high water wastage. The community reviewed and discussed alternative water supply solutions including: surface water supply from the highly polluted nearby Cauca river which was initially preferred, water supply from the Pance river which is ten kilometres away from the community or groundwater. On the basis of a review of cost involved and management and maintenance requirements the community after field visits to other communities with similar systems ultimately adopted the drilling of a new well as most feasible option. It was also decided to improve the distribution network and the in-house installations. Financial support was obtained from the Health Secretariat and Plan International. The community established three committees. A monitoring committee to keep track of work progress being in line with contractual obligations; a purchase committee which received or bought materials after asking quotations; a work organising committee which planned the work inputs from the community and organised it through identified sector leaders who distributed the work in their sector of the community. With CINARAs' support a training and orientation programme was established for inspection and repairs of in-house installations. Local plumbers particularly helped women to learn how to repair taps and toilets, which very much reduced wastage.

With construction work being completed, the community has just elected a new water committee and in a user meeting it was decided to install water meters and to establish a new tariff. This new tariff will be between US$ 2 and 3 per month and will cover the cost of operation and maintenance and the salary of a full time operator, but not the investment cost of the system. The old tariff be it for a detrimental service was only US$ 0.25 per month.

5   Conclusions

In the communities indicated above and several others in Colombia good progress has been made with increased efficiency of water. A participatory approach in which the community works together with the agencies on an equal footing, has proven very effective in bringing about the required changes. Helping communities to identify problems and making them visible for all parties concerned is what seems to be the root of problem solving. It is also encouraging to note that people are very willing to accept an increase in water tariffs, provided tariff development is transparent and good service is being provided. It is crucial as Culp and Smith (1992) stress [14] also that users need to be satisfied with the service and they should perceive the water quality as satisfying their needs and matching their reality. This implies developing a common understanding between agencies and communities for which learning projects provide excellent opportunities. In this way sustainable water supply systems can be developed which only require a minimum of external support. This enables the community to take things in hand and manage their own water supply and their own development. This has helped them to identify and solve problems amongst themselves and has enabled leadership to build on the socio-cultural history of the community concerned.

The results clearly demonstrate the importance of participatory institutional support and validate a systematic approach to problem analysis and solving primarily by the community with support from the agencies. This approach has a great potential to improve water distribution and reduce water loss in existing schemes which in turn has great impact on the production and treatment cost of water supplies.

6   References

1. Departamento Nacional de Planeación de la República de Colombia (1995). *Plan de Agua 1995-1998*. Documento CONPES 2767. Santafé de Bogotá, Colombia, Ministerio de Desarrollo Económico-DNP:UPRU.
2. ACODAL (1995). Discurso de apertura del XXXVIII congreso de la asociación colombiana de ingeniería sanitaria y ambiental, in *Revista Acodal*, No. 166, pp. 7-11, Santafé de Bogotá, Colombia, ACODAL.
3. Quiroga, R.E., Espinoza, A. (1995). Conservar los recursos hídricos, una tarea inaplazable, in: *Agua y Vida*, bimonthly journal no. 2, January-February 1995, pp. 4-5, Cali, Colombia, CINARA.
4. OPS/OMS (1994). *Plan regional de inversiones en ambiente y salud*. Análisis del sector de agua potable y saneamiento en Ecuador. (Serie Análisis Sectoriales; No. 1.) Washington, D.C., U.S.A., Organización Panamericana de la Salud/Organización Mundial de la Salud.
5. Visscher, J.T., et al. (1995). *Evaluación post-proyectos de agua y saneamiento en la república del Ecuador*. Informe final (Convenio CARE-ETAPA-SSA-IRC-CINARA), Cali, Colombia, CINARA.
6. CINARA/IDRC (1990). *Evaluación de sistemas de abastecimiento de agua con plantas de tratamiento administradas por comunidades*. Informe Final. Cali, Colombia, CINARA.
7. Quiroga, R.E. et al. (1995b). *Diagnóstico del sistema de abastecimiento de agua del municipio de Chaparral (Tolima)*. Informe de visita. Cali, Colombia, CINARA.
8. CARE-Ecuador (1994). *Planificación estratégica a largo plazo*. Quito, Ecuador. CARE-Ecuador.
9. CINARA/IRC (1995). *Informe de progreso del programa de transferencia de tecnología en abastecimiento de agua en Colombia (TRANSCOL)*. Cali, Colombia, CINARA.
10. Ordóñez, E.G. (1992). *Cooperación andina en tecnología apropiada de desinfección y análisis del agua para consumo humano*. Cuenca, Ecuador. Universidad de Cuenca.
11. FINDETER (1991). *Acueductos, plantas potabilizadoras y alcantarillados. Criterios y pautas generales para su diseño y evaluación técnica*. Santafé de Bogotá, Colombia, Financiera de Desarrollo Territorial, S.A.
12. Castilla, A. (1995). Reductores de presión en redes de distribución de agua, in *Revista Gaceta Ambiental* No. 10, pp. 5-7. Cali, Colombia. ACODAL.
13. Quiroga, R.E. (1994). *A successful water treatment rehabilitation project arising from diagnostic surveillance*. M.Sc. Thesis. Guildford, United Kingdom, University of Surrey, Department of Civil Engineering.
14. Culp, G., Smith, A. (1992). Applying total quality management, satisfying your customer's needs, in *Water Environment & Technology*, July 1992, pp. 42-46, Washington, D.C., USA, Water Pollution Control Federation.

A CHILD'S RIGHT TO WATER: THE CASE OF METERING
Children's rights and water metering

C.J. CUNINGHAME and S.K. LAWS
Save the Children Fund, London, UK.

Abstract
The right of access to water is specified in the 1989 UN Convention on the Rights of the Child. Research into the impact of water metering on low-income families in the UK shows that many families make economies which may endanger their children's health. It is proposed that a principle for policy on water charging should be that water for basic human needs should be available and affordable for all families.
Keywords: children's health, children's rights, low-income families, poverty, water charging, water policy, water metering.

1 Introduction

An adequate supply of clean water is essential to children's health. The right of access to water is specified in the 1989 United Nations Convention on the Rights of the Child, ratified by the UK Government in 1991. Access to clean water has also been a cornerstone of the UK's public health policy since the mid-nineteenth century [1].

The Save the Children Fund has long been active in work to assure access to a clean water supply for children in many countries overseas. Since the privatisation of the water industry for England and Wales in 1989, there has been increasing concern about access to water in these countries for families on low incomes. In response to this, Save the Children's UK and European Programmes Department set up a programme of research. The study described in the report *Water tight: the impact of water metering on low-income families* [2] draws attention to the social reality of water metering for children in low income families.

At present, only seven per cent of households in England and Wales have water meters. However, the Government, the water regulator OFWAT (Office of Water

Water Policy: Allocation and management in practice. Edited by P. Howsam and R.C. Carter.
Published in 1996 by E & FN Spon. ISBN 0 419 21650 2

Services) and some water companies want to see metering introduced much more widely, to replace the system of charging on the basis of rateable values. Save the Children's study was designed to examine some of the likely consequences if water metering were introduced more widely.

2   The Study

The research was primarily qualitative in nature, seeking to find out to what extent families changed their behaviour when their water was charged for on a metered basis. We asked for parents' own views and also looked at their latest bills. Seventy-one low income families living on two newly-built estates in the outer London area were interviewed. There were 147 children living in these households, 63 per cent of them under five years old. The sample was not randomly chosen, nor is it representative of all households with water meters. Instead it was designed to yield information specifically on families with children living in social housing, on relatively low incomes, who have water meters.

3   Key findings

Fifty families, 70 per cent of the sample, were taking measures to reduce their use of water.

- Common measures included sharing baths, taking fewer baths or showers, washing clothes less often, flushing the toilet less often and preventing children from playing with water.
- Other families either could not or would not save water - many cited the needs of their children as the reason they could not economise effectively.
- Twenty (44 per cent) of the bills we saw (not all the respondents let us see their water bill) showed arrears. Many families were in difficulty in paying their arrears. One family was paying weekly instalments of #30.
- With average weekly incomes of #100-#125, families would have to spend an average of about 4 per cent of their weekly budget to pay for their water. This compares with a national average of about 1 per cent. For those with arrears to pay, this figure would be higher still.
- Meters were felt to be difficult to read: only six (eight per cent) respondents had in fact read their meter.
- Only 20 per cent of respondents were satisfied with metering as a method of charging.

Detailed findings, including more on the respondents' own views on water charging, can be found in the full research report.

These families' behaviour is economically rational: they are cutting down in the areas where they use most water. Yet measures taken include a number that are very likely to have a negative impact on children's health.

Our data confirms previous findings [3] of very high levels of debt, and consequent anxiety, among low income families.

It is important to distinguish between two distinct types of problem:
- those arising from the high price of water itself;
- those arising from metering.

Some of the problems faced by the families in our sample - high arrears, high repayment levels, experience of summonses and disconnection - are shared with those on low incomes who are charged on the basis of rateable value. However, metering adds another dimension. In addition to pressure on the household budget, there is the pressure to cut back on the use of water.

Although metering seems fair - you pay for what you use - the pressure placed on consumers to economise on water does not fall equally on all in society. Those on low incomes are put under far greater pressure. The families in our sample were spending a proportion of their income on water four times greater than the national average. Metering also means that those with more children pay more for water - and respondents reported that the presence of young children made it particularly difficult to cut down on water use.

4   Policy and practice

Our findings in this research echo conclusions drawn by those concerned with SCF's work on water supply in Africa, Asia and Latin America. In areas where the chief health problems are related to poor water quality and lack of easy access to a supply, Save the Children finds that metering water is likely to have an immediate, deleterious effect on children's health. To improve supplies in such areas and then restrict access to low-income families would be self-defeating.

Why does metering matter in the UK? The fact that families on low incomes would suffer if water metering were brought in more widely has been recognised for some time [4]. However, they have been seen as a minority whose interests may not coincide with the majority. Yet four million children in Britain are growing up in poverty - almost a third of all children [5]. Increasingly, poverty is concentrated in households with children [6].

As a society, for the past 150 years in the UK, we have made a priority of access to clean water for all our citizens [7]. Historically, it has been seen as unacceptable for families not to be able to afford water. Has this suddenly changed? Do we now feel that it is acceptable for low-income families to be placed under such pressure to economise on water? It is notable that the National Rivers Authority (now part of the new Environment Agency) has recently acknowledged the need to safeguard low-income families where metering is introduced [8].

5   Principles for water policy

In Save the Children's view, water policy should accord with principles of equality of access to services and welfare, rather than following the principle of 'ability to pay'. Both metering and the implementation of cost recovery schemes (to recoup capital expenditure) may restrict access to water and engender greater disparities in community welfare.

Save the Children recommends that the following principles be taken as key reference points in developing policy on charging for water:

* Water for basic human needs should be available and affordable for all families.

* The impact on children in low-income families should be taken into account in deciding on methods of charging for water.

6   References

1. Frazer, W.M. (1950) *A history of the English public health 1834-1939*, Balliere, Tindall and Cox, London.
2. Cuninghame, C., Laws, S., and Griffin, J. (1996) *Water tight: the impact of water metering on low-income families*, Save the Children Fund, London.
3. Herbert, A and Kempson, E. (1995) *Water debt and disconnection*, Policy Studies Institute, London.
4. McNeish, D. (1993) *Liquid Gold: the cost of water in the '90s*, Barnardos, Barkingside.
5. National Metering Trials Working Group (1993)   *National Metering Trials Working Group final report: summary*, Water Services Association et al, Sheffield.
6. NCH Action for Children (1995) *Factfile '95*, NCH Action for Children, London.
7. Department of Social Security (1995) *Households below average income, 1979-1992/3*, Department of Social Security, London.
8. Frazer, W. M., (1950), *op cit.*
9. National Rivers Authority (1995)   *Saving water: the NRA's approach to water conservation and demand management*, NRA, London.

CLOSING A WATER RESOURCE: SOME POLICY CONSIDERATIONS
Closing a water resource

B. & L. CHATTERTON
Podere valle Pulcini, Castel di Fiori, Montegabbione, Italy

Abstract
The problems facing water users and national level agencies when the volumes of water available are insufficient to meet demand are discussed from the point of view of policy making and policy implementation. The term the 'closure of a water resource' is coined to capture the concepts which have to be addressed in the policy debate and at implementation. The term is also helpful in communicating to those involved in the political and technical process of 'closure' that its achievement requires a number of phases, namely discourse, policy formation, implementation and follow-up. The importance of gaining wide agreement on the part of those involved in the 'water closure' process on principles relating to water rights is also emphasised. A range of types of water right are identified. The discussion is based on Australian experience; the approach is presented as being of general relevance especially to economies in semi-arid and arid regions such as the Middle East and North Africa currently facing difficulties in meeting the water demands of their agricultural sectors.
Keywords: 'closure', politics, water allocation, water pricing, water rights.

1   The period of policy debate

Most water resources in semi-arid and arid regions such as north Africa and the Middle East are still open. That is it is still possible to extend the area under irrigation or have water supplied for other uses. However, in many cases the limited of supply have been reached or will be soon and there will be a need to close the resource. In most countries there is a period of debate as the upper limits of supply are being reached. During this period various groups within the Government bureaucracy, the political leadership and the community will debate whether the

Water Policy: Allocation and management in practice. Edited by P. Howsam and R.C. Carter.
Published in 1996 by E & FN Spon. ISBN 0 419 21650 2

resource should be closed or whether even greater efforts should be made to expand the supply.

During this period there will be an even greater expansion of demand as more and more farmers or speculators try to establish some rights to water. They will do this because they realise (probably instinctively) that water rights will have some value and they should get in while they are still available. Obviously the longer the debate continues the greater will be the expansion but the alternative of keeping the debate secret and within the Government is unfair and inevitably some people will find out and make huge profits while the average farmer will not.

A better approach is to declare a 'date' from which the debate starts and use this date to establish two levels of water rights. Water rights will be determined in the future as a result of the debate but the opening date will warn people that whatever the outcome those established before the 'date' will be treated differently to those established after the 'date'.

There are many factors influencing the patterns of increasing water consumption but the leap in consumption in South Australia (Fig. 1) between 1965 and 1975 covered the period of transition to a closed resource. From our own experience in the political debate in South Australia it would have been better to declare a 'date' in 1965 from which the debate on water allocation started and to have used this date to establish two types of water rights.

The leap in consumption in Jordan in the period since 1990 (Fig. 2) has also in a sense been due to a scramble to obtain water rights similar to those which occurred in South Australia between 1965 and 1975. Jordan has increased its water consumption by pumping the shared Disi aquifer which lies across its southern international border with Saudi Arabia. Jordan will need to use this water ultimately for metropolitan Amman. In the 1990s, however, in order to establish its 'rights' over the groundwater Jordan has been developing wells from which water has been pumped to irrigated crop production. Such water rights may not be sustainable in the long term but they are significant to establish negotiating positions.

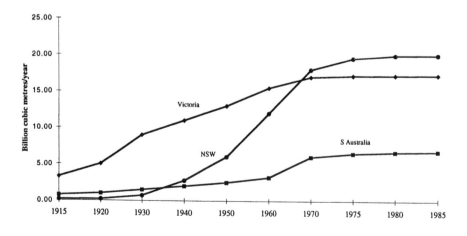

Fig. 1. Trends in state requirements from the Murray River

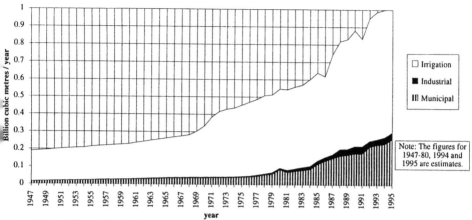

Source: Ministry of Water and Irrigation, Amman, Jordan, 1995, and author's annotation (JAA).

Fig. 2. Jordan's water consumption by sector: 1947-95

1.1 Allocating the water

It is most important not to allocate all the water that is available. It is impossible to determine in advance the number of people and the amount of water they will claim no mater how refined the statistics so it is better to allocate only a certain %age and keep some as a reserve against appeals. There are many who will appeal and there are always some genuine hard cases that should receive water. If all the water has been allocated this can only be done by removing existing allocation which will create huge political problems. If there is already a reserve it can be used. If not all the reserve is used it can be shared out as a 'bonus' to those holding water rights.

1.2 Pricing the water

Most water is under-sold. This adds to the profits of the farmer. If the farmer is able to obtain water at a much lower price than its value to him the profits of the farm will increase. The price of the water remains low because it is still an open resource. Another farmer can obtain the same cheap water and does not need to pay a high price. Once the resource is closed and the rights are distributed the water will become valuable but the increase in price will go to the holder of the water right not to the water supplier.

The value of the water right will reflect a capitalised value for the 'excess profit' that can be produced from the water. At first this is only a notional value but very quickly some of the farmers, particularly the late entrants who were really speculators, will sell these water rights and new entrant will pay cash for them. This will create huge political problems for the Government because if they wish to increase the price of water the capitalised value of the water right will fall. As long as the capital value is notional there will be little sympathy in the community but once real money has been paid the Government will be accused of destroying the farmers' capital.

The lesson to be learnt is that pricing policy must be introduced at the same time as closure or at the very least quickly afterwards. If this is not done and water rights become valuable and cash has been paid the Government may be forced to pay some form of compensation.

Government may believe that they own the water either as 'the state' or in a more indeterminate way as 'the nation' or 'the people' but this is a legal fiction as long as farmers have permanent 'tenure' of the water. If farmers have secure rights and are able to buy, sell, lease and inherit water rights they have effective ownership.

1.3 Is it possible to prevent water rights acquiring a value?

In theory it is possible to stop water rights acquiring a value by preventing farmers from acquiring security. For example water could be allocated annually by tender or on some other sort of term basis but in practical terms this is not a feasible scenario. Politically it would create huge opposition and economically it would deter long term investment. The practical reality is that farmers will have secure water rights and that they will acquire value.

2   Types of water rights

Water rights can be tied to the land, or to the farmer or can be a separate traded right.

During the debate there will be many people who will argue for water to be tied to the land or to the farmer and one of their strongest arguments will be that trading in water is wrong and putting a value on the water right is undesirable. There is a great deal of validity in this argument. It is unfair that a single generation of farmers who happened to be owners of irrigated land should receive a capital bonus. The previous generation received nothing because the resource was open and the next generation will receive little or nothing because they must first pay the present generation. Their capital bonus will only come if the value of the water rights rises faster than inflation. The practical situation is that it is unstoppable. One can set up a regulatory regime that will stop it being 'openly' traded but it will happen in an underground way which will work to the disadvantage of many farmers and the Government.

2.1 Advantages of traded water rights

The greatest benefit of traded water rights is to the inefficient farmer. This does not mean the small farmer necessarily but any farmer who is making low profits from his enterprise. He or she is able to sell their water rights and make a profit which may be greater than his current net income. If the rights are tied to the land he or she is forced to sell the land and probably their house and the new owner will then use some subterfuge to transfer the water to where the need is. If the rights are traded the farmer can simply sell them, stay in his house, perhaps use the land for something else or find some other occupation.

Another advantage for traded rights is that it will give the Government an indication of the value farmers themselves put on water and thus help to establish a price for water. The value will be arrived at in negotiations between farmers. The efficient farmer will pay to have more water and will make a profit while the inefficient will sell water and also make a profit from the transaction. The water right sale can be on an annual basis which reflects the price of this transaction, or more likely on a permanent basis which reflects the capitalised value of these annual sales. Government should be wary of using these prices in establishing a notional price for water for national accounting and other purposes. Most farmers are not as efficient as those making the purchases and to impose the marginal price of the most efficient on the whole community could prove disastrous. If some %age can be arrived at through negotiations with farmers at the early stage of introduction of traded rights, then further increases in the price of water will be as a result of farmers' own sales. High prices will dampen capital values and the system will be self adjusting to some degree. It should be a policy aim to avoid high capital values as they provide a huge bonus to one generation and an unfair burden on the next. High prices for water will reduce capital values for water rights.

2.2 Limits to trading in water
Obviously there are technical limits. One cannot trade water that cannot be supplied to the new owner. There may also be a need to provide some limits on the accumulation of water rights for social reasons if it is felt that too many small farmers are selling up and this is creating social problems, but one must treat such social issues with great caution. While it may seem desirable for the sake of social stability to reduce or prevent the drift of small farmers from the land one must balance this against the rights of the individual who, having made this decision, is entitled to the best possible price for their assets so they can start a new life or enterprise.

3   Other pricing issues

It seems that the debate over water prices is still at the stage of charging for distribution and storage. Essentially the price being considered is some form of 'cost of production' plus perhaps a profit margin or return on investment of some sort. Of course there is considerable debate about 'the plus' particularly if the water distribution has been privatised. There is also a need within this system of pricing to provide a price which reflects reliability of supply, not just the cost of the pipes and the dams. This is similar to electricity where prices are lower for interrupted supply; lower than the average cost of production. Similar pricing regimes for water could produce a better framework for deciding the level of investment in drought storage. The difference in price between 'reliable water' and 'drought interrupted water' could assist in deciding how much investment should be made in turning drought interrupted water into reliable water.

Over and above these issues is the question of the price of water itself. As we have already pointed out it is impossible to ignore this issue once the resource is closed. It is not possible to say the resource is free except for the distribution and storage fees. If access is restricted and other people wish to gain access the water will have a value even if it is heavily disguised as the value of something else - usually land. If Governments try to ignore this value and pretend that the resources is restricted but 'free' they will certainly provide large capital bonuses to the present generation of holders of water rights but it will not be 'free' water. It is better to charge a resource rent which distributes the value of the resource between the community and the holders of the rights rather than let the present generation capture the whole value.

This resource rent should go to the community whether the water is privately or publicly distributed. In fact it should be kept separate from the distribution authority in both cases and used by the community for the welfare of its people.

4   Political issues

The above discussion may sound politically unrealistic as few Governments have sufficient courage to charge realistically for water distribution and storage and are unlikely to draw further opprobrium by introducing further charges for some theoretical concept of a resource rent. Governments can make some justification for the costs of distribution and storage that will be accepted by the community who would otherwise have to pay these costs out of their taxation, but adding further charges will not be easily explained and will draw criticism as 'making a profit from national resource' or 'forcing the small farmer into bankruptcy.'

There is no doubt that it is politically easier merely to charge for the costs of distribution and storage. Perhaps the Government offers some discounts for 'interrupted supply'; or 'annual licenses' as they were called in Australia. It is also politically easier to tie the water rights to the property with many strict rules against selling water rights. The political rhetoric remains that the water is free and the charges are just to cover costs. Over a period of years the value of land with water rights attached rises considerably in comparison to land that has no water rights. There is no doubt political agitation over the issue as it becomes difficult for small farmers to find the capital to buy a farm with water or pay the high rents charged by landlords. The Government cynically avoids the flack by maintaining that legally the water is free and it cannot be held responsible for the actions of speculators and criminals who break the law. It can pass even more futile laws in an attempt to stop the value of the water being openly expressed.

An alternative scenario appears to be more politically dangerous but with some compromises could be feasible. The same charges for distribution and storage would be introduced as in the first scenario and then water rights would be made freely transferable and the values of the transfers would be openly declared. While it may be tempting to tax these values it would be a mistake as the level of taxation needed to capture some of the value of the water for the community is so high that it would drive a large part of the transactions on to the black market. It would be preferable to use these values as the basis of an extra resource charge. Let us say for example that farmers are prepared to pay $5 a cubic metre for a water right then the Government might say that it will introduce a formula based charge of 10 cents a year for water. The advantage of this approach is that farmers will first have to establish values and these will not occur for sometime after the resource has been closed. When the Government is criticised for selling the national heritage to the highest bidder it can counter that it is clawing back some of the value for the sake of the community and using it to assist small farmers or for some other community benefit.

5   Conclusion

The availability of water is becoming restricted in more and more countries because of natural supply limitations and the increasing cost of developing additional resources. Once supply is restricted water becomes a 'closed resource' and water rights can only be acquired through the purchase of existing right as new rights are no longer being created.   As countries, or sub-national level entities such as states, approach this point of total closure water rights will increase in value and national and state level Governments should take policy decisions to anticipate problems associated with the sale of water rights. If the implications of the closure of the resource are ignored there will be a large increase in the capital value of water rights which will be appropriated by a single generation of farmers. Governments should try to establish traded water rights so values are freely expressed and water can be allocated more efficiently. They should also try to moderate the inflation in the capital value of water rights for the sake of the next generation of farmers.

We have discussed the interests of farmers in particular in this paper but one must also be aware that the political debate will increasingly focus on the interests of industrialists, domestic consumers and amenity demands (recreation and tourism). These will inevitably cause conflict as demand grows and the closure of the resource bites. Governments will have to decide whether they will allow traded rights for agricultural water to be converted to these other uses and on what terms such conversions can take place.

What must not be forgotten is that the interests of farmers are bound up with food supplies for the population. Locally produced food has many advantages and in the case of fresh produce is cheaper and safer for consumers. Constructive attempts to improve dryland production of such staples as grain and meat using proven sustainable systems would help lessen the pressure from the farmers competing with other users for shares of a closed water resource.

6   References

1.   Royal Scientific Society (1996) Data on sectoral water use in Jordan, Amman
2.   Royal Scientific Society.
3.   Turrel, H. (1995) Water resource management in the Murray Basin, Paper in the SOAS Water Issues Seminar series, March 1995.

ALLOWING LOCAL PEOPLE TO COPE WITH CHANGE AND TAKE RESPONSIBILITY FOR SUSTAINING THEIR GROUNDWATER SOURCES

An awareness of a new agenda for hydrogeologists

D.M. BALL
Consultant Hydrogeologist, Dublin, Ireland

Abstract
There are a considerable number of boreholes and wells in different parts of the world which are not used. The evidence may appear to indicate technical failures but many of these groundwater developments have not been sustained for other reasons. The central Government agencies set up in many countries to take responsibility for groundwater sources and sustaining groundwater development are faltering and insecure. There is a need to shift the balance of responsibility. The responsibility for local water sources should rest with the local people, and the hydrogeologist's approach to the change of responsibility needs to be realistic.
Keywords: community, coping with change, development, hydrogeologists, infrastructure, responsibility, rural water supplies.

1 Introduction

"Water is for people." In developing groundwater supplies, there is a tendency to forget that our work relates to the needs of the people. Although in our training and practice, we embrace the politically correct concept of community participation, real contact with local people is often lost during a project as we heed the demands and agendas of funding agencies, counterparts, and our own needs.

I have worked on the development of water supplies in Europe, Africa, Middle East and Far East and I am struck by the number of dead, unused, defunct boreholes and wells that I find in villages and rural areas. Sometimes these boreholes represent a series of development projects that span decades. In the past I used to look for, and I usually found, a technical reason for these failures. As a young hydrogeologist, I felt consoled that my technical skill could spot the flaws in the work carried out before

Water Policy: Allocation and management in practice. Edited by P. Howsam and R.C. Carter.
Published in 1996 by E & FN Spon. ISBN 0 419 21650 2

me. This consolation wore thin with time, and I realised that the previous hydrogeologists had probably found flaws in the work of their predecessors. Each one of us in turn have been making technical improvements, yet each one of us repeating the pattern of the past and failing to provide a sustained water source.

I believe that however much we improve on the technical side we will always undermine our technical excellence if we ignore the human and political reality of the site.

Other hydrogeologists have said to me that we should not stray from our discipline and become socio-anthropologists. I agree, but I am not advocating that we should pretend we belong to another discipline. Instead I am saying that hydrogeologists are capable people, we have ordinary people skills, we can communicate, and we can understand complex issues and local personal issues outside our technology. These issues directly relate to our attempts to achieve sustainable groundwater development. It is in our interest to pay attention to these issues and integrate them in our work. If we wear technical blinkers we will repeat the failures of the past.

There are 3 aspects or components to a successful water development project that will achieve sustained new water sources:-

- **The People** - the hard part
- **The Hydrogeology** - the uncertain part
- **The Construction** - the attractive and obvious part

Most water projects in the Sahel during the past 40 years have focused on the construction part and used their achievements, in terms of numbers of wells dug or yields of water obtained, as the means of measuring their project's success. Many of these projects ultimately have been failures because the new water sources have not been sustained. The construction component of a water well project is not only obvious, but it is 'attractive', because it can be controlled; equipment and materials can be purchased, teams can be trained, and something measurable can be seen to be achieved.

Other projects have been more professional and gone beyond just drilling or digging holes in the ground. They have paid attention in addition to the technical and scientific aspects of the hydrogeology of the area and the individual sites. This has lead to better siting, design and construction of wells and boreholes. Many of these projects have also ultimately failed. The hydrogeology part is described as 'uncertain' because the availability of suitable aquifers and suitable groundwater cannot be predicted with certainty or controlled by man.

Projects in the early part of the post colonial era paid little attention to the people. In recent years it has become 'politically correct' to talk about "community involvement" or "village participation" but few projects have done more than pay lip service to these phrases. When the 'People' part is just an add-on or low priority aspect in a technical/construction project, the project has usually failed to create sustained new water sources. They may have been technically 'sustainable' but they were not 'sustained'.

The 'people part' is described as the hard part because it is difficult to carry out. The people part is the work with the people as they go through their process. Their process of deciding whether they wish to take on, and take responsibility for, a new water supply. It is to their agenda. It cannot be controlled.

A lot of time and work can be put into the people part with no visible or easily measurable sign of success. The temptation for the outsider is to drive this process along; to impose the outsiders agenda and project objective. Resisting this temptation is the hard part. Being there with the people as they go through their process is hard when there is always the possibility that the outcome of the good intentions and months of effort ends up with the people deciding that they cannot cope with a new water supply.

Another hard part of working with the people is that they have already been exposed to aid and development projects. Putting it colloquially; 'they know the game' - they know the rules and the role that they are supposed to play. Similarly they expect the outsider to play a predictable role. Changing the game, in such a way that the people feel they are equal partners; that they are 'empowered'; that they have the confidence to take responsibility; is time consuming and difficult.

It seems to me that hydrogeologists, water engineers and other professionals have been repeating an approach to development of groundwater for over 40 years. The approach has overcome the technical problems yet has failed to provide sustainable sources. I think that the weight of evidence that I and many others have observed across the world, combined means that we must now look in a searching manner for the reasons for these failures. I suggest that the reasons lie not just in technical failures, but in our own training, our own approach and agendas and our reticence to challenge an established pattern. Most important is our hesitance to challenge both the people who engage us, and the people who supposedly want the development of a new groundwater source; to challenge them to clearly understand what they want and who is going to take responsibility for it. The purpose of this paper is therefore to draw attention to some of the many human and structural components that make up a comprehensive approach to groundwater development.

It is widely acknowledged that it is important that the end water user is involved in water policy implementation. The purpose of this paper is to show that to achieve long term success will require a deeper change in attitude and approach by the implementing agencies and their professionals than has so far been recognised.

2   Infrastructure and Stability

In the last 6 years there has been a break up of the old post World War II order. We appear to live in a very fractious and fragmented world where old balances of power have been demolished, old concepts of Government, democracy, control and responsibility, that gave an apparent stability are now seriously questioned or discarded. Old assumptions that gave us a framework for our work, appear insecure.

The past order has had a bearing on the development of groundwater. In the past both sides of the power struggle and the old colonial powers all promulgated a notion of a Central Government which took some degree of responsibility for the development of natural resources. Laws were passed to protect groundwater or encourage its development. Agencies were set up to carry out the wishes of Central Government or local Government, and the responsibility for the protection or development of groundwater was taken by a bureaucracy that was above the people who used it.

During the 1980's many of these bureaucracies were seen to be inadequate or less reliable than necessary. Programmes or projects started but failed to be sustained. Follow through and maintenance petered out. Teams of 'experts' were sent, from supposedly developed countries, to carry out programmes of infrastructural support, and a lot of money was, and still is, put in to 'infrastructural strengthening' and training to support something seen as crumbling The assumption that there is an infrastructure with real ability to take responsibility for or support groundwater development is not valid. One of the common reasons for a Government run water supply to fail is that the pump operator had not been paid. Even in developed countries there has been a cut back in the civil service and the first thing to go are basic items such as the transport allowance for field engineers and hydrogeologists.

In the last couple of years I have noticed a growing awareness that Government, or Government agency, responsibility for water supplies is not working except in very affluent countries. There are few places where there is a reliable and adequate infrastructure. At last something that I have long recognised but to which I, in common with many of us, failed to pay sufficient attention, is becoming incorporated into strategies and current thinking. This is that in developing countries, and many developed countries, there are old traditional, indigenous systems of power, consultation, decision making and responsibility, that exist at a local level. These grass roots traditional organisation methods did not fit with the Central Government model of democracy left as a hang over from a pre-independence rule or enforced by either a western or eastern power. The failure of old style Central Government has left instability, change, uncertainty, and often a vacuum. In many places I have found there is a real opportunity for people on the ground at a local level to consider taking responsibility for the development of their own groundwater resources. I use the word 'consider' because repeated attempts by Government or international agencies to uphold or sustain their responsibility for groundwater development have not genuinely encouraged local control and initiative.

Opportunities are there for people to decide whether they really want their existing borehole or the development of a new source, and recognise that they alone must take responsibility for it.

As hydrogeologists we need to recognise this destabilisation of the old assumptions concerning power and control and recognise and encourage the shift to local responsibility through which water supplies can be sustained. We need to learn how to work within frameworks that may appear new and insecure. To see any of our work sustained we need to not only recognise the change but also find realistic ways of working on the ground. This is not going to be easy because the 'new order' does not conform to many of the convenient models and assumptions we've worked with in the past. I suggest that to find new ways of working as professionals we need look at and revise many elements of our past assumptions and the assumptions of others. Below I draw attention to some of these elements.

3   Community participation

In recent years, at all levels from Non Government Organisations to International Aid Agencies, it has been become mandatory in project documents to incorporate phrases that imply an emphasis on community participation in the development of groundwater. Terms such as 'village participation' 'community involvement' have become one could almost say 'politically correct'.

I suggest we should look closely at the term 'community' and relate it to our own experience in the development of water supplies. I have found that the term community is pushed as a convenient collective term. It is often used to imply a sense of unity amongst the people in a given area; a unity of agenda, a unity of purpose. The 'Community' is slotted into a project like an input into a mathematical groundwater model

The use of the term and it's implication of unity or cohesion is misleading. In my experience communities do not exist in this sense. I have found that what outsiders wish to conveniently regard as a community is in fact a space occupied by several groups of people often from different tribes, sub tribes, sub clans or major families. They are in fact a collection of individual people who happen to be in a particular place, at a particular time, and who may remain there for a particular duration in the future. We seem prepared to ignore the obvious that disparate people are unlikely behave as a unit in the long term for our convenience. I suggest that the use of the collective term community is an attempt, at an intellectual level, to achieve a "distancing technique". An attempt to try to distance from the nitty-gritty of working with individual people, for their benefit, on their water supply. I think we are being unrealistic if we assume that there are no power struggles, envies, individual agendas, or pre-existing balances of power that could be altered by the new water supply we intend to install.

Stripping away the concept of 'community' and looking at what lies behind it opens up the uncertainties that are associated with individuals and their agendas relating to water. It also brings up the traditional, and often ancient, linkages and relationships between the people and individuals at a particular place and the people around them.

The frequent lack of a group that conforms to our notion of a community combined with a lack of an effective Central Government infrastructure means we should re-think our approach to the development of groundwater particularly in rural areas. It is easy to say that hydrogeologists should leave it to others to sort out the community while we get on with our job. I disagree; I think that if we are concerned about our jobs being real and effective then we have to sort out the relationship between our technology and the people.

Our skill as hydrogeologists is to be able to link information, constraints and concepts from many components (e.g. geology, engineering, economics, water quality and environmental considerations) and draw conclusions. Hydrogeologists need to look at things in the round in order to feel confident that their assessments and scope of work are sound.

Our ability to look at the wider picture and link or relate many different aspects is a strength of our discipline. I suggest we shift the emphasis of our work in groundwater development to firmly relate our role and technology to the people and infrastructure.

Hydrogeologists cannot assess whether a group of people are a community, but we can challenge them to decide whether they feel ready to take responsibility for their water supply. The responsibility is upon them and not upon us. However we have to deal with the implications of their uncertainty and insecurity. We can't work at a technical level unless they decide what they want us to do for them.

4   Change and the capacity for change

There is a big difference between disaster relief work and development work. NGO's who wish to raise money from the public and Governments and aid agencies who wish to justify their involvement in an area often do not draw attention to this difference. In the context of groundwater we are implored by advertisements that for example ask us to "provide $700 that will pay for a water supply for a village for a year". These advertisements and Government announcements justifying their aid budgets for development of water supplies imply that the people in the area concerned have no water supply. In a disaster this may be correct, but in a development situation the people in all cases have existing water supplies. They may not be ideal and they may not meet WHO standards but they do exist. If they didn't have an adequate water supply then the people would not survive for more than three days.

An existing water supply means that there are existing agreements between people, checks, balances and power structures and customary behaviour that have evolved over time. There are often many sources of water exploited on a traditional and sometimes opportunistic basis, that fit with the cycle of the people concerned and often have a value greater than just the provision of water. For example many groups in the Sahel move to well known areas of saline water and saline vegetation at the end of the winter dry season. The salts remedy deficiencies in the diets of people and animals and it is also a time for gatherings and arranging weddings. All too often I find that hydrogeologists either through their terms of reference, or by default, fail to recognise the importance and value of old water supplies in their process of providing a new water supply. Two years later the hydrogeologist wonders why his new borehole is not used.

I suggest that we need to recognise the difficulties inherent in change, and that we as a profession need to become competent in helping other people to decide whether they feel able to accept change. Hydrogeologists cannot ignore this dimension of the development process and say it is for other professions such as sociologists or extension workers. These other professions are probably not available for the time necessary, nor have they the ability to explain and fully discus all the technical options in groundwater development.

If the hydrogeologist wishes to develop a sustainable water supply then before work begins the hydrogeologist must feel assured that the people are confident they can cope with the change. This statement raises the important consideration that if the people are not confident they can handle the change to a new water supply, then it may be a better option to do nothing; i.e. the zero option. The zero option sounds acceptable in theory but is difficult to carry out in practice because it involves changing the project and walking away from the objective. This brings up the question of the personal agenda and perceived role of hydrogeologists working in the field and also the constraints and agenda in their terms of reference.

5   The framework of agendas and roles during a groundwater development programme

There are many agendas influencing a hydrogeologist carrying out a groundwater development programme. From my experience they are recognised in informal discussions but with certain exceptions the limitations they impose are seldom addressed or challenged in a public forum. I suggest we as a profession need to challenge some of them inside and outside this forum.

Groundwater development work is seen as primarily a technical activity by donor agencies and Government departments and many of us. The agenda in the terms of reference is often set in terms of a number of boreholes or wells to meet a presumed need for water. There is a focus on technical achievements, there is a work programme, contracts and specifications with clear budgets for such items as drilling, testing, pumps, vehicles, etc. These are obviously important, but there is seldom a budget for listening. Similarly there is seldom a budget for waiting for the people affected by the proposed programme to reach their own decisions.

Hydrogeologists are constrained and focused on technical matters because it is difficult to budget or allocate time for the non technical considerations. To push for space and time on a project for working with the people is difficult because decision makers in offices in aid agencies and local Governments only feel secure when they are agreeing budgets for old style projects containing tangibles such as pumps, or measurable technical achievements such as boreholes. Conversely the people who set budgets feel insecure when asked to pay for intangible procedures that require time, sensitivity, patience and listening. The insecurity of budget decision makers is understandable. I suggest that hydrogeologists need to allay their fears, and convince them that tight schedules and heavy commitments to technical achievement distorts our work and inhibits real sustainable development. A way of doing this is for us to change the emphasis of our proposals and put the listening and facilitating top of the agenda, and make the technical content become dependent of the outcome of the work with the people. For an experienced hydrogeologist the technical part of the work is usually straight forward. It is the easy part; the techniques we use have been well proven over decades. The difficult part is marrying the different technical options with the wishes and capacity for change in the people.

The agenda of counterpart agencies is also a constraint. In most developing countries and all but a few developed countries there are budgetary shortages in counterpart agencies. There are cut backs in what is often seen as an unwieldy inefficient civil service. In some places the basic salary for a fellow professional hydrogeologist or groundwater engineer is barely subsistence. In this context counterparts tend to make a positive response to almost any proposed project that would involve them, pay field allowances and perhaps leave at the end serviceable transport. Large projects with a big budget for capital expenditure are most attractive. The ideas of the counterpart concerning the development of his or her country are often not expressed for fear that the external project, with its spin offs, will be compromised.

I have found that the understandable personal agenda of the counterparts often acts to distort the project at the planning stage, and may impede the progress of a sensitive project at a local scale. I refer to this not as a criticism but merely to draw attention to it for decision makers in this forum.

The agenda of the local people can also hold back a project or lock it into a pattern of repeating past mistakes. A hydrogeologist represents a donor. He or she is therefore expected to give. A hydrogeologist is also an agent of a higher authority and therefore it is expected that he or she will issue instructions and as a result take responsibility. This is a perception and a pattern that is hard to change. There are very few areas of the world that have not been exposed to a project. A project culture is pandemic. Potential beneficiaries have learnt how to argue within the old aid or development framework of international agencies or Central Government. To ask people to change their understanding of us and our role and to then decide themselves whether they want a development and can take responsibility for it, is difficult and akin to changing the rules of a game whilst the game is being played.

Finally, I suggest hydrogeologists, both new graduates and experienced old hands, should look at their own agendas. I suggest that we all gain satisfaction from showing off our latest equipment, technical skills and our ability to complete a job on time. I suggest that we enjoy being in control of our work and seeing our ideas brought to fruition. We like being master of the situation. Conversely I suggest that we would be leery of a groundwater development project where the beneficiaries have the control and we must await their decisions in their timescale. Who knows we may even have to face a decision where the people say they are not ready for our project or our innovation. In other words we have to recognise the prospect of rejection. I think we should recognise that perhaps a big block to us carrying out a comprehensive groundwater development project that is sustainable by the people, is our own unwillingness to give up control.

We recognise that we will have to give up control at some stage. We are not going to operate and maintain a village well for the rest of time. However I suggest we recognise that when the time comes, we are not going to give up control to some reliable infrastructure maintained by Central Government. It is likely that there is not going to be a smooth transition from one higher authority to another. If we are interested in seeing our efforts sustained we will have to give up control to the people who will, in reality, sustain it, i.e. the local individuals on the site. I suggest that we clarify our agenda and our roles at the start of the work and give it priority. We are still able to influence and facilitate and we have a form of control because we can say no if we feel that some idea or proposition is unworkable. However until we face actually giving up control in terms of timing and imposition of technology all of our statements about community involvement are just window dressing to conform with the political correctness of current 'project speak'.

6   Conclusion

I recommend that hydrogeologists and other water supply professionals from all countries recognise that Central Government or its agencies can only take comprehensive responsibility for the development or protection of groundwater if there is a superb infrastructure. Changes in awareness and political upheavals are causing us to become aware that there are few countries in which such an infrastructure really exists. Improvements in technology are not going to compensate for this. Hydrogeologists need to come to terms with the changes, and change our approach. I suggest it may be prudent to shift the pendulum of responsibility and to put the responsibility for sustaining a groundwater development onto the people who will use it. I suggest that we try to facilitate and advise them as they to go through this change, and we try not to distance ourselves from their very real problems. I suggest our training and literature should place a greater emphasis on exploring and dealing with the people issues of power, responsibility and control relating to water, so that field hydrogeologists and water engineers are better prepared for an important but changing role. Finally I think we should challenge our Governments and aid agencies to recognise that hydrogeology involves more than a technical fix to their perception of a water supply problem. It is time we made realistic changes to the terms of reference for our work in the development of groundwater.

WATER LAW, WATER RIGHTS AND WATER POLICY
Law, rights, and policy

P. HOWSAM
Water Management Department, Silsoe College, Cranfield University, UK

Abstract
If individual water rights can be regarded as access to a clean and adequate supply of water for basic needs, then any water policy should include the protection of such rights. The policy should be supported by a strategy that provides the means to implement policy objectives. Water laws, required to implement and enforce policy, should provide effective administrative and regulatory mechanisms at the most appropriate levels.

If the principle of basic water rights is universally accepted, i.e. by people and therefore communities, society and ultimately the state, then it is suggested that these rights should provide the focus and first priority of any water policy and supporting laws. Control should be in the hands of those closest to the issue, i.e. people and local communities with the state (and international agencies) providing only a co-ordinating, educating and information disseminating role. Such an approach to water rights and law need not conflict with the principle that water has an economic value and has to be paid for.

Keywords: administration, Common law, economic value, reasonable use, riparian rights, water law, water policy, water rights.

1 Introduction

Water is a subject that attracts many fine words and principles. For many years simple statements like "water is essential for life" have been, and still are, the centre of policy statements. Unfortunately fine sounding words is all that they will become, if they have not already. Now the agenda is much wider and other principles influence water policy; e.g. political, financial and environmental.

Water Policy: Allocation and management in practice. Edited by P. Howsam and R.C. Carter.
Published in 1996 by E & FN Spon. ISBN 0 419 21650 2

Modern principles and concepts relating to water policy include: integrated catchment management and sustainable water resources; conservation and environmental protection; allocation based on water as an economic commodity and privatisation. These principles now permeate statements on water policy at all levels, international, national, regional and local.

In European Community water policy [1], water is described as having several different functions: "Water is a basic human need for drinking, preparing food and washing. It is also an economic resource contributing to broader human needs in terms of fisheries, agriculture, industry, transport and recreation. It is a vital element of every ecosystem and every landscape as well as forming distinctive environments in its own right. It can also represent a threat in the form of floods or droughts."

Such statements will inevitably and as intended put pressure on us to address the subject of water in new and possibly radical ways. Amongst this complex inter-related agenda it is important to review the status of basic water rights. Have they been compromised or minimised by growing environmental concerns or by pragmatic economic justifications? Winpenny [2] argues that the key problem in dealing with these issues has been the failure to regard water as an economic commodity. He criticises the 'entitlement' syndrome that has historically evolved, where many people expect water to be always available or provided and at little or no cost.

Whilst few would disagree with the need to value water and to use it wisely, the current focus on economic approaches to dealing with water and water supply is tending to marginalise the rights and roles of individuals and communities. Burchi [3] has identified the fading role of private water rights and the cautious mobility of water rights from less to more economically efficient uses of water.

2   Water rights

Water rights may mean different things to different people in different circumstances. The concept of water rights has many social, religious, political and geographical overtones. In poor arid countries the emphasis is on the priority of the basic needs of people and their livestock to survive. In such circumstances problems are exacerbated where the limited water resources have become polluted. In Europe, with its wetter climate, any concern is generally over the right to good quality unpolluted water rather than to reliable quantities - the latter has largely been taken for granted. However in England for example, recent exposure to minor short term water shortages has focused the attention of some of the public on their rights to a reliable supply of water - because "we pay for it"! - not because it is a basic human requirement. This is perhaps a good example of the effect of a water policy, in this case the privatisation of water supply, on public attitudes to water.

To some the word right conjures up hard meanings like claim and ownership i.e. something that is enforced by legal entitlement. To others it has softer meanings such as interest and privilege - i.e. something that has responsibilities and obligations attached to it. This latter view could imply that duties should come before rights or in the extreme that we have no rights only duties [4]. Unfortunately today too many people are all too ready to claim their rights without being willing to accept their responsibilities.

In the UK and other European countries where water is state controlled then the only real right that an individual has is the right to buy water. This is very much in line with many who advocate that water has an economic value and therefore is a commodity that must be bought and sold - not a free right.

In the last 50 years there have been many instances where states have felt it necessary to abolish common law riparian water rights and introduce complete state control [3]. Rarely has this curtailing of historic rights undergone significant legal challenge, although the preservation, as in the UK and Australia, of minimal individual rights of use has helped to avoid conflict. Indeed few would argue against a central combined water quantity and water quality co-ordinating role for the state, but it has not been proven that states, rather than individuals or local communities, are significantly better at water allocation and management.

Within the right national framework it is possible for water rights to be maintained by local communities, water user groups or farmer co-operatives. At the local level water user associations provide the best means to cover the needs of, and resolve any water right disputes between, individuals. Any national water administration should have the ability, perhaps via a system of water tribunals or courts, to deal with those issues that risk causing harm, when they cannot be settled at the local level [5].Local groups can, at the same time provide a mechanism for the active participation of water users in the planning and management of water resources on a wider scale and at different levels under the guidance of the co-ordinating water administration body.

Similar issues arise when water rights are discussed and applied at different levels, for example upstream and downstream rights across international boundaries, where political issues may come to dominate. A review of traditional water rights and laws would suggest that it has been possible to get together and agree on ways of co-operating in the sharing and protecting of water because it is understood by all concerned that it is mutually beneficial to do so. For this to happen at other, regional, national or international, levels however more knowledge, awareness and understanding would be required. Riparian rights of individuals as established under Common law could, and already do to some extent within international law, form the basis for the rights of states. Articles 5 and 7 of the International Law Commission's Draft law on the non-navigational uses of international watercourses, talk in terms of "equitable and reasonable utilisation and participation" and of an "obligation not to cause appreciable harm to other users". Indeed customary law established in many parts of world is based on similar principles. The common sense approach that has evolved by custom and normally adopted between individuals who are close to the reality of the situation, i.e. they are upstream or downstream co-riparians, has produced means to deal with the range of issues, e.g. water resource allocation, water quality, drainage and flooding. In the latter case for example "a riparian owner has the right to raise the river banks from time to time as it becomes necessary to confine flood waters within the banks and prevent it from overflowing his land [6]." Flood prevention "work may only be done provided that it can be established without actual injury to the property of others" [7].

Under common law additional rights to water use may be acquired by a deed; by prescription or custom or by statute. Of these the most difficult to reconcile is that of rights acquired by prescription, i.e. those claimed on the basis of historic un-interrupted use [8]. In areas of limited resources this principle protects the rights of existing long term users but offers little hope for the next and new generations. The parallel at international level can be drawn as between Egypt with its long term historic claim on the use of the waters of the Nile on the one hand and Ethiopia with its emerging development and hopes for increased upstream water use from the same river, on the other.

3 Water policy

A water policy is, in simple terms, a statement of general principles governing water allocation, development and management. In relation to water rights it is relevant to point out here that a principle is defined in the dictionary as a moral, a belief or a code. Policy is usually formulated at the national or institutional level; but also occurs at all levels. A water policy developed by a small community has to address the same basic issues, including water rights, as those considered by the international community.

In all the stages, from policy formulation, through strategy development to implementation, water rights should be a key issue. Today, whilst policies can be expressed simply, the strategies required to implement them are anything but straightforward. Policy formulation may not always include full consideration of the practicable implications of effective implementation or perhaps of the long term social impact. Policies demand integration of all water issues, with political, social, technical, environmental and financial balances between different water requirements and uses, but the ability to implement integrated policies in an integrated manner is often lacking.

For instance in the UK whilst appropriately sounding public health and water policies, and supporting laws had been introduced in the late 19th and early 20th centuries it was not until 1948, with the introduction of the Rivers Board Act, that shortcomings in administration of the laws, i.e. lack of an integrated approach, were recognised. However it took another 50 years to realise that integrating the provider of water with the water regulator within the same administration (i.e. the Rivers Boards and subsequently the Water Authorities) was not an effective policy. The 1989 Water Act saw the privatisation of the water industry in England & Wales and the introduction of separate regulators.

The problem is that policy statements refer to the protection of basic rights, but this may or may not be included in any strategy and certainly could easily be ignored in the urgency of the implementers to achieve or be seen to achieve. Will the rush to impose current fashionable policies, through exhortation, exaggerated claims of doom, legal restrictions or financial penalties, lead to the erosion of basic rights? Policy is imposed on people in less developed countries for their own good - not necessarily according to their own wishes but more from the point of view of external self-promoting experts. Where economic arguments are allowed to dominate, will rights only rest with those who can afford them? Du Bois [9] points out that many traditional (common law or riparian) water rights have been lost, in Africa for instance, when economic development occurred and was given priority over individual water rights. He argues that in any case such laws and rights would not encourage efficient use of water, neither could they provide an equitable distribution of access to water. On the other hand they usually involved collective decision making by those who had to live with the circumstances.

The idea of marketable private water rights is not a new system and is used in the USA and in some Moslem countries in the allocation and control of irrigation water from qanat or falaj. In protecting individual or community water rights then developments requiring water have to negotiate with the local people most likely to be affected. Caponera [5] points out that " one advantage of customary and traditional law over written statutory law is its flexibility, making adaptation to local needs at a particular moment easier. At the users' level it is a system generally well known, respected and followed". The trend to the alternative of state control on the other hand, has inevitably cut out local decision making and allowed the introduction of externally generated priorities, often within the influence of influential and wealthy sectors of society. Vani [10] argues also that state control in some circumstances allows scope for the misuse of powers within a system which places heavy financial and administrative burdens on Government.

4 Water law

Water law can be regarded as the link between water policy and water rights. On the one hand laws may be needed to protect the water rights of individuals but equally can be introduced so as to restrict water rights and facilitate the imposition of new policy initiatives deemed to be for the public good. In either case a well conceived water law should facilitate implementation of water policy decisions [5]. A good law should promote obligations as well as rights, but there are both moral and legal obligations and rights. In an ideal world both rights and obligations should be morally acceptable. In reality laws are not always obeyed on moral grounds but rather because of a general acceptance that laws must be obeyed regardless or because of fear of legal and financial sanctions [8]. Thus laws have the power to impose the will of a few on many and indeed are widely used to do so in a range of both undemocratic and so called democratic systems. Indeed in many developed countries modern statutory water law has 'progressed' to such an extent that any reference in them to individual water rights is hard to find.

The English Common law has historically provided a means to protect the rights of individual water users but only in the case of riparian owners, i.e. those who own land adjacent to a watercourse. The rights extend to an imprecisely defined reasonable use of water. Common law is established by judgements in the higher courts which become legally binding precedents applicable to future appropriately similar cases. Riparian water rights were best summed up by Lord MacNaghten in 1893 in the John Young & Co v Bankier Distillery case [11] - " A riparian proprietor is entitled to have water of the stream, on the banks of which his property lies, flow down as it has been accustomed to flow down to his property, subject to the ordinary use of the flowing water by upper proprietors and to such further use, if any, on their part in connection with their property as may be reasonable under the circumstances. Every riparian proprietor is thus entitled to the water of his stream, in its natural flow, without sensible diminution or increase and without any sensible alteration in its character or quality. Any invasion of this right causing actual damage or calculated to found a claim which may ripen into an adverse right, entitles the party injured to the intervention of the Court".

It should be noted that such rights relate to use of the water not ownership of the water. It has long been accepted that water in a water course is in public and common ownership. The wording of a judgement by Justice Parke in 1851 in Embrey v Owen [12] is significant - " the right to have a stream flow in its natural state, without diminution or alteration is an incident of property in the land through which it passes; but flowing water is *publici juris*, not in the sense that it is *bonum vacans*, to which the first occupant may acquire an exclusive right, but that it is public and common in the sense only, that all may reasonably use it who have a right of access to it, and none can have property in the water itself, except in the particular portion which he may choose to abstract from the stream and take into his possession, and that during the time of his possession only."[6].

Thus whilst riparian rights seem to be a sound principle they are limited by the words "....all may reasonably use it who have a right of access to it, ...". What happens to those who do not "have the right of access to it". Groundwater may be an option where it is locally accessible but the principles of riparian rights have traditionally only been applicable to surface watercourses.

Despite these common law provisions for the protection of private water rights, the statements on which could easily be taken as principles of policy, water pollution was not reduced or prevented. The reasons were identified by a Royal Commission in 1867 as - few individuals could afford or were willing to take legal action against what would normally be a powerful industrial neighbour [13]. Additionally such people would have been reluctant to be witnesses against those who provided them with work.

Increasingly today in the UK, as in many countries, statutory law has become the primary means of managing and protecting water resources. Often the underlying policy behind statutory law has been based on the principles of common law and riparian rights. In many instances statutory provisions attempt to protect historic water rights. The latest 1991 Water Resources Act that controls water use and disposal by a system of licences and discharge consents, allows abstraction of up to 20 m^3 each day for domestic and some agricultural purposes without a licence.

As with water resources, water quality in the UK has for a long time been dealt with by statutory provisions. Such statutory legislation is aimed at the public in general not individuals. Howarth [13] identified the earliest legislation relating to water pollution was the 1388 Act for Punishing Nuisances which Cause Corruption of the Air near Cities and Great Towns. The Act referred to: "......so much dung and other filth of the garbage and entrails as well of beasts killed, as of other corruptions, be cast and put in ditches, rivers and other waters, and also many other places, within, about, and nigh unto divers cities, boroughs, and towns of the realm, and the suburbs of them, that the air there is greatly corrupt and infect, and many maladies and other intolerable diseases do daily happen, as well as to the inhabitants and those that are conversant in the said cities, boroughs, towns, and suburbs, as to others repairing and travelling thither, to the great annoyance, damage, and peril of the inhabitants, dwellers, repairers, and travellers." [13]. Despite a considerable fine imposed for dumping rubbish in the rivers, this legislation did not improve matters and further related laws were brought in 100 years later in 1489.

For those who have seen the 20th Century conditions in the slum areas of some developing country cities, then this 14th century description will be quite familiar. Yet as then in England, in those places now, well intended polices will not be implemented and the law will not help the vast majority of people. The sad thing is that if and when prosperity comes to these areas, possibly in the form of industrial development, conditions will only get worse. The protection of water quality and the environment has only seriously been addressed in the UK for example, in the last 20 years - some 150 years after the start of the Industrial Revolution. Why has this been so? The policies have recognised the need and legislation has been provided yet water quality has not been protected.

These circumstances cannot all be blamed on Governments. It would seem that people who live in conditions without clean water and a healthy environment have other higher priorities. The claiming of rights to clean water comes later after poverty has been alleviated. The difference between this century and the last or prior centuries however is that now there is a lot more scientific knowledge and understanding. Governments cannot claim ignorance but ignorance must be part of the reason why many people living in slum conditions in developing countries do not claim their rights. Depending upon the circumstances individuals may not perceive water rights as their top priority. This situation does not encourage Governments to monitor and ensure that policy and legislation have been properly implemented and objectives achieved.

It is increasingly the case that countries will feel it necessary to impose state control on water, thus overriding the traditional (common law) approaches to water rights. In this process whilst every effort to protect individual water rights are made, it has been the case that statutory law has not been so easily available to the individual as a means to protect their rights. To a large extent statutory water law is aimed at protecting public rights although in essence the public have had to accept a compromise between their water rights and economic prosperity. At this level the individual has little say against powerful political and wealthy financial individuals or groups and in reality fine ideals and statements of policy never get properly implemented or become a secondary consequence of any action.

5   Discussion

A look at the evolution of water rights and law in the UK reveals that similar situations are evolving in developing countries. Increasingly the emphasis of policy and the law has been the protection of water resources for the good of the state as a whole, with individual rights becoming subservient to the wider good. Individual water rights should come first in the order of priorities of any water policy and should be properly protected by law. Each group of individuals, each community should be allowed to exercise democratic control over local water resources for their benefit. It is argued that local communities must be given priority over commercial institutions in the development of water resources. [10].

Water law should be seen as an integral part of society not something above or outside it [14]. All too often insufficient attention has been given to water rights and law by many involved in water policy and planning with the consequence of an "impressive record of failure, or unintended consequences, shown by development programmes around the world"[14].   Water laws need to reflect changing circumstances with regard to limited water resources and increasing and often changing water demands, since permanent protection of historic rights will not allow fair and efficient re-allocation of water .

In some cases historic or customary practices and water rights and laws have been criticised and accused of being obstructive to economic change. Adherence to tradition was regarded as being backward. However abolition of customary rights can be destructive of the principle of user participation [10]. Indeed modern water resource policies tend to promote, but often fail to deliver, peoples participation in the management of water resources [5]. Increasingly in practice modern water rights means having the ability to pay for clean and adequate water. There are many lessons to be learnt from traditional water laws that should form the basis for reform rather than be discarded as inappropriate to modern needs and development as is often argued.

6 References

1. Anon. (1996) *European Community Water Policy* COM(96) 59. Office for 5. Official Publications of the European Communities, Luxembourg.
2. Winpenny, J. (1994) *Managing water as an economic good*. Routledge, London.
3. Burchi, S. (1991) Current developments and trends in the law and administration of water resources - a comparative state-of- the-art appraisal. *Journal of Environmental Law,* Vol.3, No.1, pp. 69 - 91
4. Finnis, J. (1980) *Natural law and natural rights*. Clarendon Press, Oxford.
5. Caponera, D.A. (1992) *Principles of water law and administration.* A.A.Balkema, Rotterdam.
6. Howarth, W. (1992) *Wisdom's law of watercourses*. 5th Ed. Shaw & Sons, London.
7. *Trafford v The King (1832) 8 Bing. 204*
8. Hart, H.L.A. (1972) *The concept of law*. Clarendon Press, Oxford.
9. Du Bois, F. (1994) Water rights and the limits of environmental law. *Journal of Environmental Law,* Vol. 6, No.1, pp.73 - 84.
10. Vani, M.S. (1995) Law and policy on water resources in Kumaon and Garhwal. *Farmer-Managed Irrigation Systems Network Newsletter* No.13, pp.9 - 13
11. *John Young Co. v Bankier Distillery COs (1893) All ER 439*
12. *Embrey v Owen (1851) 6. Ex. 353*
13. Howarth, W. (1988) *Water pollution law*. Shaw & Sons, London.
14. Spiertz, H.L.J. and de Jong, I.J.H. (1992) *Traditional law and irrigation management*. In: Irrigators and Engineers. Eds Diemer & Slabbers. pp.185-201. Thesis Publishers, Amsterdam.

AUTHOR INDEX

SUBJECT INDEX

For Product Safety Concerns and Information please contact our EU
representative GPSR@taylorandfrancis.com
Taylor & Francis Verlag GmbH, Kaufingerstraße 24, 80331 München, Germany

www.ingramcontent.com/pod-product-compliance
Ingram Content Group UK Ltd.
Pitfield, Milton Keynes, MK11 3LW, UK
UKHW021605240425
457818UK00018B/400